BRITISH NAVAL AVIATION

▼ **HMS *Argus*, the world's first aircraft carrier with a fully flushed deck, seen early in 1930 with the Blackburn Blackburns of No. 450 (Fleet Spotter Reconnaissance) Flight parked on deck. A retractable charthouse is visible forward and the palisades are up to catch any aircraft which is likely to run over the side of the deck whilst landing. (RAF Museum)**

BRITISH NAVAL AVIATION

The Fleet Air Arm, 1917–1990

Ray Sturtivant

Naval Institute Press

Published and distributed in the United States of America and Canada by the Naval Institute Press, Annapolis, Maryland 21402.

Library of Congress Catalog Card No. 89-63589.

ISBN 0-87021-026-2

This edition is authorized for sale only in the United States of America, its territories and possessions, and Canada.

Edited and designed by Roger Chesneau.
Typeset by Ronset Typesetters Ltd, Darwen, Lancashire, UK.
Reproduction by M&E Reproductions, North Fambridge, Essex, UK.
Printed and bound in Great Britain by Courier International, Tiptree, Essex, UK.

Jacket illustrations:

Front: 'The Battle of Taranto', from a painting by Robert Taylor, is reproduced by kind permission of The Military Gallery, Bath, UK.

Back: upper: An early photograph of the second production example of the Fairey Seal (K3478) flying over HMS *Courageous*, with a destroyer in attendance in the distance. The photograph was taken during the Home Fleet Summer Cruise in May 1933. (RAF Museum P.101720)

Back, centre: A deck scene on board HMS *Ark Royal* shortly before the outbreak of the Second World War. Watched by onlookers at the rails, the batsman signals with hand-held flags to a following aircraft moving up behind Blackburn Skua L2878 of No. 803 (Fleet Fighter) Squadron. (Cdr R. N. Everett)

Back, lower: Trainee telegraphist air gunners march to a lecture past Blackburn Sharks of No. 755 (TAG Training) Squadron at HMS *Kestrel*, otherwise RNAS Worthy Down, one of the stations taken over from the RAF when the Fleet Air Arm gained its independence on 24 May 1939. The aircraft in the background (K5634) carries on the fin the new-style squadron code 'X2' and an unidentifiable individual letter. (FAA Museum)

Contents

Acknowledgements

I wish to thank the staff of the Fleet Air Arm Museum for their assistance over many years. I would also like to record my appreciation for the considerable help and advice given by Mick Burrow, Dick Cronin and Eric Myall. A large number of people have helped me during many years of research into Fleet Air Arm history and I should particularly like to thank the following, whose assistance has been invaluable in the compilation of the present book: Capt. H. J. Abraham, RN (Ret.); Dave Allen; Peter Ames; Peter Arnold; Capt. E. R. G. Baker, RN (Ret.); Mrs S. Baker; Cdr F. W. Baring, VRD, RNR; Rick Barker; Joe Barr; Charles N. Bates; Lt Cdr P. N. Beagley, RAN (Ret.); Col F. D. G. Bird, RN (Ret.); Trevor Boughton; Chaz Bowyer; Lt (A) A. W. Bradley, RNZNVR; Cecil Bristow; Mollie Brown; Jack Bryant; Capt. J. A. Burnett, CBE, RN (Ret.); Raymond Burrows; Charles W. Cain; Tim Calloway; Dugald Cameron; Capt. E. S. Carver, DSC, RN (Ret.); Maj. V. B. G. Cheesman, DSO, MBE, DSC, RM; A. G. Clayton; Mrs S. Clark; Lt Cdr L. A. Cox, RN (Ret.); Cdr J. S. L. Crabb, RN (Ret.); Ernie Cromie; Bill Crozer; Ron W. Davies; Jim Davis; Fred C. Dickey Jr; Derek Day; Pat Dobbs; Tony Down; Jim Downing; Commissioned Gunner Les Dudley, RN (Ret.); Cdr R. N. Everett, OBE, RN (Ret.); the Fleet Air Arm Officers' Association; Capt. H. L. St J. Fancourt, RN (Ret.); Capt. M. Farquhar, RN (Ret.); Lt Cdr D. J. Foley, RN (Ret.); Mike Garbett; H. W. Gold; Peter H. T. Green; J. A. Greenfield; Jim Halley; Lt I. W. Halliday, RN; Marshall Hawes; Cdr R. C. Hay, DSO, DSC, RN (Ret.); Steve Hobden; Mike Hooks; Frank Hunter; Rear Admiral J. Ievers CB, OBE, RN; R. A. Joss; Donald Judd; Mike Keep; J. D. Kelsall; Lt Cdr A. Kennard, DSC, RN (Ret.); Lord Kilbracken; Lt Cdr V. M. Langman, DSC, CD, RCN (Ret); Hugh Langrishe; Lt Cdr H. J. M. Lawrence, RD, RNR; John Lawson; Lt Cdr G. E. Legg, RN (Ret.); Bob Lea; H. Liddle; Len Lovell; Brian Lowe; Fred Lynn; Lt Cdr N. C. Manley-Cooper, DSC, RN (Ret.); Mrs M. Marriott; Maj A. E. Marsh, RM; Gp Capt. R. A. McMurtrie; Jock Moffatt; Lt Cdr P. H. Moss, RN (Ret.); Lt Fred Motley, RN (Ret.); Dr E. V. B. Morton, VRD, MD, FRCPE; Cdr B. H. C. Nation, RN (Ret.); C. S. Nell; Jim Oughton; N. S. Painter, MS, FRCS; Ron Pankhurst; Cdr R. A. B. Phillimore, RN (Ret.); Lt D. W. Phillips, DSC, RN (Ret.); James Pickering, AFC, AE, FGS, FSA; Cdr J. W. Powell, DSC, RN (Ret.); Lt Cdr (A) Derek J. Price, RNVR; the RAF Museum; John Rawlings; Bill Reeks; Lt Cdr F. C. Rice, DFM, RN (Ret.); Dr. A. Robinson; George Rock; Cdr R. H. S. Rodger, OBE, RN (Ret.); Douglas Rough; Brian Shaw; Ken Sims; Rear Admiral M. F. Simpson, CEng FRAeS, FIMechE; T. L. Sirs; H. A. Smith; Vic Smith; Lt Cdr P. Snow, RN (Ret.); Cdr F. A. Swanton, DSO, DSC, RN (Ret.); the Telegraphist Air Gunners' Association; John Tipp; Reg Torrington; John Treble; Geoffrey Wakeham; Arthur Ward; L. C. Watson; Lt Cdr C. White, RNR; Ray Williams; Gordon Wright; Dick Yeo; and Paul Yockney. Grateful thanks are also due to the widow of the late Cdr Gerard A. Woods for her generosity in allowing me to use much of the material he had gathered for a proposed book of Fleet Air Arm reminiscences.

Ray Sturtivant

Introduction

British naval aviation came into being towards the end of 1910, and at the outbreak of the First World War the Royal Naval Air Service had a motley collection of aircraft and a relatively large number of trained pilots. By the time that war ended the fragile 'stick and string' machines had given way to strong and versatile aircraft, while the RNAS had been absorbed into the Royal Air Force on 1 April 1918.

The first successful take-offs and landings had, however, been made from the deck of an aircraft carrier in 1917, and further ships of this nature were under construction. Soon after the end of the war, carrier flying units were formed, and the title 'Fleet Air Arm of the Royal Air Force' was given to these on 1 April 1924. Shortly before the Second World War broke out in September 1939, the Admiralty regained control of naval aviation, which retained the term 'Fleet Air Arm' as it does to the present day.

One legacy of control by the RAF was that the FAA was equipped with semi-obsolescent machines when the Second World War broke out. The early loss of the aircraft carriers *Courageous* and *Glorious* was a great setback, but the FAA struggled on with such ships and aircraft as it had. The latter, which were only too often adaptations of land-based RAF aircraft, were soon reinforced by sturdy American types such as the Wildcat fighter and later the Avenger torpedo-bomber.

Some British aircraft gave a good account of themselves, and rather surprisingly these included the Swordfish – already due for replacement at the outbreak of war but still in first-line service when it ended – which had a multitude of successes to its credit. Notable amongst these were the night raid on Taranto, which put a major portion of the Italian Fleet out of action, and the attacks on the German battleship *Bismarck*.

The end of the Second World War inevitably led to a reduction in the size of the FAA, but it soon became apparent that further conflict was likely somewhere and in 1950 war broke out in Korea. The Royal Navy played a small but significant part in United Nations operations against the aggressor, and by the time an armistice was negotiated three years later a succession of British carriers had seen action.

Meanwhile the use of helicopters was increasing in the FAA, and these proved invaluable when they were called upon to assist in activities against terrorists in Malaya. Jet-powered fixed-wing aircraft also began to reach first-line squadrons, and in 1956 some of these were in action during Operation 'Musketeer', the brief but fateful Suez War. During 1961 the FAA afforded protection for Kuwait, then under threat from Iraq, putting ashore Royal Marine Commandos. Similar activities were undertaken the following year in Brunei, where attacks were made by Indonesian troops. The use of FAA helicopters was strengthened in 1965 when amphibious warfare ships came into service, these being complemented in 1967 by two helicopter cruisers.

Conventional fixed-wing flying eventually came to an end in 1978 with the withdrawal of *Ark Royal*, but this class of carrier was replaced by the so-called 'through-deck cruiser' equipped with a small number of vertical take-off Sea Harriers. The performance of these aircraft was quickly enhanced by fitting such ships with a 'ski-jump', one of many pioneering British carrier inventions. The Sea Harriers were soon to be put through their paces when the Falklands War broke out in 1982, and they proved an outstanding success. FAA helicopters also played a crucial part in that episode, operating from a variety of warships. Many lessons were learnt – some the hard way.

The Fleet Air Arm has since continued with similar equipment to that in use during the hostilities. Nowadays financial stringencies seldom permit the introduction of completely new aircraft, though improved versions of most contemporary types have been introduced into service from time to time.

CHAPTER 1

In the Beginning

Experiments in flying aircraft from warships were started by the Royal Navy as early as January 1912, when Lt C. R. Samson, a legendary figure in early British naval aviation, successfully flew a Short biplane from staging and trackway erected on the foredeck of the battleship *Africa* while at anchor at Sheerness. From this small beginning, and under the impetus of war, naval aircraft had within six years become an accepted part of the naval scene.

By November 1918 many hundreds of landplanes, floatplanes and flying boats were operational, dedicated to naval and coastal use. The floatplanes (or seaplanes) were often carried by various types of ship, being hoisted in and out of the sea as required. Flights were also made by ship-based landplanes, either from wooden platforms fixed above a gun turret or from lighters towed behind ships, although both of these methods were likely to lead to a watery ending unless land was within range. Vital as these early activities were, however, the origins of the Fleet Air Arm as we know it today may be traced back to events in August 1917.

A few weeks earlier, HMS *Furious* had commissioned at Walker-on-Tyne as an aircraft carrier, following the ship's conversion from a light battlecruiser. Her forward turret had been removed to make room for a 228ft long × 50ft wide flying-off deck, and during her early trials she carried three Short seaplanes and five Sopwith Pup landplanes.

Furious was a fast ship, able to maintain a steady wind speed of 31.5kt over the flying-off deck, and Sqn Cdr E. H. Dunning soon suggested that it might be possible not only to

▼ **Sqn Cdr Dunning making the world's first carrier deck landing, on HMS *Furious* on 2 August 1917. The deck party is about to rush out to hold his Sopwith Pup down, special toggles having been attached to the wings for this purpose. (Via Capt. M. Farquhar)**

► Dunning's Sopwith Pup crashed into the sea on 7 August 1917 while he was attempting to go round again, with fatal results. (Via Capt. M. Farquhar)

launch wheeled aircraft but to land them back on again. The advantages of being able to retrieve landplanes at sea were obvious, and approval for a trial was soon given. The ship was with the Grand Fleet at Scapa Flow at the time, and on 2 August an impressive assembly of gold-braided officers gathered on deck to see his first attempt.

Dunning chose Pup N6452 for the occasion, and he made what was by then a normal take-off. The ship steamed into wind, and as he came to attempt a landing she was making about 26kt; since the wind speed over the deck was about 47kt, a relatively slow approach was possible. Coming in on the port side so as to avoid the ship's superstructure, Dunning side-slipped down and centred up over the deck. A flight deck party of officers then rushed out and pulled the aircraft down by means of special toggles attached to the wings.

The practicability of landing wheeled aircraft on the deck of a moving carrier had been proved once and for all and the scene was set for carrier operations of the future, though there was much to be learnt about the arts of deck landing and deck handling. This was demonstrated very tragically only five days later, when further trials were carried out. Conditions on this occasion were less favourable, the weather being somewhat gusty. The first landing, using another machine, was carried out successfully but minor damage was caused to the elevator on touch-down and Dunning reverted to the original aircraft. This time the approach was somewhat higher. Dunning realized that he was too far down the deck to land as intended, so he waved the deck party away and started to go round again. Unfortunately, as he started to rise, the engine choked and the aircraft stalled. It dropped heavily on the starboard wheel, then started to go over the side of the ship. The deck party made a dash for it but, having been waved away, were too far off to catch it. No safety boat was launched, and it took 20 minutes for the ship to turn around and return to the spot. It was too late. Dunning had evidently been knocked out when the aircraft ditched and, sadly, had drowned by the time he was recovered.

Despite this tragic loss, Dunning's historic achievement proved without question that wheeled aircraft could both take off from and land on warships. The next logical development was a carrier with an uninterrupted flight deck, and this appeared in September 1918 when HMS *Argus*, the world's first flush-decked aircraft carrier, entered service.

CHAPTER 2

The Formative Years

The Royal Naval Air Service had ceased to exist on 1 April 1918 when it merged into the newly formed Royal Air Force. By that time it possessed nearly 3,000 aircraft and 100 airships, and had a strength of 67,000 personnel of all ranks. There were dozens of air stations, not only in the United Kingdom but in many locations overseas, especially around the Mediterranean and the Aegean. After the Armistice the naval element of the Royal Air Force was run down drastically, but the fleet carriers *Argus* and *Furious* were retained as the nucleus of a postwar carrier force and the seaplane carriers *Ark Royal* and *Pegasus* for use mainly as aircraft transports. Of the many UK naval air stations which existed in November 1918 only four were retained. Gosport was useful as a shore base convenient to Portsmouth, whilst Leuchars performed a similar function for ships at Rosyth and in the Firth of Forth. The needs of the seaplanes were met by Calshot and Lee-on-Solent, both similarly handy for Portsmouth.

Wartime aircraft flown from the carriers had included Sopwith 1½ Strutters, Sopwith Pups, Sopwith Camels and, latterly, Sopwith Cuckoos and Parnall Panthers, but the Pups and Camels were obsolete by 1919. Early in 1920, aircraft for carrier use were brought within the RAF squadron system, the first unit being No. 210 which in February 1920 formed at Gosport as a Torpedo Training Squadron, equipped mainly with Cuckoos. The following month No. 203 Squadron formed at Leuchars as a Fleet Fighter Squadron equipped with Camels and in April 1920 No. 205 formed at Leuchars as a Fleet Reconnaissance Squadron with Panthers. Finally, in October 1921, part of No. 205 Squadron broke away to form No. 3 Squadron, a Naval Air Co-operation unit equipped with the new Westland Walrus, a three-seater fleet spotter version of the De Havilland DH9a light bomber. These four units thus formed the nucleus of the early postwar first-line carrier-borne strength of the RAF. There was in addition the School of Naval Co-operation, split between Lee-on-Solent and Calshot. Providing training in operating seaplanes, this at first used wartime Short 184s until re-equipping from late 1921 with the new Fairey IIID, a reliable aircraft which continued in service for many years.

The four carrier squadrons embarked from time to time on board *Argus*, but *Furious* was undergoing extensive alterations and would consequently be out of commission for some years. In the spring of 1922 No. 210 Squadron began to receive the Blackburn Dart, a new postwar design of torpedo-bomber destined to be the mainstay in this role for several years. A few weeks later No. 203 Squadron re-equipped with Nieuport Nightjars, these being late wartime Nieuport Nighthawks modified by Gloster as stop-gap carrier-based fighters.

In the autumn of 1922 an international crisis arose in the Near East. Turkey, which had sided with Germany during the First World War, recovered quickly after the Armistice of November 1918. She had taken back much of the land occupied by Italy and France under its terms and was now beginning to threaten British interests. Her troops had crossed the neutral line established in the Dardanelles and were also concentrating ready to support agitators in Iraq. To help counteract these activities the small British force in the area was quickly strengthened. In early September six Nightjars of No. 203 Squadron were embarked on board *Argus* and shipped to the Dardanelles; two weeks later *Ark Royal* was used to transport an RAF squadron of Bristol Fighters, whilst *Pegasus* brought an RAF flight of IIID seaplanes from Malta. Most of the RAF units remained in the region until the crisis ended in August 1923, operating as the Constantinople Wing, but the Nightjars returned home in *Argus* in December 1922 after spending three months ashore at Kilia.

A planned expansion of the carrier force led to a rethink about the nature of the units which would operate from them and on 1 April 1923 came a further reorganization. Out went the concept of the squadron as the basic carrier aircraft formation and in its place came a series of flights, each normally equipped with six aircraft. Replacing the rather haphazard squadron numbers, the new flights were to be allocated standardized numbers in blocks according to their intended purpose. The

▼ Supermarine Seagull III N9647 '41' amphibian flying boat of No. 440 Flight seen ashore at Hal Far aerodrome, Malta, in 1924. The type was not a great success, giving way shortly afterwards to the Fairey IIID, but it laid the foundations for the ubiquitous Supermarine Walrus. (FAA Museum)

fighter units would in future be known as Fleet Fighter Flights, numbered from 401 onwards. The first of these, No. 401 Flight, formed at Leuchars, being initially equipped with the Nightjars formerly used by No. 203 Squadron, later to be replaced by Fairey Flycatchers. The latter, another successful postwar design, became the standard aircraft for this type of unit, equipping No. 402 Flight when it formed at Leuchars on 1 April 1923.

The next numerical series of new units comprised the Fleet Spotter Flights, which initially took over the Walrus aircraft of No. 3 Squadron, and these were numbered from 420 onwards. Nos. 420, 421 and 422 Flights all formed at Gosport at this time, but No. 422 soon re-equipped with another postwar design, the whimsically named Blackburn Blackburn. This type also reached No. 420 Flight in early 1925, but No. 421 instead received its competitor, the Avro Bison. Neither of these machines gained any points for their looks, the Blackburn having a particularly bulbous appearance.

The 440 series was reserved for Fleet Reconnaissance Flights, Nos 441 and 442 Flights both forming on 1 April 1923 at Leuchars from the Panthers of No. 205 Squadron and re-equipping the following year with Fairey IIIDs. No. 440 Flight, however, formed at Lee-on-Solent on 1 May 1923 equipped with Supermarine Seagull Mk. III amphibian flying boats, but these were not a great success, and eighteen months later they too gave way to IIIDs. A nucleus of No. 443 Flight also formed at Leuchars on 21 May 1923, but this did not become effective until 1925, again with IIIDs. Finally, the torpedo-bombers of No. 210 Squadron formed the basis of the 460 series of Fleet Torpedo Flights, both Nos. 460 and 461 forming on 1 April 1923 at Gosport equipped with Darts.

Argus was still the only fleet carrier in commission, being then fitted with fore-and-aft deck wires to help aircraft maintain a straight course after landing. This system was dropped two years later and thereafter the pilot made his approach after being given clearance by the Affirmative Flag, and by a shutter operated from the ship's island. He then used his own judgement, cutting the engine on passing the after end of the flight deck and gliding down to come to rest – in the early days without the benefit of brakes, although generally a rope safety barrier was raised during landing to prevent his running off the forward end. There was little spare room on deck, so as each aircraft landed it had to be quickly struck down via the lift into the hangar, to allow the next machine to land on.

Meanwhile No. 403 Fleet Fighter Flight had formed at Leuchars on 1 June 1923 with Parnall Plovers, this type being a less successful competitor of the Flycatcher which did not stay long in service (though it also equipped No. 404 Flight when it formed there a month later). Another new unit was No. 423 Fleet Spotter Flight, which came into existence at Gosport on 21 November 1923 with Bisons, a few Walruses also being used for a time.

On 1 April 1924, exactly a year after these new carrier-borne flights had begun to form, they were given the collective title 'Fleet Air Arm of the Royal Air Force', soon abbreviated in practice to the now familiar 'Fleet Air Arm'. Shortly afterwards FAA aircraft began to adopt distinctive markings for visual identification purposes. Each parent carrier was allocated a particular colour to be used in a diagonal or vertical fuselage band on all its aircraft. Thus aircraft of *Argus* flights were to be painted with green bands and those of *Furious* red, and when the new carriers *Eagle* and *Hermes* came into service their aircraft would be painted with black and white bands respectively. For individual identification, each aircraft also bore a one- or two-digit number (officially known as a Fleet Number), superimposed on the fuselage bands and often also carried on the wings. This aircraft numbering system has, with some modifications, continued until the present day, though the carrier colours have been abandoned and three-digit numbers adopted.

Originally laid down as the Chilean battleship *Almirante Cochrane*, HMS *Eagle* commissioned in February 1924 after a lengthy conversion. The new carrier emerged from the shipyard with a full-length flight deck, equipped with lifts, and with its superstructure, or island, to starboard, this layout becoming the basic pattern for all aircraft carriers up to the present day. She was ready for service by May, when her flights embarked for service in the Mediterranean, these being Nos. 402 with Flycatchers, 422 with Blackburns, 440 with Seagulls and 460 with Darts. She returned home at the end of the year for a short refit, leaving Nos. 422 and 460 Flights in Malta; No. 402 went to Leuchars, but No. 440 went to the School of Naval Co-operation to learn to fly new IIIDs.

By November 1924 *Hermes* was also ready for service – the first ship designed specifically as an aircraft carrier to be commissioned. She took *Eagle*'s place with the Mediterranean Fleet for a time but being a small carrier could carry only the Flycatchers of No. 403 Flight and the IIIDs of No. 441. *Eagle* returned to Malta in March 1925 and *Hermes* then sailed for home, taking No. 441 Flight with her but leaving No. 403 behind. *Hermes* sailed again from Portsmouth in June 1925 and, after picking up the IIIDs of *Eagle*'s No. 440 Flight in Malta the following month, continued on for the China Station, the IIIDs disembarking when the carrier called in at Alexandria en route. After spending some time at Hong Kong, *Hermes* returned to Malta in March 1926.

Meanwhile, in September 1925, *Furious* recommissioned, flush-decked, after a four-year programme of modernization. An innovation was the fitting of a round-down at the after end of the flight deck, to improve air flow and also to give pilots greater confidence when landing on, and this feature later became standard on other carriers. Being a much larger ship, *Furious* was able to embark the Flycatchers of No. 404 Flight, the Blackburns of No. 420 Flight, the three Bisons of No. 421A half-Flight, the three IIIDs of No. 443A half-Flight and the Darts of Nos. 461 and 462 Flights.

Thus, at the time the Fleet Air Arm came into existence on 1 April 1924 *Argus* had been the only carrier actually available, but within eighteen months she had been joined by *Eagle*, *Hermes* and *Furious* to bring the new service up, albeit briefly, to the planned strength for the early postwar years. These ships were due to be joined later by *Courageous* and *Glorious*, but in October 1925 *Argus* had to go into Chatham Dockyard for extensive repairs after spending more than six years in full commission; she was relieved in the Atlantic Fleet by *Furious*.

The first deck landing ever made at night came on 6 May 1926, when Flt Lt Gerald Boyce landed a Blackburn Dart of No. 462 Flight safely on the deck of *Furious* off the south coast of England. The deck was brightly floodlit, and the affirmative signal for landing was also illuminated. Further night trials subsequently took place aboard the same ship in the Firth of Forth.

At this time *Eagle* was serving with the Mediterranean Fleet, and Cdr R. H. S. Rodger, RN, spent much of his earlier Fleet Air Arm career there with her:

In October 1926 I joined No. 460 Flight in HMS *Eagle*. On arrival at Malta we flew ashore to Hal Far aerodrome. Hal Far was quite a small aerodrome at that time, and in the middle of it was a little house, owned by a Maltese who for years wouldn't sell. Later, in May 1929, we had a pageant there, with various kinds of demonstration flying. I was a qualified

▲ Avro Bison II N9848 '21' of No. 423 (Fleet Spotter) Flight, with the distinctive vertical white fuselage identification band of HMS *Hermes*, flying near the ship in the Mediterranean during the summer of 1926. (RAF Museum)

armament officer by then, and I decided we would practise bombing this house. I told the aircrew that the house was not to be hit with the practice bombs, but they must make it hell for the owner, which we did. We all thought it was very amusing, and the fellow got so distressed that he eventually did sell it. Then I had a lovely time bombing it properly.

We also did a lot of practice night flying at Hal Far. The wind line for landings was illuminated by buckets containing paraffin flares, more paraffin being poured on occasionally to keep them alight. I did one bad night landing there, when my left wheel collapsed and I went in on my left wing tip, which in fact was rather fortunate as all the flares were on my right. Those were pioneer days at Hal Far, and when we did night flying the gunners used to try to locate us by sound. They had an aerial rangefinder with earphones at each end, and a sound indicator, which was interesting.

I reckon I am probably one of the few people who can honestly say he has taken off from an aerodrome in a certain compass direction (which was about south-west) and, without altering course, landed again on the same aerodrome in exactly the same direction. Hal Far was on the edge of a 200ft cliff, and when there was a strong wind from the south-west, the wind went vertically upwards until it curved over. One day I took off in a Dart, flying at about 30mph, then the vertical flow gave me extra height in a wind speed exceeding 30mph and I found myself flying backwards over the ground to land normally! Several of us then did this, just for the fun of doing it.

I remember an occasion in 1928 when an aircraft carrier was to leave the United Kingdom for Malta with empty aircraft hangars. Permission was given to fill the empty hangars with motor cars owned by officers serving in Malta.

In September 1926 *Hermes* returned to the China Station. She was ordered to travel at best speed to help deal with bandits and pirate junks, carrying the Flycatchers of No. 403 Flight and the IIIDs of No. 440 Flight. The Flycatchers exchanged their wheeled undercarriages for floats on arrival at Hong Kong. *Argus* came back into commission in January 1927. She had now been fitted with palisades, these being hinged metal and rope constructions extending from each side of the flight deck, to catch aircraft in danger of going over the side of the ship while landing on. A troublesome step in the after end of her flight deck had been removed and, like *Furious*, she was now fitted with a round-down.

A further crisis at that time in the Far East brought a need for reinforcements, and *Argus* immediately sailed for the China Station as part of the Shanghai Defence Force, which also included RAF units. Chinese revolutionary forces led by Generalissimo Chiang Kai-shek had overrun several large towns and were threatening Shanghai, which had a large British population. *Argus* took with her the three Flycatchers of No. 404B half-Flight and the three IIIDs of No. 443B half-Flight, and en route also embarked at Malta the IIIDs of *Eagle*'s No. 441 Flight. Many of these aircraft operated ashore from Shanghai racecourse, using an improvised 400yd strip parallel to the grandstand. Air patrols were carried out around the settlement, which became surrounded by rebel troops.

In the Kowloon peninsula at Hong Kong another landing strip was set up at Kai Tak so that aircraft from *Hermes* could operate ashore. Kai Tak was to become a permanent shore base for the Fleet Air Arm and later the RAF and in more recent years has been extended to become Hong Kong's international airport. The Fleet Air Arm also had available in the area at that time the three IIID seaplanes of No. 444 Flight, which operated from the cruiser *Vindictive*, with the more northerly anchorage at Wei-hai-Wei as a shore base, the latter being also used in later years by aircraft from *Hermes* when the Fleet sailed north to escape the heat of Shanghai and Hong Kong during the summer months.

Later in 1927 the Chinese Nationalist forces regained control of the Shanghai area, and the Defence Force then disbanded. *Hermes* sailed home for a refit in September, and in November *Argus* was also able to withdraw, spending four months in Hong Kong before reaching Portsmouth in early May 1928. *Vindictive* remained on station until March 1928, when she too went home, *Hermes* having returned East by then.

By this time another new carrier was ready to join the Fleet. *Courageous* commissioned at Devonport in February 1928, and when her flights embarked in May they carried blue fuselage identification bands. She was the first carrier to be fitted with transverse arrester wires, a system which, although much developed, remains in use as the standard means of stopping fixed-wing aircraft; she was also provided with a lower flying off deck in the bow, a feature later repeated in *Glorious*. The largest Royal Navy carrier to date, *Courageous* had six flights, mostly newly formed, comprising Nos. 404 and 407 with Flycatchers, Nos. 445 and 446 with Fairey IIIFs (successors to the IIIDs) and Nos. 463 and 464 with Darts. In June she sailed for Malta to join the Mediterranean Fleet, cruises being later made to the Aegean. The introduction of the versatile and sturdy IIIF led to a new combined fleet-spotter-reconnaissance task. The pure fleet-spotter category accordingly became obsolete, and in April 1929, to conform with the system, the four 420-series flights were renumbered in the 440 series.

In August 1929 trouble flared up in Palestine, where Arabs were making raids on Jewish villages. *Courageous* was despatched to the area and two days later she was off Jaffa with a full complement of aircraft as well as a battalion of troops and supporting transport. These were all disembarked, her flights going to a desert landing strip at Gaza from where they attacked Arab villages and made deterrent flights against Arab raiders and their camels until re-embarking four weeks later.

Cdr Rodger was involved in this episode:

◀Fairey Flycatcher N9905 '6' of No. 404 (Fleet Fighter) Flight, with a diagonal red fuselage band, leaving the flying-off deck of *Furious* in 1926. Its individual code marking, or fleet number, is carried on a diagonal red fuselage band, this colour identifying the parent carrier. (FAA Museum)

▲ **Fairey IIID floatplane S1108 '40' from No. 445 Flight, the last machine of this type to be built. Attached to the battleship *Resolution*, with the Mediterranean Fleet, it was wrecked on 7 March 1928 when, during an air pageant at Calafrana seaplane base, Malta, it dropped several bags then overbanked and struck the water. (RAF Museum)**

On 28 August 1929 we flew from *Courageous*, off Haifa, to the Imperial Airways aerodrome at Gaza. Palestine was then a British Protectorate, and the Arabs were raiding Jewish villages. At Gaza food was something of a problem, but the locals started a fire in a trench and cooked for us a young calf with a rod through it, rather like a spit, twisting it in the flames. This was very tasty. While we were there we did a big formation flight over Jerusalem, afterwards dropping leaflets.

Then there was a southern patrol from Gaza to Beersheba, and I also flew to the Sinai Desert to see what it was like. On 2 September I was selected to drop proclamation leaflets on Jericho, refuelling at RAF Ramleh, near Jaffa, before returning to Gaza. When I was refuelling I discovered a little water leak, and I used chewing gum to fill the hole temporarily! After dropping the leaflets I realized that I was 1,000 feet below sea level and it occurred to me that this was a chance to really get one up on some submarine officers who were then serving in *Courageous*. We often used to fly down low above the water and roll our wheels along it, so I decided to do this along the Dead Sea. On my return I said 'I have flown my aeroplane lower than you can get your bloody submarine'. 'Oh no you haven't', they said, 'A drink on it?'. 'Yes', I replied, 'Dead Sea, 1,000 feet below sea level. Can you beat that anywhere in the Mediterranean?'

On one occasion we did a demonstration flight over Constantinople in the form of a crescent with a star in the middle.

The last of the planned new carriers was ready by October 1929 when HMS *Glorious* was commissioned, this having an island as did later carriers. Her allotted carrier colour was yellow, borne by the Flycatchers of Nos. 405, 406 and 408 Flights, the IIIFs of Nos. 441 and 447 Flights and the fast new Blackburn Ripon torpedo-bombers of Nos. 461 and 462 Flights when they all embarked in March 1930. The ship joined the Mediterranean Fleet three months later but, before sailing, No. 405 Flight was involved in trials aboard *Furious* for the next generation of FAA fighters: the Hawker Hornet, Armstrong Whitworth Starling, Fairey Fleetwing and Vickers 177 were all involved in deck-landing trials. None of these was successful, but the first-named was developed to produce the sturdy Hawker Nimrod.

Dan Baker, an observer who was later Commander (O) in *Courageous* at the time she was sunk, gives these impressions of that period:

I started flying in the Navy in January 1926, having previously done three months' training in ground subjects, signals, gunnery and navigation. In the Navy this latter was dead reckoning – we never did any celestial navigation. Our training was at an RAF base, and all our instructors were RAF. Most of the observer instructors, who were indeed the only instructors we had because the pilots simply flew the aircraft, were former air gunners of the old RNAS who had eventually come to commissioned rank in the RAF. Their main subject to us was W/T [wireless telegraphy], training us to be able to handle an aircraft set and transmit and receive, and teaching us the Morse code at the speed at which one operates in an aircraft.

We had a few old Fairey IIID floatplanes, with great wooden floats, and also a few single-engined Supermarine Seagull amphibians, precursors of the Walrus. The Seagulls were fitted with old Napier Lion engines which suffered severely from hiccups due to water leakage as their water jackets used to rust through. All the Fleet Air Arm aircraft in operational use at that time in the carriers were Napier Lion-engined and no one really liked them very much because of this water leak business, which constantly caused forced landings at unexpected moments.

In one incident, about a month after we had started flying training at Lee-on-Solent, we had a forced landing in a IIID floatplane during very heavy weather about 20 miles south of Swanage. Of course one float punctured, and she turned on her back at once and floated on the remaining float. That sort of thing was happening much too often, so nobody regarded the Lion engine as reliable and yet it went on for a good many years.

The provision of aircraft for the Fleet Air Arm was through the Air Force, who owned the whole thing – you might say it was a taxi service owned by the RAF, chartered by the Navy. The provision of naval aircraft was, in my opinion, most seriously delayed, being given a bottom priority. After all, you must remember that the number of RAF first-line squadrons at that time was so small that papers like the *Daily Mail* christened the RAF 'The Royal Ground Force' because they were so seldom able to take to the air. So many of the new types for the Fleet Air Arm were modifications of RAF general-service aircraft, which meant they were three or four years behind their coming into service in the RAF by the time they got to us in the Navy. They were also pretty unsuitable, not having been specifically designed for the Navy. One exception, though, was the single-seater Blackburn Dart torpedo aircraft. This had no application to the RAF and in strong winds you could see it quite visibly flying backwards because its speed was so terrible. It was superseded by the Blackburn Ripon, which was in effect a two-seater Dart, slightly streamlined. The Ripon could carry an observer and W/T operator, so the torpedo striking force could be independent, whereas previously the single-seat Dart torpedo-carrying aircraft had to be led to its target and back again by a reconnaissance aircraft of the Fairey IIID type with a pilot and observer.

The RAF provided 30 per cent of the flying personnel and 100 per cent of the maintenance personnel, and the RN and RAF flyers worked as a team in the squadrons, in maintenance and in the carriers. We on the naval side regarded the RAF flying personnel as one of ourselves and I think they felt the same towards us, but at the same time, professionally, there is no doubt that a number of them regarded it as a waste of time as far as their RAF career was concerned, and showed lack of interest.

The early people in the Fleet Air Arm were, however, thought to be a bit eccentric by the general run of the Navy, who considered themselves to be essentially a big-gun Navy to which aircraft were a rather ridiculous addition. In the view of the gunnery officers, they might be helpful in lieu of cruisers for reconnaissance but could never do damage to an enemy fleet or even to a single ship because they would always be shot down. (My own view was that the anti-aircraft shooting of the Fleet was totally lamentable!)

We had plenty of towed drogues, and a tow drogue flight used to go round with the Fleet, this being rather a plum job as they always lived ashore, so everybody was jealous of them. They had a very safe and unblemished life because I have never seen the shoot carried out on the drogue where the anti-aircraft shell burst went closer than 200 or 300 yards astern of the drogue, let alone the towing aircraft. They later progressed to a radio-controlled Queen Bee which used to stumble around the Fleet at a fairly modest height of about 5,000 feet, doing an honest 48 knots. The lack of efficiency in the anti-aircraft defences of the fleet was criminal. I think it was brought out in the war, where until we got radar-controlled anti-aircraft gunnery systems the number of hits on German aircraft was sweet Fanny Adams.

▼*Furious* at sea, with Flycatcher fleet fighters ranged on deck ready for flying off. The palisades are erected at the sides of the deck and the forward wind break is upright. The lower flight deck has its wind break lowered. (Gp Capt. R. A. McMurtrie)

CHAPTER 3

The Clouds Darken

The postwar pattern of naval aviation was now well established but the year 1930 saw several changes. In January *Courageous* left for a refit, to be replaced in the Mediterranean Fleet later in the year by *Glorious*; in March *Argus* went into reserve, not to be used again for six years; and in June *Furious* went to Portsmouth, then to Devonport for nearly two years. *Courageous* took the place of *Argus* in the Atlantic Fleet in September and in the same month *Hermes* returned from the China Station for another short refit before sailing once more for Hong Kong two months later. Then in May 1931 *Eagle* was also decommissioned for a refit.

During the 1920s, in continuation of a practice adopted towards the end of the First World War, various trials had been carried out in operating wheeled aircraft from wooden platforms mounted on the main guns of large warships. These activitives had their drawbacks, however, and more promise was shown by the development of ship-mounted catapults driven by compressed air or a cordite charge. Ships which were so equipped could now carry reconnaissance seaplanes, able to be flown off whilst the ship was under way.

By the autumn of 1930 sufficient progress had been made for No. 443 Flight, which had previously served on board *Furious*, to be rededicated as a catapult flight operating Fairey IIIF seaplanes from the battleship *Valiant* and the cruiser *York*; it was also equipped with a few Flycatchers to operate from the cruisers *Emerald*, *Enterprise* and *Kent* in the East Indies and on the China Station. When ashore in the United Kingdom aircraft of the catapult flights went to the School of Naval Co-operation at Lee-on-Solent, which acted as their shore base. At about the same time No. 444 Flight, formerly aboard *Vindictive*, also became a catapult flight, operating at first from the cruisers *Dorsetshire* and *Norfolk*. In August 1931 these two catapult flights were reorganized, so that No. 443 became responsible for supplying seaplanes to ships of the 2nd Cruiser Squadron whilst No. 444 undertook the same task for battleships and battlecruisers.

Further warships were being fitted with catapults and in mid-1932 *Glorious* lost Nos. 407 and 447 Flights when these too were redesignated catapult flights. No. 407 Flight then operated new Hawker Ospreys from ships of the 4th Cruiser Squadron on the East Indies Station, whilst No. 447 Flight flew IIIFs with the 1st Cruiser Squadron in the Mediterranean Fleet. The Osprey was a two-seater fleet reconnaissance aircraft, and its single-seat counterpart from the same stable, the Hawker Nimrod fleet fighter, entered service around the same time. These two, both based on RAF aircraft designs, gradually re-equipped all the Flycatcher flights. Other new types were also on the way, and a Fairey Seal seaplane reached No. 444 Flight in December 1932 for use aboard HMS *Valiant*.

Speeds of aircraft were increasing as newer types came into service. The friction-type arrester gear, originally fitted to *Courageous* to pull up aircraft when they landed on, had not proved entirely satisfactory and experiments had continued in order to improve on this system. The main difficulty was the lack of control of the pull-out of the wire when the aircraft's hook engaged it but the problem was finally solved by fitting the ship with a hydraulic controlled system during a refit at the end of 1932. This equipment was proved in trials early the next year and later fitted to other carriers.

By now the nature of the Fleet Air Arm, which had grown to a strength of 27 flights, had changed considerably from that envisaged when it had first formed. The existing structure was proving unwieldy, especially with the increasing size of carriers, and on 3 April 1933, therefore, all the carrier-based flights were regrouped as squadrons, only the catapult flights retaining their identities – at least for the time being.

The Fleet Air Arm was still part of the Royal Air Force at that time, so to avoid duplication with the nomenclature of existing RAF units the new squadrons were allocated numbers in a fresh series beginning at 800. Continuing previous practice, the numbering system was subdivided, fighter squadrons being numbered 800 onwards, torpedo-bomber squadrons 810 onwards and spotter-reconnaissance squad-

rons 820 onwards. Each squadron would generally have either nine or twelve aircraft, depending mainly on the size of the parent carrier: a larger ship would have three such squadrons and a smaller one only two. The allocation of unit numbers depended initially on the carrier to which a squadron was allocated. Thus *Courageous* had Nos. 800, 810, 820 and 821 Squadrons, equipped respectively with Nimrods/Ospreys, Darts/Ripons, IIIFs/Seals and IIIFs/Seals. *Furious* was allocated Nos. 801, 811 and 822 Squadrons whose respective mounts were Nimrods/Ospreys, Ripons and IIIFs, whilst *Glorious* had Nos. 802 (Nimrods/Ospreys), 812 (Ripons) and 823 (IIIFs). The smaller *Eagle* carried just two squadrons, No. 803 with Ospreys and No. 824 with IIIFs. *Argus* was still in reserve at that time, but *Hermes* was due to leave the Far East for a refit and therefore did not adopt the new squadron system for either of her two flights, Nos. 403 and 440. When she was relieved soon afterwards by *Eagle*, No. 440 was absorbed into No. 824 Squadron whilst No. 403 became a catapult flight with the 5th Cruiser Squadron, remaining on the China Station.

During 1933 and 1934 the IIIFs were gradually replaced in the carriers by Seals, and in 1934 the Darts and Ripons gave way to a radial-engined version of the Ripon, named the Baffin; in the catapult flights Ospreys became the standard equipment. More important, however, in the longer term, was the receipt early in 1934 by No. 444 Flight of a prototype Supermarine Seagull V amphibian flying boat for trials aboard the battleship *Nelson*. These tests were not without their difficulties but they proved the value of this different concept of a catapult aircraft and led

◄ **The view from a Fairey IIIF coming in to land aboard *Furious*, with the red and white 'Affirmative' signal showing. The palisades have been erected and the wireless masts are lowered horizontally outside the ship. In the foreground, immediately following the round-down, can be seen the ship's deck-level exhaust grids and at the forward end of the flight deck are the grab-crew in readiness to hold the aircraft down. (Gp Capt. R. A. McMurtrie)**

directly to the rugged and ubiquitous Supermarine Walrus which, known affectionately as the 'Shagbat', was to become used extensively for this and other purposes in the Second World War.

In October 1934 No. 824 Squadron in *Eagle* on the China Station was renumbered to become No. 825 Squadron. At the same time a new No. 824 Squadron formed at Upavon for *Hermes*, with Seals. That ship sailed shortly afterwards to relieve *Eagle* on the China Station, taking over No. 803 Squadron on arrival. Her aircraft were now given green bands, this colour having become available with *Argus* still out of commission.

At the end of 1934 No. 820 Squadron aboard *Courageous* became the first unit to receive Blackburn Sharks, a new torpedo-bomber which was to prove not very successful, mainly because of engine problems. The re-equipment of catapult flights continued during 1935. In January No. 444 Flight began trials with the Walrus on board the battleship *Nelson* and No. 447 Flight partially replaced its IIIFs with Ospreys, No. 443 being similarly re-equipped four months later. In June the shore base for disembarked catapult flights was changed from Lee-on-Solent to Mount Batten, an RAF flying boat base at Plymouth, and in August No. 445 Flight re-formed as a catapult unit, equipped with Ospreys for the 3rd Cruiser Squadron in the Mediterranean.

Baffins were the new equipment of No. 811 Squadron when it rejoined *Furious* early in 1935, and the same type equipped 'A' Flight of No. 820 Squadron in August when it sailed with *Courageous* to the Middle East during the Italian invasion of Abyssinia, as did the newly re-commissioned *Glorious*. Both ships disembarked their aircraft on arrival at Alexandria, but the war did not spread and in the early part of 1936 the FAA squadrons were withdrawn from Egypt. Among the many RAF personnel serving aboard *Glorious* in 1935 was Cecil Bristow, who was attached to No. 825 Squadron:

> In August 1935 sanctions were declared against Italy and most of the Mediterranean Fleet departed Malta for Alexandria, leaving Grand Harbour strangely empty. All that summer it seemed that the island's Commissariat had been bringing its larder up to date and we were fed on corned beef morning, noon and night in some form or other and were by then heartily sick of it. Our TAG's lament was 'Roll on *Glorious* and let's have some decent food'. *Glorious* duly arrived from the UK on 28 August – and our first main meal on board was a corned beef salad! The first indication of her nearness had been when Hal Far was suddenly flooded with aircraft, Nos. 802 and 823 Squadrons having flown off to stretch their legs. The carrier had undergone a major refit which included extending the flight deck aft over the quarterdeck, supported by four tubular girders in 'W' formation, building extra cabins aft so that the quarterdeck was raised in line with the lower deck, making her readily identifiable from her sister ship *Courageous*. She had also had accelerators installed.
>
> On 2 September all four squadrons – Nos. 802, 812, 823 and 825 – flew aboard. This seemed to take up most of the day, Nos. 812 and 825 being especially long-winded as they were joining *Glorious* for the first time and all ground handling both on deck and striking below was done by raw crews. I was detailed for the rear party of four ratings and an NCO to despatch the aircraft from Hal Far, and we could see the carrier steaming back and forth off shore as she received each squadron. This was my very first sight of her (or of any other carrier if it came to that!).
>
> It was evening before we received word that all were aboard and we gathered up our tool kits and other servicing aids and were transported to Grand Harbour. A duty rating met us on deck and led us to the bedding store, it now being 10 p.m. (I was yet to learn how to tell the time by bells and watches). Most people were turned in, and we learnt the hard way that it wasn't the 'done thing' to bump when passing beneath an occupied hammock! Our guide had left us and we knew not where we were. Quite by accident we stumbled upon the hangar and, right or wrong, we 'crashed' there on the hangar floor (sorry, deck), bewildered and hungry. Next morning, we late arrivals were 'piped' to report to the Master at Arms for 'joining routine'. 'Yes, Chief', I said when at last I had found the right place. Talk about the bloke who coughed in the chemist's shop – there was a deathly hush all around followed by a 10-minute spiel with not a word repeated, and I gathered that though his three cuff buttons make him look like a CPO he wasn't one, and it would pay to rapidly recognize collar badges in future!
>
> The hangar deck was abandoned as a sleeping place and I was duly allotted 18 inches or so of space above the mess table, soon learning to trust the simple knot used when slinging my hammock and to lash up with the seven regulation loops and stow. New words began to appear in our vocabulary and stairs and ceilings became ladders and deckheads etc. – but who on earth invented the word 'heads'? I digress.
>
> Our second day aboard was spent by playing 'draughts' with the aircraft, getting practice in ranging up and striking down, stowing and, of course, lashing down, so alien after years on aerodromes. No. 802 Squadron with its Nimrods and Ospreys was housed in the upper hangar forward of the front lift shaft. No. 812's Baffins and No. 823's Seals shared the remainder of the upper hangar and No. 825's IIIFs were in the lower hangar, on the same level as the battery deck. Being housed in the lower hangar added considerably to the length

of time it took the squadron to 'land on' and strike down twelve aircraft after a flying programme; angled decks and aircraft parks forward of the crash barrier were yet to be thought of. Each IIIF would land on, disengage hook (for a while we had one aircraft with no hook fitted and one or two had no braking system), be taxied forward and 'spotted' on the forward lift, wings folded, and be struck below. It took a deck-handling party of seven squadron ground staff (no specific flight-deck crew). Six ratings would lift the rear fuselage clear of the deck and set the tail skid (!) into a locating box mounted on a two-wheeled barrow in the hands of a corporal. The six ratings then took up positions on the wings: one stood at each wing-tip to hold back the mainplanes, two others mounted the lower wings at the root-end to unwind the upper wing attachment bolts whilst the remaining two unwound the lower wing bolts. These four would then assist the men at the wing-tips to fold back the wings and lock in position (none of your hydraulic operated affairs).

Our best time ever for thus handling twelve aircraft was 20 minutes, steaming into wind all this time. How the U-boats would have loved that! Trying to save split seconds when operating the lift led to at least two mishaps. Once when the lift was just on its way up it caught the tips of the lower propeller blade before the aircraft was far enough into the hangar. The lower blade was dead vertical and the aircraft wheels began to lift clear of the deck before the prop tip curled. This meant a propeller change and a shock-load test on the prop shaft. In the second mishap the corporal on the lift, holding the tail-barrow, let go the handle before the hangar corporal had grasped it and the handle shot upwards. This was my aircraft, and I had a late session in the hangar changing rudder and elevators!

To continue, we reached Alexandria on 2 September and three days later *Courageous* arrived to reinforce the Fleet, having made the passage from the UK in a record 5½ days. All squadron ratings had to take turn as mess cooks – drawing all meals for their mess, serving them, washing up and cleaning their allotted section of the mess deck. This caused no little inconvenience in the hangar where we should be servicing our aircraft. The CO's solution to this was to appoint the seaman 'Killick' and the six ABs who did general duties in the squadron

to be permanent mess cooks and excused practically any other requirement of them. At first they were a little peeved but this soon vanished when, having a lot of spare time on their hands, they organized a squadron 'dhobi firm', for remuneration of course, first washing our overalls then progressing to all our laundry. It was reputed they never drew any of their service pay for the rest of the commission!

Towards the end of September my IIIF (fitted up for drogue-towing) plus a second aircraft for 'spotting' purposes were put ashore at the RAF station of Aboukir, close to Alexandria, to enable the major Fleet units get in some firing practice without the carrier having to leave harbour each time. On one such flight the black puffs appeared to be much closer to us than the towed target and we rocked quite a bit. On another flight we were privileged to see a 'battlewagon' fire a broadside, something not often seen from above and it really was a fantastic sight. We were also involved with night flying, spending quite a few nights over Alex doing dummy attack approaches to get some practice.

Italy finally declared war on Abyssinia on 3 October and security was greatly increased all round. On October 18 the Italian liner *Ausonia* caught fire at sea off Alexandria and put in to Alex harbour for shelter and help. In spite of strained relations fire-fighting crews were provided by British naval units but to no avail as the fire had too great a hold. Eight days later she was a hulk and still burning.

In December an unfortunate accident occurred aboard *Courageous*. She had just cleared Alex harbour en route to Malta when one of the hangar fire screens, a huge asbestos curtain with a lead weight along its base, broke from its stowed position in the deck-head and fatally injured one of the squadron's flight sergeants. *Courageous* put back into Alex, put the body ashore and departed again. He was buried in the British Military Cemetery, *Glorious* supplying the various funeral parties, the cortège passing through deep ranks of local onlookers. There were some unsavoury rumours about the accident and I resolved that if I ever became a flight sergeant when I grew up I would be rather circumspect in my behaviour.

Following the return of *Courageous*, *Glorious* sailed for Malta on 22 December and all squadrons disembarked to Hal Far next day. After enjoying our Christmas ashore we all re-embarked on 1 Jan. 1936 and returned to Alex. Everyone was shattered at the news later that month of the death of King George V – a big loss to the Royal Navy, who regarded him as the 'Sailor King'.

Cecil also tells the sad tale of an accident the following year:

On 23 August all squadrons re-embarked, and next day we set off on our autumn cruise and exercises. There was a nasty incident during one 'range'. As a corporal armourer of No. 823 Squadron was passing behind one aircraft its pilot, about to take off, began to rev up and the slipstream blew the corporal off-balance. He instinctively raised his hand to steady himself and the propeller of the aircraft behind sliced off his hand, flinging it overboard to float like a glove. A Royal Marine bystander in the nets saw what had happened, and whipping the injured arm behind its owner, assisted him to the sick bay just below the flight deck, and he was on the operating table before the wound lost its numbness and he could begin to feel pain. (As a sequel to this, some years after the war my wife and I were in London viewing a display of Royal Wedding presents – Princess Margaret's I think – which were guarded by a party of the Corps of Commissionaires. Noticing one was wearing the Atlantic Star ribbon I asked him if he had ever served on carriers. And, cutting it short, he turned out to be the above Marine!)

▼Hawker Nimrod II S1621 '504' of No. 800 (Fleet Fighter) Squadron around 1933. It bears the diagonal blue fuselage band of HMS *Courageous*, with the squadron badge in gold on a black fin. This machine was eventually lost on 12 February 1935 after colliding with another Nimrod during a mock attack on a Fairey Seal. (Via J. D. Oughton)

Further re-equipping of catapult flights occurred during 1936, commencing in January with the arrival of Ospreys in No. 444 Flight, which in March also received Sharks and new Fairey Swordfish. Shortly afterwards the Walrus reached No. 407 Flight and then No. 403, but on 15 July all these flights lost their identities when they were reorganized into a new 700 series. Under the new numbering system flight numbers were allocated in blocks according to the type of ship, commencing with Nos. 701 and 702 Flights in battleships, followed by No. 705 Flight in battlecruisers and then Nos. 711 onwards in cruisers. This last sub-series adopted the number of the parent cruiser squadron as the last digit of the flight number. No. 720 Flight was allocated to cruisers of the New Zealand Division, being given four Walruses, and equipment was soon standardized on this type in most of the cruiser flights. No. 701 Flight received some Sharks and a Seal towards the end of 1936.

More carrier squadrons re-equipped during 1936, commencing in March with the issue of Sharks to No. 821 Squadron on board *Courageous*, followed in June by the re-equipment of No. 822 Squadron in *Furious* with Seals as a temporary measure pending the arrival five months later of Sharks. By this time, however, both the spotter-reconnaissance and torpedo-bomber squadrons were beginning to standardize on the Swordfish and were therefore reclassified as torpedo-spotter-reconnaissance squadrons. The first to do so was No. 825 Squadron in *Glorious* in July 1936, followed in October by No. 811 Squadron in *Furious*, then Nos. 823 and 812 in *Glorious*.

Early in 1937 *Eagle* went back into service after a spell in reserve and embarked No. 813 Squadron with Swordfish before sailing for the China Station to replace *Hermes* which was

▼ **Hawker Osprey III floatplane K3642 '067', from the cruiser *London* with the 1st Cruiser Squadron in the Mediterranean Fleet, flying over Alexandria during 1936. Piloted here by Lt E. G. Clutton, RN, the machine was flown by No. 447 (Fleet Spotter Reconnaissance) Flight until it came to grief on 22 May 1936 when, fitted out as a landplane, it stalled and crashed on take-off from RAF Aboukir, catching fire on impact. (RAF Museum)**

K
3642

◀ **Supermarine Walrus K8345 of No. 711 (Catapult) Flight being catapulted from the cruiser *Devonshire* towards the end of 1936. The ship was then part of the 1st Cruiser Squadron with the Mediterranean Fleet. (RAF Museum)**

due for a refit. No. 803 Squadron disbanded when *Hermes* departed but No. 824 transferred to *Eagle* and re-equipped with Swordfish, which aircraft was already showing the promise it was to fulfil throughout the war. No. 810 Squadron on board *Courageous* received obsolescent Sharks in April 1937 but five months later these too gave way to Swordfish, which very soon was also equipping No. 822 Squadron in *Furious* and Nos. 820 and 821 in *Courageous*.

Life aboard *Hermes* in the mid-1930s is vividly illustrated by these recollections from Commissioned Gunner Les Dudley, RN (Ret.):

> *Hermes*, with a displacement fully loaded of about 13,000 tons, was the smallest of our naval carriers and operated mainly in the Far East, where her time with the China Fleet alternated with that of *Eagle*. She had a complement of approximately 700 officers and men and recommissioned on 1 November 1934, following an extensive refit during which she had spent time at both Chatham and Devonport Dockyards. Vice Admiral Sir Eric J. A. Fullerton inspected the ship on 7 November and later in the day we sailed from Devonport to Portsmouth. On arrival, RAF stores, Seal aircraft and personnel of 824 Squadron, which included some pilots, observers and other members of the Fleet Air Arm, were embarked and preparations made for our departure to the China Station. Other consignments were also taken aboard for various ships and naval ports; one of these was a pack of hounds which we were taking to Gibraltar.
>
> On passage to Gibraltar, evolutions for emergencies were practised frequently. It was a mixed ship's company, consisting of naval, Royal Marine and RAF personnel, who were destined to make this their home for the next two and a half years. Initially, it was strange to see officers and men in RAF uniform in our midst. They had to learn about the ways of the other two services and the nautical language common to them. The pipe 'up spirits' caused some consternation and perhaps was thought to be an ecclesiastical command, whilst the pipe 'hands to make and mend clothes' would bring forth sailors with sewing baskets and knitting needles. The sailors and Marines in their turn were to hear such jargon as 'flat spin' and 'being shot down in flames'. In a very short time, though, the RAF personnel fitted in extremely well with the remainder of the ship's company, and friendships were soon formed. Good natured reference by sailors and Marines to the RAF men was that of 'crabfats', whilst they were soon to refer to the other service's members as 'fish-heads' and 'bootnecks'.
>
> Following our journey out from the UK, during which we had embarked Ospreys, stores and personnel of No. 803 Squadron, we arrived in Hong Kong in early January to become an integral part of the China Fleet. Our stay here lasted from January to May 1935. The ship went to sea for two or three days a week to do exercises with other ships of the Fleet, deck landing practices and working up to reach peak efficiency. The flying took place from Kai Tak airport on the mainland. Although not completed on our arrival, it was used by the Royal Air Force and the Far East Aviation Company and also by other smaller airlines that were developing in South China at that time. When we went to sea our machines of Nos. 803 and 824 Squadrons came out from the airport to land and take off again frequently, performing their deck landing practices.
>
> It was during one of these days at sea that we became involved in one of the piracy incidents that were known to take place in these waters. We received a signal to search for the SS *Tungchow*, a small coastal steamer carrying both passengers and cargo. She was on passage from Shanghai to Hong Kong and was overdue. Our planes took part in the search, and she was eventually located off Bias Bay, a notorious pirate lair, in the hands of pirates, and was subsequently returned to her owners intact. Although there had been a number of children on board, the only casualty was the shooting of one of the Russian guards which the vessel carried in order to try and prevent such acts of piracy.
>
> During our stay in Hong Kong celebrations for the Silver Jubilee of King George V took place, and both Nos. 824 and 803 Squadrons gave displays of formation flying and aerobatics in their Seals and Ospreys. Following these, in May we left to join the rest of the China Fleet at Wei-hai-Wei, which would be our base for the summer months.
>
> We regularly spent time at sea, carrying out exercises with the rest of the China Fleet. Some of our planes were fitted with floats and this enabled flying to take place whilst we were at anchor. The ship's crane hoisted the planes in and out as required for flying duties.
>
> On 5 August 1935 we left Chemulpo to meet the rest of the Fleet returning from their various cruises, and carried out combined exercises, with our aircraft much in evidence. This entailed being divided into Red and Blue Fleets. We successfully fought our way through the opposing Fleet and eventually anchored during the evening of 9 August. We were then due to remain at Wei-hai-Wei until 23 September, but at the end of August news was coming through in connection with the Italian-Abyssinian situation. Various ships of the Fleet were leaving harbour suddenly for unknown destinations, and as the days went by an air of uncertainty prevailed.
>
> On 12 September it was our turn to sail, and as we looked out to sea from our anchorage in Four Funnel Bay we could tell that we were in for a rough trip, and so everything that was movable was secured with lashing. This was particularly necessary with all the planes parked in the hangar below the flight deck. The Captain explained the position of affairs in Europe: we were heading for Singapore with all despatch at a speed commensurate with the

oil fuel we had in our tanks to complete the journey. It was obvious that we had to get there as quickly as possible, to be on station for a quick move westward, which at that time looked inevitable.

The hangar now was a scene of great activity, servicing all the aircraft as the planes had had a heavy flying programme at Wei-hai-Wei, taking part in gunnery and other exercises with various ships of the Fleet. Fitters, riggers and other tradesmen were occupied non-stop, as they transformed seaplanes into landplanes, the violent motion of the ship not helping them in the tasks they performed, the ship being then on the edge of a typhoon.

As we steamed nearer to Singapore conditions improved and we were able to review the damage. Several boats had suffered, guardrails carried away and slight damage to three or four aircraft. Air fans that had ceased to do their job needed new motors and a complete overhaul.

During this trip our movements were secret as we were not in direct communication with ships or shore, having maintained 'W/T silence'. We could pick up messages, but no one could determine the course and speed of the ship. Arriving at Singapore on 19 September, we anchored at 0300, and shortly afterwards an oiler came alongside to replenish our much depleted oil fuel stocks. As daylight came we saw anchored around us HMS *Berwick*, HMS *Cornwall* and two destroyers, all from the China Fleet. These in turn left, until only *Cornwall* and ourselves remained at the anchorage. Other naval ships had called, but were soon on their way again. Owing to the political situation, the movements of ships were unknown. Both our squadrons were flown off to the RAF station at Seletar, where they were able to get their training that otherwise should have taken place in Hong Kong.

It was early in November that planes participating in the air race from England to Australia were expected to arrive in Singapore. Broadbent was the first to be seen flying over, but didn't land. Kingsford-Smith was also due that same evening, but didn't show up. Melrose, who had been overtaken by Kingsford-Smith on the journey, opted to remain in Singapore instead of going on to Australia, so that he could help in a search if necessary.

As Kingsford-Smith had not appeared early on 9 November, No. 205 Flying Boat Squadron flew off to search for him. Melrose in his plane joined in too. When it became known that they were unsuccessful, all RAF machines, including our squadrons, joined in the general search which ensued. This went on for about three weeks without success. Further search was taken over by Quantas Airways. Eventually the search was terminated but no trace was ever found of this intrepid pilot or his passenger.

With the situation in Europe becoming more settled, it was announced that the date of our sailing for Hong Kong was to be 25 February 1936, and on that date we embarked the aircraft and personnel of our two squadrons, Nos. 803 and 824. The passage to Hong Kong took five and a half days. After a couple of days the temperature dropped and we were again in blue uniform and dispensed with our tropical rig. On Monday morning a destroyer came from Hong Kong to attend on us for flying duties, and in the afternoon the squadrons flew off to Kai Tak. At about 1600 we anchored in Hong Kong harbour after an absence of nearly ten months.

We then sailed for Shanghai. The first signs that we were approaching the mouth of the Yangtse was that many miles out to sea, and beyond the sight of land, the colour of the water changed from a greyish blue to a dirty yellow. We entered the river, and after travelling some forty-five miles we reached Woosung, where we anchored for the night. It is here that the Whangpoo river joins the Yangtse. On 14 October we weighed anchor and commenced our journey up the Whangpoo to Shanghai. A few miles from the city centre we came to the busy outskirts and here activity on the river increased greatly. A short distance further on, and still some two miles from the heart of the city, a continuous line of merchant ships and warships of many nationalities were moored in the middle of the river. Our eventual berth as 'guardship' was a buoy just off the Bund, and close to the city centre. At this time the berth was occupied by the flagship HMS *Kent*. We tied up at a wharf nearby until she sailed, and we then moved out to the buoy.

Due to the unsettled state of affairs between the Chinese and Japanese at Shanghai, there was a large number of Japanese warships in evidence. We assumed that they were there to protect the interests of their nationals. During this stay we learned the news that King Edward VIII had abdicated. We were also told that our last cruise of the commission was to be to the south. In February 1937 we were due in Singapore to eventually welcome the arrival of our much awaited relief, HMS *Eagle*, and, shortly after that, our homeward passage to the UK. It was with these thoughts in mind that we enjoyed the third Christmas of our commission, in Hong Kong, where it was much cooler than the two previous ones we had in the Singapore area. It was with a great deal of excitement that we welcomed our relief, and following a quick 'turn-over' we sailed for home on 25 March, reaching Devonport on 3 May. Our anticipated leave was delayed, however, as we then had to paint ship and prepare to take part in the Royal Review at Spithead on 20 May 1937.

Around that time the 'batsman' – officially the Deck Landing Control Officer – was introduced. The DLCO's task was to stand at the side of the flight deck during landings, and indicate with table-tennis type bats in each hand what changes if any the pilot should make in his approach, and when he should cut the engine of his aircraft, waving him off to try again if necessary.

CHAPTER 4

The Navy Regains its Air Arm

▼ Hawker Ospreys of No. 800 (Fleet Fighter) Squadron ranged on the flight deck of HMS *Ark Royal* a few months before the outbreak of the Second World War; one machine has just taken off. Shortly after this photograph was taken the squadron re-equipped with Blackburn Skuas. (RAF Museum)

Ever since the RNAS had been amalgamated into the RAF on 1 April 1918 the Royal Navy had made repeated efforts to win back its air arm. Success finally came after the question had been referred to arbitration, and on 21 July 1937 Sir Thomas Inskip, in what came to be known as the 'Inskip Award', recommended to the Cabinet that the Navy have full control of its aircraft, training and organization. It was to be nearly two years, however, before this could be properly implemented, and even longer before the last RAF ground crew ceased to be required. The title 'Fleet Air Arm of the Royal Air Force' was to be dropped, and the service would become officially the 'Air Branch', but in practice the term 'Fleet Air Arm' never went out of use and indeed was officially readopted in 1953.

Colonel F. D. G. Bird, RM (Ret.), was one of a small number of Royal Marine officers in the Fleet Air Arm at this time. He recalls:

> I entered the Royal Marines at the age of eighteen as a probationary second lieutenant and completed the normal three years' training, after which one joined one of the larger ships of the Fleet as a lieutenant. My first ship was the battleship *Resolution* in the 1st Battle Squadron, Mediterranean Fleet, with instructions to take passage to join her at Malta in the aircraft carrier *Courageous*. That was early in 1935, and in those days, both ashore and afloat, the RAF featured prominently in naval aviation. All the aircraft maintenance, about a third of the air crew, and various appointments were the responsibility of the RAF.
>
> On the way to Malta there was plenty of flying, and I had little to do but watch it and like what I saw. The aircraft – Seals, IIIFs, Ospreys and Nimrods – did not seem to be as quaint then as they do now in retrospect. I must have decided then that aviation was going to be the thing for me. There was an atmosphere in the ship which doubtless lives on in carriers and is particular to naval aviation circles. It was not just a devil-may-care attitude to the chanciness of defying gravity and of flying single-engined aircraft over the sea that gave rise to this ethos: it may not have been unconnected with the metallic charm of the six shillings a day flying pay – a welcome addition to the standard daily rate of thirteen shillings and sixpence.
>
> After the statutory one year in *Resolution* I went with a request to the Captain (J. H. D.

Cunningham) to be considered for flying training. There were then still senior officers who considered aeroplanes in HM ships to be nothing more than a nuisance which interfered with routine, but Captain Cunningham was not one of them, and he forwarded my request. My Royal Marine father required more convincing that to fly was better than to be a gunnery officer, but he came round in the end.

And so to the Royal Air Force at No. 1 Flying Training School at Leuchars in Scotland, for flying training. Of the naval pupils a proportion spent eight months in two terms at Leuchars, and then went south to become torpedo-spotter-reconnaissance pilots; the remainder stayed for a further term to be trained as fighter pilots. I don't know how it was determined who did what, though I had an uneasy feeling that it was thought to be imprudent to condemn observers to fly behind certain pilots. I became a fighter pilot.

In flying training, as in other forms of training, the psychological relationship between instructor and pupil, I am sure, plays an important part in the outcome of success or failure. I know that I progressed happily with some and went backwards, less happily, with others. I was lucky to have as my initial instructor Flight Lieutenant Heber-Percy – a gentle man and a patient one. He had an aeroplane of his own at Leuchars, a Leopard Moth I think. He also had a Sealyham which used to fly with him, and for a long time claimed more flying hours than I had.

We flew the venerable Avro 504N for the first term; a less than flattering comment in my flying log book by the Chief Flying Instructor, Wing Commander Noakes, reminds me that I did not handle it all that well. For the second term we progressed to the delightful Hawker Hart (T) and were allotted new instructors. Sergeant Pilot Cordern took me on for that term, which was either my good fortune or enlightened casting. We got on very well, to my satisfaction if not to his. Inter-cockpit communication was by voicepipe, the Gosport tube of World War I, and the upstairs/downstairs communication of yore. Sergeant Pilot Cordern's quiet comment shortly after take-off that the engine temperature seemed to be falling a bit was enough to remind me that I had forgotten to wind in the radiator, and was in distinct contrast to Flight Lieutenant Cracroft, another instructor, who would demand with a shout 'What about your bloody radiator? Blast you!'

The third and last term included two weeks at RAF Calshot learning to handle floatplanes. Many cruisers and battleships at that time carried an aircraft of some kind for which the pilot needed a subtle combination of

▶ HMS *Eagle* steaming near Gibraltar in the late 1930s with both aircraft lifts lowered. The ship's origins as a battleship are apparent in the lines of the hull, and the heavy seaplane crane is an indication of her intended role as a seaplane carrier. A more recent addition is the high-angle director system installed on the foremast. (RAF Museum)

airmanship, seamanship and good luck successfully to complete a sortie.

Still under training, the next step was a period with No. 801 Squadron, based at Eastleigh and equipped with one of the many Hawker Hart variants, the Osprey, navalized by the addition of folding wings, an arrester hook and an inflatable dinghy. The squadron was attached to the training carrier *Furious*, in which many pupils were introduced to deck landing, the real thing after much dummy deck landing ashore, and all other aspects of the operation of aircraft from carriers. Initial deck landings included a number of arrivals without the benefit of arrester wires. We returned to Eastleigh as fully fledged naval pilots considered fit for first-line squadrons. I joined No. 800 Squadron, also based at Eastleigh.

There the RN were cuckoos nesting on the east side of the grass aerodrome, with the Vickers Supermarine factory and the Hampshire Flying Club on the west side. On the southern boundary was the Municipal Crematorium from which the periodical puff of smoke from its chimney was a cautionary reminder at take-off when the wind was in the south. There was no runway then, our aircraft were housed in canvas hangars and the naval personnel were quartered in wooden huts, relics of the Kaiser's War.

No. 800 Squadron was at that time equipped with Ospreys and Nimrods and our floating home was *Courageous*. For some obscure reason it was not unusual, if a squadron had an RM officer on the strength, to make him Squadron Adjutant, for which I was duly earmarked. Soon after I joined the squadron we migrated north to Evanton, not far from Leuchars, for our annual firing and bombing practice camp. We paused on the way to refuel and have lunch at RAF Catterick whence, later, I got a mess bill for our lunch referring to *x* naval officers, *x* RAF officers and one 'party in khaki' – presumably me!

The CO of No. 800 was Lieutenant Commander H. A. Traill. He arranged that during the 1938 spring cruise in the Mediterranean we would fly off in the vicinity of Alexandria to Amman in the Transjordan, where his brother in the RAF was CO of No. 14 Bomber Squadron. We landed there by sub-flights in formation, as was the customary procedure, but somersaulting over on to one's back, as I did, was not so acceptable! After three or four days in Amman, snowbound of all things, we returned to Ismailia, I as a passenger in the rear cockpit of Squadron Leader Traill's Gordon. Back on board I was somewhat shaken to see a signal referring to the cost of getting my Nimrod back to Alex by train. The bill, quoted in piastres, had more noughts on it than I care to remember.

On return to UK, the squadron transferred to the one-time RAF station at Worthy Down, north of Winchester. Soon after that we had to surrender our Nimrods and re-equip completely with Ospreys, these with their folding wings being acceptable to the slimmer lifts of *Ark Royal* which we were soon to join.

After the spring cruise we re-equipped again, this time with Skuas, and still at Worthy Down. Built by Blackburns in the robust fashion of that manufacturer, the Skua, described as a fighter/dive-bomber, and the Navy's first monoplane, was a bit un-nimble as a fighter but steady indeed in the bomb-dropping dive. As to deck-landing, one felt mahout-like, perched high on the top of an elephant, with an excellent view of where you were going, which is handy for deck-landing.

Meanwhile the Swordfish, primarily a carrier-based torpedo-spotter-reconnaissance aircraft, had also reached a catapult unit in September 1937 when No. 701 Flight took over four aircraft from No. 812 Squadron, though No. 702 Flight had to be content with a few Seals until more Swordfish became available for this purpose about a year later. However, 1937 also saw the gradual replacement in light cruisers of most of the Ospreys by the new Fairey Seafox light reconnaissance seaplane, with four flights receiving the new type between June and November, these being Nos. 714, 718, 716 and 713, in that order. No. 712, on the other hand, replaced its Ospreys with Walruses. The home shore base for all these flights reverted to Lee-on-Solent at the end of that year.

By now the TSR and catapult squadrons had completed their re-equipment, but new aircraft for the fighter squadrons were not yet available. Towards the end of 1938 *Furious*, which had been used for a time as a deck-landing training carrier, was paid off and replaced in this role by *Courageous*, which then took over her squadrons, Nos. 801, 811 and 822. No. 801 Squadron began at this time to replace its Ospreys with the Gloster Sea Gladiator, the last biplane fighter to join the Fleet and yet another adaptation of an RAF machine – in this case an obsolescent one.

The squadrons given up by *Courageous* when she changed her role were in their turn taken over by the new fleet carrier *Ark Royal*, which was sufficiently large to need in addition several new squadrons. This modern ship had two hangars, one above the other, able to accommodate 70 aircraft. Her flight deck was fitted with transverse arrester wires, a hydraulic catapult forward and a mechanically operated barrier forward. Two fighter units were carried: No 800 Squadron was re-equipped with Blackburn Skuas whilst No. 803 Squadron re-formed for this new carrier, initially using Nimrods and Ospreys but soon converting to Skuas. The Skua, which could operate as a dive-bomber, was the Fleet Air Arm's first operational monoplane, being all-metal and fitted with a retractable

▼Blackburn Skua IIs of No. 803 (Fleet Fighter) Squadron from *Ark Royal* flying along the south coast during the summer of 1939. (RAF Museum)

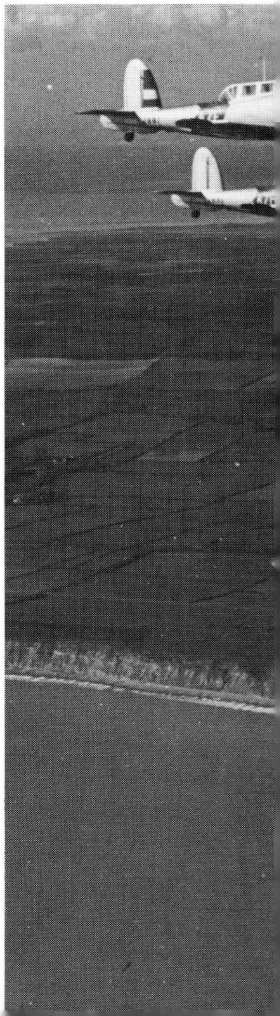

► Fleet Air Arm ordnance artificers inspecting a multiple pom-pom aboard *Ark Royal* in 1939. Nicknamed 'Chicago pianos', these weapons could put up a considerable barrage of ammunition but wartime experience later proved them to be somewhat ineffective. (RAF Museum)

▲ **A meteorological officer aboard *Ark Royal* in 1939, ready to track a 'met' balloon just released by a rating. (RAF Museum)**

undercarriage, but it was never a great success and was later relegated to target-towing duties. Four Swordfish units were also carried aboard *Ark Royal*, these being Nos. 810, 814, 820 and 821, and all the ship's aircraft carried her new colours, consisting of parallel stripes of blue, red and blue.

The 'Inskip Award' took real effect on 24 May 1939, on which date the Royal Navy gained practical control of its own aircraft and shore bases. The headquarters of the Fleet Air Arm was to be at Lee-on-Solent, which like all naval shore establishments was given a ships' name, in this case HMS *Daedalus*. RAF stations taken over at this time included Donibristle (HMS *Merlin*), Ford (HMS *Peregrine*), Gosport (lodger facilities only) and Worthy Down (HMS *Kestrel*), and then Eastleigh (HMS *Raven*) from 1 July. First-line squadrons retained their 800-series numbers, and catapult units kept the numbers 700 onwards, many of the latter having by then been elevated to squadron status. New training units, some taken over from the RAF, were given second-line squadron status, and these were numbered 750 onwards.

By the time war broke out on 3 September 1939 the Royal Navy had in full commission the carriers *Ark Royal, Eagle*, *Furious*, *Glorious* and *Hermes*, as well as *Argus* and *Courageous* in use as training carriers; in addition, nearly 50 capital ships had by then been equipped with catapults. New stations were under construction at Arbroath, Crail and Yeovilton, to become HMS *Condor*, HMS *Jackdaw* and HMS *Heron* respectively. The first-line squadrons numbered sixteen, and there were eleven catapult squadrons and a seaplane squadron, plus eleven second-line squadrons. The pre-war aircraft identification system had, for security reasons, been dropped in favour of letter/number combinations of various kinds, plain numbers not being used again until the end of the war.

CHAPTER 5

The Phoney War

▼ **Fairey Swordfish K8867 'G3P' of No. 812 Squadron ashore from HMS *Glorious* at the naval camp at Dekheila, the prewar Alexandria airport, late in 1939. This station became HMS *Grebe* in September 1940 and as such was the focal point and main base throughout the war for all FAA activities in the Eastern Mediterranean. (Cdr R. N. Everett)**

The first few months of the Second World War were known at the time as the 'Phoney War', action being very limited. The German Army sat behind the fortified Siegfried Line, whilst the French Army faced it behind the Maginot Line, supported by the British Expeditionary Force. RAF activity was generally limited to a few raids plus a lot of leaflet-dropping. At sea, however, things were rather different.

At that time *Ark Royal* and *Courageous* were with the Home Fleet, whilst *Furious* was engaged in deck-landing training in the Firth of Forth, *Argus* was in reserve at Portsmouth and *Hermes* had recently recommissioned following a refit. *Glorious* was serving with the Mediterranean Fleet and *Eagle* with the Far East Fleet. In addition, the seaplane carrier *Albatross* was on its way to Sierra Leone with the Walruses of the recently formed No. 710 Squadron, which would soon be carrying out anti-submarine patrols off the coast of West Africa and protecting Allied shipping in the vicinity of the important refuelling port of Freetown.

The lessons of the earlier world war had not been entirely forgotten, and to counteract the new U-boat menace *Courageous* and *Hermes* were assigned to the North-West Approaches and *Ark Royal* to the South-West Approaches. The war was only eleven days old, however, when *Ark Royal* was fortunate to survive a very near miss by the German submarine *U-39*. *Courageous* was less lucky only three days later, on 17 September, when she was hit by three torpedoes from *U-29*, 17 officers and 464 ratings being lost as she sank and Nos. 811 and 822 Swordfish Squadrons being wiped out at a stroke. This was a terrible blow, and as a consequence the remaining carriers were withdrawn from vulnerable anti-submarine work.

On the credit side, the first Fleet Air Arm success of the war was claimed on 26 September when Lt B. S. McEwen, RN, in a Skua of No. 803 Squadron from *Ark Royal*, shot down one of three Dornier Do 18 flying boat shadowers over the North Sea. This was in fact the first German aircraft to be shot down by any of the British Services during the Second World War. The Fleet then made for Scapa Flow, but its position had already been reported and at about 1400 several Heinkel He 111 bombers appeared. Their main target was the carrier, and although one bomb dropped

just ahead of the ship her captain fortunately managed to steer her clear with only a shaking from the explosion. The pilot of the German aircraft, Adolphe Francke, claimed to have sunk the ship and was awarded the Iron Cross and promoted to *Oberleutnant*. His claim, though mistaken, was not unsupported, as German reconnaissance aircraft later came across two British cruisers, mistook them for the two battleships which had been accompanying the carrier and assumed that as *Ark Royal* was not astern of them she must have gone down. This was to be the first of many German claims to have sunk this new carrier.

Cdr R. A. Phillimore has vivid recollections of this event:

> My diary for 31 August 1939 records: 'In the afternoon we received three signals: 1. Raise steam with the utmost despatch and report when ready for sea. 2. Fire is to be opened on any aircraft which cannot be identified. 3. All remaining shells and warheads are to be fused. Prepare for war.' This was the last entry in my diary for there were orders that in wartime no serving personnel were allowed to keep a diary.
>
> Some days after war had been declared, a small force of the *Ark Royal*, *Repulse*, *Rodney* and a flotilla of destroyers was operating half way between the Orkneys and Norway. A signal was received that a Hudson aircraft would be closing the Fleet – the USA had recently made some Lockheed Hudsons available to Coastal Command and most of us had never seen one. It duly appeared, low down, and was passing some message by Aldis when we were aware that three aircraft were nearly vertical above us. One of them went into a near-vertical dive over the *Ark Royal*, dropped a bomb at about 1,000 feet and made its getaway below the level of the tops of the masts, while all the close-range weapons of our force were trying to train quickly enough to fire at it and avoid hitting the other ships. Then, when it was near the horizon, it would climb again and stand by for another run.
>
> My action station was in the armoured tower, providing a front seat at a most spectacular display. My recollection is that the three aircraft attacked singly, each carrying out three runs. It was dramatic in the extreme, with the *Ark Royal* taking violent evasive action as soon

as a plane was committed to a dive and with the *Rodney* and *Repulse* doing their best to conform. No hits were scored on either side, although Captain A. J. Power reported that the last bomb had broken crockery and taken off some paint from the ship's side of the *Ark Royal*.

This was one of the many times the Germans claimed to have sunk the *Ark Royal*, almost certainly because shortly afterwards she, with some of the destroyers, left for Rosyth, while the rest of us returned to Scapa. Not seeing her, they thought they had sunk her.

In the Mediterranean things were rather quieter, as Lt Cdr A. Kennard recalls:

▼ **Blackburn Skuas on the hydraulic catapult of HMS *Ark Royal*, somewhere in the South Atlantic in November 1939, watched by a crowd of onlookers. The port windshield is raised and the radio masts are lowered. The carrier was then part of Force K, searching for enemy raiders. (Cdr R. N. Everett)**

During the summer of 1939 I was serving in No. 810 Squadron with Swordfish and was due for a move. To my surprise and great pleasure I was appointed to the flagship of the West Indies Squadron, which I think was then one of the 'Town' Class cruisers and carried a Walrus. I was sent to Lee-on-Solent to carry out a Walrus conversion course. My instructor was 'Butch' Judd who had a fiery red beard and an even hotter temper. However, I succeeded in being converted to Walri in spite of Butch trying to remove his control column in order to strike me over the head for not doing what he wanted me to do.

I had just completed the conversion course, towards the end of August, when my appointment was cancelled and I was told to join *Shropshire* in the Mediterranean, but nobody knew where in the Med . . . I was eventually told to join the troopship *Dorsetshire* to proceed to Gibraltar. It was fairly obvious by then that war was inevitable as one's departure was somewhat fraught and exciting. I was unmarried, so had no worries in that direction.

We duly arrived in Gibraltar on 2 September. The next day, when the news came through, it was decided that the colour of the ship should be changed from white to grey before proceeding further east. This was done in record time by professionals and amateurs, and the ship sailed about three days later for Malta. We arrived safely in Grand Harbour and still no sign of *Shropshire*, so I went to Alexandria. *Shropshire* at last arrived and I duly joined along with the new executive officer, Peter Gornall, a well-known naval cricketer. Before the boat came alongside I looked up at the Walrus sitting on its catapult and realized that the next time I flew I would be shot off that catapult at sea, having had only one previous experience, and that under dual control instruction.

Shropshire had been ferrying British troops from Marseilles to Alexandria and having done several trips at high speed had completely run out of booze in the wardroom. Fortunately this defect was put right before we sailed for Capetown through the Suez Canal.

I found that my observer was Lieutenant Commander 'Jenks' Harrison, who was considerably senior to me, I being then a junior two-striper. Jenks eyed me with considerable suspicion as did most observers on getting a new pilot and particularly one they had never heard of before. I gathered that 'Jenks' had had some nasty moments with his previous pilot so quite naturally was apprehensive about the new one.

As far as I can remember, we had practically no flying between Suez and the Cape as we were required at our destination as soon as possible. We then started on the novel routine of going to action stations every day at dawn. After a few days in Simonstown we started on the job we had been sent out to do. This was to carry out patrols in the South Atlantic, primarily to try and intercept German ships which had taken refuge in South West African ports and were endeavouring to return to Germany. Our partner on these patrols was the *Sussex*, also carrying a Walrus.

Whenever the weather was suitable for a Walrus to carry out a 'slick' landing, Jenks, Thorogood and I scoured the ocean for anything we could find. Jenks' navigation was superb and we invariably sighted the ship after three-hour patrols, exactly when he said we would. *Sussex*'s Walrus was not so lucky, and we spent 9½ hours in one day looking for it without success, involving three launches and three slick landings. There were fairly numerous alarms when ships were reported as having sailed, but we never had the excitement of finding one. Our instructions on sighting an enemy merchant ship were to stop it by the usual method of shots across the bows and then prevent the crew abandoning the ship or scuttling it.

One day, to our surprise and pleasure, we found a ship which looked to be German. I dived down to a few hundred feet and Thorogood fired across the bow with the Vickers K gun. She was not much of a ship – one funnel amidships and the usual fore and aft castles of a tramp steamer. Her name was *Adolf Leonhardt*. She soon stopped and the crew proceeded to man one of the only two lifeboats. To prevent this we fired some shots near them, whereupon they all went to the boat on the other side of the ship. It takes a little time for a Walrus to fly round to the other side but we just managed it in time to loose off a few more rounds and sent them back where they had come from. This game went on a few more times until they eventually managed to get their boat in the water followed by a second one.

We reckoned it would be a good hour before *Shropshire* arrived on the scene so decided to board and capture the ship before she sank, as the crew had obviously opened the cocks. The sea was calm and only a low swell, so alighting on the water was no trouble. I taxied close under the boat falls, which were dangling in the water, and Thorogood made a jump for it and shinned up the tackle with a white ensign under his arm. (Great forethought on Jenks' part to carry a white ensign with us). Thorogood, the telegraphist air gunner, having hoisted the ensign above the Nazi flag, proceeded to see what was on board. He appeared on the upper deck and bombarded us with oranges and a framed picture of Hitler!

Shropshire duly arrived and immediately sent a party of engineers on board to see if they could save the ship. Alas, it was too late. Our 'captive' had been somewhat short-lived! *Shropshire* then stood off and gave the 8-inch guns some live practice, accompanied by some blistering comments from Captain A. W. Bisset, RN! The crew of the *Adolf Leonhardt* were a fairly motley collection and included a dog and a monkey, all safely delivered to Cape Town at the end of that patrol.

▼ A busy scene aboard *Ark Royal* while briefly in dock at Portsmouth early in 1940. Cases of ammunition and stores are seen awaiting stowage, RAF uniforms being still evident at this stage. Being hoisted inboard by the ship's crane is a Swordfish (P4199) for No. 821 Squadron, still bearing the floats and markings of its former unit, No. 702 (Catapult) Squadron in the battleship *Resolution*. (RAF Museum)

Early in October *Ark Royal* was despatched to the South Atlantic, her place in the Home Fleet being taken by *Furious*. The latter then sailed with the battlecruiser *Repulse* to afford cover for the first Canadian troop convoy from Halifax, Nova Scotia, eventually reaching the Clyde on 17 December. *Ark Royal* meanwhile had become a part of a new fleet code-named 'Force K', which also comprised the battlecruiser *Renown* and a screen of four destroyers. *Hermes* was now operating out of Dakar whilst *Glorious* was covering the Aden area and later the Indian Ocean.

Apart from *Furious*, these carriers were largely engaged in searching for German commerce raiders. In October Swordfish from *Ark Royal* sighted the somewhat notorious *Altmark*, a supply vessel for the pocket battleship *Graf Spee*, but incorrectly identified her and she got away on that occasion. Less lucky was SS *Uhenfels*, which they spotted a few weeks later and was subsequently taken in prize by British destroyers.

The loss of merchant shipping in the South Atlantic made it apparent that a surface raider was somewhere around, and Force K was well

placed to search her out. *Ark Royal*'s Swordfish and Skuas carried out many patrols without success, but it was calculated that the enemy ship would at some stage have to put into Uruguay to refuel and the cruisers *Ajax*, *Achilles* and *Exeter* therefore sailed for the mouth of the River Plate to try to intercept her. At first light on 13 December they spotted *Graf Spee*, which immediately opened fire on them at a range of ten miles.

All three cruisers normally carried catapult spotting aircraft but that of *Achilles* happened to be ashore for overhaul at that time and *Exeter*'s two Walruses were soon put out of action by shell splinters. Similar damage had also been inflicted on one of the Seafoxes of No. 718 Squadron aboard *Ajax* but the other, though whipped badly by blast from the ship's turrets, successfully catapulted off at 0637. Crewed by Lt E. D. G. Lewin, RN, and Lt R. E. N. Kearney, RN, the aircraft climbed to 3,000ft, where cloud cover was available if required. They saw *Exeter* falling behind, having been slowed down by damage, but *Ajax* and *Achilles* continued to give chase at 31kt, the fall of shot being reported by the Seafox, which closed in at one stage before hastily withdrawing on being hit by anti-aircraft fire though having stayed long enough to report at least thirty hits.

Graf Spee then sought refuge in Montevideo, where daily reconnaissance flights reported her continued presence, until at around 1730 on 17 December she weighed anchor. Anticipating renewed battle, *Ajax* and *Achilles*, now accompanied by *Cumberland*, another cruiser, sailed towards Montevideo and Lewin took off, expecting to resume the task he had so successfully carried out four days earlier. There being no sign of the German ship emerging, however, he was ordered to leave the spotting position over *Ajax*'s starboard bow and report on the movements of the enemy warship and the attendant merchant ship *Tacoma*. Just before sunset Lewin saw several spots of light forward and aft and initially thought that these were caused by gunfire but soon realized that in fact she was being scuttled. At 2054 the aircraft was able to signal '*Spee* has blown herself up'. For their vital role in this drama, Lewin was awarded the Distinguished Service Cross and Lt Kearney was mentioned in despatches – these the first of many awards gained by members of the Fleet Air Arm during the Second World War.

No carrier had participated in the Battle of the River Plate, as the action became known, but the decision of *Graf Spee*'s commander, Captain Langsdorff, to seek refuge and

►A successful outcome to an encounter with a Junkers Ju 88 near Scapa Flow on Christmas Day 1940 by No. 804 Squadron from Hatston. Attacked by the three aircraft of Red Section, led by Lt R. H. P. Carver, RN, flying some of the Fleet Air Arm's first Grumman Martlet Is, it ended up in a bog one mile south of Loch Skail. (Capt. H. L. St J. Fancourt)

▼A Fairey Swordfish of No. 818 Squadron awaiting launch from the starboard catapult aboard *Ark Royal* in the South Atlantic in 1940. The aircraft is loaded with six 100lb anti-submarine bombs and is protected from cross-winds by the raised starboard windshield. (Cdr R. N. Everett)

eventually scuttle her was undoubtedly influenced by the knowledge that *Ark Royal* and the remainder of Force K were in the vicinity. *Ark Royal* was in fact at Rio de Janeiro, just over a day's sailing away, at the time of the scuttling, but on hearing the news she headed back for Freetown, from where she continued to search the South Atlantic for the next six weeks. On 8 February 1940 she left for home, engaging during the voyage in a hunt for six German merchant ships attempting to return to home ports; five of these vessels were sunk by the carrier's Swordfish off the Spanish coast. U-boats lay in wait for her in the Bay of Biscay, but she managed to evade these, docking at Portsmouth on 15 February.

After a five-week refit *Ark Royal* sailed on 20 March for the Eastern Mediterranean carrying only her Swordfish squadrons, which flew ashore on reaching Alexandria to work up on night flying over the desert. The Skuas of Nos. 800 and 803 Squadrons had been left ashore at Hatston in the Orkneys, to help protect the nearby Home Fleet anchorage at Scapa Flow, in company with the Sea Gladiators of No. 804 Squadron, which had formed there some weeks earlier for that purpose.

The 'Phoney War' ended abruptly on 9 April when news came through that Denmark and Norway had been invaded. The next day *Ark Royal* and *Glorious* were ordered to make for Gibraltar at best speed in order to rejoin the Home Fleet. On the same day Dornier Do 17s and Heinkel He 111s carried out a series of attacks against towns and shore positions in the Scapa area and the Sea Gladiators of No. 804 Squadron had a very active time, scoring a number of hits and shooting down one of the Heinkels. This squadron was to have a very lively time in the defence of the Orkneys and Scapa Flow for some months to come, later being re-equipped with Grumman Martlets.

CHAPTER 6

The Norwegian Campaign

The German invasion of Denmark and Norway began at dawn on 9 April 1940 and within twenty-four hours the whole of Denmark and the main Norwegian airfields and ports had been captured. One of the key factors in this lightning operation was the use of air power, airborne landings being made simultaneously at vital places in both countries.

At the time of the invasion the Royal Navy had no carriers in home waters. *Furious* was lying at Greenock, but this was on the wrong side of Scotland, and she had only just completed a programme of refitting and repairs, all her squadrons being ashore. She was quickly sent to sea, the Swordfish of Nos. 816 and 818 Squadrons flying aboard from Campbeltown as she sailed down the Clyde, but they would have to remain without fighter protection as there was no time to embark the Skuas of No. 801 Squadron from Evanton.

It had been reported that German cruisers were in Bergen harbour, and the only possibility was to mount a land-based attack against them from Hatston in the Orkneys. The Skuas of No. 800 Squadron were already there, and they were joined by those of No. 803 Squadron which were flown up from Wick. At 0500 on 10 April the two squadrons set off on the 600-mile round trip, the aircraft loaded with 500lb bombs. On arrival at Bergen they found that two of the ships had already left, only the 6,000-ton *Königsberg* remaining anchored alongside the Skoltegrund Mole. No. 803 Squadron, led by Lt W. P. Lucy, RM, went in first, climbing to 8,000ft before diving down at an angle of 60 degrees amidst heavy anti-aircraft fire, followed by No. 800 Squadron under Capt. R. T. Partridge, RM.

The attack lasted just three minutes, but in that short time the aircraft achieved three direct hits and twelve near-misses, one of the latter exploding beneath the water and blowing a large hole in the side of the ship. The *Königsberg* caught fire and her magazines soon exploded, a pall of smoke rising high into the cloudy morning sky as the attackers flew off into the mountains, having made the first successful air attack by any nation on a major warship, for the loss of only one aircraft – Skua L2923 of No. 803 Squadron, crewed by Lt B. J. Smeeton, RN, and Midshipman F. Watkinson.

Furious arrived in Norwegian waters the next day, promptly mounting a torpedo attack against two German warships in Trondheimfjord. This was the first such major attack of the war, but insufficient account was taken of the available depth of water and all the missiles grounded in shallows. The ship remained in the Narvik area, but another attack the same day was thwarted by a snowstorm, two aircraft failing to return to the carrier and another crashing on deck while attempting to land. *Furious* continued operations for the next two weeks before returning to Greenock on 29 April.

Meanwhile the battleship *Warspite* entered Ofot Fjord on 13 April, escorted by nine destroyers, and at 1152 she catapulted off one of two Swordfish seaplanes of No. 700 Squadron. Loaded with two 100lb and two 250lb anti-submarine bombs and piloted by Petty Officer F. C. 'Ben' Rice, with Lt Cdr W. L. M. Brown, RN, as observer and TAG Leading Airman M. G. Pacey, the aircraft

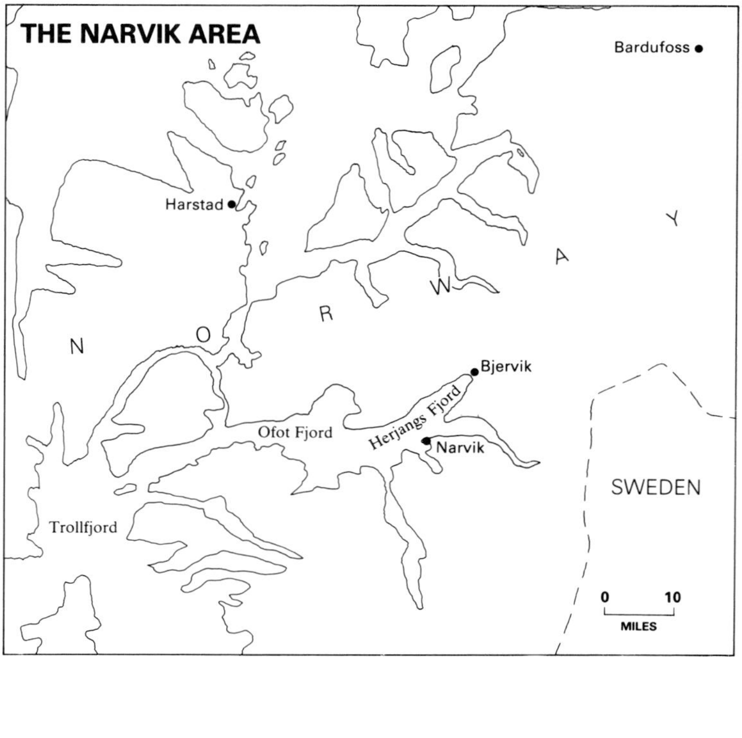

(L9767) headed in the direction of Narvik and Bjervik, seemingly in a tunnel, with water below, low clouds above and steep cliffs either side. They first sighted a German destroyer, but this quickly withdrew when a British destroyer opened fire on her. Then, turning up the narrow Herjangs Fjord towards Bjervik, Rice spotted a U-boat, which later turned out to be *U-64*, anchored near the jetty. As he dived down to 300ft to drop his bombs, Pacey raked the conning tower with his guns. The TAG's fire was too late to prevent retaliatory fire from damaging the tailplane, but Rice's first bomb had scored a direct hit on the submarine's bows, and within half a minute it was sinking. The aircraft managed to return safely to the ship (and in fact survived for another four years).

On 22 April *Glorious* and *Ark Royal*, having arrived home four days earlier, sailed for Norway with the task of providing support for the British and Norwegian forces at Aandalesnes and Namsos. *Glorious* also carried the eighteen obsolescent RAF Gladiators of No. 263 Squadron, likely to be better suited than more modern fighters for operating from any small Norwegian landing ground still not overrun. On 24 April these were flown ashore to a landing strip which had been prepared on Lake Lesjaskog, near Aandalesnes, and the fighters from the two carriers commenced patrols.

Next day the Swordfish took off for a raid against targets in the Trondheim area, accompanied by Skuas operating in the dive-bombing role. *Glorious* left the scene late on 26 April but the *Ark Royal* squadrons made further attacks in the same area on the 28th, including a strike on Vaernes airfield which inflicted considerable damage. A number of aircraft were lost in these attacks, including several which ran out of fuel returning to the ship – which was then operating more than 100 miles from the mainland – though most of the crews were rescued.

Two crew members who were very fortunate to survive were Capt. R. T. Partridge, RM, the CO of No. 800 Squadron, and his observer Lt R. S. Bostock, RN, who were shot down by a Heinkel He 111 during an offensive patrol. Successfully landing on a frozen lake, they set fire to their Skua aircraft (L2940) in order to destroy its IFF equipment, then made their way to Aandalesnes, where they were rescued by HMS *Manchester* and taken home to rejoin their squadron. Thirty-five years later the remains of their machine were recovered by a naval diving team and are now preserved in the Fleet Air Arm Museum at Yeovilton.

Ark Royal pulled out the following day and returned briefly to Scapa Flow, where she refuelled and replaced her lost and damaged equipment. *Glorious* rejoined the Fleet on 1 May and her Sea Gladiators defended her against enemy attacks during that afternoon before she too returned to Scapa. On 5 May *Ark Royal* was back in action, her aircraft operating in support of the Allied

▼ Fairey Swordfish 'U4B' of No. 816 Squadron from HMS *Furious* on a reconnaissance flight over Norway during 1940. In April that year squadron aircraft made the first airborne torpedo attack of the Second World War. (Arthur Ward)

Expeditionary Force in the Narvik area. During the next few days a number of aircraft were lost, although most crew members were again saved. Among those not so fortunate were the crew of Skua L2925 of No. 803 Squadron, which on 14 May was shot down in the entrance to Ofot Fjord, the lives being lost of both Lt Lucy, who had sunk the *Königsberg* five weeks earlier, and his observer Lt M. Hanson, RN.

Four days later *Furious* and *Glorious* returned to the scene, both now laden with aircraft. The Walruses of No. 701 Squadron were flown off *Glorious* to land at Harstad for communications and reconnaissance duties, followed on 21 May by the RAF Hurricanes of No. 46 Squadron, which landed at Bardufoss together with the Gladiators of No. 263 Squadron from *Furious*. No 263 had re-equipped after losing all its aircraft three weeks earlier, the new machines having been flown aboard by Fleet Air Arm pilots of No. 804 Squadron.

Furious returned to Greenock on 26 May and disembarked her squadron, but in her place *Ark Royal* sailed from there for Scapa four days later, arriving in Norwegian waters on 2 June. Allied land forces had in the meantime achieved moderate success, Narvik having been temporarily retaken on 28 May, but it was becoming increasingly obvious that an evacuation would be necessary. The first withdrawals were made on 4 June, covered by aircraft from *Ark Royal*, which three days later took aboard the five surviving Walruses of No. 701 Squadron. On that same day *Glorious* embarked the remaining Gladiators and Hurricanes from Bardufoss, but in the meantime *Scharnhorst*, *Gneisenau* and other German ships were making their way towards Harstad in order to attack the Allied base there the following night. In the afternoon of 8 June they sighted *Glorious* and her escort of two destroyers. The latter set up a smoke-screen to aid the carrier's escape, but to no avail. She was quickly hit by gunfire, and all three British ships were sunk: *Glorious* went down at 1740, taking with her all but 43 of the 1,515 officers and men of the Royal Navy and Royal Air Force aboard.

One of the destroyers, however, had managed to hit *Scharnhorst* with a torpedo, resulting in her putting into Trondheim for repairs, and on 13 June *Ark Royal* put up fifteen Skuas of Nos. 800 and 803 Squadrons to attack her and other German warships in Trondheim-fjord. Each machine was armed with a 500lb bomb, but the element of surprise was lost because a planned simultaneous attack by RAF Beauforts with an escort of Blenheim fighters was made too early. The Skuas consequently encountered heavy flak and only seven aircraft returned, the two squadron commanders being among those lost – Capt. R. T. Partridge, RM, of No. 800 Squadron in Skua 'A6A', whose aircraft was shot down by Messerschmitt Bf 109s, and Lt Cdr J. Casson, RN, of No. 803 Squadron in 'A7A' (possibly L2991).

►The oil sheds of Tromsø as seen from a Fairey Swordfish from *Furious* in April 1940. (Gordon Wright)

Rear Admiral Ievers participated in this campaign. He recalls:

> The Norwegian campaign was one in which I was involved from start to finish. On the day Norway was invaded HMS *Glasgow* was patrolling off the Norwegian coast. I was then the Flight Commander of the Walrus flight on board and was flown off to look for a German pocket battleship reported to be nestling in the fjords there. After three hours' fruitless searching we returned to *Glasgow*'s last position to find she had left in a hurry under German air attack. We flew back to Molde and taxied up to the jetty where we were met by the harbourmaster. Having told him our problem he said 'Oh well, you're in good company because *Rodney*'s Walrus is here already and we also have a German floatplane which landed here this morning and which we have captured. They are up the fjord some fifteen miles'. We took off and flew up the fjord, where we found not only the *Rodney*'s Walrus and its pilot, Lieutenant Clem Bateman, but a very modern looking Arado floatplane and a very antiquated Norwegian seaplane sheltering under the lee of the fjord out of the incessant stream of German aircraft flying overhead.
>
> We eventually managed to get in touch with the Admiralty on the Walrus's radio at night and were able to tell them where we were and what we were doing – we must have used a code of some sort. After four or five days there was a favourable easterly wind and we set off for the Shetlands, which was the nearest point in the

◀ **A view of a Norwegian fjord as seen from the cockpit of a Fairey Swordfish of No. 816 Squadron flying from *Furious*. (Arthur Ward)**

United Kingdom. The Arado was sent off ahead with *Rodney*'s observer in the back. It was twice as fast as we were, and there was no point in keeping him with us doing 80 knots. Shortly after departure the wind went round to due west and started to blow Force 6 to 7. We went down lower and lower on the water until we were flying at about 100 feet to lessen the wind effect. After some three and a half hours with no Shetlands in sight, we decided to ask Hatston for a D/F bearing which was immediately forthcoming and told us 'You are bearing 090', which meant that not only had we missed the Shetlands but we were about to miss the Orkneys as well.

However, that was very helpful and we altered course to make Hatston. After some four and a half hours airborne and with fuel gauges showing virtually empty, out of the sky came a flight of three Sea Gladiators from No. 804 Squadron, which had been scrambled to investigate the bogeys approaching from the east! They proceeded to riddle the wretched Norwegian seaplane full of holes. Besides the Norwegian pilot there were three or four of his countrymen crowded in the back seat but mercifully none of them was hit. I decided the best thing was to get down on the water, which we did, being by then in the lee of the islands, and we taxied the last three or four miles rather ignominiously and beached the aircraft. The Arado meanwhile had flown straight into the Shetlands and landed at Sullum Voe without being challenged at all, with German markings and the lot. It always struck me as wonderful – the British get shot down and the German comes in unscathed!

The next day Bateman and I were flown down to London in the back seats of two Ospreys and spent the day being debriefed on the situation in southern Norway, culminating in a session with Winston Churchill, to whom I did not endear myself in replying to his question about the Norwegian reaction to how things were going by saying very tactlessly that all they wanted was to see a lot more British soldiers on the ground.

I rejoined *Glasgow* almost immediately and by a strange coincidence our first task was to proceed to Molde and escort King Haakon and the Norwegian Government plus all their gold reserves to north Norway. This time, the Germans having got wind of the operation, this lovely town, which was almost entirely wooden built, was a sheet of flames – a sad sight after my recent visit. However, the two cruisers escaped without damage and proceeded northwards, disembarking our distinguished guests and their money at Tromsø.

The Royal Navy had by now built up a task force and naval headquarters in Harstad and I was disembarked there to operate with the RAF. My boss was a very famous character, Wing Commander 'Batchy' (Atcherley) of Schneider Trophy fame, and a wonderful man to work for. As a young lieutenant I was always addressed as 'Admiral'. Very good for the morale!

Atcherley's task was to survey the country for potential fighter airfields and then to prepare them for operation. In the event we settled for three. The first was at Skaanland, just south of Harstad, but this wasn't very successful because it was so boggy and every time an aircraft landed there on the Sommerfeld track which had been laid it went on its nose. We then prepared an airfield at Bardufoss. There was a lot of work to be done by the local labour force and I remember flying their wages up from Harstad and dropping them on the site while it was being got ready. In a short time it was levelled off, aircraft shelters prepared and the Hurricanes moved in. Incidentally it was still in use up to quite recently.

Finally we found an ideal site on the other side of North Cape at the head of Laksefjord. This was really in Lapland, and there was nobody there except a very attractive little postmistress and a few Lapps. We left my telegraphist air gunner, Naval Airman Hunt, to get the thing

cracking, and we went back to Harstad. When we returned a fortnight later the whole place had been transformed. Hunt had got hold of the postmistress who in turn had got hold of all the locals and they had prepared the most marvellous airstrip. It was absolutely perfect and was the only part of the area that wasn't snowbound. Hunt had really done the most tremendous job. He was quite happy where he was but we took him back and he was decorated on the field by the Earl of Cork and Orrery, Admiral Boyle. I imagine that Hunt's good work was approved of by the Germans, who must have used his airfield against our Murmansk convoys later on.

Once it became obvious that we would have to evacuate north Norway, Atcherley summoned me up to Bardufoss where he thought I might be of some assistance to the RAF, as they would have to embark in a carrier for passage home. I spent the last few days with the squadrons and although my knowledge of deck-landing in Hurricanes was nil I was able to give them some rudimentary rules to follow. When it came to the evacuation I took the Group Captain in charge of RAF operations in north Norway, a chap called Moore, while Atcherley went off in one of the troopships from Harstad.

We followed the Hurricanes out to *Glorious* and circled around while they landed on, the only damage being one broken tailwheel, which was a remarkable feat of skill on the part of the squadron pilots. I then landed on with my Group Captain and was awaiting instructions for being struck down below when a chap came down from flyco and said 'Sorry, there's no room for you – you'll have to go on to *Ark Royal*'. I objected strongly because I wanted to stay with the squadron but I was overruled and given a course for *Ark Royal*, where I landed-on some forty minutes later. Some thirty-six hours afterwards the news came through to *Ark Royal* that *Glorious* had been sunk. I suspect that I was the last person to land on and fly off from her deck. A lucky escape. Norway was over for me, but not for those unfortunate air crew from *Ark Royal* who on our way back to the United Kingdom had to take part in that expensive and abortive attack on the German Fleet at Trondheim. What a waste of valuable aircraft and invaluable experienced air crew.

This virtually ended the Fleet Air Arm's carrier involvement in the campaign. An attempt was made at a land-based attack on 21 June when six torpedo-equipped Swordfish of Nos. 821 and 823 Squadrons flew off from Hatston, word having been received that *Scharnhorst* was on her way back to Kiel for repairs. This met with no success, however, the crews being quite out of practice at this specialized form of attack, and as they turned for home two aircraft were shot down.

During September and October 1940 *Furious* launched strikes against targets at Trondheim and Tromsø by the Swordfish of Nos. 816 and 825 Squadrons, escorted by Skuas of No. 801 Squadron, but little was achieved. The October attacks included the first night torpedo attack to be made by a full squadron, but No. 825's effort was handicapped by a lack of detailed information about possible targets.

Elsewhere the Walruses of No. 701 Squadron had been transported to Iceland by *Argus* in late June 1940 for anti-submarine and reconnaissance patrols after the British occupation of that country to forestall a possible German invasion.

▼ *Ark Royal* under attack from three high-level German bombers on 1 May 1940. Her evasive action leaves a sharply curving wake as she heads into the wall of water and spray resulting from a stick of bombs. (Via Cdr R. N. Everett)

CHAPTER 7

Action in the Mediterranean, 1940

Whilst the Royal Navy had been kept busy in Norway, an equally unsuccessful struggle had taken place in France, culminating in the withdrawal of British ground forces through Dunkirk. A small part was played in this by six turreted Blackburn Rocs of No. 801 Squadron which helped to provide air cover operating from Detling in Kent. At the same time, shore-based Swordfish carried out attacks against U-boats, E-boats and enemy transport in the English Channel. Following the evacuation the Admiralty offered the RAF the loan of volunteer trainee fighter pilots for the coming defence of the British Isles. As a consequence, 58 naval pilots participated in the Battle of Britain, flying Spitfires and Hurricanes with RAF squadrons, and eighteen were killed. On 16 August 1940, during the battle, HMS *Daedalus*, otherwise RNAS Lee-on-Solent, was one of many aerodromes on the south coast to be the target of concerted Luftwaffe attacks, and many casualties were caused.

Taking advantage of the deteriorating situation, Italy declared war in support of the Germans on 6 June 1940, presenting an immediate threat in a quite different area. She had a large fleet, which included six battleships, though no aircraft carriers, whereas the Royal Navy by now had *Eagle* back in the Mediterranean, recently returned after a refit at Singapore. She was a relatively small ship, however, being able to carry only the eighteen Swordfish of Nos. 813 and 824 Squadrons plus a small number of defending Sea Gladiators. The obsolete *Argus* might have been there, but only the previous day she had sailed for Greenock from Gibraltar, having spent six months engaged in deck-landing training off Toulon. The only other Fleet Air Arm presence in the Mediterranean at that time was a limited number of Swordfish seaplanes and Walrus amphibians embarked in various warships.

No. 767 Squadron, a second-line unit which had been carrying out deck-landing training aboard *Argus* from a base in the south of France, suddenly found itself on operational service, and on 19 June the squadron's Swordfish carried out a bombing attack on Genoa and on Italian lines of communication. The new first-line status was officially recognized when, after moving to Malta, it was renumbered No. 830 Squadron, subsequently playing a vital part in the defence of that beleaguered island. On 8 July *Eagle* sailed from Alexandria with the British Fleet and the

▼ The remains of the control tower and hangars at Lee-on-Solent after a dive bombing attack by German Stukas on 16 August 1940 during the Battle of Britain. Heavy casualties were suffered in this raid, which was one of several carried out that day on south-coast aerodromes. (Capt. H. L. St J. Fancourt)

▲ **A Gloster Sea Gladiator of No. 806 Squadron landing aboard *Illustrious* in the Eastern Mediterranean in November 1940. (Official)**

next day her aircraft were in action. The Sea Gladiators, flown by Swordfish pilots, fought gallantly against a succession of Italian raids and over the next eight months shot down a total of seven enemy aircraft as well as damaging three others.

In the changed circumstances there was now a pressing need to augment the air defences of Malta and a special RAF flight was therefore set up in July at Abbotsinch to provide reinforcements in the shape of Hurricanes. One of those involved in the first attempt, Operation 'Hurry', was Jim Pickering:

In the summer of 1940, after completing a course of fighter training with No. 7 Operational Training Unit at Hawarden, I was posted to No. 64 Squadron at RAF Kenley. At the end of the month, however, I was told by the CO to report to No. 418 Flight at Uxbridge with all possible speed and the aid of his staff car. His official instruction was that this was a temporary secondment, but unofficially, and wise in the ways of the services, he advised me not to rely on an early return to Kenley. Several of us were flown to Hullavington in communication aircraft, issued with a new Hurricane each and told to make our own way to Abbotsinch (Glasgow), where a reception committee covered with gold braid told us to take the wings off our Hurricanes and load them on to barges. There was much tut-tutting when we said we had never done such a thing and in any case we had no tools. Such a situation had not been envisaged.

Our gloom increased when we were escorted to a grey hulk that we recognized as the *Argus* and directed to the grotty locker room on the starboard bow which we had occupied before and told we would all sail to an unrevealed destination in a few days and would not be allowed ashore. However, several RAF junior officers came aboard, who had also previously been on attachment to the FAA and had, like us, been seconded to No. 418 Flight. They did not know either why they were aboard the *Argus*, but we managed to find the usual leaky clerk who told us we were being shanghaied to Malta.

Having flown Hurricanes to Glasgow, we only had our overnight kit and created enough fuss to get ashore and buy some essentials. We also made it clear to the 'Jaunty' that we would not tolerate the living conditions imposed upon us in the past, for which we were marched in front of the naval officer we had previously nicknamed 'Piggy'. In our twelve months of service we had, however, learnt a thing or two. We were personnel of No. 418 Flight RAF, not the crew of the *Argus*, we told 'Piggy'. If our services were required on board we would receive instructions from our own officers, whom we would also expect to ensure that our accommodation and conditions were commensurate with our rank and responsibilities. 'Piggy' caved in and agreed with our point of view but the 'Jaunty' concealed his feelings with a spontaneous performance of covert malice that would have earned him an Oscar in Hollywood. We were provided with two pretty useless seamen as mess orderlies, did our fair share of watch-keeping and played cards until we docked at Gibraltar.

The *Ark Royal* was also at Gib with many old friends aboard and we celebrated our joint presence in gallons of Tom Collins – the then-trendy embalmer – before sailing eastwards into the Med under the escort of seemingly the entire West Mediterranean Fleet.

We were eventually briefed for our mission. 'You will fly off tomorrow to RAF Luqa, Malta, in two flights of six, each flight being led by a Skua. Captain Ford, RM, is senior navigator in the leading Skua, which will be flown by Sergeant Ayre.

We were briefed about the airfield at Luqa and our route around Pantellaria and action to take in the event of enemy interception or forced landing in the sea. (A Sunderland flying boat was to follow our route shortly after.) When we came to the intended take-off point we found it was beyond the flying range of Hurricanes. The briefing officer showed his displeasure at our ridiculous quibble and lack of knowledge of the aircraft we were flying. He produced *Jane's All the World's Aircraft* and pointed out its statistical information on Hurricanes. They had, said *Jane's*, a maximum speed of 325mph and a maximum endurance of three hours. With the promised tail wind tomorrow, said the briefing officer, you should be safe for 1,000 miles and our distance from Malta would be much less than that. If the Skua could do this with two crew, then the Hurricane could certainly do it with only a pilot.

Even 'Piggy' looked uncomfortable at the prospect of the briefing turning into a mutiny, and in the end it was agreed that radio silence would be broken to obtain endurance figures from the Air Ministry. Later in the day we were informed without explanation that take-off had been delayed for twenty-four hours whilst the fleet sailed further eastward. It was not a popular decision because we were bombed by Italian aircraft during the day, though without any hits on any ship.

Aircraft were ranged before dawn and they finished up with the Skuas in front of each flight of six Hurricanes. The leading Skua had therefore the shortest take-off run. The ramp on the bows of the *Argus* bumped it into the air at too low an airspeed for comfort and at an obviously too steep an angle of attack. It sank slowly below the level of the *Argus*'s bows and out of my sight gasping for air. I was next off and scores of permutations of circumstances cascaded through my mind. We had no plan of action if the lead Skua pranged on take-off. If a Hurricane had trouble on take-off the pilot would bale out and hope to be picked up by one of the escort ships. Survival from ditched monoplanes was less likely. If this happened en route to Malta the lead Skua's TAG would send a Morse signal of the position to the Sunderland flying boat.

However, the lead Skua did not hit the sea. Harry Ayre carried out a balancing act that kept it just above the water whilst it built up enough flying speed to climb, and Bats waved me off before either he or I could see the Skua, but all was well. The Hurricane leapt from the deck even without full throttle. We formed up into a vic formation of seven aircraft in one wide circuit of the *Argus* and headed eastward into the sun on a fine clear day, with the north coast of Africa just discernible in the distance on our starboard beam. The second flight then had deck space to open out and start their engines and set course later without problem.

The flight was exciting with anticipation but uneventful. On arrival at Luqa, however, Robertson beat up the airfield and, knowing nothing about hot air having less lift, completed his ostentatious display with a heavy landing that collapsed one leg of his Hurricane. We expressed our own disapproval before the Air Officer Commanding had his say. When the second flight arrived the lead Skua made the same mistake as Robertson (without the beat-up) and collapsed both legs.

Back in the easier informality of an RAF station at that stage of the war we were asked to await the arrival of the AOC, Air Commodore Maynard. (In the Navy we would have been marched in front of whoever had been ordered to see us.) 'Please be seated', said the AOC. 'I must first congratulate you on the completion of your task which, even allowing for the two landing accidents, was more successful than we could have hoped. It was an immensely complicated operation to reinforce the defence of Malta in this way. It was ordered from the highest level and its success ensures it will be the pattern for future reinforcements. Secondly', said the AOC, 'I have some news for you. You are being retained here to re-form No. 261 Squadron with your aircraft, the Hurricane already here, and the Gladiators *Faith*, *Hope* and *Charity*. This will be the island's sole air defence.'

Uproar broke out. We were only on secondment to No. 418 Flight, we said. Our squadrons in the UK were expecting us back. We had no tropical kit. There was a Sunderland at Kalafrana Bay waiting to fly us back to Gib. The AOC sat patiently until protests started to subside. He seized the initiative. 'If you will kindly be quiet', he said, 'I will be able to telephone Kalafrana to tell the ship to leave without you.' And he did just that. Few of us returned to the UK and even then it was more than three years later.

An identical reinforcement [Operation 'White'] was attempted in November 1940 with twelve RAF pilots who had flown through the Battle of Britain. It was identical up to the point where the same briefing officer decided where the aircraft would take off. The RAF pilots, unused to naval ignorance of aircraft, accepted the briefing without question. One Skua and four Hurricanes reached Malta on the last dregs of their fuel. The other Skua landed in Sicily. One Hurricane pilot was picked up from the sea by the Sunderland flying boat. The rest were lost.

This failure was not of method but of

execution. The really massive fighter reinforcement of Malta in 1941, 1942 and 1943 was carried out by the procedures pioneered by No. 418 Flight in 1940.

Arrival at Malta terminated my contact with the FAA except for one further Malta episode. This was the arrival, presence and departure of HMS *Illustrious*. We had three serviceable Hurricanes and one serviceable Gladiator and tried to provide some air cover to the badly damaged vessel. By then all aircraft were regarded as hostile and anything within range of its guns was fired at. After she arrived in Valetta harbour there were three major raids estimated at 180 aircraft, 140, and 120, mostly German aircraft. Eric Kelsey was last seen chasing a Ju 87 into the *Illustrious*'s box barrage.

It was reported after the *Illustrious* had got away on 20 January 1941 that since the outbreak of hostilities with Italy in June 1940 the Malta defences had accounted for 87 enemy aircraft confirmed shot down, 24 probably shot down and 34 more were known to have been damaged. In the same period (and excluding pilots lost on the second *Argus* reinforcement) No. 261 Squadron lost eleven fighters in action, but four of the pilots were saved.

The strength of the Mediterranean Fleet had been greatly increased on 2 September 1940 by the arrival of *Illustrious*, the new fleet carrier. Two days later her aircraft attacked airfields on Rhodes, following this up by raids on Benghazi on 17 September and Leros on 14 October. Fitted with 3in-thick deck armour and modern radar, *Illustrious* carried, in addition to Nos. 815 and 819 Swordfish Squadrons, the Fulmar two-seat fighters of No. 806 Squadron equipped with eight wing guns. The latter accounted for more than twenty enemy machines during the ensuing months.

With two carriers available the possibility opened up of an attack on the Italian naval base at Taranto, where the presence of the Italian Fleet was causing a large number of British ships to be tied to that theatre. The raid was originally scheduled for Trafalgar Day, 21 October, but had to be postponed owing to a hangar fire in *Illustrious*. Cloud cover brought a further delay, then Eagle was found to have sea-water in her petrol supply system following damage during Italian dive-bombing attacks and became unavailable. Five of her Swordfish were consequently transferred to the other carrier and the Fleet finally left Alexandria on 6 November. RAF photographic reconnaissance four days later revealed the Italian Fleet, which included five battleships, to be still in harbour.

The following day, 11 November, *Illustrious* sailed to within 170 miles of Taranto and at 2100 the first strike of twelve aircraft took off, six armed with torpedoes and the remainder with bombs, two of the latter group also carrying flares. Each aircraft was fitted with long-range tanks to increase the overall range to 400 miles, and, to save weight, no air gunners were carried. Flying through thin

◀ A Swordfish being loaded with a torpedo aboard *Ark Royal* prior to the attack on Oran on 3 July 1940. The torpedo is about to be wheeled under the aircraft's fuselage, where it will be jacked up into the dropping position. (Via Cdr R. N. Everett)

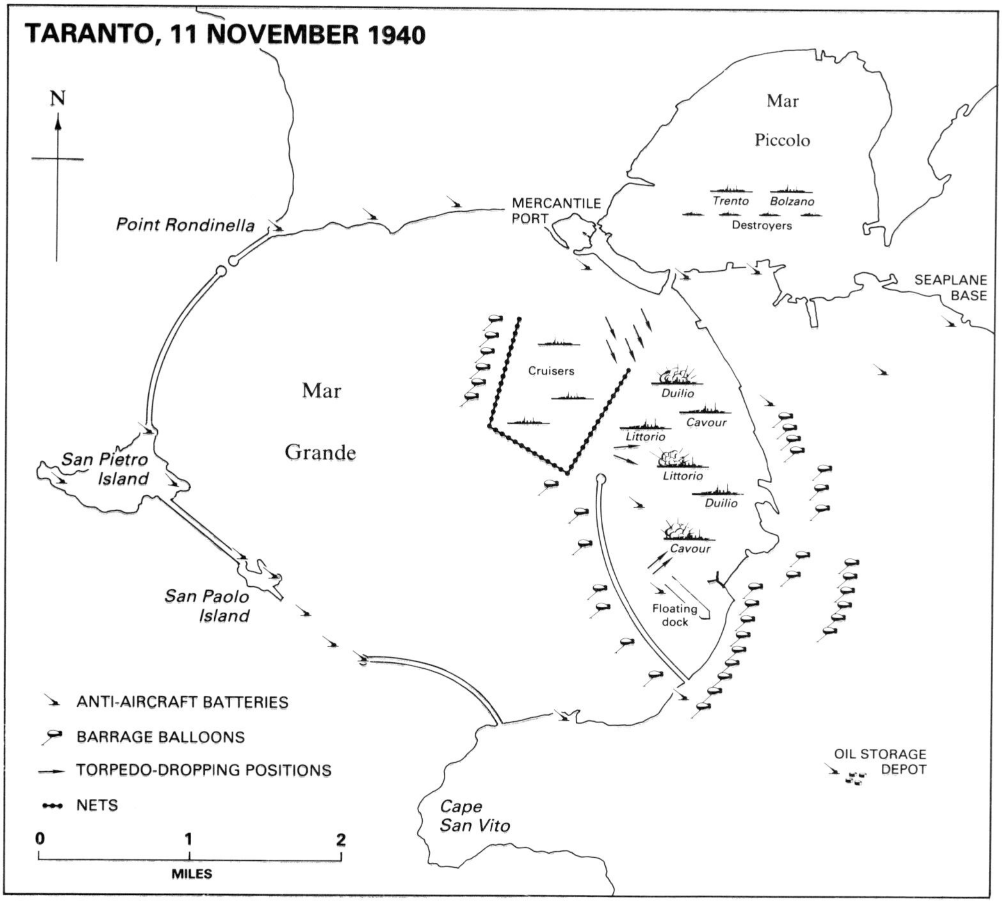

cloud, three of the bombers and a torpedo-carrier strayed from the main force but continued to press on independently. Two hours later the first aircraft arrived, and a flare was dropped to the east of the harbour, after which this aircraft joined with the other flare-dropper to set fire to oil tanks in a dive-bombing attack. The leader of the force, Lt Cdr K. Williamson, RN, of No. 815 Squadron, then led the next three aircraft over San Pietro island, his own machine ('L4A') being shot down by flak just after releasing its torpedo, which tore a 27ft hole in the battleship *Conte di Cavour*, causing it to list badly. Despite this loss the other two aircraft in this sub-flight ('L4C' and 'L4R'), piloted respectively by Sub-Lt (A) P. D. J. Sparke, RN, and Sub-Lt (A) A. S. D. Macauley, RN, continued with the attack, encountering intense anti-aircraft fire and having to weave through a balloon barrage to attack the battleship *Andrea Doria* unsuccessfully.

The next sub-flight had better luck, coming in from a more northerly direction, and Lt N. McI. Kemp, RN, in the leading aircraft ('L4K') dropped his torpedo at the new battleship *Littorio*, blowing a large hole in the starboard bow. This ship was also hit by Lt (A) H. A. I. Swayne in the next aircraft ('L4M'), this time on the port quarter, and she was soon settling down by the bows. Swayne was followed by Lt M. R. Maund, RN, from one of the *Eagle* squadrons (in 'E4F'), whose torpedo failed to hit the flagship *Vittorio Veneto* at which it was aimed.

It was now the turn of the bombing force, led by Capt. O. Patch, RM, in 'E5A'. He and his observer. Lt D. G. Goodwin, RN, found the targets difficult to identify but they dived on two cruisers from 1,500ft, followed by another Swordfish which dropped its bombs across four destroyers, the third machine in this wave bombing a seaplane hangar after failing to find its original target in the Mar Piccolo. Meanwhile a further striking force of nine aircraft was on the way, having taken off half an hour after the first force under the leadership of Lt Cdr J. W. Hale, RN, of No. 819 Squadron (in 'L5A'). Two of the four bombing aircraft carried flares, the other five

◀ **Swordfish K8403 '4M' of No. 813 Squadron made a forced landing at Scarpanto during a raid on Rhodes during the night of 3/4 September 1940. The aircraft and crew were captured by the Italians.**

machines being equipped with torpedoes. One turned back after its auxiliary fuel tank became loose and another took off twenty minutes late having had temporary repairs following a minor taxying accident.

The pattern was repeated, with flares being dropped shortly before midnight. Both Lt Cdr Hale and Lt (A) F. M. A. Torrens-Spence, RN, in 'L5K', aimed their torpedoes at *Littorio*, which was already settling from the earlier attack, and one of them hit her again in the bow. Lt T. W. G. Wellham, RN, in 'E5H', aimed at *Vittorio Veneto* but was twice hit by flak and his torpedo achieved no results. However, Lt (A) C. S. C. Lea, RN, in 'L5H', struck the *Cavour* Class battleship *Caio Duilio* amidships, the explosion making a large hole which resulted in both forward magazines being flooded. The machine ('E4H') flown by Lt G. W. L. A. Bayly, RN, was shot down by wild gunfire as he followed Hale into the attack, this being the only loss to the second wave of torpedo-bombers. Lt Clifford's machine ('L5F') arrived on the scene fifteen minutes after the other aircraft had left, to be met by a hail of fire as he dived through the balloon barrage to bomb a cruiser, but he got away safely to reach *Illustrious* at 0239 next morning.

The carrier now turned back to Alexandria, her air crews having accomplished a famous victory long to be remembered. Its immediate effect, however, was the withdrawal of the remains of the Italian fleet to Naples, leaving the British fleet much greater freedom to operate in the Mediterranean and enabling two battleships to be released to other spheres.

◀ **The remains of Lt Cdr Williamson's Swordfish ('L4A') photographed by the Italians the day after the fateful attack on the Italian Fleet in harbour at Taranto.**

CHAPTER 8

Force H and West Africa

The fall of France and the consequent loss to the Allies of her navy left unguarded a number of areas in the Mediterranean, and to cover the gap several British ships were hastily brought together as the nucleus of a new naval formation known as Force H. It was constituted under Vice Admiral Somerville on 28 June 1940. The carrier strength of this famous Force consisted initially of *Ark Royal*, which had arrived at Gibraltar from Norway five days earlier after a brief three days at Scapa. The flagship was HMS *Hood*, and also in the Force were two other battleships, *Valiant* and *Resolution*, both carrying Swordfish seaplanes of No. 700 Squadron. Two cruisers and eleven destroyers made up the remainder of the Force, whose ships were continually changing, with several of the cruisers carrying No. 700 Squadron Walruses.

The French Fleet, lying at anchor in the Algerian port of Oran, posed a potential threat and attempts to neutralize it by diplomatic means failed. At dawn on 3 July, therefore, the new Force sailed from Gibraltar and after many hours of abortive negotiations opened fire at 1753 on the ships of the former ally. Swordfish from *Ark Royal* made both bombing and torpedo attacks, but met with little success, and three of their number were lost in addition to two Skuas. The attacks continued for several days and included a torpedo strike against the battleship *Dunkerque* by six Swordfish of No. 820 Squadron on 6 July which caused severe damage. Salvos from the British ships also inflicted heavy damage on the French ships.

In the meantime *Hermes* had been shadowing the new French battleship *Richelieu* off the west coast of Africa. On 2 July the carrier called in at Freetown but her quarry was by now at Dakar in French West Africa and the chances of catching her at sea were slim. *Hermes* therefore sailed north on 5 July and three days later positioned herself off Dakar for a torpedo strike by Swordfish of No. 814 Squadron. Six aircraft attacked soon after dawn and, flying through AA fire between two rows of merchant ships, managed a single hit. The damage did not appear too serious, and further operations were planned, but in fact there was considerable flooding aft, the propeller shaft was twisted and the steering gear was out of order. It was to be another year before *Richelieu* was ready to put to sea again, local repair facilities being minimal.

Following her efforts in North Africa *Ark Royal* had sailed for the central Mediterranean, where her aircraft were soon in combat with the Regia Aeronautica off Sardinia. On 9 July a Cant 506 seaplane was spotted and brought down by a section of No. 800 Skuas led by their Commanding Officer, Lt R. M. Smeeton, RN, attacking in line astern. They were too late, however, to prevent the seaplane radioing that it had spotted the Fleet, and later that day Force H was attacked by forty Savoia Marchetti SM 79 bombers in three waves. More than a hundred bombs were dropped, but as a result of the efforts of the defending Skuas of Nos. 800 and 803 Squadrons no damage was inflicted, two of the attackers being brought down and two others damaged. Capt. E. S. Carver recalls:

> I can say a little about the very early days of fighter direction. I was serving as senior observer in No. 800 Squadron (Skua fighter/dive-bombers), *Ark Royal*, in 1940–41 and one of our consorts in Force H based on Gibraltar was *Sheffield*, one of the earliest ships to be fitted with an air warning radar – Type 79, I think.
>
> On our sorties eastwards into the Mediterranean on offensive operations and/or escorting convoys to reinforce Malta we were the target for Italian Air Force Savoia Marchetti SM 79 bombers after we had been located by Cant Z.506 or Z.501 reconnaissance floatplanes. Our fighter defence organization worked out something like this. *Sheffield* would detect a shadower or a group of aircraft on her radar and pass its bearing and range to *Ark Royal* by flag hoist to avoid breaking W/T silence. Our signal officer in *Ark Royal*, Charles Coke, would put this into a simple code and pass it to the fighter patrol (later CAP) leader by H/F W/T. The leader's observer would then pass the data to his pilot by Gosport tube and, if necessary, plot a course to intercept.
>
> A fighter patrol was normally a sub-flight of three aircraft, of which the lead aircraft carried an observer and the other two a telegraphist air gunner. All three aircraft would therefore receive information about enemy aircraft.

There would be at least another sub-flight at standby on deck and others at short notice.

One of our problems at this time was with voice communications. The Skua had a TR9D H/F voice set as well as the T.1083/R.1082 H/F and M/F W/T set. The trouble lay largely with our 'Carbon' microphones which, when switched on, picked up so much engine and slipstream noise that transmissions became very difficult to read. Even 'intercom' between crew members was better by 'tube' than through the TR9. Communication between aircraft in formation was frequently by 'zogging' – visual, Morse signals made with the raised forearm. When electromagnetic microphones and, of course, VHF came in shortly after this period the problem was resolved.

The lack of height-finding by the Type 79 didn't matter too much. The SM 79s, as I recollect, always high-level bombed from about 12–15,000 feet and the shadowers always shadowed from either nought feet or just below cloud base. The Skua could only catch the Savoia if it had a good height advantage but could overhaul the Cants, particularly the 501s.

On 2 August twelve of the carrier's Swordfish made a night raid on Cagliari in southern Sardinia – the first such attack on Italian soil. Twelve machines took off at 0230, three armed with mines and the remainder with bombs, though one of the latter aircraft hit the ship's island with its starboard wing and the three crew members perished when it went over the side. The remaining bombers and the mine-layers split into two groups but both lost their way, delaying the intended dawn commencement of the attack. The first to arrive were the three mine-layers, under the leadership of Lt R. N. Everett, RN, and they succeeded in dropping their mines from fifty feet, undeterred by splashes from 6in shells fired by coastal batteries. They were quickly followed by the surviving bombers, led by Lt Cdr G. B. Hodgkinson, RN, which attacked the local aerodrome and seaplanes afloat in the harbour, inflicting heavy damage. One Swordfish (P4117) was lost to a defending fighter, but a Cant 501 was forced down by nine Skuas as the rest made their way back to the ship.

Two further attacks were made on Cagliari on 2 and 3 September, known respectively as Operations 'Smash' and 'Grab'. In the first of these raids parachute flares were dropped by nine Swordfish, though these turned out to be superfluous because of the 'flaming onions' put up by the enemy AA. Damage from the previous raid was clearly visible and in the dive-bombing attack part of a military headquarters was destroyed and aircraft parked on the ground were hit. The following day's attack was less successful owing to low cloud formations and mist in the valleys. Flares were dropped by four aircraft and one of the searchlights was eliminated, then two aircraft attacked what appeared to be a night-landing flare path, but the remainder unloaded their bombs into the sea as they made their way back to the ship. A final raid on 9 September inflicted further damage under heavy fire, but all the aircraft returned safely.

Ark Royal now made for Freetown, where she arrived on 16 September, embarking two French Caudron Luciole training aircraft two days later. On 21 September she sailed with Force M, having taken aboard four Swordfish

▼A Swordfish of No. 814 Squadron from HMS *Hermes* being towed by a team of bullocks whilst ashore at Ouakam, near Dakar in French West Africa, about February 1940. Such primitive methods of moving aircraft by animals were, of necessity, quite common in both the Middle East and Far East. (Cdr J. H. Dundas)

of No. 814 Squadron from *Hermes*. Heading for Dakar, the Force was accompanied by General de Gaulle and a Free French force hoping to make an unopposed amphibious landing. On arrival two days later the Caudrons were flown off to announce the arrival of the French leader but attempts to arrange a peaceful settlement were unsuccessful. Operations commenced the following day but the results were disastrous, the attacking force suffering considerably more damage than the defenders. Five Swordfish failed to return from the main attack and another four aircraft were lost before operations ceased on 26th. The carrier then returned home to refit at Liverpool and her obsolescent Skuas were discarded for the new Fulmars of No. 808 Squadron.

Cdr J. S. L. Crabb, RN (Ret.), then a lieutenant with No. 814 Squadron, recalls this episode. On 23 September he was involved in dropping leaflets, but the Vichy French were in no mood to surrender and operations were planned for the following day. These included a strike against *Richelieu*, it not then being appreciated how badly she had been damaged in the earlier attack:

> I turned out very early to be on the top line for anything that might turn up but our machine was not down for any blitz. First of all six Skuas were flown off to attack the French battleship *Richelieu* and three cruisers. After that six Swordfish were sent off, I think to bomb the battery on Cap Manuel. The third attack was to be carried out by six machines from our squadron against the batteries at Cap Manuel and Goree, but our machine (P4217) was not down to go.
>
> However, I went to breakfast about 0630 and Lt Godfrey-Faussett came up and said 'Afraid you've got to go in our place on the next blitz as our tail wheel has burst while ranging. Your machine is being ranged now'. So I went and got hold of Lt T.W.B. Shaw to find out what was happening and he said we should fly off at about 0730, that his sub-section was going to bomb the Cap Manuel battery and that we were to lead the other sub-section against the battery on Goree, getting back to the ship on our own or joining up with one of the other aircraft, who all had beacons. We were being armed with four 250lb SAP [semi-armour-piercing] bombs and eight Cooper 20lb bombs for use against personnel.
>
> So I whizzed around getting everything ready and information from the Air Office, managing to forget of course what call-sign we should use. I got down rather late to the machine which was being run up and no sooner had I got in than my pilot, Lt H. H. Jackson, said we were all going to attack the *Richelieu* instead. This didn't sound too good, though little did I realize what we were in for. I found that Jarvis hadn't got our call-sign either. We had a frantic dash around the other air gunners and eventually got hold of a list of call-signs. While we were waiting to take off, five Skuas came back from their attack, and I feared the other might be lost but I heard later that it got back.
>
> We took off at 0740 and climbed up to 8,000ft above the ship. There was considerable haze straight away, making the air-to-ship visibility bad, but there were no clouds. I saw three Swordfish come back to the ship while we were climbing and thought, 'Heavens, are the other three lost? Things don't look so good'. Actually the other three did get back later, though I didn't know this.
>
> It took 70 minutes to get up to 8,000ft, dúring which time we made visual signs to the aircraft on our starboard side (L7696) confirming our

▼ A flight of Swordfish of No. 814 Squadron ashore at Ouakam, near Dakar, around February 1940. Only a few months later the squadron's aircraft were to be in action against the French Fleet in the same region. (Cdr J. H. Dundas)

call-sign. This machine's crew were Sub-Lt G. M. M. C. Wheeler, RN, pilot, Sub-Lt A. L. Cross, RN, observer, and Dawson, air gunner. Wheeler had been best man at Jackson's wedding. At about 0850 we set off towards Dakar, sub-sections in line astern. It was a lovely day, blue sky, sun shining and everything in the garden lovely, but from our point of view it couldn't have been worse – there was absolutely no cover and the French would be fully wide awake so there would be no surprise. Not having done this sort of thing before, my feelings on the matter as we approached the coast were pretty apprehensive but they would have been more so if I'd had more previous experience! Funnily enough, the thought of being taken prisoner never entered my head.

We made a landfall just north of Cap Manuel soon after 0900 and the battery there opened fire immediately. We went into line astern and proceeded towards the harbour where the *Richelieu* was lying alongside the oiling jetty. She opened fire too, also the cruisers. I was keeping a good look-out for fighters – the thought of them coming across us was ghastly! As we made our way towards the *Richelieu* the fire got better and better. The Cap Manuel battery had started a long way short but they soon got the height very accurately and the bursts were unpleasantly close.

While in line astern, the machine astern of us got a direct hit, killing Wheeler and severely wounding Cross. The machine started to climb out of control but Dawson managed to bale out and came down in the sea off Les Iles des Serpents. He had tried to get Cross out but couldn't manage it. The machine spun in and exploded on hitting the sea.

That wasn't at all pleasant, and I thought that at any moment the same thing might happen to us. We had got over the harbour now and Jackson started his dive and I set the 'Mickey Mouse' bomb distributor. My feelings at this time were of complete fright – I crouched on my seat and peered over the port side at the *Richelieu* and it really was an unpleasant sight. Her deck seemed to be a mass of flame from HA and short range weapons. I didn't see how they could fail to hit us and just nerved myself for the inevitable end. Having nothing to do was very trying.

Jackson let go the bombs at about 2,500ft and I watched them go down and fall in the water just outside the jetty. It was then that I felt a very hot feeling underneath the aircraft and I thought I had been hit in the backside, but on feeling it I found all was well. Jarvis however sang out that he had been hit, though I couldn't make out where. Actually a piece of shrapnel had cut through his shoe, inflicting a slight wound in the foot.

To make our getaway we continued in a shallow dive, full out – about 140 knots! – straight over the *Richelieu* towards the bay. In the bay the cruisers and flying boats on the surface were firing at us but it was the only way open to us. We got over the *Richelieu*, and I

◀ **A Swordfish of No. 818 Squadron descending on one of *Ark Royal*'s three lifts in 1940. (Author's collection)**

thought we really stood a chance of getting away with it, when Jarvis tapped my arm and pointed to the port upper mainplane. There to my horror I saw a small red round hole and one could see that the whole of the inside of the wing was on fire.

It would obviously be only a short time before the whole of the wing was blazing, probably exploding the petrol tank. We were by then far too low to bale out so I sang out to Jackson to land in the sea. He'd already decided to do that and we glided down, getting heavily fired at by the flying boats and cruisers. I had got my tail strap hooked on and braced myself against the landing, hoping to high heaven that we got down before the machine was all ablaze and also that we should not get hit again.

Jackson brought her down very nicely indeed and I suffered no ill effects at all. The most noticeable things were the sudden silence and suddenly being up to one's waist in the water, the machine having gone straight up on her nose. I hastily undid my harness, heaved the Syko coding machine and naval aircraft code over the side and stepped out of the machine into the delightfully warm water. Jarvis had left his place of duty without permission, the silly ass having forgotten to have his tail strap hooked on, with the result that he shot through the air and landed up about ten yards ahead of the machine.

Jackson was OK and got out but meanwhile one of the flying boats was still machine-gunning us and the bursts were very close indeed. I thought this a bit offside and started to swim away from the machine. Luckily they soon stopped firing.

The machine showed no signs of sinking but floated with about six feet of the tail out of the water. The dinghy had not come out on its own, so we all got hold of the wire strap and heaved away at it, but nothing happened and we had to give up, thinking it had probably been burnt, which actually was the case.

We were about one and a half miles from the shore so I thought the best thing to do was to try and swim there and if possible lie low until Dakar was taken. I didn't like the idea of swimming much because I knew there were hundreds of sharks about and blood was coming from Jarvis's foot. However, we set off, keeping close together. At this time there was a first class battle going on round the harbour. Fifteen-inch shells were falling amongst the shipping in the Roads and straddling the *Richelieu* in the harbour. The three cruisers were steaming at full speed to and fro across the bay and the *Richelieu* was firing full bat. It was an inspiring sight and I only hoped that we shouldn't collect any 'overs' from our ships.

They were then picked up by one of four big French flying boats that were taxying up and down to defend the beaches, ending up in a prisoner-of-war camp.

▼ ***Ark Royal*, off Cape Spartivento in the afternoon of 27 November 1940 with all guns blazing, emerges unscathed from a wall of water after thirty bombs had been dropped nearby from Savoia-Marchetti SM 79 bombers. Some of the bombs have fallen only 30yd away. (Via Cdr R. N. Everett)**

By early November *Ark Royal* was back at Gibraltar and in the ensuing months saw further action against various types of target. One notable raid occurred on 2 February 1941 when her Swordfish attacked a power station and dam at San Chiar d'Ula in Sardinia. Take-off was at 0600 and there was a gusty wind, but the eight aircraft departed safely in the dark and flew to the target through heavy rain and hail, with ice forming on the wings. Seven found their target but one was shot down and two had to jettison their torpedoes owing to icing. The other four dropped their missiles successfully, the best drop being made by Sub-Lt (A) R. S. Charlier, RN, of No. 810 Squadron in L2766, who had flown all the way from the coast at 50ft and consequently avoided enemy fire until making his attack. Unfortunately no damage to the dam could be seen.

Hermes in the meantime was engaged in trade protection duties in the Indian Ocean, her aircraft undertaking searches and convoy protection off East Africa. In February 1941 support was provided by her aircraft for advancing land forces in British Somaliland, and in April 1941 she was called upon to escort a troop convoy from Bombay to Iraq, where a change of power had put a pro-German group in authority. No. 814 Squadron Swordfish disembarked to Shaibah for a time in May and the ship remained in the Persian Gulf for several weeks after the rebels had been overcome before returning to the Indian Ocean in July.

Among Force H's most important tasks was the escorting of convoys through the Mediterranean, and in particular the ferrying of aircraft to Malta. In mid-April 1941 *Argus* arrived at Gibraltar with 26 Hurricanes, which were then transferred to *Ark Royal*, to be flown off three days later under Fulmar escort to help them navigate safely to their destination. The next such operation was similarly successful, 21 Hurricanes being flown off to Malta on 21 May, and during that year eleven such operations were made, with *Argus*, *Ark Royal*, *Furious* and the new carrier *Victorious* all being involved at various times.

This activity was to end suddenly and tragically for *Ark Royal*, which left Gibraltar on 10 November on a further ferrying trip. *Argus* flew off her Hurricanes on the 12th and the ships turned back to Gibraltar. The following day brought fine weather and there appeared to be little danger to the Force, but at 1541, as the last of fourteen Swordfish was preparing to land on *Ark Royal* after a training exercise, there was a loud explosion under the

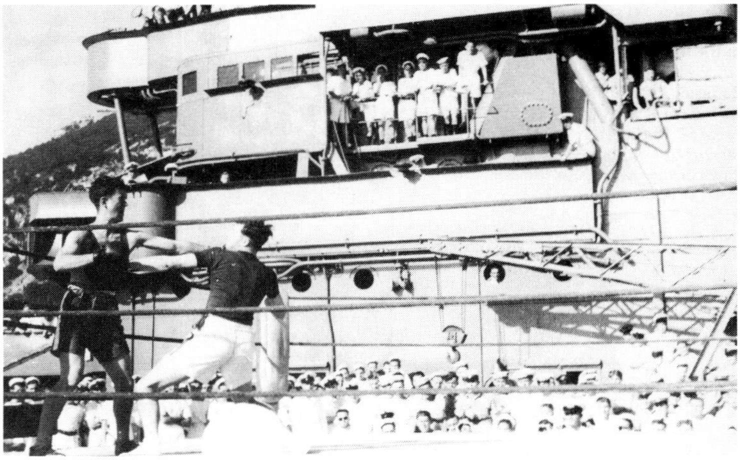

starboard side of the ship's bridge. *U-18* had apparently approached unseen and struck the carrier with a single torpedo when she was only 30 miles from her destination. She had been travelling at 18kt and the damage inflicted was such that within three minutes she had a 12-degree list. Efforts to tow her into Gibraltar continued throughout the night but at 0613 she turned over, sinking shortly afterwards. Only one life had been lost in the explosion, and the other 1,540 members of her company were taken off safely. Some of her aircraft survived to reach North Front aerodrome at Gibraltar, including four Fulmars of No. 807 Squadron and also the Swordfish of No. 825 Squadron, which was in the air at the time of the attack.

Around this time Jock Moffat was serving in Swordfish with No. 818 Squadron:

> Towards the end of 1941 the squadron had been working up at Machrihanish. Their Lordships wanted two aircraft to go on the *Argus*, to do convoy duty to Gibraltar, and I was sent with McWilliam. I can't remember the other pilot but I believe the other observer was Penrose.
>
> We picked her up in Greenock. The Commander (Flying) tried to get us to go off the catapult, which had never been used since the outbreak of war, but we were spared that. We weren't very enthusiastic, so eventually they decided not to try it.
>
> Just before we set sail we took on board a party of Petty Officer Wrens – Signals I think. A very fine bunch who were on passage to Gibraltar. They were the first young ladies to be taken on one of His Majesty's warships – I believe the original party went down in a previous convoy. The skipper gave over his quarters to the whole lot of them and made the necessary arrangements that they fed there, and everything else. They certainly helped to relieve the boredom of a usually tedious trip!
>
> We had been out about a week in very changeable weather, and whether there had been a submarine scare or not the Commodore

◀ **The ship's crew watches a boxing match in progress on the flight deck of *Ark Royal* while she lies alongside at Gibraltar during her spell as part of Force H. In the background is 'Jumbo', the ship's crane, which was used for removing crashed aircraft from the flight deck. (Cdr R. N. Everett)**

decided that one of our aircraft should drop a couple of depth charges astern of the convoy on this particular day. The date was 7 October 1941 and I was the one who happened to be in the air [in V4556], my crew being Midshipman McWilliam and Leading Airman Clark. I went to a suitable distance astern of the convoy – a distance from which I thought that a submarine might be able to shadow a slow-moving convoy – made the necessary switches in the cockpit, said 'OK, this is it, here we go,' and pressed the old tit.

The next minute there was a hell of an explosion and the aircraft shot up about two or three hundred feet in the air. It was flinging itself around the sky like a well-done seagull with a pellet up its 'how's your father' and didn't know where to go. I realized that something had happened that shouldn't – I thought somebody must have fired at us or something.

I grabbed hold of the stick and wrestled with the thing as much as I could. I remember that the only way I could get any sort of flight into the Stringbag was to push the stick with all my strength against the dashboard, and that gave us some sort of equilibrium. I had to use my foot as well, and when I took it off the rudder bar and looked down I could see the sea!

The wings seemed to be rather shredded and the lower mainplanes appeared to have no skin on them at all. I thought the best thing I could do was to head for the ship. I tried to make contact with the back cockpit but wasn't able to, so I put my hand in the air and made the sign of a pistol. McWilliam must have read it, or whether he did it on his own I don't know, but he fired a red Very, and we headed – though that's hardly the word – towards the *Argus*.

I found that although I could get up to about 300 feet it was a hell of a job to get down again. It kept up a sort of porpoise action, and there was no way I could get the nose down at all, so I had to work on the throttle. I was going to get on that deck somehow, though, and the only way I could do this was to get back down on to the water, so I slewed my way down. I could see the ship in the distance and headed for the round-down. I wasn't going to wait for the ship to get into wind. Just as I got to the round-down I opened the throttle, up over the top, whipped the throttle back and dropped us on to the deck. I was lucky enough to pick up a wire, and there we were – a bit shattered.

I remember I switched off and looked down below at my feet. There was nothing there but the deck, and the next thing I saw was two legs dangling underneath the plane and McWilliam appeared. He climbed out underneath the plane, and just as he did so I noticed that the skipper and Commander (Flying) were heading towards us. I thought, 'I'm going to sit still for a second. I'm not rushing out into this lot'. So I sat there with the engine switched off.

The next thing I saw was the skipper waving his arms and Mac standing to attention, five feet nothing of red patch Middy, with his board under his arm. Then the skipper got stuck into poor old Mac, saying 'What the hell did he mean coming on to his ship like that, what kind of flying was this and what the hell did he mean by landing on in that manner?' And I always remember McWilliam turned round and said, 'For Christ's sake, Sir, be reasonable,' and the skipper's face went as red as a beetroot. His mouth opened and nothing came out, and he just turned and walked away and left Mac standing there. I thought it was quite something, the way he had stood his ground.

When I did get out there was petrol pouring out and, looking underneath, there was a great big chunk of depth-charge. It had gone past my legs and into the tank. Luckily those self-sealers didn't explode. There was no bottom left: all the canvas had come out of the bottom of the plane and most of the lower mainplanes as well, so that's how the air gunner and McWilliam dropped down below instead of coming over the side.

I went down to the wardroom and had suitable refreshment quietly slipped to me and then managed to get changed. That evening, on the quarterdeck, I was suitably comforted by one or two of those nice young ladies, who had seen the whole thing from the deck. So it turned out all right in the end!

▶ **Swordfish P4219 '5A' of No. 818 Squadron is bombed up aboard *Ark Royal* during 1940. (Cdr R. N. Everett)**

CHAPTER 9

Catapult Ships

During the latter part of 1940 Allied shipping was increasingly menaced by German long-range bomber aircraft operating out of captured aerodromes along the western coast of Europe, from south-west France to northern Norway. There were mounting losses from attacks by Junkers Ju 88s, Heinkel He 111s and especially the four-engined Focke-Wulf Fw 200s, which also called up U-boats once they had sighted a convoy.

No carriers could be spared to combat this threat, and as a temporary expedient the Admiralty decided to have aircraft catapults fitted to a number of merchant ships; fighter aircraft were still in desperately short supply at this time, but the danger to shipping was so great that this solution was forced upon them. The unfortunate pilot knew when he was launched that unless he was within range of land, which was seldom likely, he must inevitably abandon his aircraft at the end of the patrol and hope that after baling out he would be picked up from the sea by a nearby vessel.

In all, five ships were selected to be fitted as catapult ships at this time, four naval vessels, *Ariguani*, *Maplin*, *Patia* and *Springbank*, which were known as fighter catapult ships, and the merchantman *Michael E.* The Fleet Air Arm unit selected for embarkation was No. 804 Squadron, which since its formation had spent most of its life ashore in the Orkneys, apart from brief periods in *Glorious* and *Furious*. In early February 1941 it moved down to Yeovilton where it exchanged its Martlets for Fulmars and Sea Hurricanes modified for catapulting. Working up under Lt Cdr P. H. Havers, RN, the squadron pilots went to Gosport and later Farnborough for catapult training. The Hurricanes were former RAF aircraft specially modified by Hawker for this task, and many had seen service in the Battle of Britain.

As working up advanced, aircraft were flown to Sydenham, near Belfast, which by June had become the squadron's main base. *Patia* was sunk off the mouth of the Tyne before coming into service, but the other four fighter catapult ships began operating from Belfast, where the aircraft were loaded on to the forecastle with some difficulty. Rather handily, the aerodrome was fairly near, and the machines could be towed to and from the ship through the streets, their wings being removed for this purpose and re-fitted on arrival. Also pressed into service for a time was the First World War seaplane carrier *Pegasus*, originally named *Ark Royal* and now the Fleet Air Arm's catapult-equipped training ship.

The first of these vessels to join an Atlantic convoy was the *Michael E.*, which sailed on 27 May 1941 carrying two Sea Hurricanes. This type of vessel was to be known as a catapult-armed merchantman (or CAM-ship), and the honour of being the first pilot to be involved in a live launch from a CAM-ship fell to Sub-Lt (A) M. A. Birrell, RN, in W9276, but only four days out the ship was torpedoed by a U-boat and sunk. He and Sub-Lt (A) E. J. Clark, RNVR, the pilot of W9277, were among those rescued after spending 20 hours in the boats, and after being taken to America both men returned to the United Kingdom.

Meanwhile eastbound convoy HX129 had sailed from Halifax, Nova Scotia, accompanied by *Springbank*. Towards the end of the voyage, on 10 June, PO F. J. Shaw, RN, was launched in Fulmar N4065 after an Fw 200, but the enemy aircraft escaped into cloud. Fortunately the convoy was by then nearing the Irish coast and Shaw had sufficient fuel left to make a safe landing at Belfast.

Less lucky were the crew of Fulmar N4038 from *Pegasus*, which, whilst escorting convoys SL78 and OG67, launched them after an Fw 200 on 7 July. They failed to intercept it, then headed towards Aldergrove in poor visibility, but the TAG, LA E. F. Miller, was unable to make radio contact with the available homing assistance. Flying in cloud, the aircraft flew into the Kerran Hill, near Southend on the Kintyre peninsula, Argyll, killing both crew members. The pilot was Sub-Lt (A) T. R. V. Parke, RN. This sad episode marked the end of *Pegasus*' duties as a fighter catapult ship, and five days later she disembarked her remaining Fulmars to Belfast for the last time.

On 3 August 1941 occurred the first and only successful attack from a fighter operating from a Royal Navy catapult ship. *Maplin* was some 400 miles south-west of Cape Clear on her way to pick up convoy SL81 when an Fw 200 of KG 40 operating out of Bordeaux/Mérignac was spotted ten miles astern, very low on the horizon. Within six minutes the ship had launched a Hurricane piloted by Lt (A) R. W. H. Everett, RNVR, a very tough character who had been a steeplechase jockey (he won the 1929 Grand National on Gregalach at odds of 100-1). He had a lengthy chase after the Fw 200 but eventually pressed home from both beam and astern, concentrating his fire on the enemy's engines. His windscreen became obscured by engine oil, which made him think at first that he had been hit, but in fact the oil was from the Focke-Wulf, which he eventually set on fire to crash some 30–40 miles from the convoy.

Everett now had the unwelcome task of trying to save his own skin. He was homed back, and after two unsuccessful attempts at baling out he alighted safely near the destroyer *Wanderer*. He did not use the aircraft dinghy, being soon picked up by *Maplin*. On 1 October he was awarded the DSO for this achievement but he sadly lost his life on 29 January 1942 off Anglesey while ferrying an elderly Hurricane to England. It is likely that he was attempting another ditching but unfortunately the rescue services were slow to be alerted and his body was washed ashore several weeks later.

Ariguani was in action on 27 August when Sub-Lt Birrell, late of *Michael E.*, was launched in Fulmar N4072 against an Fw 200 which he chased for 45 miles. Because of low cloud he had to be guided by radar, and after the enemy had fled he headed for Ireland, eventually landing on a beach in Eire. He escaped internment by persuading the local police that he had no guns, which he was only able to do because the fabric covering the wing gun ports was still intact, he never having had the opportunity to get in a shot. After twenty minutes, having borrowed a supply of petrol, he was permitted to fly off again, making his way across the border to land at Eglinton, near Londonderry, where the aerodrome was at that time still under construction.

On 14 September Sub-Lt (A) C. W. Walker,

▼ A Hawker Sea Hurricane of the Merchant Ship Fighter Unit poised on the catapult of a merchantman. (FAA Museum)

RNVR, was launched in Hurricane W9215 from *Maplin* while she was escorting convoy HG72. Four days later a Fulmar from *Springbank* was in action whilst escorting convoy HG73. Piloted by Lt (A) B. F. Cox, RNVR, the aircraft attempted an attack on an Fw 200 but was foiled because of faulty ammunition, only one of the guns being operative. The enemy made good his escape in cloud and the Fulmar then landed safely at North Front aerodrome, Gibraltar. It was around this time that an advanced base was set up there, with a pool of six Hurricanes and two Fulmars.

The squadron commitment was reduced on 27 September when *Springbank* was sunk. Another attack was made on 4 October by Lt R. A. Bird, RN, his Fulmar being launched from *Ariguani* about 400 miles west of Ireland while escorting convoy OG75. He made a successful interception, inflicting damage on the Fw 200, but could not complete his kill as the quarry escaped into cloud. He subsequently ditched near a destroyer, but its attempts to pick him up were unsuccessful and he was eventually rescued by his own ship somewhat the worse for wear. He was unaccountably killed some time afterwards when his aircraft dived into the ground during air-to-ground firing practice.

By this time the fighter catapult task was in the process of being transferred to the RAF, which in May 1941 had set up a Merchant Ship Fighter Unit at Speke, near Liverpool. Outposts were established at Nova Scotia, Archangel and Gibraltar, and when at full strength the unit had sixty aircraft, all Hurricanes, to man the 34 merchant ships equipped with catapults. No. 804 then gradually wound down its catapult activities. *Ariguani* returned to normal duties on 27 December, but *Maplin* continued until May 1942, after which the squadron regrouped as a normal carrier-based unit, subsequently flying later versions of the Sea Hurricane.

Ten operational launches had been made by Fleet Air Arm pilots and all had been successful in chasing away the shadower although only one of these had actually been shot down. The MSFU continued to operate in this role until it was disbanded at Speke on 7 September 1943.

In addition to these activities numerous catapult flights were made by Fairey Seafox and Vought Kingfisher aircraft of Nos. 702 and 703 Squadrons from light cruisers and, later, armed merchant cruisers. The Kingfishers of *Corfu* Flight in No. 703 Squadron, for example, flew 143 sorties in the South Atlantic in ten months, often in bad weather, yet none of these aircraft suffered any damage despite the fact that on only two occasions was the sea sufficiently calm to dispense with a slick of oil from the ship to calm the waves for the pick-up on their return. *Cilicia* Flight bettered this by carrying out nearly 200 sorties during eleven months of operations; such flights were in addition to similar searches made by carrier aircraft from *Hermes*.

▼ A Seafox floatplane of No. 702 Squadron being hoisted out from the armed merchant cruiser HMS *Asturias*. Aircraft of this type made numerous flights from such ships, searching for disguised German raiders in the Indian Ocean and South Atlantic. (Tony Down)

CHAPTER 10

The Mediterranean and Malta, 1941–1942

Early in December 1940 the Western Desert Force under General Wavell advanced from Egypt into Cyrenaica and the Italians were soon in full retreat. Both *Eagle* and *Illustrious* were in action during the month, mounting an attack on Italian transport at Bardia on the 12th and launching Swordfish bombing attacks later in the month on Rhodes, Stampalia and Tripoli. On the 21st nine Swordfish from *Illustrious* sank two Italian merchant vessels in a daylight operation off the Tunisian coast, the only loss being P4075 'L5Q', piloted by Lt (A) D. C. Garton-Stone, RN, of No. 819 Squadron, which could not be found after a search; the other crew members were Lt J. H. R. Medlicott-Vereker, RN, and TAG NA1 W. E. Sperry.

The Italians' retreat was a setback to their German allies, who quickly brought large numbers of aircraft down to Sicily from all parts of Europe. Malta was to be the main target for their activities, but first they turned their attention to *Illustrious*. On 7 January 1941 the carrier put out to sea from Alexandria, in company with *Warspite* and *Valiant*, to take over from Force H the task of escorting a convoy bound for Malta and Greece. The Mediterranean Fleet accepted responsibility for the convoy during the morning of the 10th and headed for Valetta's Grand Harbour with No. 806 Squadron's Fulmars patrolling overhead.

Soon after 1000, Italian aircraft appeared on the scene and the carrier then came under almost continuous attack. The Fulmars succeeded in shooting down two of the initial attackers and drove off the remainder, but after an hour they were low on ammunition. When the first wave of a large force of Ju 87s appeared on the scene at 1230 there were no Fulmars in the area, those still aloft having left in pursuit of two SM 79s towards Sicily. Owing to a delay of four minutes in obtaining permission from the flagship for the remaining Fulmars to take off, the last of these was only just leaving the deck as the first bombs were falling. The dive-bombers dropped from 12,000ft, and their initial rate of climb of only 1,200ft per minute meant that the Fulmars stood no chance of reaching them in time.

Within six minutes the Stukas had wreaked havoc on the carrier. Evading the heavy anti-aircraft fire put up by the Fleet, they succeeded in striking the after deck several times with bombs, scoring two hits on the lift. The engines remained working, though conditions were terrible in the boiler-rooms, but for three hours the ship was almost out of control with several fires blazing. During this time Italian bombers made another attack, then at 1600 the Luftwaffe returned, but the Fulmars, which had refuelled at Malta, beat off all but one of the enemy, the latter unfortunately dropping another 1,000lb bomb near the after lift. The fires flared up again, but the ship was now within 40 miles of Malta and at 2215 she succeeded in docking although the fires were not put out until the following morning. Casualties were heavy and almost a third of the air crew who had successfully attacked Taranto two months earlier had either lost their lives or were seriously wounded.

Thirteen days later, despite further attacks by the bombers of Fliegerkorps X while she was undergoing temporary repairs, *Illustrious* was sufficiently seaworthy to make for Alexandria, where she arrived two days later. Here she remained for six weeks until she had been patched up enough to sail to America for rebuilding. She eventually left for Port Said on 3 March, and after a long voyage through the Suez Canal and calling in at Cape Town and the West Indies she docked on 12 May at Norfolk repair yards, Virginia, where she remained until work was completed at the end of November.

Lt Cdr Pat Beagley gives this account of his experiences at that time:

> After the *Illustrious* was bombed I flew ashore – I was airborne at the time and the ship was obviously u/s. We started operating from Hal Far with No. 830 while the *Illustrious* was being repaired and as a bloody great bomb hit my aircraft that took care of me – fortunately I wasn't in the aircraft at the time. We went down into caves at Malta and, when the ship was ready, as a leading airman I was detailed to help sail the ship back, and I think I'm one of the few sailors who bailed out a carrier with a bucket on the passage from Malta to Alexandria. When we got to Alexandria we

◀ **A Swordfish comes into land on HMS *Illustrious*, watched by a member of the emergency fire crew clad in a fireproof asbestos suit. (RAF Museum)**

were equipped with new aircraft and went up to the desert.

By early 1941 *Eagle* was badly in need of a refit but with the effective loss of *Illustrious* she had to await the arrival of the new carrier *Formidable*, which did not reach Alexandria until 10 March, a week after *Illustrious* had left. On the 27th a report was received from a Malta-based Sunderland of No. 230 Squadron that a force of Italian warships had been sighted 80 miles south of Sicily, apparently making for the route travelled by convoys passing between Alexandria and Greek ports. The Mediterranean Fleet promptly put to sea and at 0720 the next day an Albacore on reconnaissance from *Formidable* sighted the enemy force of four cruisers and seven destroyers. Two hours later the Italian warships changed course westward to join up with the flagship *Vittorio Veneto*.

At 1000 six Albacores of No. 826 Squadron took off from *Formidable* led by Lt Cdr W. H. G. Saunt, DSC, RN, with two Fulmars of No. 803 Squadron providing fighter cover. Their orders were to attack the Italian cruisers but after a flight of 100 miles they sighted the *Vittorio Veneto* with an escort of destroyers. Diving in two sub-flights through heavy AA fire, the Albacores carried out their attack without casualties, the Fulmar escort destroying one of two Ju 88s which appeared on the scene. Half an hour later three Swordfish of No. 815 Squadron arrived from Maleme in Crete and attacked the enemy battleship, but no strikes were observed. At about this time *Formidable* was preparing a second striking force of three Albacores and two Swordfish, armed with torpedoes and escorted by two Fulmars. These were eventually sent off at 1350 under Lt Cdr J. Dalyell-Stead, RN, the CO of No. 829 Squadron, and at 1525 they sighted the enemy flagship south of Cape Matapan, which was to give its name to the ensuing naval battle. Diving out of the sun in two sub-flights, the Albacores went in first and one of their two torpedoes succeeded in hitting the battleship, slowing her down to 8kt although she was later repaired sufficiently to be able to increase speed and make her escape. The leader of the attack was the only loss suffered by the aircraft taking part in the whole of the day's operations.

At dusk a final attack was mounted with every available aircraft. Six Albacores and two Swordfish took off from *Formidable* under the leadership of Lt Cdr Saunt, and also joining in the attack were two Swordfish from Maleme which followed in behind the others to avoid confusion. The aircraft went down independently from 1930 over a period of a quarter of an hour to the combined hazards of an intense barrage, searchlights, a smoke-screen and a false cloud horizon. In a courag-

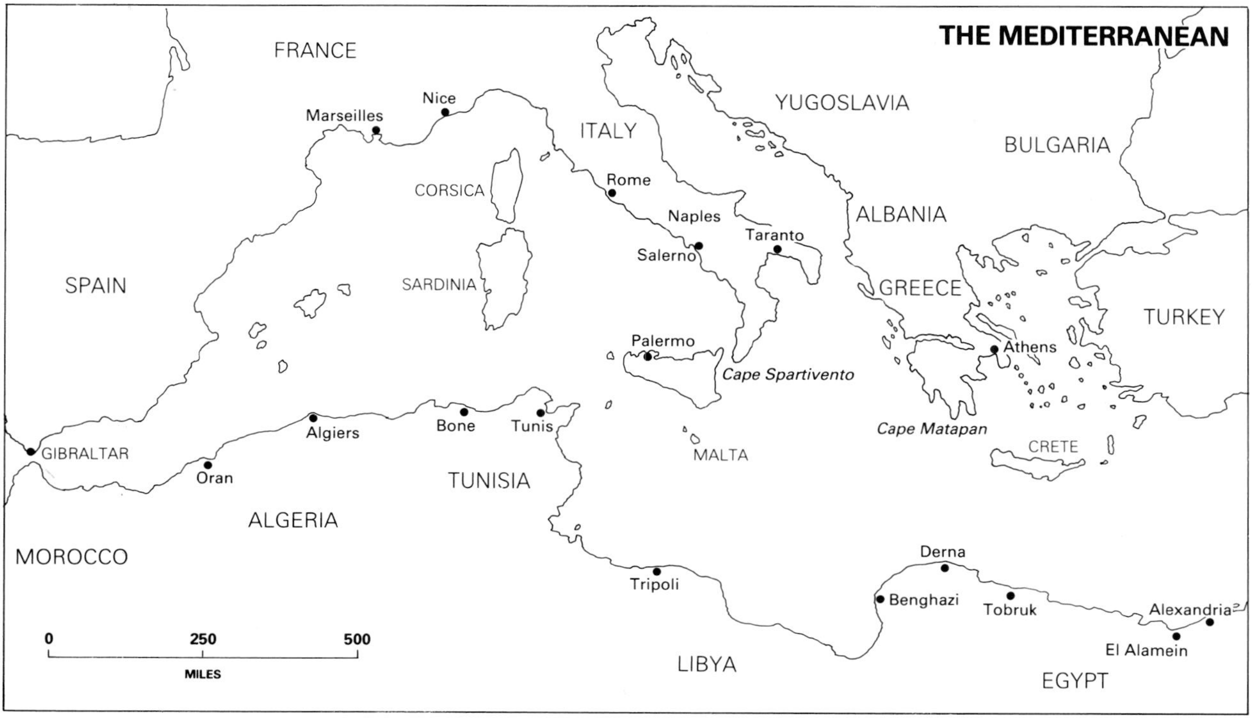

eous attack Lt F. M. A. Torrens-Spence of No. 815 Squadron put his torpedo into the cruiser *Pola*, stopping her engines and causing a power failure. In a subsequent bombardment the Fleet sank the *Pola* and her two sister-ships *Zara* and *Fiume*, which had stopped to help her, in addition to sinking the two destroyers. This victory was to have the important result of reducing the capacity of the Italian Fleet so that it later was prevented from interfering with the transport to Greece of an expeditionary force and its subsequent evacuation.

Lt Cdr 'Ben' Rice, then a rating pilot, flew a Swordfish seaplane (K8863, named *Lorna*) with *Warspite* Flight of No. 700 Squadron at that time. His aircraft was engaged in observing and shadowing the Italian Fleet during the battle, making two sorties. His observer was Lt Cdr A. S. Bolt, DSC, RN, and the TAG was PO M. G. Pacey. Here is Ben's account of the second sortie:

At 1950 we were relieved by an Albacore from *Formidable* and we took departure for Suda Bay at 2,000 feet. After about half an hour I enquired when we might expect a landfall, and where, as I was getting interested by this time since it was rather dark. Up comes '2113 Ákra Spátha, height 1,214 feet'. So I further enquired, 'Where is Ákta Spátha, Sir?' 'It is the north-west tip of Crete.' At about five past nine I observed a large black mass ahead to starboard which I reported to the observer who informed me that it was the mountain range on the north-west tip of Crete, highest point 2,454 feet. At 2113 we passed over Ákra Spátha.

I then suggested to Lt Cdr Bolt that we ask Maleme, which was about ten miles south, if we could land on the grass there. He then told me we might damage the floats doing this! An understatement on his part, I thought! So he suggested, as we had flare-floats, we go and alight in Suda Bay. I had landed and taken off from here a couple of times in daylight so I knew the harbour. We set course for Ákra Malchas lighthouse (negative light). On arriving I turned south for Suda Bay. Lt Cdr Bolt gave me a wind of 250 degrees 10 knots, and I then turned into the Bay on this heading at 1,000 feet and dropped the flares on the 'Mickey Mouse' at 100-yard intervals (I forget the correct name for this bomb-dropping distributor) outside the boom. Report from the back seat: 'Flares gone, first one burning brightly'. Don't muck about, they only burn for five minutes, high ground to port 2,000 feet. Turn to port on to 070 degrees, all flares burning, turn again to port about one mile from the first flare, losing height. Flare path right ahead. Better than Air Traffic put out and much quicker. Line up and sit down by number two flare, time 2125.

After about two minutes all the flares went out, and it was dark! Next question from me, 'What do we do now?' From the navigator: 'We are now waterborne. Steer 310 degrees for the boom gate.' (Young lookers take note, know where you are, all the time). Pacey climbed up on to the centre-section and, he using the Aldis lamp as a headlight, we taxied at about 20 knots on this heading for a distance of about five miles which seemed to me to take a long time.

► **An urgently needed Spitfire for the RAF, seen just after taking off from HMS *Eagle* for the long flight to Malta. (Cdr F. W. Baring)**

◄ **A Swordfish of No. 824 Squadron from North Front aerodrome, Gibraltar, taking off from the American carrier *Wasp* on 1 April 1942 during a Malta convoy. (Fred C. Dickey Jr)**

> Every time I throttled back, the Aldis lamp went dim as our battery was getting low. At about 2200 we identified ourselves to the patrol vessel on the boom. He enquired by light 'What type of vessel?', to which we replied 'Floatplane'. His amazement was illustrated by the switching on of an enormous searchlight which confirmed our statement. He opened up the boom gate and we taxied into harbour and met a motor boat from HMS *York* which guided us to a mooring for the night, then took us to HMS *Carlisle*. Total time airborne 8 hours 20 minutes, including 2 hours' night.
>
> Furthermore, as there was a shortage of spares, we had surrendered our instrument flying panel to the carrier squadron and the aircraft was fitted only with a primitive turn and bank indicator, P.10 compass (they were still using these in Sea Princes but called it a P.12) and the old type altimeter fitted with one needle giving about one inch of movement for every thousand feet.

They returned to Alexandria on 30 March via Mersa Matruh. For this operation Lt Cdr (later Rear Admiral) Bolt was awarded a bar to his DSC, and Rice and Pacey were both mentioned in despatches.

Meanwhile the Fleet Air Arm had been in action in operations from both Greece and Crete. At the end of January 1941 No. 815 Squadron, which had been without a ship since *Illustrious* retired for repairs, sent a flight of six aircraft to Maleme, Crete, under Lt Cdr J. de F. Jago, RN. Its task was to keep the Italian Navy from the Aegean, the Swordfish making attacks on shipping and carrying out anti-submarine patrols. Early in March they were joined by the Fulmars of No. 805 Squadron under the command of Lt Cdr A. F. Black, RN, which later added Sea Gladiators, Buffaloes and Hurricanes to its strength as aircraft became scarce. The fighters were soon in action and on one occasion three Fulmars intercepted a large number of SM 79s with an escort of CR 42s, but on account of thick cloud only one aircraft made contact, shooting down one enemy aircraft and damaging two others before colliding with a fourth. This was the first combat in which Sub-Lt (A) R. C. Kay, RNVR, and his air gunner LA D. R. Stockman had engaged and tragically both were killed.

In mid-March the Swordfish moved up to Greece, first at Eleusis Airport near Athens and then to an advanced base at Paramythia. On 13 March, the day the aircraft arrived, the first raid was made on shipping in Valona harbour but the unit's CO in P4083 failed to return from the trip, he and the squadron's senior observer, Lt J. A. Caldecott-Smith, RN, as well as their air gunner, LA P. N. Beagley, being taken prisoner after being shot down.

Pat Beagley has this to say of the events leading up to his capture:

> After a few operations from the desert we went to Crete. I was in No. 815 Stringbag squadron at Maleme, and they were short of Fulmar air crew in Nos. 805 and 806 Squadrons for some reason, so we used to get detailed to go across and fly with them. We did two or three patrols there.
>
> I can remember seeing the chippy making an airscrew for a Fulmar out of wood from a tree he had cut down not too long before. It didn't work, but the patches in the Fulmar's wing were wood doped over. The Swordfish were very short of wheels and the chief Tiffy used to make wheels of a sandwich of steel plate and a piece of rubber for the tyres. It was a bit bumpy but it used to work all right.
>
> Then I found myself detailed to go into Greece. We went up to a place called Paramythia and we were having a go at the Italian ships in Valona. Valona is a fairly large harbour, almost the size of Portsmouth. We were operating with an RAF Blenheim squadron and RAF Gladiators.

Anyhow, we went off one night, and had to climb with a torpedo on board. The mountains were fairly tall and we came over the top of the mountain with a great struggle and got caught in searchlights. The CO, Lt Cdr Jago, opened his taps up, and a bloody great flame came out of the exhaust, which made it easy to keep the searchlights on us, but we got away with that. We were doing a run-in with the 'fish' and suddenly the whole of the bottom of the aircraft caught fire so we went into the drink. I think it may have been a magnesium flare, but it may even have hit the torpedo underneath. Anyhow, we went into the sea and got in our dinghies, all three of us.

We were all right. I had minor injuries, scratched knees and so on, and I can remember bobbing up and down in the water for about four hours, chewing pink signal flimsies and spitting them over the side. The idea had been that after we had finished the attack we were to make a signal to the Fleet that we were attacking destroyers, or bombing, or something like that, so consequently we had all the radio frequencies and call-signs of the whole of the Mediterranean Fleet.

Dawn arrived, and some Italian MTBs came and picked us up and took us down in the cabin and dried us out. They were quite good about it. Then Caldecott-Smith, the senior observer, remembered he had a revolver which he had bought in Alex, so he said 'I think I'd better offer this up to the Italians'. They were all crowding round us – I think we must have been in the Captain's cabin – but as he pulled out the gun four of them promptly disappeared up the ladder. However, he handed it over by the butt, and all was friendly again.

When we got ashore we were taken to be interrogated in Tirana, which was the main Italian fighter base, and some sweet-smelling Italian with long hair and a couple of babes on his arm came along to look at us, and it turned out he was the local ace. About a day later, though, there was a great bang on the airfield, and apparently this chap had gone in. We all cheered when we heard what had happened, which didn't amuse the Italians at all.

Beagley later spent a lengthy period in captivity.

Lt Torrens-Spence then took over command of the squadron, which continued to make attacks on shipping at Valona, Durrazo and Brindisi, the last raid being on 1 April when a laden ammunition ship lying in Valona harbour was torpedoed by the new CO and promptly blew up.

By the middle of the month the German advance had forced the squadron to return to Eleusis, having accounted for five merchant vessels and seriously damaged five others. On the 20th they were back at Maleme with No. 805 Squadron, but only temporarily as they then withdrew to Dekheila to regroup. The fighters remained at Maleme for another month, operating against overwhelming odds, but by 17 May they were reduced to one serviceable Hurricane and two days later they withdrew, eventually joining No. 815 Squadron at Dekheila, near Alexandria.

Meanwhile *Formidable* had again been in action. On 21 April nine Albacores took off for Tripoli, where they engaged in spotting for a bombardment by British battleships against the town and the ships in the harbour. Considerable damage was caused in the early morning attack, from which all the aircraft returned safely. In a further exercise, early in

◄ **Surrounded by sandbags, an Albacore of No. 815 Squadron stands ready in Cyprus for a torpedo strike, about August 1941. (Dennis Phillips)**

May, the TSR aircraft took part in anti-submarine patrols and armed reconnaissance whilst the ship was helping to escort a Malta convoy, and seven enemy aircraft were shot down by fighters.

Lt Cdr N. C. Manley-Cooper was serving in *Ark Royal* in the Mediterranean at this time:

> In early May 1941 air-to-surface vessel radar (ASV) arrived on 820 Squadron. Nobody thought this new invention would really work but it was put into my aircraft and thus I became the first ASV operator in the Mediterranean Fleet. The equipment was quite bulky, taking up most of the cockpit space underneath and in between the pilot and observer.
>
> On 17 May we took up Vice-Admiral Somerville for an ASV demonstration: he was quite interested in wireless and wanted to see this new development for himself. My pilot on this occasion was Sub-Lt Mike Lithgow, later to become well known as a test pilot. We first had a little practice, and I was able to bring the aircraft out of the clouds right over the ship. The Admiral was very impressed by this, and asked to see for himself how it was done. We put him into my cockpit and showed him what to operate whilst I leaned over from the TAGs cockpit. Unfortunately he put his hand on the wrong knob, in which there was a lot of electric current, and he promptly shot up to the extent of the G-string holding him in! After he had recovered from this we flew in cloud close to the Fleet, and I said 'Sir, there is your flagship'. We came out of the cloud and there was *Renown*. 'Dead easy, isn't it?' he said – having just suffered a very nasty electric shock!

Returning to Alexandria on 12 May, the Fleet sailed again on the 25th and the following day squadron aircraft made a surprise bombing and strafing attack on Scarpanto airfield. During the afternoon a force of Ju 87s and Ju 88s appeared from North Africa, and although these were attacked by the two Fulmars patrolling at the time, with four of the Stukas being claimed, bombs hit *Formidable* both fore and aft and her hull was damaged by bombs which had exploded nearby. She limped back to Alexandria the following day and, like *Illustrious* before her, was found to be too severely damaged for the limited local repair facilities. On 24 July she sailed eastward towards the Suez Canal, reaching Portsmouth, Virginia, on 25 August and remaining there under repair until being released on 7 December, soon after *Illustrious* had sailed. For the next three years there were to be no armoured carriers in the Mediterranean.

The island fortress of Malta now became even more important, and the Fleet Air Arm was to play its part here too. From July 1940 the Swordfish of No. 830 Squadron (formerly No. 767 Squadron) at Hal Far undertook the protection of Mediterranean convoys and carried out attacks on enemy shipping. The aircraft went into battle immediately after arrival, carrying out a raid on an oil refinery and tanks at Augusta in Sicily on the night of 30 June/1 July. In a similar raid on 14 August Swordfish L9741, piloted by Sub-Lt (A) D. S. Edmondson, RN, with Naval Airman R. Pearson as air gunner, crashed in the target area; and L2854, piloted by Lt D. W. Waters, RN, with Leading Airman S. D. Harris, also failed to return, the crew being taken prisoner-of-war.

Aircraft were also subjected to attacks on

► **An aircraft of an Albacore squadron, probably No. 830, based in Malta during 1941–42 for mine-laying, bombing and torpedo attacks. (Via J. D. Oughton)**

the ground. In a raid by 100 enemy bombers early in March 1941 at least 60 reached Hal Far, destroying three of the squadron's Swordfish and rendering all the others temporarily unserviceable. On the 19th of that month another machine was lost when K5939, piloted by Sub-Lt (A) D. Grant, RNVR, failed to return from a raid on Tripoli, and other losses occurred during the year as the aircraft were engaged in attacks on enemy shipping both by day and night.

One of the original pilots of No. 767 Squadron, still with No. 830 Squadron in April 1941, was Petty Officer (A) Charles Wines, who had been one of a relatively small number of rating pilots trained during 1939–40. He had been involved in various night attacks, but this stage of his career ended abruptly on the night of 1 April when he was piloting L7689 'B', with Leading Airman L. M. 'Bungy' Edwards as air gunner. In the Gulf of Hammamet, Tunisia, they sighted a northbound convoy and attacked a merchant ship with their torpedo, which was seen to strike the vessel just under the bridge. While taking evasive action their aircraft was repeatedly hit in the fuselage and fuel tanks with pom-pom and small-calibre gunfire from an Italian destroyer and from merchant ships. Their engine then seized up, and they had no option but to make a crash-landing on the beach at Hammamet. The crew made no attempt to set fire to the aircraft as it carried nothing which was on the secret list and it had been rendered a complete write-off by gunfire and the subsequent crash-landing. They were then interned in Tunisia and Algeria, Wines being released in November 1942 following the North African landings. He returned to first-line service later in the war.

One night towards the end of July a convoy of six enemy vessels was attacked by squadron Swordfish off the island of Lampedusa and two were sunk, the remainder being attacked the next morning by RAF Blenheims. In October No. 830 Squadron was joined in this work by the Albacores of No. 828 Squadron, but this unit suffered many losses, being reduced at one stage to only four aircraft. 'Nat' Gold,

▼ Albacore '4P', piloted by Lt Cdr Torrens-Spence, the Commanding Officer of No. 815 Squadron, comes to an untimely end in Crete about August 1941. (Dennis Phillips)

▲ **Fairey Albacore X8942 of No. 828 Squadron loaded up at Hal Far aerodrome, Malta, in late 1941 or early 1942. This aircraft went missing from an operation on 23 March 1942, all three crew members being lost. (W. N. Jones via M. Garbett)**

then a telegraphist air gunner with No. 830 Squadron at Hal Far, recalls:

Not all operational torpedo attacks were successful, some only resulting in frustration and extreme anger. At one period we ran out of torpedoes. Fortunately or unfortunately, our Maltese armourers remembered there were several 1914–1918 Great War torpedoes stored at Grand Harbour, and some were brought to Hal Far and prepared with slight modifications for use on our next operation. They were a lot smaller than the present-day ones, looking harmless and toylike. To our amazement and horror, however, when they entered the water they went round in circles.

I was never quite certain whether the newer Duplex torpedoes, which had a magnetic warhead, were all that they were cracked up to be. When they entered a magnetic field of a ship they exploded, and from the air looking down one could see a large dark blue circle of light radiating outwards in larger circles of lighter hues of blue. It was assumed that the ship had been damaged, unlike a contact head where a definite result could be seen, as I experienced on one operation – the ship exploded and disintegrated.

On 14 July 1941 nine Swordfish took off in the early hours of the morning in search of a convoy but failed to locate it. On the return journey dawn came, it was now daylight and slightly misty, and through the mist could be seen two merchant ships and a destroyer line astern. This was not the convoy we had been looking for, but our CO considered they were worth having a go at and gave the signal to break formation and attack. This was my first experience of a daylight operation.

The ships did not appear to be moving very fast – their bow wave hardly disturbed the water. We were to attack last, but, as each aircraft attacked, every torpedo missed and not a shot appeared to have been fired. Our turn came and my pilot decided to attack the leading merchantman – I stood by with gun at the ready to strafe after passing over the ship. I did not feel the usual uplift when the torpedo dropped away, and instead of passing over the ship we banked hard to port. Loud curses came over the Gosport tube from my pilot – 'The bloody torpedo has hung up – have a look to see if you can see it'. I hung over the side as far as the slipstream would allow me but couldn't see it. I reported to my pilot and he replied 'I'm going round again', so we commenced our second run – and the same thing happened. My pilot decided not to chance his luck a third time, so we carried on to catch up with the rest of the squadron.

We re-formed into three flights of three aircraft and kept close to one another. As we had no R/T I 'zogged' a message to the TAG in the aircraft next to ours. (To 'zogg' is to hold the palm vertical and jerk it up and down to simulate dots and dashes.) I asked if our torpedo was still there and if it looked secure. Back came the reply 'Still there and appears secure'. I reported this information to my pilot.

As we approached Malta the sun was still rising – a wonderful sight, far larger than seen at home. Our next worry – would we be attacked by fighters? Fortunately this did not materialize, and Malta appeared in the distance looking very small but becoming gradually larger – a welcoming scene. As we crossed the coast the leading flight commenced a shallow dive and then pulled out, climbing to perform the 'Prince of Wales feathers', the flight on our port side the same and we followed. I wondered what would happen to our torpedo, but it remained securely fixed.

During de-briefing we were told that all three ships were already sunk by our destroyers and were resting on a sandbank! I could see a smirk on my pilot's face as we were praised for bringing our precious torpedo back, thus saving £2,000.

In March 1942, while serving at Dekheila with No. 821 Squadron, Lt Cdr Manley-Cooper took part in a delivery flight to Malta:

That beleaguered island had already received many Hurricanes, these being flown off from carriers, but there was now a need for Swordfish reinforcements. A number of 'Blackfish' were available, this being the Blackburn-built version, and it was proposed to try to get them first to El Adem by way of Tobruk, then across the Mediterranean.

About six of these machines were fitted with a saddle tank in the rear cockpit, positioned vertically over the top of what was normally the air gunner's cockpit, where the observer sat for this trip. There was also a torpedo-type tank between the undercarriage legs, to give as much range as possible. The pilots and observers were a mixed bag, selected from among the three Swordfish squadrons then at Dekheila, and my pilot was Sub-Lt Dunkerley, whom I did not know. On 5 March we had a four-hour practice endurance flight in V4369. Five days later we left Dekheila in pairs. Setting off at 1130, we reached Sidi Barrani at 1400, then left again at 1655, arriving 1 hour 40 minutes later at El Adem, where the Long Range Desert Group was waiting for us. They gave us a meal and fully refuelled all our tanks during darkness from large petrol drums. They then put out goose-neck flares to mark the runway for take-off, and at 2245 we set off again in V4369.

It was a long journey, and very warm and tiring – Dunkerley went to sleep twice and I had to wake him up! By this time we had become accustomed to flying long distances, but there was always the danger that the wind direction might be different from that forecast. To find the wind one would drop a flare-float in the sea, fly on for *x* minutes, then turn back 180 degrees and take a bearing of the smoke float as we flew past it. Then we would again turn back 180 degrees and take a fresh bearing. We hadn't been able to spare the time for this on our way to Malta, but this did not matter too much as experience told us what the wind force probably was from the appearance of the waves. We could also drop flares and take back bearings to give us some idea of the relative wind direction.

At first the aircraft were able to keep in touch by W/T but near the end of the trip we encountered heavy rain and at 0534 we parted company. Six minutes later I was able to get a D/F bearing of 296½, so we changed course and within nine minutes sighted the island. We were then instructed to delay our arrival as there was an air raid in progress, but after flying around for a while we were allowed to land quite safely at 0552, after a journey which had lasted 7 hours 7 minutes.

This extraordinary exercise was only partially successful, unfortunately, costing us about three or four of the aircraft involved. Bertie Birse found himself over what turned out to be Sicily and tried to land on a German airfield before realizing his mistake. Another blew up over the coast at Tobruk, probably due to a spark catching an overfilled saddle tank. Afterwards, the survivors were flown back to Cairo in an RAF Wellington.

On 26 March 1942 Nos. 828 and 830 Squadrons were amalgamated to operate as the Naval Air Squadron, though retaining their separate identities. They took a heavy toll of enemy shipping, probably in the region of 400,000 tons by the end of 1942, but by

▼ Photographed from an 'I' Class destroyer, the last moments of HMS *Eagle*, sinking in the Mediterranean on 11 August 1942 after being hit by four torpedoes fired from *U-73* during Operation 'Pedestal', a fast convoy to Malta. (H. Liddle)

that time No. 830 had no aircraft left. Replacements were received, but at the end of March 1943 it combined with No. 828 Squadron and ceased to exist as a separate unit. Three months later No. 828 departed for North Africa, disbanding at Monastir on 1 September 1943.

Meanwhile, at the western end of the Mediterranean, the Swordfish of No. 812 Squadron, which was without a floating base after the loss of *Ark Royal*, were engaged in blockading the Gibraltar Straits during the closing weeks of 1941. Following re-equipment, and a brief spell in *Argus* for anti-submarine patrols, the squadron disembarked to North Front aerodrome for night anti-submarine operations. From 27 November it mounted a continuous patrol of one aircraft between 1900 and 0900, four of the nine aircraft being by then fitted with R.3039/T.3040 type ASV radar. They covered an area within a radius of fifteen miles to the west of Cape Spartel, an alternative being an area to the east of Almena Point. Each patrol lasted two hours, and seven sorties were therefore required each night. The radar sets enabled several attacks to be made against U-boats. Attacks were made against either *U-432* or *U-569* on 15 December, and against either *U-569* or *U-532* the following day, and then on 19 December a depth charge fell in the sea just ahead of a large swirl during an attack on *U-202*. In all, five enemy submarines were damaged during a three-week period, and on the night of 21/22 December came the first night sinking of such a vessel. Sub-Lt (A) Wilkinson, RN, Lt (A) Plummer, RNVR, and LA Oppenheim in aircraft 'A' succeeded in destroying *U-451* with a depth-charge attack off Tangier, only one survivor being picked up afterwards. The squadron's efforts, and those of their daytime counterparts, succeeded in preventing any U-boats from making passage through the Straits until the spring of 1942.

In the Eastern Mediterranean the Fleet Air Arm provided support during the Syrian Campaign in July 1941, Nos. 815 and 826 Swordfish Squadrons being particularly active with anti-shipping sorties from Cyprus, when attacks were made against Vichy French ships. The anti-submarine defence of this region was later carried out by the Walruses of Nos. 700 and 701 Squadrons.

Malta was still very badly in need of fighter aircraft for her defence and from March 1942 *Eagle*, accompanied on several occasions by *Argus* or USS *Wasp*, made a series of difficult ferry trips to deliver a total of 275 Spitfire Vs during the next four months, only six of these vitally needed aircraft being lost en route. In June 1942 a more hazardous operation was mounted, Malta's general supply position being by then very bad. Convoys were therefore despatched simultaneously from each end of the Mediterranean, that from the eastern end being code-named Operation 'Vigorous' and the other Operation 'Harpoon', which included *Eagle* and *Argus*. Both convoys were heavily battered by attacks from the Luftwaffe and Italian E-boats, and after receiving a report that the Italian battle fleet was out Rear Admiral Vian reluctantly turned back the westbound convoy, which had already lost two merchant ships and two of the escorting destroyers to air attack. The eastbound convoy continued, however, despite grievous losses, but only two merchant ships reached their destination, to unload 25,000 tons of supplies.

By the beginning of August only 80 Spitfires were left in Malta and it was decided to mount a single westbound convoy under the code-name Operation 'Pedestal'. *Furious* was to carry 38 Spitfires and there would be fourteen fast merchant ships, escort being provided by two battleships, seven cruisers, twenty destroyers and the fleet carriers *Eagle*, *Indomitable* and *Victorious* with a total of 70 fighters aboard in addition to 42 Swordfish and Albacores. The convoy passed through the Straits of Gibraltar during the night of 9/10 August but on 11 August *Eagle* was sunk by *U-73*, which fired four torpedoes when she was about 80 miles north of Algiers. The carrier went down in under eight minutes. The next day both *Victorious* and *Indomitable* received direct bomb hits on their flight decks; their armour saved the ships from destruction, but *Indomitable* was sufficiently damaged to need several months of repairs in the United States. Thirteen of the defending fighters were lost, but thirty of the attacking aircraft were destroyed, no fewer than five of these on 12 August by Lt R. J. Cork, DSC, RNVR, of No. 800 Squadron (*Indomitable*) flying a Sea Hurricane IC. Only five merchant ships eventually reached Malta, two in a sinking condition, but they included the tanker *Ohio* and their combined cargoes, amounting to 55,000 tons of supplies, were sufficient to save the island.

In all, 764 aircraft were ferried to Malta between August 1940 and October 1942, comprising 361 Hurricanes, 385 Spitfires, 11 Albacores and 7 Swordfish. Of these, 718 reached their intended destination, 12 having to return to their respective carriers and 34 being lost en route.

CHAPTER 11

War in the Desert

Not all the Fleet Air Arm's wartime first-line activities were carrier-based. After the withdrawal of *Formidable* from the Eastern Mediterranean, as a result of two direct hits during a German bombing attack off Crete in May 1941, most of her Fulmar and Albacore aircraft were disembarked to join up with the RAF in the Western Desert, making an invaluable contribution to the campaign in that arena. The Albacores of No. 826 Squadron first started operating there in early June as guests on RAF airfields. Accommodation was often primitive, consisting mainly of tents, and maintenance and servicing were difficult, the latter generally being done at night when the metal had cooled off sufficiently to be touched.

No. 826 Squadron's first priority was to become fully self-sufficient and mobile so that it could get away from Alexandria and establish its own base much nearer the front line. It was essential for the unit to have its own transport, which the RAF, though it needed the FAA aircraft and crews, could not supply. Neither could the Navy, so the CO, Lt Cdr J. W. S. Corbett, RN, went to Cairo, calling on every military office that might conceivably have a lorry to spare; at the same time other No. 826 officers combed the messes and hotels in Alexandria. Thus the squadron acquired all manner of useful vehicles, the prize item being a large Italian diesel lorry and trailer 'found' in Alexandria one evening by an observer sub-lieutenant. This proved invaluable for carrying bombs from dump to aircraft – much better than anything the RAF had.

Now their own masters, the six Albacores of 'X' Flight were sent forward from Dekheila to Ma'aten Bagush on 31 July to engage in anti-submarine patrols along the coast. They were replaced on 15 August by 'Y' Flight, but twelve days later the whole squadron became based there.

Around that time a Royal Navy Fighter Squadron was also set up, under the command of Lt Cdr A. F. Black, RN, to afford protection to convoys sailing between Mersa Matruh and Tobruk. The unit was a temporary amalgamation of Nos. 803, 805 and 806 Squadrons, all of which had also served in *Formidable* and whose pilots had just returned from operations in Crete and Syria. It left the base aerodrome at Dekheila, near Alexandria, on 17 August and set up headquarters at Sidi Haneish South, near Mersa Matruh, where it came under the control of the RAF. Its equipment comprised eight Grumman

▼ A Grumman F4F-3 (Martlet) of No. 805 Squadron comes to grief in the Western Desert around August 1941. The machine still bears its US Navy number, though it was possibly later given the British serial number AX733. (Via Geoff Wakeham)

Martlets of No. 805 Squadron, originally ordered by the Greek Government and at first still bearing their US Navy airframe numbers, plus sixteen borrowed RAF Hurricanes operated by the other two squadrons. In addition to covering convoys supplying the besieged Army formations at Tobruk, aircraft carried out attacks on German land forces and helped to escort RAF bombing raids.

The unit was in combat for the first time on 21 August when Sub-Lt (A) J. M. MacDonald, RN, of No. 805 Squadron in a Martlet was attacked by two Bf 109s. He was able to evade his attackers without sustaining damage but when he succeeded in getting one of them in his sights nothing happened as he had forgotten to select the master gun switch. On the same day Lt H. P. Allingham, RNR, of No. 806 Squadron was flying at 20,000ft when he sighted ten Bf 110s at half that height. Diving to the attack he put in five short bursts, claiming one as a probable after seeing it go down in a steep dive. Five days later the squadron suffered its first loss when Hurricane Z4052, piloted by Sub-Lt (A) G. B. Pudney, RNVR, of No. 806 Squadron was shot down into the sea in flames by a Bf 109.

Operations were also carried out from forward aerodromes. On 7 September the unit's aircraft were taxying to dispersal after refuelling at Sidi Barrani when about ten Fiat G.50 fighters appeared and carried out strafing attacks on the several landing grounds in that area. With no time to take off, pilots hastily scrambled out to take cover as best they could, fortunately without casualty, though one of their aircraft burst into flames and another two were badly damaged. Another aircraft was lost on 15 September when Martlet AX731 took off at night from Sidi Barrani North without aerodrome illumination, whilst enemy ground forces were approaching, and crashed 600yds from the boundary, killing the pilot, Sub-Lt (A) L. K. Harper, RNVR.

A success was scored on 28 September by Sub-Lt (A) R. W. M. Walsh, RN, of No. 805 Squadron in Martlet 'C' when he was attacked and hit by three G.50s. He outmanoeuvred the enemy aircraft and attacked one of them, from which he saw pieces falling before it went down in a steep dive, later to be credited as destroyed.

On 14 November the Hurricane elements moved forward into the desert, first to LG109, and then to LG123 and LG128 near Fort Maddelena, on the Libya-Egypt border, where they came under the control of No. 285 Wing RAF. Six days later Sub-Lt (A) P. N. Charlton, RN, shot down two of three Ju 87s destroyed by the unit before his Hurricane was fired on by a 'friendly' Tomahawk, forcing him to crash-land in the desert. He returned to the squadron the next day. Lt (A) W. J. Pangbourne, RNVR, of No. 806 Squadron was killed on 20 November when his Hurricane (V7858) was shot down by enemy aircraft five miles south of El Adem.

In a fighter sweep on 23 November Sub-Lt (A) G. R. Henderson, RNVR, and Sub-Lt (A) A. R. Astin, RNVR, both of No. 803 Squadron, each claimed Bf 109s as probables, and Sub-Lt (A) J. F. Knee, RNVR, of No. 803 Squadron and Sub-Lt (A) P. Fell, RNVR, of No. 806 Squadron inflicted damage on G.50s, the latter possibly destroying the machine he attacked. Lt D. P. Z. Cox, RN, of No. 803 Squadron (in 'B') and Sub-Lt (A) A. J. C. Willis, RNVR, of No. 806 Squadron (in V7308 'C') failed to return from the day's operations, the latter crashing at Bir el Gu. On that same day the Martlets of No. 805 Squadron were also engaged, Sub-Lt (A) R. W. M. Walsh, RN, of No. 805 Squadron spotting two Savoia SM 79s coming in to carry out a torpedo attack on HMS *Glengyle* when he was at 4,000ft. He was too high to prevent the attack but he dived down through an AA barrage, followed closely by his No. 2, Sub-Lt (A) J. R. Routley, RNVR, and chased the enemy aircraft out to sea, claiming one as a probable and the other as a possible. December 1 was another busy day, with Sub-Lts Diggens, Dennison and Wood each shooting down a G.50 whilst Bf 109s were probably damaged by Sub-Lts Dick and Charlton, the latter damaging yet another machine, either a Bf 109 or a Macchi C.202.

On 12 December the unit moved to Tobruk, and on the 28th Sub-Lt (A) A. R. Griffin, RNVR, in Martlet 3895, attacked a formation of four SM 79 torpedo-bombers 50 miles north of Ras el Milh, near Bardia, while on convoy patrol. He succeeded in shooting down one machine and forcing two others to jettison their torpedoes but was himself shot down and killed while attacking the last machine. On 25 January 1942 an He 111 was intercepted by two patrolling No. 806 Squadron Hurricanes piloted by Lt Allingham and Sub-Lt (A) B. H. C. Nation, RN, and inflicted damage but the enemy aircraft escaped. The following day the RN Fighter Squadron moved to LG05 at Sidi Barrani, disbanding as such just over a fortnight later. Nos. 803 and 806 Squadrons then re-equipped with Fulmars, with which they flew overland to Ceylon, where three months later they joined *Formidable* and *Indomitable* respectively.

Meanwhile the desert Albacore squadrons had been no less active. Cdr Jeff Powell, who ten years later was to become the CO of No. 826 Squadron, recalls:

No. 826 had set up a routine of carrying out minor inspections of aircraft on the desert airfield, whilst major inspections would be done at Dekheila, where a small maintenance flight was stationed for the purpose. At the same time the air crew from machines being inspected could take a couple of days' leave in Alex, the Nile Delta or in Palestine.

Everything had to be moved large distances over the rocky desert terrain – petrol, bombs, flares, rations, water. The water ration was just a few pints each day per man for washing/cooking/drinking. It was brackish – no partner for gin or whisky – and the tea it made tasted appalling. But every few months the Navy arranged for a tanker to bring forward a liquid called 'sweet water' with a ration of half a pint per man, which was merely what you and I now draw from the taps!

Ma'aten Bagush was about 150 miles west of Alexandria and only a few miles from RAF Advanced HQ, enabling the closest co-operation to be maintained with the latter. This co-operation became ever closer, with the CO calling directly on RAF HQ for the night's operation orders, and continued as the front moved back and forth and airfields changed hands. Indeed, No. 826 soon enjoyed a rather special relationship with Air Vice Marshal Coningham and his staff, being welcomed as something more than just another squadron. This is reflected in the citation for the CO's Distinguished Service Order, 'the value of whose Squadron cannot be over-estimated'.

Though often frowned upon as slow and out of date, the Albacore soon proved its usefulness for the type of warfare now being waged in the Western Desert. Cruising at 90 knots very quietly (with the sleeve-valve radial Taurus II in coarse pitch) and with the under surfaces painted matt black, they were ideal for locating and dive bombing pin-point targets at night (Afrika Korps ammunition dumps, transport or tank laagers or dispersed aircraft), using the same dead-reckoning navigation technique over the near featureless desert as they had previously over the sea. Their slow speed actually helped them to avoid AA guns and searchlights who always fired ahead – not believing that anything could fly so slowly! If their initial flares did not show up a suitable target, they would carry out a square search exactly as they would at sea, using flares to illuminate the expanding search area. They worked in small teams with some aircraft loaded mainly with bombs (usually six 250lb GP plus four flares) and others with more emphasis on flare dropping – carrying up to 36 flares when no bombs were carried.

To obtain maximum range for certain targets they would take off from Ma'aten Bagush with

►Albacore N4319 '4F' of No. 826 Squadron running up at an aerodrome in the Western Desert. The aircraft is loaded with four 250lb depth charges. (M. Langman)

◀No. 805 Squadron, at this time based in the Western Desert, proudly boasts 100 per cent serviceability for its Grumman Martlets, 7 June 1942. The unit is ready to provide fighter protection for Operation 'Harpoon', a vital eastbound Malta convoy. (Author's collection)

full weapon/flare load and top up with fuel at one of the landing grounds right up by the Eighth Army front line. In order to achieve the maximum blast effect from their bombs they required them to explode above the desert surface – this before the days of more sophisticated proximity fuses. Accordingly they adopted the simple expedient of screwing a 3ft iron rod on to the front of each bomb so that they would explode that distance above the desert and produce the most damage on dispersed aircraft, MT [motor transport] etc. In the early days the advanced landing ground was generally Sidi Barrani (or 'The Wire' as it was called, since it marked the border between Egypt and Cyrenaica), but as the Army moved forwards and then retreated, so the forward airstrips changed. When the Army advanced during a major push, such as Operation 'Crusader', the entire squadron moved forward from Ma'aten Bagush with all their tents, maintenance vehicles and MT to establish bases further forward, including their own mobile torpedo unit of several very heavy vehicles for carrying torpedoes, always kept with the squadron in case the Navy wished to reclaim it for more ordinary type naval warfare!

At one time No. 826 were as far forward as Benghazi (Berca airfield) though in this case shortly afterwards moving back to Bu Amud about ten miles away to the east of Tobruk. At the time they left Berca, having loaded the trucks with all their worldly goods, they could almost see the whites of the German eyes as they started the 'strategical retreat', which eventually ended up fairly near to that old 'Wire' once again. From the time the British forces entered Benghazi in early January until the Germans re-entered the town was only about three weeks!

During this short spell in Benghazi the squadron did revert to naval flying duties for twenty-four hours, when it was reported that an Italian convoy had sailed from the Gulf of Taranto bound for Tripoli with a strong naval escort including the battleship *Duilio*, three cruisers and escorting destroyers. The prime target was the 13,098-ton Lloyd-Triestino liner *Victoria*, carrying a Panzer division, which torpedo-carrying Beauforts had attacked earlier in the day and much reduced her speed. A flight of five Albacores, led by Lieutenant Commander Jack Corbett (in T9241), took off armed with torpedoes from Berca at 1610 on 23 January 1942 and sighted the battleship/troopship force towards sunset, accompanied by an air escort of Ju 88s.

Corbett was shot down during his attack but Lieutenant 'Ferret' Ellis obtained a hit on *Victoria* below the for'ard funnel and she sank at 1910. Sub-Lieutenant Johnny Brown hit and damaged an escorting destroyer. Ellis's aircraft was hit by flak but got back safely to Berca, from where he organized a search for Lieutenant Commander Corbett and his crew the next morning. This unfortunately produced no sighting but they were later picked up by an Italian hospital ship. Directly after returning from this search, because of rapidly advancing German forces, the squadron had to move back

◀ **A desert-based Swordfish of an unidentified squadron flies over the coast. It carries a 'cucumber' mine, somewhat similar in appearance to a torpedo but with a fixed head. (FAA Museum)**

from Benghazi to Bu Amud. Ellis received an immediate award of the DFC for his part in this attack.

Life in the desert was a vastly different existence from the comfort of dining in the wardroom, always assured of a bath and clean linen when on board. At Ma'aten Bagush there was the luxury of two ramshackle wooden huts for air and ground crews to eat and relax in, with ridge tents as 'cabins', each pilot and observer sharing. As most of the operational work took place at night they had to sleep for part of each day and then after doing the normal squadron administrative work they could in the afternoon drive a few miles to the nearby sea for a swim (or try and wash using salt water soap!), then make some furniture for the 'cabin' out of empty boxes or race captured German BMW motorbikes around the airfield or other harmless pursuits – stupid pastimes but relaxing from the perpetual night by night pressure on average-age 22-year-olds as they scoured the desert to attack Rommel's land forces.

No. 826 developed night flying to a fine art. The airfield always had a 'dummy' some ten or fifteen miles away at a known bearing and distance which was changed nightly. The dummy had a permanently lit (by night) flarepath which returning air crew could see and make for, then steer for home along the known bearing. When the aircraft was right overhead the real flarepath would be lit. It consisted of a line of ordinary electric torches on wooden bases cocked up at an angle of about five degrees and facing the direction of approach; the torches having a directional focus, they could only be properly seen by a pilot coming in to land in the right direction. As a further aid to night navigation the RAF provided one or two light beacons visible up to 20 or 30 miles whose positions were changed every few weeks. They must have helped foe as well as friend, but they were most useful.

No. 826's technique in flare illumination of their own targets over land, which was developed from a similar use of flares for illuminating shipping targets during torpedo attacks or targets ashore during bombardment by naval gunfire, was first used in the desert in August 1941. During the next few weeks the technique was improved and, following a discussion between the Squadron CO, Lieutenant Commander Corbett, and Group Captain 'Freddie' Guest, it was suggested to RAF Headquarters that the Wellingtons might like No. 826 to try illuminating one of their targets. The proposal was duly made, and, on the understanding that No. 826 would find and fully illuminate a target such as an airfield for thirty minutes, it was agreed that a trial be carried out. The trial was duly staged on 6 September 1941 and was followed by a full-scale operation on 10 September, on Martuba airfield (between Derna and Bomba Bay), Lieutenant Commander Corbett piloting the No. 826 Albacore with Lieutenant M. G. 'Pinkie' Haworth as observer on each occasion.

The trials were successful but it may have been lucky that on the first operation Corbett and Haworth failed initially to find the target and it was the Wellingtons who found it and dropped the first flare. Thereafter the Albacore illuminated Martuba according to plan while the Wellingtons bombed it. However, the initial error in navigation by No. 826 and the finding of the target by the Wellingtons made it quite clear that their skill in navigation was never in doubt; all they wanted from No. 826 was illumination which the squadron was able to provide on many occasions thereafter, including, on 27 November 1941, a very carefully planned 'Illuminating Tmimi for Wellingtons' (this cryptic comment taken from the CO's log book) which included a planned bombing strike on Tmimi in support of a parachute drop from Bombay aircraft by SAS men commanded by the legendary Lieutenant (as he was then) David Stirling, Scots Guards, the founder of the SAS. Due to 10/10 very thick cloud over the target and high winds, this first ever parachute operation by the SAS was a disaster.

Meanwhile No. 815 Squadron worked in support of the Eighth Army and carried out spotting for fleet bombardment from forward landing grounds. Throughout the closing months of 1941 these two squadrons also continued their night bombing of enemy transport and landing grounds, as well as flare-dropping and target-indication for RAF bombers, and torpedo and bombing attacks on enemy shipping. A number of air crew were lost in these activities, particularly by No. 826 Squadron. On 13 December 1941, for instance, T9151 piloted by Lt (A) T. I. Harray, RN, crashed into a Blenheim while taking off at night, he and his crew being killed when their bombs exploded. Two nights later N4319 piloted by Sub-Lt (A) K. W. Jones, RNVR, failed to return from a bombing operation on Derna aerodrome.

In March 1942 the two desert Albacore squadrons were joined by No. 821, recently arrived from the United Kingdom, and on 23 May this new arrival carried out a mine-laying operation in Derna harbour. A few days later it provided illumination for a night attack on tanks in the Tmimi area and early in June similar work enabled night attacks to be made on enemy airfields at Derna and Martuba. Various types of operation continued for the next few months, including the bombing of mechanical transport and tanks, spotting and illumination for bombardment and the occasional anti-shipping strike. Aircraft frequently had to return from these operations with low oil pressure because of maintenance problems caused by the dust and sand.

Jeff Powell remembers another such operation on 23 May 1942 as part of intensive attacks prior to a push by Rommel which started on 26 May and was later to take him into Egypt and up to El Alamein. Jeff was flying with Bobby Bradshaw and the target was Martuba again:

> Soon after dark two Albacores took off with 36 flares apiece, and 1½ hours later reached their estimated position of the target. As the initial flares illuminated only desert, we carried out a square search dropping flares every two minutes. On the third leg we found what we were looking for – including a good number of camouflaged German aircraft (Junkers and Messerschmitts). We then continued to illuminate at four-minute intervals whilst orbiting that airstrip at 7,000 feet. After a wait which seemed like hours as the precious flares were being used up, bomb flashes below us plus faint silhouettes of Wellingtons above at 10,000 feet showed that they had reached the target, having flown from their base nearly 500 miles away near the Suez Canal and refuelling at Fuka en route. They attacked in two waves of about twelve aircraft each. All the Albacores and Wellingtons returned safely from what the German official report called 'extensive damage caused by wave after wave of unidentified aircraft'.

Thus, nearly a year before the RAF Pathfinder Force was formed in UK under Air Commodore Bennett in August 1942, No. 826 Squadron had pioneered in the Western Desert the tactic of a small team of specialists seeking out and illuminating targets for attack by others.

The period from the end of May to October 1942 was one of the busiest as well as the most varied of the squadron's desert career. On 21 May there was a role reversal when No. 826 Albacores carried out an unsuccessful night torpedo attack on a convoy south-west of Benghazi, but this time with Wellingtons providing the flare illumination. The week

► Albacore N4378 '4H' of No. 826 Squadron, based at Blida, armed with a torpedo during a coastal patrol. On 6 March 1942 this aircraft, piloted by Sub-Lt A. Barnett and with Sub-Lt T. Goddard as observer, failed to return from a strike. (FAA Museum)

after Rommel started his advance from the line Tmimi to Bir Hacheim, No. 826 Squadron evacuated Bu Amud, but during the following week successive night attacks were made on Tmimi airfield and twice on shipping in Derna harbour as well as standing by for a torpedo attack on the Italian fleet off Tobruk.

After Rommel's capture of Tobruk on 21 June the Squadron evacuated Sidi Barrani followed by two night mine-laying operations in Tobruk harbour. There followed three consecutive night operations, the first providing flare illumination for Wellingtons of mobile columns at Sidi Barrani, and two attacks on MT between Sidi Barrani and Mersa Matruh, as Rommel advanced. In between these two operations Ma'aten Bagush Satellite was evacuated and the squadron completed its full circle of the desert back at Dekheila in Alexandria where it had disembarked from *Formidable* just over a year ago. At this point, although no orders were issued, the panic and confusion was such that the squadron were warned to expect to be told to fly either east towards Iraq or south towards Sudan!

Neither of these disasters happened, however, since Rommel's advance was halted at Alamein on 30 June. From then on the squadron, operating from Dekheila, went out night after night bombing everything and anything between Alamein and Mersa Matruh, including its old homes at Fuka and Bagush. The flying time from Dekheila to Alamein was no more than 30 minutes so that it was not unusual for crews to do two or even three operations a night. These operations sometimes took the form of searching out concentrations of troops and MT by flare-dropping and then dive-bombing them, or by providing the much practised and highly successful search and illumination for Wellingtons to cause havoc with their heavy load of bombs.

Donald Judd remembers an incident of near disaster in one of these raids which turned out 'successfully'. It was his second operation of the night – destination Alamein. He took off from Dekheila with six 250lb bombs with stick attachments and four flares. However, he hit an obstruction before he was completely airborne and had to make a forced landing in the sea just off the end of the runway. This happened to be some 30 yards off the beach and just opposite the wardroom. With the thought of the bombs and flares underneath them the crew swam faster than they had ever done before and, being so close to the wardroom, were able to have a quick Scotch before going along to the de-briefing!

The extent to which these desert operations developed is shown in the No. 826 Squadron diary, which records that in the four months leading up to the Battle of El Alamein no fewer than 12,000 flares were dropped by the squadron's Albacores. A comment by a member of Rommel's staff in late 1941 is of interest. He wrote: 'Our greatest inconvenience is the nightly precision bombing of our forward concentrations. This is a new development and one to which we have, as yet, no answer'. Air Chief Marshal Sir Arthur Tedder, the AOCinC, noted 'their magnificent work with and for the Wellingtons', also saying 'there is no doubt that these continuous night attacks were one of the decisive factors in crushing the enemy's attacks' and later that they 'may well prove to be a turning point in the war in Africa'. The RAF official account of the Middle East Campaigns records that No.

►Albacore T9172 '4L' of No. 826 Squadron, in mid-1942. On the night of 15 August 1942 this aircraft was shot down by enemy anti-aircraft fire during a raid on Mersa Matruh harbour. The two crew members, Sub-Lt T. J. McLister and Sub-Lt K. Chapslow, spent seven hours in a dinghy and then had nine days of freedom ashore before being taken prisoner. (T. L. Sirs)

◀ **Bombing up an Albacore of No. 826 Squadron in the Western Desert. (M. Langman)**

826 'not only performed their usual task of flare-dropping but dive-bombed the enemy, wrecking vehicles and causing a considerable number of fires . . . with their accumulated experience of operating over the desert by night they worked in close co-operation with the ground forces for the dive-bombing of enemy armour in the battle area'.

Lt Cdr N. C. Manley-Cooper has these recollections of No. 821 Squadron at that time:

> From April 1942, now flying Albacores, we took part in night bombing and also mining operations in Tobruk harbour. Our ground forces were on the retreat, and by the time Montgomery came out in August 1942 the Eighth Army was back in El Alamein. On a number of occasions we dropped flares on enemy motor transport and other targets. There were usually about 15–30 Wellingtons flying overhead, and once we had found what they were looking for they would proceed to bomb from 5,000–6,000ft.
>
> To find a target at night we would first fly to a point on the coast, find the wind, then fly south to where the Army had told us the enemy forces might be coming round. We would then call up the Wellingtons to flood the area with bombs, which could be rather risky for us as occasionally one of us was hit by their bombs coming down. We pioneered this method of marking targets at night, which was later adopted by the RAF for their Pathfinder Force.
>
> On 1 September a German offensive commenced and David Foster and I were the first people to spot the enemy advance. We had taken off the previous night at 2135 to illuminate enemy MT and at 0300 saw them coming round south of Alam Halfar. We estimated that there were between 1,500 and 2,000 vehicles and proceeded to drop flares, after which the Wellingtons bombed them heavily. The advance was eventually stopped, and the British counteroffensive started at El Alamein on 20 October. David Foster and I were up again that night and saw the barrage commence at 2200. We then dropped flares to help the British bombers.

No. 826, meanwhile, had continued its activities. From 12 May it engaged for some weeks in anti-shipping patrols, mine-laying and intensive bombing attacks on enemy forces during the Eighth Army's retreat to El Alamein. On 9 July nine aircraft flew 250 miles behind enemy lines to a landing ground in the desert, where they refuelled from an RAF Bombay transport then proceeded to deliver a night attack on an enemy convoy sailing towards Tobruk, claiming one ship as being probably sunk.

As stated by Lt Cdr Manley-Cooper, on 20 October 1942 the Allied Air Forces commenced heavy attacks on enemy airfields and other targets in preparation for a counter-offensive, and three days later a powerful artillery barrage signalled the start of the Battle of El Alamein, which was to turn the tide in the Western Desert. All three Albacore squadrons were still in the region, though No. 826 had temporarily withdrawn to El Birna for a period of torpedo training, returning as the battle commenced. After taking part in the initial break-out, No. 821 was withdrawn to Malta at the end of November, No. 826 departing in February 1943 for similar operations in Algeria with the British Army. Nos. 815 and 826 Squadrons continued to operate with the advancing Armies until disbanding in July and August 1943 respectively.

CHAPTER 12

Escort Carriers

By the late 1930s, with the likelihood of another war with Germany, it was realized how vulnerable the British Isles were to blockade at sea by submarine. As had been experienced in the First World War, the self protection of merchant ships by arming them was one answer but, as had been found by the Royal Naval Air Service, aircraft were an even greater deterrent.

The suggestion had been put forward that merchant ships carry their own aircraft, using rudimentary flight decks similar to those used on various warships in the earlier conflict. The idea was shelved, but with the outbreak of war, then the stationing of German aircraft anti-shipping units in France following the occupation and the subsequent heavy losses of Allied shipping, these thoughts came to the fore again.

The Director of Air Material at the Admiralty, Capt. M. S. Slattery, RN, put forward a plan to fit the simplest possible flight deck and landing equipment to suitable merchant ships, for the operation of fighter aircraft. As a stop-gap he suggested that catapults be fitted to merchant ships (see Chapter 9). In the meantime the US Navy was keeping a keen eye on the Royal Navy's struggles and suggestions were made on the same lines, of using merchantmen hulls for conversion to auxiliary carriers. By late 1940 Winston Churchill had taken up the cause, suggesting to President Roosevelt that US shipyards build auxiliary carriers for the Royal Navy, and early in 1941 the US Navy found two merchant ships suitable for conversion. The go-ahead was given and in March 1941 the transformation began of what were to become USS *Long Island* and HMS *Archer* (or BAVG-1), the first being completed in less than three months.

In the meantime a suitable ship had been found in the United Kingdom, in the shape of the German merchantman *Hannover*, a vessel of only 5,537 tons which had been captured early in the war, and this was selected for a more ambitious conversion. On 17 January 1941 work began on giving her a flight deck with two arrester wires and a barrier. The deck was small and there was no space for a hangar, but the conversion was the best that could be done in the circumstances. She was completed in July and initially given the name *Empire Audacity*, the prefix *Empire* being common to all wartime-built British merchant ships. However, this was soon dropped, and by the time she embarked six Martlets of No. 802 Squadron from Machrihanish on 10 September she had become HMS *Audacity*.

Audacity sailed from the Clyde four days later to act as escort for Gibraltar-bound convoy OG74, and on 16 September No. 802 found themselves in action. Red Section were on patrol when a U-boat was sighted, and the aircraft dived to attack with machine-gun fire, forcing the submarine to submerge before it had an opportunity to fire a torpedo at the convoy. A similar attack was made on the 19th, but the first real success came on the 21st of the month when two Martlets of Black Section, piloted by Sub-Lt (A) N. N. Patterson, RN, and Sub-Lt (A) G. R. P. Fletcher, RNVR, were scrambled after an Fw 200 which was attacking the rescue ship *Walmer Castle*. Under heavy fire from the enemy aircraft, they went in at close range, Patterson going in first, followed closely by Fletcher who had only fired 35 rounds from each gun when the tail unit of the large aircraft broke off completely, the machine plunging in to the sea with no survivors. It was around this time that the Fw 200C-3 version was coming into service with KG 40 at Bordeaux/Mérignac, with a strengthened rear fuselage and rear wing spar and other improvements including the bomb load, engines and armament.

The carrier completed the return voyage safely but she was not to survive long, being sunk by two torpedoes fired by *U-751* on 21 December while escorting homebound Gibraltar convoy HG76. During its short existence as an escort carrier fighter squadron, No. 802 had succeeded in destroying five Fw 200s, damaged three more and driven off another in addition to its activities against U-boats. On the debit side it had lost its Commanding Officer, Lt Cdr J. M. Wintour, RN, shot down in BJ516 by an Fw 200 on 8 November; and Sub-Lt (A) G. R. P. Fletcher,

▲ **HMS *Biter* at anchor. (Via Derek Price)**

RNVR, was shot down by *U-131* while attacking her on 17 December. Numerous Martlets had been damaged in these activities, and for a time only one was serviceable, but the new concept had proved its worth, as evidenced by the fact that Admiral Dönitz had ordered his U-boat pack to concentrate their efforts on *Audacity* when attacking HG76.

Four more escort carriers were by this time under conversion in America, for supply under Lend-Lease arrangements. *Avenger* (BAVG-2), *Biter* (BAVG-3), *Charger* (BAVG-4) and *Dasher* (BAVG-5) were similar to *Archer*, *Charger* being retained by the US Navy to train FAA air crew in US waters. These American-style designations denoted the type of vessel, 'B' indicating British (the customer), 'A' auxiliary vessel, 'V' heavier than air aircraft and 'G' aircraft carrier. The designation was later altered to CVE, meaning carrier/heavier than air/escort.

On 19 March 1942 four Swordfish of No. 834 Squadron embarked in *Archer* at Charleston, and she then sailed with a fast convoy to Freetown, which was reached on 3 April. Here she embarked two Martlets of No. 882 Squadron from *Illustrious*, the other four aircraft of this squadron (which should have comprised *Archer*'s fighter element) being earmarked to remain aboard *Illustrious* for the forthcoming Madagascar operation. Interminable mechanical problems delayed departure, but the ship eventually sailed for Cape Town on 15 May, only to be again delayed by further engine problems on arrival.

On 8 June she staggered out of port bound for Greenock but misfortune still dogged her. A Swordfish dropping a message about a raider was shot down while flying over an American ferry station at Ascension Island, another went over the side with the loss of her TAG and yet another crashed into the barrier. Then a 250lb bomb exploded while being loaded into the walkways, killing nine armourers and injuring ten others. One aircraft was set on fire, but the hangar spraying equipment was effective in preventing the damage from spreading further. The ship reached Freetown intact but by now her mechanical problems were such that she had to divert to New York for repairs, arriving on 15 July after breaking down again in mid-Atlantic. She returned to service in November with No. 834 Squadron once more aboard her after spending several weeks working up at Floyd Bennett Field, and she then took part in the North African landings, ferrying 25 P-40 Warhawks of the USAAF to Morocco. In 1943 she embarked the Swordfish of No. 819 Squadron and the Wildcats of No. 892 Squadron but in August that year she was again taken out of service for engine repairs and never saw active service again.

The standards of fuel arrangements in the

◀ **A Swordfish of No. 811 Squadron takes off from the flight deck of *Biter*. (Via Derek Price)**

▼ ***Charger* was originally earmarked for the Royal Navy but was soon returned to the US Navy for use in training Fleet Air Arm air crews. Several squadrons spent short periods aboard her whilst working up in US waters. (Via P. H. Dobbs)**

early ships left a lot to be desired, as highlighted by the tragic loss of *Dasher* when she blew up off the Isle of Arran with heavy loss of life on 27 March 1943. The explosion was subsequently attributed to a carelessly dropped cigarette end igniting petrol from a leaky valve. This led to a belated tightening-up of fuel safety arrangements to bring them nearer to British practice, and all new escort carriers received from the United States were subject to intensive modification before they were allowed to enter service with the Royal Navy.

Lt Cdr (A) Derek Price, RNVR, was involved in two incidents with No. 811 Squadron in HMS *Biter* during 1943:

The first tale starts in the centre of the storm-tossed Atlantic Ocean with a convoy (HX237) homeward bound through a sea infested with packs of German U-boats. Things were a bit dicey, but in addition to the normal destroyer and corvette screen the convoy had the protective services of the Swordfish of No. 811 Squadron. Flying from HMS *Biter*, they patrolled round the convoy, hoping to attack U-boats if seen, or at least keep them submerged to prevent attack.

In the early evening of 10 May 1943 Swordfish HS160 took off to carry out a Cobra dusk patrol round the convoy. The driver was Sub-Lt (A) Mike Wargent, RNVR, a good friend of mine; I was the 'looker' and LA Crinkley dealt with the wireless. It was a pleasant evening with a mild swell and reasonable visibility – but after an hour or so the weather closed in suddenly. The time to return arrived; at the limit of visibility – away from the direction of the convoy – we saw the white wake of some vessel (or U-boat?) on the surface and decided to go and have a look. 'A bit daft', said my listener, 'what with not much

petrol left and all that.' 'You're right', I said (but there was no knowing what it was, and duty came before danger!)

Approaching the unknown after some time, we circled a fast merchant ship whilst I interrogated by Aldis and determined a friendly vessel. This had taken more time and petrol than anticipated and Wargie decided we couldn't get back to *Biter* on the few pints left. The only solution was to ditch and hope the ship would stop to pick us up. Not certain, though, because there might have been a U-boat around and a stationary ship could be torpedoed.

Anyway, Wargie landed us like a feather, scarcely a jolt, and we floated gently in the swell about a quarter of a mile on the ship's starboard bow. She stopped, and a boat was launched and made its way towards us. A wire is fixed along the starboard side of the observer's cockpit in a Swordfish. When pulled, a large dinghy is automatically inflated and emerges from above the mainplane. I pulled violently several times, with negative results except for blood flow from my fingers and a view of the bones of the finger joints! Luckily our small dinghy worked – we held on to it and swam away from the sinking aircraft, within 20 minutes being lifted into the whaler and wrapped in blankets. I was rather cold in the water. My next conscious memory was waking up in sick bay, wearing Red Cross pyjamas, drinking soup and feeling grateful that the Captain of HMS *Cheshire* – an independently routed AMC with a hold full of ping pong balls – had kindly paused to rescue us in spite of the danger. Back to Gourock with the odd watchkeeping stint.

The second story began at 1210 on the 8 June 1943 when Swordfish HS437 of No. 811 Squadron took off to carry out a Cobra patrol at 20 miles round the convoy, HX242, somewhere in the Atlantic and homeward-bound. It was fairly rough – Sub-Lt Mike Wargent was driving, LA Crinkley with the wireless and gun, and I was dealing with the navigation etc. After 2 hours 40 minutes of sea and sky we prepared to land, with Ollie Campbell waving the bats on deck. All went well until the last few seconds, when, due to

▼ HMS *Searcher* makes a sharp turn to port. (FAA Museum)

unforeseen circumstances, the stern rose violently and slammed us amidships. The aircraft broke its back and the rear end fell into the sea, being churned up efficiently by the propellers whilst the three of us in the remaining part of HS437 went 'A over T' along the deck.

We were very lucky. I damaged my chest but the others survived intact. A week's leave with the right arm in a sling, being greeted like a wounded hero, helped to soothe the pain!

All the later American-built escort carriers were fitted with catapults, although not all British aircraft were capable of taking advantage of these, having been designed for the older British accelerator. As increasing numbers of escort carriers became available they were earmarked for specific duties. About half were retained for the original task of trade protection but a dozen were allocated for assault and fighter-escort duties. For this latter purpose they were mostly equipped with fighter squadrons, taking part in a series of actions from late 1942 until the end of the war, although some carried torpedo-reconnaissance aircraft and operated in a general-purpose role.

Nearly all escort carriers undertook aircraft ferrying duties from time to time but seven of them were engaged primarily in this essential work, mainly delivering American-built naval aircraft to Royal Navy establishments in the UK and overseas. In addition the British-built escort carrier *Pretoria Castle* and the American-built *Ravager* spent most of their time in deck-landing trials and training duties in the Clyde estuary and its environs. After the war the survivors of the 38 American-built carriers were returned to the United States under the Lend-Lease arrangements (although *Biter* was transferred to the French Navy in 1945) and most were reconverted for merchant service.

▶▼Avenger JZ159 'C' of No. 846 Squadron, piloted by Sub-Lt D. A. Thomas, failed to gain height and had to ditch after take-off from HMS *Trumpeter* in Scapa Flow on 31 August 1944. (J. A. Greenfield via F. C. Lynn)

CHAPTER 13

Norwegian Operations

In June 1941 the Germans invaded the Soviet Union, immediately adding to the burdens of the Royal Navy. To assist the new allies a strike was planned on the northern German-occupied ports of Kirkenes and Petsamo by aircraft from *Furious* and *Victorious*.

The two carriers left Scapa Flow for Iceland on 23 July accompanied by two cruisers and six destroyers. Two days later they arrived at Seidis Fjord where they refuelled, sailing for Norway the next day. The strike was scheduled for the 30th, but the element of surprise was lost when an enemy aircraft spotted the force shortly before take-off. Petsamo was the target for *Furious*, which launched nine Albacores of No. 817 Squadron and nine Swordfish of No. 812 Squadron, accompanied by an escort of six Fulmars of No. 800 Squadron. When the aircraft arrived at the target they found relatively slight opposition; there were few ships in the harbour, a small steamer becoming the sole victim of their torpedoes for the loss of one Albacore (N4250) and two Fulmars (N4029 and X8624).

The force from *Victorious* had even less fortune. The defences at Kirkenes were prepared, and such few ships as were in the harbour were on the move. Amid heavy flak, and under attack from enemy fighters, the twenty Albacores of Nos. 827 and 828 Squadrons attacked their target but sank only one small ship and set fire to another, for the loss of eleven of their number. Two of the escort of nine Fulmars of No. 809 Squadron were also lost, although the unit claimed one Bf 109 and two Bf 110s. The naval force then withdrew to Scapa Flow via Seidis Fjord.

Furious was now detached for duty elsewhere but *Victorious* remained in service with the Home Fleet, escorting convoys to Iceland and Russia. During these duties two strikes were made on Norway, both on shipping in the Bodø area. For the first of these the ships left Scapa Flow on 23 August and anchored in Sardam Bay, Spitzbergen, a week later. After two days there the fleet sailed and on 3 September a Do 18 flying boat was shot down by a No. 809 Squadron Fulmar. The strike set off on the 12th with the Albacores of Nos. 817 and 832 Squadrons involved and they succeeded in sinking two merchant vessels in Glomfjord without loss to themselves or their

◀ Sea Hurricanes of No. 880 Squadron flying in formation during 1941. Four aircraft of this squadron joined *Furious* in July 1941 to provide air defence during an attack on the Arctic port of Petsamo, the squadron CO, Lt Cdr F. E. C. Judd, RN, being successful in shooting down an attacking Dornier Do 18. (Cdr R. N. Everett)

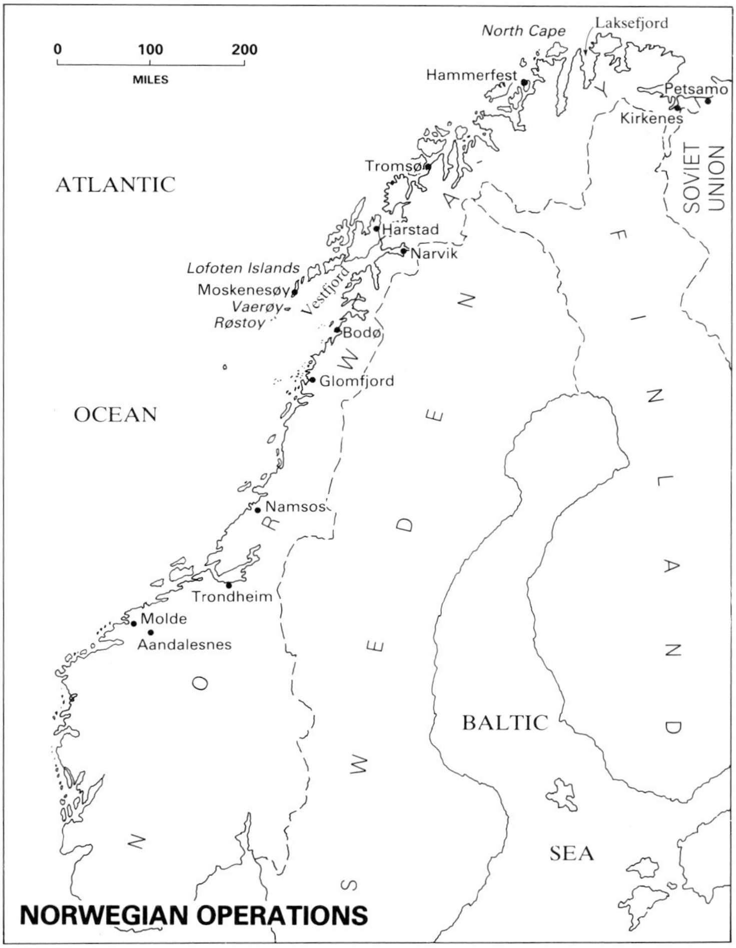

fighter cover. By the following day the ship was back at Scapa Flow. A similar raid in the same region in October was equally successful, the only casualties being two Albacores which crashed on the flight deck after receiving anti-aircraft damage. No further attacks of this nature could be made for some time as there was no spare carrier strength and the range for land-based FAA aircraft was far too great. *Victorious* continued making trips to Iceland and Russia until July 1942, when she went into dry dock at Liverpool.

The contemporary diary of No. 832 Squadron deals at some length with the September 1941 attack:

2 September. At 0230 the force left Sardam Bay and steamed south towards the North Cape. It was the intention to intercept a convoy which was steaming north from Tromsø towards Hammerfest and thence to Kirkenes, and attack it either with bombs or torpedoes or possibly both. Twelve aircraft were to be used, six from No. 817 Squadron and six from No. 832 Squadron. The aircraft of the former (Force B) were to be armed with torpedoes and were to search the 'inner leads' south of Hammerfest, 'sweeping' (as much as an Albacore can sweep!) northwards. Those of the latter (Force A) were to carry bombs and were to search the 'inner leads' southwards to the South Cape towards Hammerfest; if the convoy was not sighted, and no other shipping was found, they were to attack oil tanks situated about three miles south of Hammerfest.

3 September. At 0030 the two striking forces were flown off. No. 832 Squadron were represented by Nos. 1 and 2 sub-flights. The weather was all too clear and it was obvious that, after passing the North Cape, we were not going to escape detection for very long. The sky was deep red in the east and the aircraft, silhouetted against it, must have been visible for a great distance. From position 71° 28′ N 22° 10′ E we reached the North Cape after seven minutes' flying. We continued beyond, intending to sweep south. Went into the north entrance of the 'inner leads'. Details of the coastline were becoming clearer every minute, as the sun came nearer the horizon. In more peaceful circumstances one would have called it a glorious dawn. At 0415 approx. we sighted the convoy about 12 miles distant. Under prevailing conditions the CO decided not to attack as we would have been spotted a long way off and would have been 'dead meat' for any flak-ship. As it was, they had probably detected our presence already and the Ju 88s may have been on their way. We turned round therefore and set back to the carrier, jettisoning our anti-personnel bombs on the way. Force B was back some time before us.

Next day the ships ran into fog, but by 7 September preparations were being made for an attack the following day:

7 September. The force in company with CinC steamed eastwards all day towards the flying-off position for the operation. There was a high wind with thick fog patches. Four small striking forces were to search an area of the Norwegian coast from north of Bodø to south of Glomfjord. Primary targets were to be shipping. Secondary target for striking forces C and D (No. 827 Squadron sub-flights) was the power station at Glomfjord. Three striking forces were to carry 6 × 250lb GP bombs and the fourth (No. 817 Squadron) torpedoes. The main purpose of Forces C and D's secondary mission was to immobilize the Nauvig aluminium works, which was entirely dependent on the power of the power station. Flying crews retired early to be called at 0300. Aircraft were to be ranged at approx 0230. At 2300 the weather was poor. High gusty wind and intermittent snow and hail showers prevailed. The sea was high.

8 September. The weather continued to be rough. The striking forces were ranged at 0230. At about 0315, in gusty high wind, a violent roll and severe gust caused the aircraft on deck to

take charge resulting in damage to four of the squadron aircraft (including '4G', the standby). One of No. 817 Squadron's aircraft was also damaged. The net result was that three aircraft took off at 0525 (Reconnaissance sortie. Crews were '4K' Lt Keppel, Lt Shrubsole, LA Fuller; '4B' Sub-Lt Williams, Mid. Burbidge, LA Gibbs; '4R' Sub-Lt Barnes, Sub-Lt O'Shea, LA Stott). Due to the prevailing bad weather the aircraft were unable to form up and proceeded independently.

Aircraft '4K' searched Bodø harbour and the leads to Glomfjord. In the harbour a ship of 1,000 tons was unsuccessfully attacked. Light AA fire was encountered and close-range weapon fire, three bullets passing through the fuselage just aft of LA Fuller. Lt Keppel secured some excellent photographs of the Bodø area which ought to prove of considerable value if any further attacks are carried out in the area. Aircraft '4B' attacked a vessel and set it on fire, and last saw attempts being made to beach it. The attack delivered was high bombing from a cloud about 2,000 feet above the target.

As the general evidence suggests that further shipping is in the operational area, the CinC ordered a further striking force to be flown off at about 1100. Aircraft were to be armed with 6 × 250 GP bombs.

The second striking force consisting of five squadron aircraft were airborne at 1110. The first sub-flight, '4B' (Lt Cdr Plugge, Lt Stenning, LA Vaughan), '4Q' (Sub-Lt Brown, Mid. Harvey, LA Farrar) and '4R' (Sub-Lt Eyre, Sub-Lt Evans, LA Hollowood) proceeded in company up the centre of Vestfjord as far as Staevan and then into the leads. There they unsuccessfully attacked the *Haakon Adalstein* (1,500 tons). One stick straddled the ship and the crew were seen to abandon the ship although no hits were observed. An enemy aircraft identified as a Heinkel He 115 floatplane was observed about one mile to the westward and to proceed up Skiten Fjord. Mutual respect!

A second sub-flight, '4C' (Lt King, Lt Seccombe, LA Lovell) and '4H' (Sub-Lt Sayer, Sub-Lt Hopkins, LA Weldon) parted company in a snowstorm off Rostoy Island. '4C' proceeded up the west side of Vestfjord to 68° north. A vessel of 2,000 tons was unsuccessfully attacked. Light AA fire from the ship's escort almost severed the upper starboard mainplane and LA Lovell was slightly injured in the back by shrapnel. Lt King did excellent work in getting the aircraft back safely and was unfortunate in his landing when after an emergency cross-wind touch-down the aircraft collapsed. No one sustained any injury as a result. '4H', having sighted no shipping in the Vestfjord, dropped bombs on the W/T station on Rostoy Island. The stick missed the station but hit the jetty. All aircraft having been landed on, the ships set course to the westward, hands having been closed up at action stations since 0600.

Three days later preparations were being made for further attacks:

11 September. Day spent in preparation for the attack to be carried out on the morning of the 12th. The plan for the attack was as follows. At 0100 the ship was to be in a position some 60 miles NW of the south of the Lofoten Islands. There were to be three striking forces, 'A', 'B' and 'C'. 'A' was composed of six aircraft from No. 817 Squadron and was armed with Mk XII torpedoes. They were to sweep up the Vestfjord from the south of the Lofoten Islands towards Narvik and sink any shipping they found there and return. Force 'B' armed with Mk. XII torpedoes, was to consist of No. 2 Flight of No. 832 Squadron and these aircraft were to accompany Force 'A' up the Vestfjord, where they were to break off and search the

► Wildcat JV720 'QY' of No. 853 Squadron's Fighter Flight, piloted by Lt W. A. Storey, after floating into the barrier while attempting to land on HMS *Queen* on 17 March 1945. The squadron, which was primarily equipped with Avengers, carried out a number of strikes against targets in the months before VE-Day. (Via Ray Williams)

◄ **A Barracuda of No. 828 Squadron seen on a raid over Norway and loaded with an armour-piercing bomb. (FAA Museum)**

leads southwards towards Bodø. If they found nothing they were to attack shipping in Bodø itself and thence return. Force 'C', consisting of six aircraft of No. 832 Squadron armed with six 250lb SAP bombs, were to attack a power station and aluminium works near the head of Glomfjord, south of Bodø.

12 September. When the striking forces were ready to take off there was a brilliant moon, and it seemed that weather conditions were going to be ideal. There was a light wind, and the sea was calm.

At 0103 Force 'A', closely followed by Force 'B', took off and set course for the Lofoten Islands. Very soon they had sighted the chequered outline of their landfall and after 45 minutes' flying they passed over Moskensøy Island and then set course to make good a track of 075. Visibility was excellent but the moon was becoming obscured by the clouds from the landward side. At 0222 Force 'B' parted company from Force 'A' and struck south. Force 'A' continued up Vestfjord. They sighted one small vessel, which they sank, and two others, which they attacked but failed to hit. It was bad luck that they didn't find bigger fry. The same may be said of Force 'B' which found nothing in the leads inside Landegode and finally arrived off Bodø at 0249. The three aircraft then proceeded independently.

The crew of 'L' sighted a vessel of about 600–900 tons moored off the mole which bounds the western end of the inner harbour and this was attacked. Unfortunately it was too dark to observe any results, but the crew of 'K' considered that 'L's torpedo exploded prematurely and this is likely. Connolly then machine-gunned a warehouse on the south side of the harbour where there were many lights showing. Indeed, from the black-out point of view, Bodø put up a very bad show. During the search navigation lights had been observed all round the coast and all showing the advertised characteristics.

The crew of 'M' sighted a vessel of some 2,000 tons in the inner harbour and O'Shea fired his torpedo through the actual entrance. Again results were not observed but the air gunner claims he saw a red glow around the hull of the

ship, but again it is doubtful whether the torpedo actually exploded. During all this time the anticipated 'flak' had not materialized at all, and throughout the attack was entirely unopposed.

Meanwhile the crew of 'K' had sighted a ship alongside the wharf and the warehouse which Connolly had machine-gunned. Shrubsole fired his torpedo at this ship and observed an explosion to one side of it. He claimed that he saw the warehouse collapse. He then machine-gunned it in the hope of starting a fire. All three then returned independently to the ship, 'M' joining 'L' after passing the Lofoten Islands. They landed on between 0345 and 0400. Results were disappointing in that it was impossible to assess them accurately but we trust at least that we had the pleasure of getting the local Hun garrison out of their beds a lot quicker than usual and considerably earlier too.

Force 'C' did very well indeed although they left minus one aircraft, the engine of which failed to start. At 0208 they passed between Vaerøy and Røstoy heading towards Glomfjord. After this they climbed and crossed the coast at 6,000ft. Over the target area cloud formation made conditions somewhat difficult and the five aircraft broke up. The leader in '4C' decided to climb to 4,000ft and from there was able to make out the power station quite clearly. He dived to attack but the flash of his bombs prevented him from seeing the result of his stick, and therefore he can make no claim. He then flew off down the fjord and set course for Røstoy where he arrived at 0243. There he attacked the D/F station with 40lb anti-personnel bombs but these fell over. He then set course for the carrier and landed on at 0415.

Aircraft '4B' attacked the aluminium works and the crew claimed that their first stick fell across the target. They were unable to observe the second one. They likewise proceeded to Røstoy but, having no bombs left, were unable to attack. They landed on the carrier at 0420.

Aircraft '4F' likewise went for the aluminium works and observed fires on leaving the target area. At 0338 they arrived over Røstoy and, as a result of their attack, claimed a direct hit on the D/F station. They landed on the carrier at 0418.

Aircraft '4G' followed '4F' and observed the latter's bombs fall. As they went in Shaw said he saw two rocket pyrotechnics fired from the ground to a height of some 5,000 feet. They were probably some sort of air-raid warning. Bombs were observed to fall among the buildings. At 0432 '4G' arrived over Røstoy Island. Buildings on a small island were attacked with 40lb bombs but no results were observed. They landed on at 0416.

Aircraft '4H' dropped bombs on the aluminium works amongst the debris left by the other aircraft. Apart from this no accurate results were seen. After leaving the coast they formed up with '4F' and at 0337 arrived over Røstoy. A dummy run was made over the D/F station and then an attack was made with 40lb bombs. These were claimed as direct hits. They landed on at 0420.

This attack seems to have been a success in that it was more possible to observe results. Likewise no opposition whatsoever was encountered. All three striking forces managed to achieve complete surprise. Thus ended 832 Squadron's first crack at the Hun.

▲ The German U-boat depot ship *Black Watch* under attack by aircraft of Nos. 853, 846 and 882 Squadrons from the escort carriers *Queen*, *Trumpeter* and *Searcher* on 4 May 1945. This was the final operation by the Home Fleet in the Second World War. (FAA Museum)

It was not until early 1944 that further operations were made on Norwegian coastal targets. By then the Royal Navy had escort carriers available for this task, able to carry Avenger strike aircraft and Wildcat fighters each with sufficient range to carry out extensive strikes from offshore carriers. These were augmented on occasion during 1944 by fleet carriers, with *Furious*, *Implacable*, *Indefatigable* and *Victorious* all participating at various times. Their greater capacity and better organization and facilities resulted in their gaining credit for a greater part of the damage inflicted in this activity though this in no way belittles the efforts of the escort carriers.

These operations continued until the end of the war, over thirty raids being made during 1944 and 1945. The last was on 4 May 1945, only four days before VE-Day, when 44 Avenger and Wildcat aircraft of Nos. 853, 846 and 882 Squadrons, respectively from the escort carriers *Queen*, *Trumpeter* and *Searcher*, attacked Kilbotn, near Harstad, blowing up a depot ship and sinking a U-boat.

CHAPTER 14

Operation Torch

With a reversal of fortunes, the German desert forces under General Rommel were retreating steadily westward by the autumn of 1942. By that time the Americans had built up their air and ground forces in Britain and were keen to see them in action. The decision was reached, therefore, to mount a joint Anglo-American invasion of Vichy French-held territory in North Africa.

The operation was given the code name 'Torch' and was set for 8 November. The Fleet Air Arm was given a vital role in support of the amphibious operation, no fewer than four of the Royal Navy's available fleet carriers participating. These were the elderly *Argus* and *Furious*, the repaired *Formidable* and the new *Victorious*, which between them carried thirteen squadrons equipped variously with Martlets, Seafires, Fulmars and Albacores. Also involved were three Sea Hurricane-equipped escort carriers, *Avenger*, *Biter* and *Dasher*. In all they carried more than 160 British aircraft, mainly fighters, in addition to 136 aircraft with the American contingent. The British aircraft were painted up with 'Torch Star' markings in place of the usual roundels and the words 'US Navy' instead of 'Royal Navy' on the rear fuselage: it was thought there would be less opposition from the Vichy French if they appeared to be American.

The carriers left the Clyde at different times over a period of nine days between 22 and 30 October, patrols being flown en route to Gibraltar. To add to the element of surprise the main invasion force sailed in fifteen convoys, hoping to give the impression that these were normal Mediterranean convoys.

▼ An Albacore of No. 820 Squadron aboard *Formidable* is loaded up with six 250lb bombs for a raid on Fort d'Estrées, Algiers, during Operation 'Torch'. Thirty out of the 36 bombs dropped by the squadron scored direct hits. The aircraft carries spurious US Navy markings. (Frank Hunter)

◀ **A dummy French fighter found on Tafaroui aerodrome, Oran, during Operation 'Torch'. The French evidently wanted their fighter defences to appear greater than they really were. (Cdr F. W. Baring)**

This plan was completely successful and the enemy had no inkling of the invasion until the troops actually landed.

The armada was divided into three task forces, one American and two British, with additional cover for the latter being provided by Force H. The Americans formed the Western Naval Task Force and their objective was Casablanca; the Central Naval Task Force, which included *Biter*, *Dasher* and *Furious*, was to attempt to take Oran, whilst the Western Naval Task Force, with *Argus* and *Avenger*, was earmarked for Algiers. *Formidable* and *Victorious* were in the Covering Group, attached to Force H.

The ships sailed through the Straits of Gibraltar on 6 November, RAF Hudsons and Sunderlands undertaking anti-submarine patrols. The carriers sent up fighter patrols but the only aircraft spotted was a French Potez 63 flying at 10,000ft over Force H. Maintaining the deception, the convoys continued to sail eastwards during the 7th, but in the night they all turned south at a predetermined time.

The first landings took place at 0100 on the 8th with the smaller carriers lying nearby, waiting to fly off their fighter patrols at dawn to provide cover for the troop transports. No opposition was met although flares were dropped on Force H during the night by enemy aircraft. The first aircraft up were two Albacores of Force H, sent off at 0530. Fifteen minutes later four Martlets of No. 882 Squadron were despatched from *Victorious* to the military airfield at Blida and on arrival fired at two French aircraft about to take off, only light AA fire being encountered. Forty-two aircraft were then sent off from four carriers against Vichy airfields at La Senia, Maison Blanche and Tafaroui. Eight Albacores from No. 822 Squadron (*Furious*) and a Fulmar which had been attached to the squadron attacked La Senia and succeeded in destroying five hangars and 47 aircraft. During this attack they were fired on by nine Dewoitine D.520s but escorting Sea Hurricanes from *Biter* and *Dasher* shot down five of these, one success being shared with the rear gunner of an Albacore. Unfortunately only four Albacores returned from this raid, one of those lost being the Commanding Officer, Lt (A) J. G. A. McI. Nares, RN, whose aircraft (BF665) was shot down in flames by AA fire.

At 0800 four more Martlets of No. 882 Squadron left *Victorious* for a fighter patrol over Blida, led by Lt (A) B. H. C. Nation, RN, in machine 'C'. There was a little AA fire as they approached the target but on flying round the airfield they could see a large number of dispersed aircraft, and AA gunners manning, but not firing, their guns, whilst farm-workers in the surrounding fields were waving their handkerchiefs. Nation promptly radioed that the French appeared to have given in and were ready to surrender. The ship's Air Staff were at first dubious, asking him to check that he really was over Blida, which he had no difficulty in confirming since the name was in the middle of the airfield in large letters. After some debate as to who should accept the surrender, he received a message from his Admiral that he could land 'if he thought it safe to do so'.

Leaving the other three aircraft to cover his approach and landing, he touched down without incident and taxied towards the hangars, where he switched off his engine. Climbing out, he drew his revolver and ordered one of the assembled officers to take him to the Station Commandant. An elderly general rose from his desk and found himself looking down the barrel of a revolver. He was allowed to make one telephone call, and then he wrote on a piece of paper torn from a writing pad 'La base de Blida disponible pour l'atterrissage des armées alliées [Blida base is at the disposal of the Allied armies for landing purposes]' and he handed this to Lt Nation. The airfield was then taken over by a group of American Rangers who had just arrived. This episode is modestly recorded in Nation's flying log book as 'Fighter patrol over Blida drome. Landed and accepted surrender of same from French general. Then to Maison Blanche and on to Vic'. The following day he attacked and damaged a Ju 88 while engaged in a patrol over the fleet in Martlet FN153.

◀ **Sub-Lt P. C. Heath's Swordfish DK757 '4H' of No. 813 Squadron after being set on fire by Focke-Wulf Fw 190s in a low-level bombing and machine-gun attack on Bone airfield on 31 December 1942. (Cdr F. W. Baring)**

The Seafires were also active, and it was in the course of the operation that the first success was achieved by this new type of aircraft. The six Seafire IICs of No. 885 Squadron had joined *Formidable* in the Clyde as she sailed and their main task on the invasion day was to patrol over Maison Blanche. While patrolling above Mers-el-Kebir harbour, Sub-Lt A. S. Long, RNZNVR, of this squadron saw a French Martin 167 bomber which he promptly attacked, sending it down in flames. No. 807 Squadron Seafires from *Furious* covered the landings at Oran, finding themselves engaged in a fight with a formation of D.520s which they were able to outperform to such effect that Sub-Lt G. C. Baldwin, RN, shot down one, two others being claimed by the remainder of the squadron. No. 807 also destroyed about twenty aircraft on the ground.

The Albacores were also extremely active. One force of six bombed and silenced a naval fort at Jethée du Nord which was bombarding two destroyers attempting to crash through the boom at Algiers. Soon afterwards other Albacore strikes performed a similarly successful task on Fort du Perré, which was troubling a force of commandos to the west of the city, and also on Fort Matifou.

Late on the 10th the carriers moved to within four miles of Algiers and *Argus* sent up a patrol of three No. 880 Squadron Seafires. They sighted fifteen Ju 88s at 20,000ft while still climbing but were unable to prevent their making a dive-bombing attack on the ship. Three more Seafires were ranged on the deck but they could not take off as the ship had no opportunity to steam back into wind; they were all damaged in the attack, one losing its tail, but none of the pilots suffered any injury.

Aircraft were busy the whole time, patrolling, bombing, carrying out reconnaissance, dropping leaflets and undertaking other tasks to create diversions, and there were

▲ **Martlet IV FN121 of No. 893 Squadron, resplendent in US Navy-style markings for the occasion, about to take off from *Formidable* during Operation 'Torch'. (Via Col F. D. G. Bird)**

many incidents. Sub-Lt (A) L. P. Twiss, DSC, RNVR, of No. 807 Squadron was one of a formation of Seafire pilots carrying out a reconnaissance of the road between the airfields at Lourmel and La Senia which shot down one of a formation of seven D.520s which attacked them. Afterwards he landed alongside a column of American tanks and climbed from his cockpit to ask if they needed any help. The commander asked him to look for troop movements on roads to the south-east and south-west, and after flying over that area he returned to report that none were to be seen. Being then short of petrol he flew off and landed at Tafaroui, not knowing whether it had been captured. The French were in fact leaving, but although he was not attacked his tailwheel broke on landing. Nothing daunted, he replaced it with one from a nearby crashed aircraft, siphoned petrol from another and then returned to his ship the next morning having slept the night under the wing of his aircraft.

The operation was proving a success and the land forces were advancing so rapidly that the need for naval air support was much reduced by the second day of the invasion. Seafires patrolled the beaches during a fresh landing at Bougie Beach, east of Algiers, and fighters and Albacores were active over Oran where further landings were made. By now Tafaroui had been occupied by USAAF Spitfires flown in from Gibraltar and consequently the carriers prepared to withdraw. On the 10th *Avenger* went in to Algiers harbour for repairs, transferring four Sea Hurricanes next day to *Argus*, which remained on patrol in the area and was subjected to several attacks.

Once the land forces were firmly established the convoys began to withdraw, covered by their escort carriers. However, tragedy struck on the 15th when a torpedo from *U-155* hit *Avenger* while she was escorting convoy MFK 1 and, primarily as a result of the lower American fuel and fire protection requirements for these early CVEs, she blew up with the loss of all but seventeen of her crew; both Nos. 802 and 883 Sea Hurricane Squadrons consequently ceased to exist. Submarines remained active in the area, and two days later *Formidable*, which had spent a couple of days back at Gibraltar, put to sea again. During the day one of its No. 820 Squadron Albacores patrolling east of the Straits succeeded in torpedoing *U-331*, which was suffering from the previous attentions of a Walrus and three Hudsons of No. 500 Squadron operating from Tafaroui.

CHAPTER 15

Mediterranean Landings

By early 1943 the tide had turned in North Africa, with British forces pressing on from the east and the new front going well in Vichy French territories. It was too early to contemplate an invasion in northern France, but at a summit conference held in January it was decided that there were now sufficient resources available in the Mediterranean for an attack on Sicily.

Four months later the Tunisian campaign was over, which meant that an invading force could rely on air support from that country and also from Malta, each of which would be within striking range, thus reducing the necessity for full carrier support. *Formidable* was the only fleet carrier left in that arena by then, but the reduced Italian Fleet still posed a danger, and the repaired *Indomitable* arrived at Gibraltar on 23 June to support her in Force H.

Fleet Air Arm involvement in the landings, which took place on 10 July under the code-name Operation 'Husky', was minimal. *Indomitable*, however, was put out of action on night of 15/16 July when a Ju 88 torpedo-bomber was mistaken for a returning Albacore, its missile hitting the port side and causing extensive damage to a boiler room. Accompanied by *Formidable*, she limped into Grand Harbour then after ten days' temporary repair work made her way to Gibraltar, where on the 29th she unloaded all her aircraft before sailing to America, not emerging from Norfolk dockyard until the following April.

Sicily was completely occupied within two months, and on 3 September the Eighth Army crossed over the Straits of Messina to the Italian mainland. On that day secret negotiations with the Italian Government were successfully completed, bringing them into the Allied cause and thus avoiding the necessity for a slogging series of battles upwards from the foot of Italy.

German forces were still well established in Italy, however, and a leapfrogging operation was planned for a landing at Salerno, south of Naples, to be code-named Operation 'Avalanche'. This time considerable air support would be needed, and *Illustrious* was now allocated to Force H to replace *Indomitable* so that with *Formidable* she could take on the Italian Fleet, should it put in an appearance, and also provide air defence for the assault carriers. The latter formed Force V, with over 100 fighters (mainly Seafire IICs), aboard *Attacker*, *Battler*, *Hunter* and *Stalker* as well as *Unicorn*, a light fleet repair and maintenance carrier not normally used operationally but which for 'Avalanche' carried about sixty aircraft.

Early on 8 September the two fleets sailed north, Force H around the west of Sicily and Force V through the Straits of Messina. The Italian Fleet sailed south the following day and surrendered, leaving Force H free to concentrate on providing additional support for the beach-head. Force V had the task of providing cover for the landing troops, and the first of twenty Seafires took off at dawn on the 9th for a patrol lasting an hour and a half. This pattern was to continue, with Seafires taking off at hourly intervals.

The intention had been that the land forces would take Montecorvino airfield, so that from the second day British and American land-based fighters would take over, but the unforeseen presence of a resting Panzer division in the area prevented this. Instead, an improvised airstrip was hastily built at Paestum, though the Seafires could not avail themselves of this until the 12th, putting a heavy strain on Force V, which had not been planned for continuous air operations.

Seafire undercarriages tended to be rather fragile and an additional handicap was that many of the squadrons had relatively inexperienced pilots, combining, with a lack of wind over the flight decks, to produce an excessively high accident rate. The worst affected was No. 899 Squadron in *Hunter*, which lost thirteen machines in three days, and the Captain of that ship ordered six inches to be cropped off each propeller blade to reduce 'pecking' caused by the tips hitting the deck when the arrester hook engaged the wire. This innovation proved so effective, and resulted in so little loss of performance, that it became a standard feature of the Seafire.

In the first three days over 700 sorties were flown, despite increasing unserviceability

►Hellcat JV179 'ES' of No. 800 Squadron, piloted by Sub-Lt J. G. Pettigrew, comes to grief while attempting to land aboard *Emperor* on 3 November 1944 during the final phase of the Aegean operations. (Author's collection)

among the aircraft. The Seafires were too slow to catch the Bf 109s and Fw 190s which put in an appearance, and therefore there were few combat successes, but they had a considerable deterrent effect on the German fighter-bombers, causing many of them to discontinue their attacks or drop their bombs wide of the beach-head.

On the 12th the assault carriers were at last able to put 26 Seafires ashore to Paestum. Conditions there were somewhat hazardous, but the aircraft coped magnificently, only one machine being lost, through brake failure on landing. The next day they re-embarked and the ships sailed to Bizerta. The landings successfully completed, and the Italian Fleet having ceased to be a threat, both Force V and Force H were then disbanded. This allowed both *Formidable* and *Illustrious* to rejoin the Home Fleet, and the Fleet Air Arm had little part to play in that theatre for the next nine months.

On 6 June 1944 the Allied forces invaded Normandy, but by that time the battle in Italy was running into stiff opposition from the Germans. A landing was planned in southern France to relieve pressure from this Italian front, originally to have taken place in June as Operation 'Anvil'. Following a decision instead to wait for the vital Normandy beach-head to become well established, it was post-poned until August and renamed Operation 'Dragoon'.

In the meantime a number of naval pilots and their aircraft were put ashore to operate with Desert Air Force squadrons in Italy, undertaking close support of the Army, bombing and tactical reconnaissance work. On 21 June eight Seafire L.IICs of No. 809 Squadron flew from Blida to Capodichino to be divided amongst Nos. 92, 145, 417 and 601 Squadrons in No. 244 Wing and No. 7 Squadron, South African Air Force, in No. 7 SAAF Wing, which was operating as part of the Desert Air Force. The following day nine similar aircraft of No. 879 Squadron from *Attacker* joined No. 7 SAAF Wing, to be shared among Nos. 1, 2, 4 and 7 SAAF Squadrons.

During 'Dragoon' the Fleet Air Arm was to repeat the role it had played at Salerno, Nos. 4 and 7 Fighter Wings this time flying a miscellany of Seafires, Wildcats (as the Martlets had been renamed) and the new Hellcats from the ships of Task Force 88. The latter included the assault carriers *Attacker*, *Emperor*, *Hunter*, *Khedive*, *Pursuer*, *Searcher* and *Stalker*, plus two American CVEs. *Hunter* and *Stalker* were to come under US Navy control in Task Group 88.2, and the remainder constituted Task Group 88.1.

By early August the carrier force was assembled off Malta where it carried out exercises whilst assault shipping was prepared. The first troops went ashore between Frejus and St Raphael around dawn on 15 August, meeting comparatively slight opposition, most of the German forces having been drawn off to Normandy. The Luftwaffe was largely con-spicuous by its absence and the naval fighters

◀ **Sub-Lt Painter's Hellcat JV105 aboard *Emperor* off Khios in September 1944. He flew the aircraft, whose temporarily applied invasion stripes are gradually disappearing, on a number of operations both in southern France and the Aegean, including a bombing and strafing attack on Leros harbour on 3 October 1944. (N. S. Painter)**

were able to roam freely and widely, attacking shore defences and road, rail and river traffic in addition to bombardment-spotting for the participating warships.

Carrier accidents were considerably fewer than in 'Avalanche', despite similar conditions prevailing, though there were a number of operational losses. On the 17th Lt (A) L. G. Lloyd, RNVR, of No. 807 Squadron, flying Seafire L.III fighter-bomber NF606 from *Hunter*, crashed into the sea after being hit by flak off Toulon. Three days later Seafire LIIC MB314 of the same squadron, piloted by Lt E. V. Speakman, RN, crashed over the bow while attempting to land after suffering flak damage. Other pilots were lost while attacking targets, one being Sub-Lt (A) D. A. Cary, RNVR, of No. 899 Squadron from *Khedive* in Seafire L.III NF661, who flew into a hillside while carrying out a low-level attack on enemy mechanical transport on the 18th. These losses were fairly typical of the casualties suffered by the squadrons before the carriers withdrew towards the end of the month.

This task completed, there was little work left for the Royal Navy in the Mediterranean and its surrounding waters though there were still a few pockets of resistance in the Aegean. The Germans appeared to be withdrawing from the area by mid-August and the Royal Navy was given the task of cutting off their retreat. Operations commenced on 9 September and ten days later fighters from *Attacker*, *Emperor*, *Khedive* and *Pursuer* dropped 26,000lb of bombs on Rhodes without loss. Numerous attacks were made against enemy transport on islands in the region by Seafire, Wildcat and Hellcat fighters of Nos. 4 and 7 Naval Fighter Wings operating from these carriers and also *Hunter*, *Searcher* and *Stalker*. Athens was occupied early in October and the final sorties were flown by No. 800's Hellcats from *Emperor* over Milos on 5 November.

CHAPTER 16

Operations against Enemy Raiders

The sinking of *Graf Spee* had eased the menace of German capital ships but others remained and U-boats were a constant threat to the vital supplies of food and other cargoes from America. The available carrier strength was too stretched to cover all the requirements for air cover over Atlantic convoys, which for the most part could only be met at first by the comparatively few Walruses of No. 700 Catapult Squadron aboard the larger warships.

When war broke out the Germans had been building a new battleship, *Bismarck*, and by the spring of 1941 she had completed her sea trials, posing a threat to Allied shipping in the Atlantic. Aware that she was ready to go to sea, the RAF carried out photographic reconnaissance sorties over the Baltic to track her movements. She was eventually sighted on 20 May making her way between Danish islands leading to the Kattegat and Skagerrak, accompanied by the cruiser *Prinz Eugen* and several destroyers, and the following day she was seen heading for Bergen. Bad weather prevented an RAF bomber force from sighting its quarry, and on the 22nd conditions had deteriorated further. However, the crew of a Fleet Air Arm Maryland of No. 771 Squadron volunteered to carry out the search, and the aircraft took off from Hatston in low cloud, piloted by Lt (A) N. E. Goddard, RNVR, with Cdr G. A. Rotherham, RN, as his observer and TAG Milne as the third crew member. They eventually ran into clear weather near the Norwegian coast and first searched the Korsfjord area, where the ships had been last sighted, and the Bergen Fjord, flying through heavy flak, but their efforts were fruitless and

◀ **One of the small number of Martin Marylands flown by the Fleet Air Arm. They were used only by No. 771 Squadron, a Fleet Requirements Unit based at Hatston in the Orkneys, the crew of one of which was responsible for making the vital report that the German battleship *Bismarck* had broken out into the Atlantic. (FAA Museum)**

Milne radioed the observer's report that the ships had evidently broken out.

Within hours the Home Fleet had sailed north, accompanied by the new fleet carrier *Victorious*, which had only embarked her first aircraft eleven days earlier and had had no opportunity to work up her squadrons. She was thus equipped only with the six Fulmars of No. 800Z Flight, which were already embarked, and nine Swordfish of No. 825 Squadron which embarked as she sailed; other squadrons had been earmarked for her, but only the Albacores of No. 828 Squadron were readily available, at Hatston, and these flew to Sumburgh in the Shetlands the next day. They were attached to Coastal Command at the time, however, and although trained and standing by for this express purpose, permission for their release arrived too late for them to embark.

On the 23rd the cruisers *Suffolk* and *Norfolk* sighted *Bismarck* heading south-west in the Denmark Strait between Greenland and Iceland and other ships then headed for that area, a Walrus of No. 700 Squadron from *Norfolk* shadowing the enemy ship between snow showers. The following morning *Hood* and the newly commissioned *Prince of Wales* joined in the attack but *Bismarck* promptly fired on them, sinking *Hood* with heavy loss of life. *Prince of Wales* was also hit, but managed to damage one of the enemy's fuel tanks with a near-miss before breaking off. The Home Fleet meanwhile sailed towards a position south of Iceland, and Force H with *Ark Royal* was on the way from Gibraltar but had a considerable distance to travel, so it was essential to slow down *Bismarck*.

In order to carry out an air attack *Victorious* was detached from the main hunting force during the afternoon of the 24th, escorted by four destroyers. The sky was still light at that northerly latitude as all nine No. 825 Squadron Swordfish took off at 2210 under the leadership of Lt Cdr (A) E. Esmonde, RN, the squadron commander. No. 800Z Flight had the task of maintaining contact with *Bismarck* for another attack at dawn and they sent up three Fulmars at 2300, another two relieving them at 0100. At 2327, after a flight of 120 miles through squalls, an ASV contact was made with *Bismarck* at a range of sixteen miles. Contact was lost as cloud increased, but *Norfolk* informed Esmonde visually that the enemy ship was to the north-west. Surprise was lost when they were spotted at a range of six miles, and the resulting flak was so intense that Esmonde's aircraft was hit when still four miles from the target.

On its final approach the squadron split into three sub-flights which attacked independently. Having had his starboard lower aileron damaged, Esmonde abandoned his original plan of leading in the first sub-flight and instead decided to attack the port bow whilst in a good position. Lt P. D. Gick, RN, abandoned his first attempt with the second sub-flight and, flying low over the water, made his way to a better position, evading the worst of the fire. Lt (A) H. C. M. Pollard, RN, also led the third sub-flight away from the barrage and although one of his aircraft became detached the other two went in to the attack. The air gunners fired at the ship's superstructure and gun positions as they turned away and one hit was observed. Esmonde's TAG was ordered to signal *Victorious* 'Have attacked with torpedoes. Only one observed'. This hit, which had been made by Gick's lone attempt from the west, had sent up a column of water amidships, followed by a cloud of heavy black smoke. In fact little damage was done by the torpedo, which hit the ship's armoured belt, but the stress set up by the German battleship's constant evasion in the attack widened the split already caused by *Prince of Wales* and fuel losses now became a major problem. The Swordfish all reached the carrier safely, though not without difficulty, but two of the Fulmars failed to return.

Contact was lost the following morning and a planned dawn strike was called off. Instead the Swordfish flew off in bad weather in an unsuccessful hunt for their prey, two failing to return to the ship although fortunately both crews were rescued. *Bismarck* was eventually sighted at 1030 on the 26th, by a Coastal Command Catalina, making for refuge at Brest. Heavy AA fire drove away the Catalina but at 1114 the ship was sighted by a No. 810 Squadron Swordfish from *Ark Royal* piloted by Sub-Lt (A) J. V. Hartley, RN, with Sub-Lt (A) P. R. Elias, RNVR, as his observer. Seven minutes later another *Ark Royal* Swordfish also spotted her and the two aircraft maintained contact until relieved by another pair, this tactic continuing until late at night.

In terrible conditions, fourteen Swordfish now set off from *Ark Royal*. Unhappily they were not warned that *Sheffield* was in the area and she suddenly found herself the target of their attack, but skilfully her captain succeeded in evading the torpedoes launched by eleven of the aircraft.

In the evening a second strike was launched with fifteen aircraft of Nos. 810, 818 and 820 Squadrons, led by Lt Cdr T. P. Coode, RN, the CO of No. 818 Squadron. The weather was still appalling, but all the attacking aircraft succeeded in finding *Bismarck*, including one which had lost touch while flying in cloud. Intense fire forced some of the aircraft to turn away at first, but all the attackers dropped their torpedoes and at least two hit their target, one striking the ship aft and causing such severe damage to her propellers and rudders that she was unable to steer a steady course. A third strike the following morning proved unnecessary – gun attacks throughout the night by the Home Fleet having so reduced the enemy that a torpedo from the cruiser *Dorsetshire* was sufficient to sink her – and the Swordfish jettisoned their torpedoes.

The remains of the German ship were found in 1989, and it was suggested that she might have been scuttled, but Capt. Edmund Carver, in a letter published in *The Daily Telegraph* on 28 June 1989, wrote:

> I must state that if she succeeded in scuttling herself it was quite a remarkable feat, or chance, of timing. As the observer in a Fleet Air Arm Swordfish crew flying from *Ark Royal*, my pilot and I were circling a few hundred feet above *Bismarck* during her final minutes. We saw *Dorsetshire* approach, fire her last torpedo into *Bismarck*'s port side and, within seconds of this hit, watched the battleship capsize to port and then founder.

Lt Cdr Manley-Cooper recalls:

> A Catalina has always been credited with finding the *Bismarck,* but I wonder if it was actually first seen by the crew of one of our Fulmars which had developed a radio fault and was therefore unable to make a report until it returned to the ship.
>
> After the sighting, three Swordfish squadrons were sent up, led by Lt Cdr Stewart-Moore. I was flying No. 2 in my squadron, and looking into my ASV set, when up came a blip on the screen. As far as we were aware there was no other ship in the area, so we naturally assumed it to be *Bismarck*. We zigzagged to let the leader know, then Stewart-Moore led us all down into the attack. The ship saw our approach, however, and took effective evasive action so that none of our torpedoes hit her – which turned out to be extremely fortunate as it was actually HMS *Sheffield*! There were

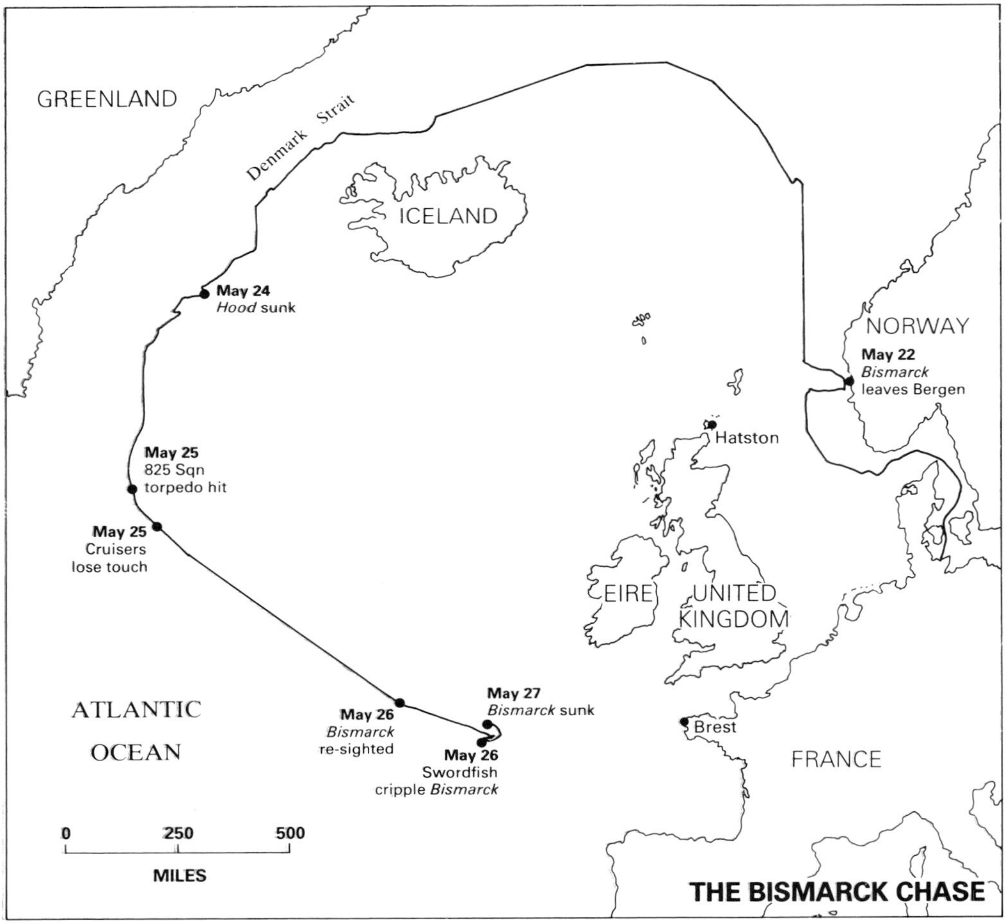

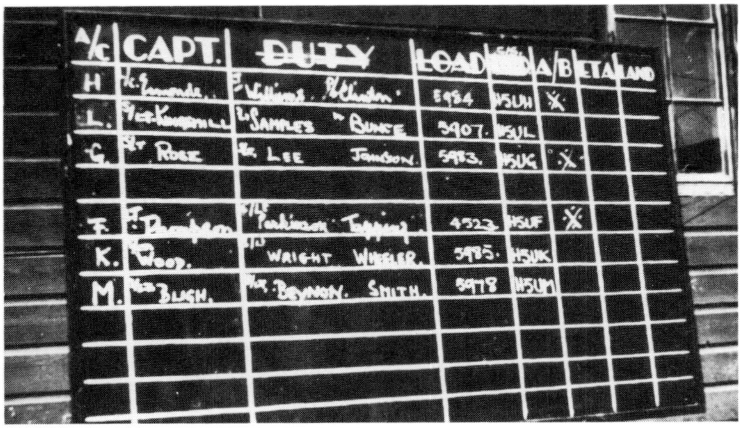

▲ **The briefing board for the gallant but fruitless attack by six Swordfish of No. 825 Squadron, led by Lt Cdr Esmonde, on *Scharnhorst* and *Gneisenau* during their dash up the English Channel on 11 February 1942. (H. J. Abraham)**

> recriminations on our return, of course, but we were not to blame as we had not been told she was around, and were entitled to assume any ship sighted would be *Bismarck*.
>
> One good thing did come out of this episode, though. We had all used Duplex-headed torpedoes, and those which had been dropped had all porpoised in the rough sea and blown up. After assessing the situation we were fitted up with contact-type torpedoes, and off we set again, led this time by Lt Cdr Tim Coode, CO of No. 818 Squadron. Our instructions this time were to report to *Sheffield*, who would signal *Bismarck*'s bearing and distance by lights. We were to fly at the regulation height, then drop down to let off our torpedoes. However, the air was so cold that several aircraft, including ours, fell out of the sky with engines stopped, only picking up again at about 7,000ft when they had de-iced in warm air. Eventually my ASV, which was still the only one we had at that time, picked up *Bismarck* and we saw her steaming up towards us. The three squadrons had by that time split up and came in to attack from different directions, the enemy ship getting a mopping with torpedoes coming from different directions. I saw our torpedo explode aft, but one or two others hit it too, and I have no idea which one did the main damage.

This highly skilful action still left *Scharnhorst* and *Gneisenau* at Brest, where they were joined on 1 June by *Prinz Eugen*, and here they were subjected to the attention of Bomber Command.

In January 1942 the remnants of No. 825 Squadron re-formed at Lee-on-Solent, again commanded by Lt Cdr Esmonde. Fears that the German ships might break out led to the squadron moving on the morning of 4 February to RAF Manston in Kent, where they were put on five minutes' readiness for what was expected to be a night attack. On 11 February Esmonde attended an investiture at Buckingham Palace, where he received a well-deserved DSO for his part in the *Bismarck* action.

That night the German ships took advantage of poor weather to leave harbour with a heavy escort, and with fighter protection standing by. At 1055 the next day Esmonde received the news at snowbound Manston, by which time the ships were well up the English Channel. It was therefore necessary to mount an attack as soon as possible and at 1220 six Swordfish took off, rendezvousing ten minutes later with a cover of only ten Spitfires from Biggin Hill, far fewer than had been planned. German fighters soon put in an appearance, and the attackers dodged their cannon fire as best they could.

Esmonde, leading the first sub-flight in W5984 'H', was hit by a ricocheting shell while flying at 50ft and part of a wing was shot away, causing him to steer an erratic course, but an Fw 190 soon completed the damage and he went into the sea. The next aircraft, W5983 'G', was piloted by Sub-Lt (A) B. W. Rose, RNVR, whose air gunner, LA A. L. Johnson, had been killed. Rose had himself been hit in the back by a shell splinter and the petrol tank had been struck by cannon fire, but he succeeded in dropping his torpedo at a range of 2,000ft. He then managed to get his aircraft up to 1,200ft but petrol was streaming out at such a rate that it was obvious he could not reach the coast, so he ditched, he and his observer, Sub-Lt (A) E. Lee, RNVR, being rescued by MTBs. In the third aircraft (W5907 'L'), Sub-Lt (A) C. M. Kingsmill, RNVR, also managed to drop his torpedo, his TAG, LA D. A. Bunce shooting down an enemy fighter before being shot down themselves, both they and their observer, Sub-Lt (A) R. M. Samples, RNVR, being picked up later by an MTB. The second sub-flight consisted of Lt (A) J. C. Thompson, RN, in V4523 'F', Sub-Lt (A) L. R. Wood, RN, in W5985 'K' and Sub-Lt (A) P. Bligh, RNVR, in W5978 'M' and their crews. They took violent evasive action as they progressed towards the target and were last seen flying through heavy flak and attacks by fighters as they passed over the escorting destroyers.

For his part in this attack Esmonde was posthumously awarded the Victoria Cross, the first to be gained by a member of the Fleet Air Arm. The four surviving officers, Kingsmill, Lee, Rose and Samples, all received the DSO, and air gunner Bunce the CGM. The other members of this gallant force, who all lost their lives, were mentioned in despatches. Vice-Admiral Ramsay, Flag Officer Commanding Dover, wrote: 'In my opinion the gallant sortie of these six Swordfish constitutes one of the finest exhibitions of self-sacrifice and devotion to duty that the war has yet witnessed.

CHAPTER 17

Arctic Convoys

One consequence of the Soviet Union's entry into the war was the necessity to provide her with military equipment and supplies, most of which could only be sent by sea. The Royal Navy therefore took on the thankless task of escorting convoys through the Arctic to ports in northern Russia. At first such convoys formed up in the Icelandic port of Hvalfjord but in March 1942 they switched to Reykjavik. In September 1942, however, the departure point was moved to home waters, Loch Ewe being used until shortly before the end of the war in Europe when the Clyde became the starting point. During 1942 the ships headed for either Archangel or Murmansk but after 1942 they all aimed for Kola Inlet.

The first such convoy left Hvalfjord in August 1941 under the code-name 'Dervish', arriving at Archangel ten days later. After that a numbering system was adopted, outbound convoys being PQ1 onwards in sequence, and the corresponding returning ones QP1 onwards. From December 1942 this system was changed for security reasons, so that eastbound convoys were numbered JW51 to JW67 and westbound ones RA51 and RA67. In retrospect it seems surprising that these and other types of convoy were numbered in sequence when random numbering might have provided more security.

Capt. J. A. Burnett, CBE, RN, (Ret.), was involved in several of the early Arctic convoys as the Meteorological Officer in HMS *Victorious*:

> The current 'Pilot' for the Kola Coast was misleading rather than helpful and even stated that along the coast 'fog could be dispersed by gunfire'! It also included the statement that cloudy weather was prevalent with a southerly wind, not what was experienced for the ill-conceived and disastrous strike on Kirkenes (and Petsamo) by No. 827 Squadron when there was no worthwhile target and casualties were approximately 50 per cent in the perfectly clear conditions.
>
> In fact, weather data were still conspicuous by their absence in 1941–42. On my first Russian convoy I took frequent sea temperature readings east of Spitzbergen, so on the second one, about a month later, I knew within narrow limits where to find the cold tongue extending south to the east of Spitzbergen. That turned out to be fortunate, for we were shadowed after making a tentative foray towards northern Norway and we were due to rendezvous with, I think, HMS *Argus* laden with fighters for Russia. With a warm southerly wind again it was easy to forecast the quickest way to find fog, in which we steamed for about three days, going as far north as 78 degrees and eventually

▼ Fulmars of No. 809 Squadron on the flight deck of HMS *Victorious* in the Arctic Ocean. (Official)

approaching Russia to fly off fighters by steaming almost due south fairly close to the west coast of Nova Zemlya.

The Russians never co-operated. For each convoy, I was supposed to receive reports but there was never a direct report. There was one convoy when, at the critical time, the nearest weather report was for 800 miles away!

Somewhat surprisingly, casualties to the early convoys were minimal, only one merchant ship being lost out of more than 100 which had sailed up to the beginning of March 1942. After that, however, losses brought about by attacks from both U-boats and German aircraft steadily mounted, the worst being in June 1942, when PQ17 arrived at its destination with only thirteen of the original 36 merchant vessels still afloat. Fleet Air Arm support during such convoys was restricted to catapult flights by Walrus aircraft of No. 700 Squadron from the escorting cruisers. The crew of Walrus P5706 from HMS *Norfolk*, piloted by Sub-Lt (A) R. Wignall, RNVR, with observer Sub-Lt (A) G. R. N. Riley, RNVR, and TAG LA G. Gibbons, were lucky to survive when PQ17 was ordered to scatter whilst they were in the air. They managed to find one of the escorts, HMS *Palomares*, and land alongside it, their aircraft then being towed more than 400 miles to port.

The chastening experience with this convoy led to a complete change in strategy. Icelandic

◀ **A U-boat off the Russian coast turns to keep her eight Oerlikon guns at the rear of her conning tower trained on an attacking Swordfish (from No. 816 Squadron aboard the escort carrier *Chaser*), about March 1945. (Vic Smith)**

departures were abandoned and improved air cover was provided, the latter in the shape of the new escort carriers now appearing on the scene. The 40 merchant vessels and their escorts in convoy PQ18 finally left Loch Ewe on 2 September, to be joined seven days later off Iceland by *Avenger* carrying eighteen Sea Hurricanes of Nos. 802 and 883 Squadrons as well as three Swordfish of No. 825 Squadron.

Lying in wait in northern Norway was the strengthened Luftflotte V, hoping to emulate its successes against PQ17. Their first attack began on the 12th but the inexperienced Sea Hurricane pilots had made the mistake of chasing after Bv 138 shadowers and the unguarded convoy soon lost eight merchant vessels to torpedo-carrying He 111s. The lesson had been learnt, however, and when a further succession of attacks came in over the next two days the defenders stayed close to the convoy. The Hurricanes were continuously in action, breaking off only to land, refuel and re-arm before going up once more to rejoin the fray. Only one defending aircraft was lost to the enemy, though three had the misfortune to be brought down by defending fire from merchant vessels. In return, however, they shot down five He 111s and Ju 88s and damaged 21 more during the three days of operations, with no further losses to the convoy.

Equally effective had been the activities of the small Swordfish force. They had dropped depth charges on sixteen U-boats and jointly with the destroyer HMS *Onslow* were credited with the destruction of *U-589*. Total German losses in the air were 41, many victims falling to the intensive AA fire, and this type of attack was largely abandoned as a consequence. Later convoys were mainly subjected only to the attentions of U-boats, which were inhibited by the likely presence of escort carriers, and no more convoys suffered so grievously as had PQ17 and PQ18.

In practice, had the Germans but known it, the Royal Navy would be in no position to spare escort carriers for this task for quite some time, all those available being needed for the North African landings. *Dasher* was to have accompanied JW53, which left Loch Ewe on 15 February 1943, but after only two days she was so badly damaged in poor weather that she had to turn back. Not until JW57, a year later, was another escort carrier available for this duty.

Colonel F. D. G. Bird, RM (Ret.), recalls of his two-month spell as Commander (Flying) aboard *Formidable*:

> I was appointed, temporarily, Commander (F) of *Formidable* vice Ermen, who had been given a pierhead jump to another appointment on promotion to Captain. That all happened so quickly that he had time to turn over to me with not much more than 'You've got her, Birdie'.
>
> However, in the usual mid-winter weather in the far north, *Formidable* left the Clyde for the Arctic Circle and my spectacular swansong. On a pitch black night, and in half a gale, the Albacores flew off to carry out a practice dummy night torpedo attack, after which they started to land on again. While they were away the night had become even more windy, and after one bad arrival amongst a pom-pom the next Albacore ploughed hard and fast into the bottom of the island. Unable to see at all clearly what was happening below me on the flight deck and expecting the crumpled Albacore to burst into flames, I ordered 'Up windscreens'. Various aircraft had been parked temporarily in such a way that as the windscreen came up they brought with them a number of Albacores doing them a good deal of damage. It was a night to remember. The Captain by then was Phillip Ruck-Keene, and his only reaction to my clottish mutilation of precious Albacores was to arrange for the control of the windscreens to be wired up during night flying. He put my bungling down to inexperience as Wings.

On 16 February 1944 No. 816 Squadron embarked its eleven rocket-armed Swordfish and six Wildcats aboard *Chaser* in Scapa Flow. The convoy of 43 ships left Loch Ewe four days later and the carrier joined them the next day, two cruisers and seventeen destroyers being also in attendance. The weather for the Swordfish crews in their exposed cockpits was appalling at that time of year but they made several attacks against the fourteen U-boats which were awaiting the convoy, though without success other than to keep them at bay. Reaching Kola Inlet on 28 February, the convoy started the return journey as RA57 on 2 March and this time the Swordfish had better luck. Two days out they damaged *U-472* with rocket fire, leaving the U-boat to be finished off by HMS *Onslaught*. A similar attack the next day put paid to *U-336* and another on the 6th disposed of *U-973*. When the carrier returned to Scapa on the 9th it had lost only one of its brood of merchant vessels, on the journey home.

The tide had now turned, and equally successful was convoy JW/RA58, which left Loch Ewe on 27 March. By now it was possible to spare two escort carriers, *Activity* carrying the seven Wildcats and three Swordfish of No. 819 Squadron whilst *Tracker* had aboard the twelve Avengers and seven Wildcats of No. 846. Five days later *U-355* was sunk in a joint attack by HMS *Beagle* and one of the Avengers, and on 3 April *U-288* was claimed by the Swordfish and Avengers. By the time the return convoy reached Loch Ewe on the 14th three more U-boats had been attacked and six shadowing aircraft shot down without the loss of any merchant vessel.

The next convoy, accompanied by *Activity* and *Fencer* carrying fourteen Swordfish and sixteen Wildcats, was equally successful. A Bv 138C shadower was shot down by a Wildcat on 1 May, on which day *U-277* was claimed by a Swordfish of No. 842 Squadron from *Fencer*, which squadron also sank *U-674* and *U-959* the following day as well as attacking eight other U-boats before the carrier docked at Greenock on the 5th.

The first convoy to sail from the Clyde was JW/RA64, also code-named Operation 'Hotbed', which left on 3 February 1945 escorted by *Campania* and *Nairana* (both of which revived famous names of First World War seaplane carriers). *Campania* was fitted with a new design of air warning radar and both ships carried the latest Swordfish Mk IIIs as well as Wildcat Mk VIs. Another innovation was the presence of an obsolescent Fulmar AI-fitted night fighter aboard *Campania*. The first success came three days later when a No. 813 Squadron Wildcat from *Campania* downed a Ju 88 shadower. An attempted attack the next morning by twelve Ju 88 torpedo-bombers was thwarted by the attentions of No. 835 Squadron's Wildcats from *Nairana*, one being shot down by an escorting corvette. No further such attacks materialized over the next two days, although German aircraft were seen at times, nor did the Swordfish succeed in finding the U-boats which were assumed to be in the area. The Fulmar was of little help on this occasion, however, its radar giving trouble when it attempted to track a shadower and the aircraft crashing heavily on subsequently landing.

Ju 88 torpedo-bombers renewed their efforts on the 10th, making a series of attacks from different directions, but *Campania*'s new aircraft radar was equal to the occasion and gave ample warning for the convoy to take evasive action and the defending fighters to get into the air. The Wildcats had a hectic time, many being fortunate not to fall to the ship's gunfire, and by the time the last of the enemy had been seen off No. 813 Squadron could boast only one serviceable aircraft. On the return journey the U-boats had some early success before the convoy became scattered in a hurricane-force gale. On the morning of the 20th it was still in process of re-forming when at around 1000 the radar detected more enemy aircraft, which turned out to be another force of 25 Ju 88s. These dropped many torpedoes, but sufficient warning had been given for none of the weapons to claim a ship and the Wildcats bagged three of the attackers as well as two probables and a possible. The remainder of the convoy eventually reached Loch Ewe safely on 28 February, having sailed through more gales.

One final convoy sailed after VE-Day, JW/RA67 being escorted by *Queen* when it left Scapa on 14 May as a precaution in case a U-boat commander had it in mind to violate the German surrender. Fortunately no trouble was encountered, though the Avenger and Wildcats of No. 853 Squadron carried out a number of protective patrols.

▼ Wildcats and Avengers of No. 846 Squadron on the icy deck of *Trumpeter* during a North Russian convoy in March 1945. (Peter Ames)

CHAPTER 18

Tirpitz Operations

With the losses of first the *Graf Spee* and then the *Bismarck* the main strength of the German Navy became somewhat depleted, but it nevertheless remained a formidable opponent for the Royal Navy. Foremost among its armoury was the battleship *Tirpitz*, which might at any time sail out to decimate Atlantic and Arctic convoys. Throughout the war a number of attempts were made to prevent this happening by both the Royal Air Force and the Royal Navy, the latter service being first involved in March 1942 during the passage of Arctic convoy PQ12. Air cover for this was provided by the fleet carrier *Victorious*, which had aboard her the Albacores of Nos. 817 and 832 Squadrons and the Fulmars of No. 809 Squadron. Word came through on 7 March that *Tirpitz* had broken out of her refuge at Trondheim and was thought to be somewhere in the area of the convoy. The Albacores made efforts to sight her, as did the two spotting Walruses of No. 700 Squadron aboard the cruiser *Kenya*, but it was not until two days later that their efforts were rewarded.

At 0630, having received further news of the enemy ship being in the vicinity, six Albacores took off to search for her. Just over an hour later they were followed by twelve similar

▼ Wildcat pilots of No. 882 Squadron aboard the escort carrier *Searcher* are briefed for a flak-suppression mission prior to the first strike against *Tirpitz* in Norwegian waters. (RAF Museum)

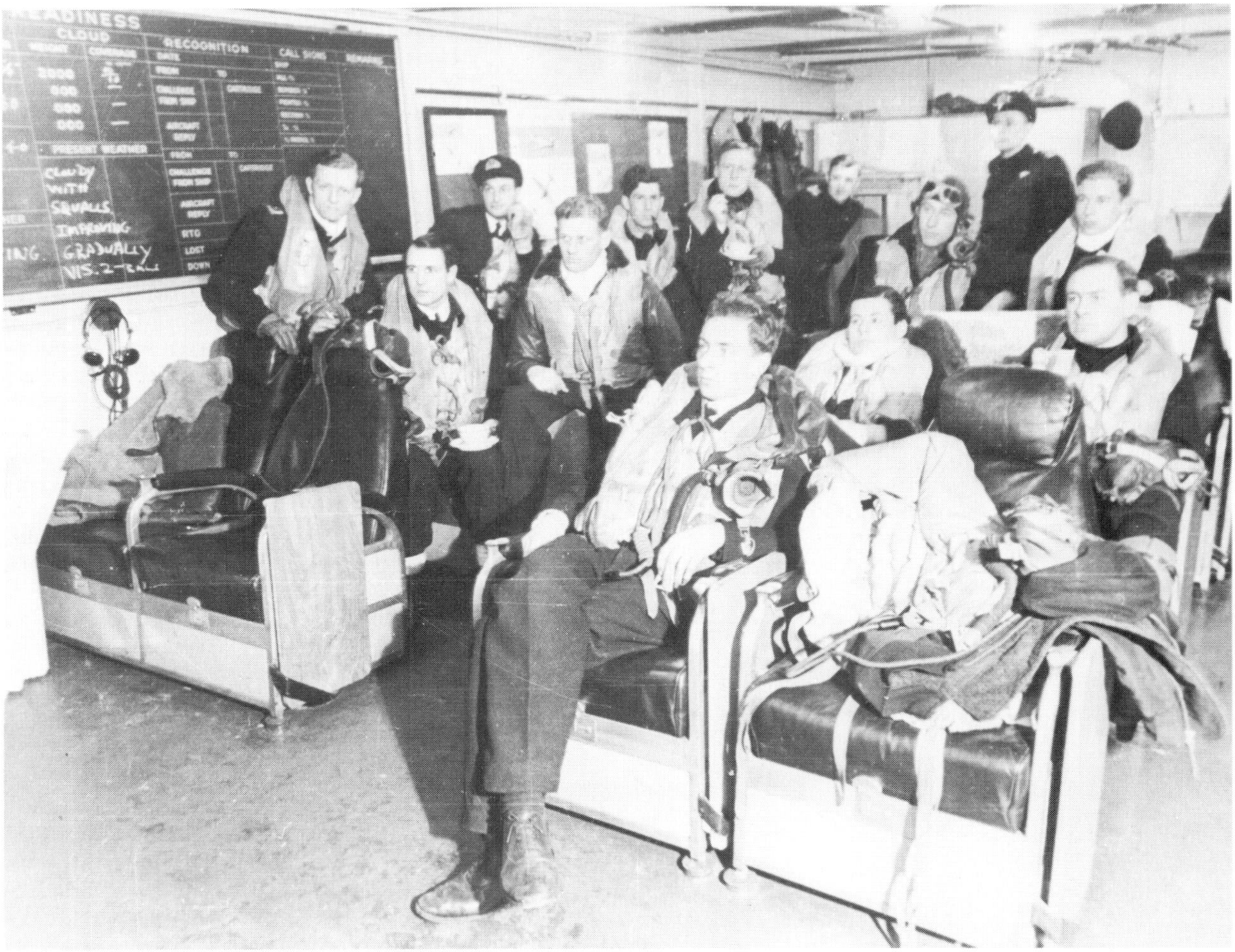

aircraft from both squadrons, loaded up with torpedoes and led by Lt Cdr W. J. Lucas, RN, the Commanding Officer of No. 832 Squadron. The first sighting was made at 0815 by aircraft '4F' of No. 832 Squadron and soon afterwards the attacking aircraft started to climb above the cloud. The sub-flights were ordered to attack independently and the first three dived on to the starboard bow amid heavy flak, dropping their torpedoes on the port bow as the ship came towards them at a range of around 1,000yds. The other three sub-flights followed in quick succession but had difficulty seeing their target because of thick smoke and two aircraft were shot down after completing their attack. The manoeuvring by the enemy ship succeeded in avoiding all the missiles, and *Tirpitz* then made for Vestfjord, which she reached only two hours after the raid, depriving the Fleet Air Arm of the opportunity of a second strike.

This extract from No. 832 Squadron's diary tells the story of that day's events:

> *9 March 1942.* We were woken at 0530 and we knew something was in the wind. Apparently a signal had been received early that morning giving a position of the *Tirpitz*. The search aircraft took off at 0630. The crews were Sub-Lts Miller, Browne and LA Lindley; Sub-Lts Willott, Barnes and LA Gibbs; Sub-Lts Connolly, Harvey and LA Pert. The striking force consisted of '4A', '4B' and '4C' normal crews, '4M' (Sub-Lts O'Shea, Johnson and LA Robertson), '4R' (Lts Stenning, Friend and LA Vaughan), '4P' (Sub-Lts Shepherd, Brown L and LA Hollowood) and '4G' (Sub-Lts Eyre, Shaw and LA Lovell).
>
> At 0735 the striking force, accompanied by five aircraft of No. 817, took off (the approx position of take-off was 69° N 6' E). After forming up on the port bow the formation (832 and 817) set course 120° N, which if we saw nothing would eventually take us to Røstoy Island. However we hadn't been in the air more than 40 minutes when at 0815 we received the first sighting report of the enemy from aircraft '4F'. This was followed by our first amplifying report, giving the position, course and speed of the *Tirpitz*. The great accuracy of these reports soon enabled Lt George in aircraft '4A' to pick the enemy up on their ASV. At 0840 the *Tirpitz* was sighted on the starboard bow.
>
> The weather had cleared considerably by then and visibility was anything up to 30 miles. Cloud base was at 4,000 feet. The squadron started to climb and soon we were above the clouds with the *Tirpitz* about 15 miles away. The order 'sub flights act independently' was given and the four sub-flights widened out. We were guided on to the target by ASV but at 0920 the first sub-flight '4A', '4B' and '4C' dived to the attack with the enemy on its starboard bow below. As soon as the first sub-flight came out of the clouds the enemy opened fire and they encountered heavy flak during the dive. They dropped on the port bow at approx. 1,000 yards with the *Tirpitz* turning towards them.
>
> The second, third and fourth sub-flights then dived to the attack, just after the first sub-flight had successfully turned away. No. 4 sub-flight followed the first sub-flight down and dropped on the port beam as the ship was steadying up from her vigorous turn to port. This was followed up by Nos. 2 and 3 sub-flights who came in out of the sun on the starboard side of the enemy who put the wheel hard over to starboard, and appeared to avoid all torpedoes. The target was thickly obscured by smoke and it is doubtful that a hit would have been seen. During the attack '4P' was hit and crashed into the sea. One aircraft of No. 817 was also hit and set on fire and likewise crashed. We set course for the carrier and landed on at 1030.

This turned out to be the only time *Tirpitz* was ever caught in the open sea. She was rightly regarded by the Germans as a big enough threat by her very presence and was prudently ordered to remain in shelter in future whenever British carriers were in the immediate area. She did come out once, for a planned attack on the ill-fated PQ17 convoy, but hastily turned about on learning that *Victorious* was with the Home Fleet.

The next opportunity arose early in 1943, when it was proposed to mount a night attack by Swordfish from *Dasher*. The planned raid on the enemy ship in her lair at Altenfjord never materialized, however, as on 27 March the escort carrier blew up suddenly while off the Isle of Arran in the Firth of Clyde. The loss was afterwards ascribed to an avgas explosion.

Another year was to pass before a fresh attack could be mounted, this time in much greater strength, under the code-name Operation 'Tungsten'. By now more modern aircraft were available in the shape of Fairey Barracudas, and these practised on a dummy target in the seven-mile-long Loch Eriboll in north-west Scotland. Two TBR wings were involved, the 8th and 52nd, their four squadrons being regrouped for the raid to allow each wing to take off simultaneously from the two carriers involved, Nos. 830 and 831 embarking in *Furious* and Nos. 827 and 829 in *Victorious*. Extensive fighter cover was to be provided by Vought Corsairs of the 47th Wing in *Victorious* and Seafires of Nos. 801 and 880 Squadrons in the other carrier, as well as Hellcats and Wildcats from the escort carriers *Emperor*, *Fencer*, *Pursuer* and *Searcher*. Anti-submarine patrols would be carried out by No. 842 Squadron Swordfish in *Fencer*.

As a subterfuge, *Victorious* and her accompanying ships, known as Force I, at first pretended to be acting as escort for the outward-bound convoy JW58, sailing from Scapa on 30 March 1944; Force II, which included *Furious*, sailed at the same time but by a more direct route. In the afternoon of 2 April the two Forces came together, then re-formed and were renamed, the two fleet carriers then joining Force 7 and the escort carriers Force 8. The first Barracudas to take off from the two larger carriers were those of the 8th Wing, which departed at 0424 next day, shortly after their escort of No. 1834 Squadron Corsairs. Fighters taking off from all the escort carriers around the same time formed a massive display of discouragement for the enemy.

Tirpitz was still in Altenfjord, and as luck would have it she was on the point of leaving her anchorage there for the first time in six months, having spent that time being repaired after a midget-submarine attack. Caught by surprise, she was destined never to make this trip. She had no time to put up a protective smokescreen and the Hellcat and Wildcat pilots were given a clear view of her as they came down over the surrounding hills to machine-gun the battleship and nearby flak emplacements, the Corsairs remaining high at 10,000ft as a precaution against the appearance of enemy fighters.

This was the opportunity for which the Fleet Air Arm had long waited and they made the most of it, the first wave of Barracudas, led by Lt Cdr R. S. Baker-Falkner, DSC, RN, diving down to score six direct hits with its bombs. By this time the second wave was on its way, similarly escorted, and these aircraft too had a field day (despite a smokescreen having been put up in the meantime), scoring eight further direct hits with several other probables in the two raids. Considering the circumstances the losses were minimal, only two Barracudas failing to return. The aircraft had done their work so well that a further strike planned for the following day was called off, which was something of a relief to the jubilant but exhausted crews.

Tirpitz was now down but by no means out, and more effort was called for in the following months. Poor weather led to the cancellation of a proposed raid on 26 April, and on 15 May Barracudas from *Furious* and *Victorious* were

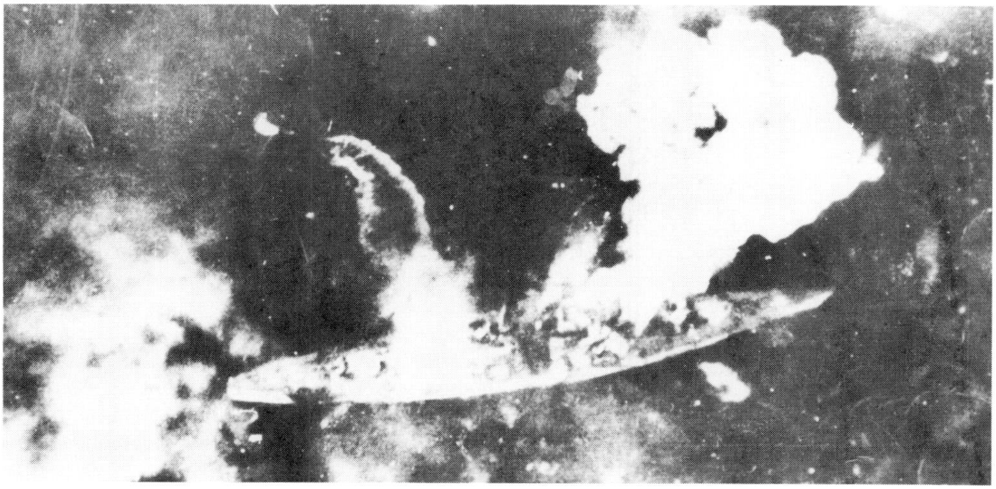

► ***Tirpitz*** **under attack during Operation 'Mascot'. (Via Dennis Phillips)**

◄ **An early example of a 'ski-jump'. A Barracuda of No. 830 Squadron, heavily laden with a 1,600lb bomb, about to take off up a special ramp aboard HMS *Furious* for the Operation 'Mascot' raid against *Tirpitz* on 17 July 1944. (FAA Museum)**

recalled when on the way to their target, which was obscured by heavy cloud. Bad weather similarly prevented a planned raid on 28 May.

By mid-summer, however, conditions had improved and it was possible to mount a further strike on 17 July 1944 under the code-name Operation 'Mascot'. Again using Barracudas, the carriers this time were *Formidable*, *Furious* and the recently completed *Indefatigable*, no escort carriers being involved on this occasion. Fighter support was to include No. 1841 Squadron Corsairs aboard *Formidable* and the new Fairey Fireflies of No. 1770 Squadron aboard *Indefatigable* as well as Seafires and Hellcats from *Furious*. Anti-submarine patrols were again provided by three Swordfish of No. 842 Squadron, now with *Fencer*. The Germans, however, had learned from their previous experience and erected an observation point on one of the nearby mountains. As soon as the striking force of 44 Barracudas and 48 escorting fighters was spotted, word was relayed to the ship, which promptly put up a thick pall of smoke with the result that the best the attackers could achieve was one near-miss.

Further strikes were planned for late August, under the code-name Operation 'Goodwood'. Again four Barracuda squadrons were involved, Nos. 826 and 828 (*Formidable*), No. 827 (*Furious*) and No. 820 (*Indefatigable*), the ships also carrying an impressive array of Corsairs, Seafires, Hellcats and Fireflies; two escort carriers were available in the shape of *Nabob* and *Trumpeter* carrying Avengers and Wildcats. The first strike ('Goodwood I'), on the 22nd, was totally unsuccessful, the Barracudas being unable to reach their target because of cloud, and although the Hellcats dropped their bombs hopefully through this they achieved nothing. An evening strike by the Hellcats alone ('Goodwood II') was equally abortive and the day was sadly marked by *Nabob* becoming a casualty after being hit by an acoustic torpedo from *U-354*. Somehow the ship managed to limp back home after a voyage of more than 1,000 miles but she never saw action again.

Rather more successful was 'Goodwood III,' on the 24th, when 33 Barracudas carrying 1,600lb armour-piercing bombs and some Hellcats and Corsairs carrying smaller bombs succeeded in attacking from several directions in order to confuse the AA fire. Despite the now inevitable smokescreen the ship was hit by a 500lb bomb and a 1,600lb bomb, the latter successfully penetrating the armoured decking. It should have inflicted considerable damage, and might possibly have sunk the ship, but it failed to explode – a frustrating outcome for the air crews who had at last reached their target only to have all their efforts wasted by a faulty missile.

Bad weather prevented further attempts during the next few days but a final raid ('Goodwood IV') was possible on the 29th. Once more it was the same old story, however, the enemy gaining sufficient warning to be able to put up a thick smokescreen and the consequent blind bombing all being wide of the target. It was left to the RAF to finish the task, *Tirpitz* finally ending her life at the hands of 12,000lb 'Tallboy' bombs dropped on 12 November 1944 by RAF Lancasters of Nos. 9 and 617 Squadrons (the latter the famous 'Dambusters'). It is debatable, however, whether the enemy ship would have been available to them as a static target but for the earlier efforts of the Fleet Air Arm.

CHAPTER 19

MAC-Ships

Early in 1943 a new type of aircraft-carrying ship appeared on the scene. A year earlier the Admiralty had decided to augment the air cover afforded to Atlantic convoys by introducing dual-purpose ships. Two grain-carriers were to be modified by fitting them with a flight deck and hangar and a minimal amount of operating equipment. These ships, intended to travel in the main body of the convoy rather than with the escorting warships, would carry their normal cargoes and were given the designation merchant aircraft carriers, soon shortened to MAC-ships.

The first such conversion, *Empire MacAlpine*, was launched on 23 December 1942 and commissioned on 14 April 1943. She sailed for Halifax on 29 May with westbound Atlantic convoy ONS9, carrying four Swordfish of No. 836 Squadron, which then had its headquarters based temporarily at Ballyhalbert in Northern Ireland. The vessel was involved a month later in a collision with the merchantman *Empire Ibex* in a return convoy but was repaired and continued to operate until the end of the war when it was reconverted to become the MV *Derrynane*.

Swordfish were used exclusively for this work, three or four aircraft being carried on each MAC-ship, and proved a highly successful deterrent. At first each ship was to be served by a different squadron: when *Empire MacAndrew* sailed in July 1943 she had four Swordfish of No. 840 Squadron aboard, whilst No. 838 Squadron embarked all its four aircraft in *Rapana* for trials on 2 August. However, further MAC-ships were by then under conversion, some of these being tankers, and the organization threatened to become too complex. Accordingly the aircraft were all put under the parentage of No. 836 Squadron, Nos. 838 and 840 being disbanded on 13 August to become flights within No. 836, which now had its headquarters at Maydown near Londonderry. Also absorbing elements of Nos. 833 and 834 Squadrons, No. 836 had an initial strength of 27 aircraft, this figure increasing rapidly over the next few months as further MAC-ships commissioned so that 80 aircraft were on strength by early 1944 to man a total of nineteen vessels. There was a single exception to the amalgamation. In June 1943 No. 860 Squadron had formed with Dutch crews to operate from the Dutch tanker MAC-ships *Gadila*, *Macoma* and *Acavus* and it was allowed to retain its separate identity though soon came within the general control of No. 836. The MAC-ship flights, each with three or four aircraft, were allocated separate identification letters between 'A' and 'Z', the flight letters 'F', 'O' and 'Z' being earmarked for the three components of No. 860 Squadron.

The new ships were an immediate success. The role of their aircraft was primarily to keep U-boats away from convoys and so prevent them from having an opportunity to attack, and the effectiveness of the concept was such that, throughout the remainder of the war, no U-boat ever made a successful attack against a convoy which included a MAC-ship. Although no U-boats were sunk outright, many were sighted and twelve direct attacks were made. One Free French submarine was sunk – *La Perle* on 8 July 1944 by an aircraft of 'T' Flight from MV *Empire MacCallum*. The last contact made between a U-boat and a MAC-ship aircraft appears to have been on 20 April 1945 when an aircraft of 'Z' Flight from MV *Empire MacAndrew*, with convoy ON298, dropped two depth-charges on a periscope sighting position.

The hazards of this aspect of the Fleet Air Arm's wartime activities are well illustrated in this account of an incident on 26 June 1944 by John Treble, who was then the senior observer of 'V' Flight on board MV *Acavus*, serving under Lt (A) A. E. Payne, RNVR:

> On the night of 25th June 1944, in a westbound convoy on the Grand Banks about three days out from Halifax, we received a situation report that a dozen U-boats were within 80 miles of the convoy. Sub-Lt Nick Carter, our batsman, was due to fly next and Ted Payne, the CO, who was my regular pilot, was to take his turn at batting. To fly off its hours to inspection, Swordfish 'V1' (LS436), my own kite, was to be flown and Wally Martin, the air gunner, and myself were to go with Nick.
>
> We'd had some experience of the weather off the Grand Banks, particularly the fog blankets which could arise almost instantaneously and

▲ **The view from the rear cockpit of a Swordfish of 'B' Flight of No. 836 Squadron just after take-off from MV *Empire MacDermott*. The photograph was taken shortly before VE-Day. (G. E. Legg)**

without warning, but the Air Staff Officer's qualms on that score were outweighed by the possibilities of a sighting. At 0200, although there was no horizon, the stars were visble, and it was decided we should fly, but we were warned to scuttle for home if the visibility worsened. 'V1' and 'V3' flew off in the dark at 0245, the convoy going 230° at 9½ knots, the wind 165° at 9 knots. The *Adula* also flew off two aircraft. We were carrying a full load of rockets with a depth charge in the crutch and the plane would only cruise decently at 70 knots. First track was 097 for 80 miles. The weather was hazy but dawn was approaching and seemed to promise an improvement. There was plenty of low cloud and we had to fly at 200 feet. In view of our low speed and the ever-present possibility of fog I decided to cut down our main leg to 60 miles. After 40 miles we noticed layers of cloud forming into sheets below us. I pointed this out to Nick, saying I thought it was a big fog forming and suggested we should return. Nick thought we should press on for a little while, but after a few minutes the weather closed in completely and so I gave him a course back to the ship, which was then some 55 miles away, and sent a signal 'Unfit returning'.

About eight minutes after turning we started to fly out of the fog into quite clear weather. However, we then received a signal from the ship ordering us to return, but I could not tell whether it had been sent on the strength of my message or conditions at the ship. The *Adula*'s aircraft were out of touch and we attempted to pass the message through to them.

At 40 miles I picked up the radar beacon on my ASV radar, headed the aircraft on to it for home and sent my ETA. The pilot dropped his depth charge and I removed the rocket projectile fuses. (This latter seemed doubtful in the light of after events but I certainly recall it although it may have only been my thoughts and not my deeds.)

Acavus told us on the R/T that she was clear astern of the convoy and ready to talk us on. Nick set the ship's course on his gyro and I tried conning him down on the BABS. This was a blind landing scan using the ASV screen, little tried and less trusted, but since visibility was virtually nil there was nothing else.

At nine miles from the ship we ran into really thick weather which shook us somewhat. It seemed to be solid fog from sea level up to 400 feet. We asked for a QFE, set the pilot's altimeter and he managed to find a slit in the muck and descend to a minimum safe height which would clear any shipping. The fog now was very dense and we must have homed from downwind to within 100 yards of the ship without seeing anything. I got the pilot to steer further downwind so that we could turn and approach the ship in the proper direction. Such a course would take us into the convoy, but since we thought the altimeter would be correct Nick flew sufficiently high to clear any masts and it didn't matter. Our first indication of altimeter trouble was when the pilot and gunner saw part of a ship. Only its bows with a gun platform on it could be seen in the fog. It was very close indeed and apparently at the same level or above us. The pilot pulled up and reset his altimeter by estimation from this event.

We then homed again on to the ship using the 2-mile scale and descending as the range decreased. This time we saw part of the ship as we went dead over her but in the fog only about a third of the deck was visible at a time. We went away downwind once more and homed again. We sighted some smoke floats giving the width of the ship but saw no wake or streamer although she was very near. We flew past without seeing her and Nick did a 360-degree turn to bring us round on to her again. He lifted the nose high up into a deck landing position and descended with the intention of crash landing or ditching alongside if we couldn't make the ship.

We were very near the ship – I estimated about 250 yards by radar – and I left the screen to brace myself for whatever was coming. We hit without warning, very gently: the pilot just saw it coming, gave the kite full engine and brought the tail down hard. In accordance with normal practice the AG and I had our harness off and were not strapped in. He was thrown out forward as we touched, and hit the sea unhurt about 40 feet ahead of the plane. There was no water in my cockpit and I pulled my Mae West and grabbed the dinghy. I looked over at the pilot who was also unhurt and was tucked well down in the cockpit trying to sort out his dinghy. We both saw the aircraft dinghy emerge from the upper wing and I shouted to Nick to get out, swimming away on the starboard quarter as I was afraid of getting caught up. Nick seemed to be taking far too long and I shouted at him again to get clear and swim out in the open.

My Mae West hadn't inflated. I tried to blow it up but it needed far too much effort for a guy in the water. Fortunately I had partially inflated it in the cockpit and this helped a bit. I could see Martin up forward and he too looked OK and well clear. Then several distinct flames and puffs of smoke went off in succession on the port wing and I rather think some went off to starboard as well. I supposed it was the rockets and I remember wondering whether they would drill Martin. They didn't. I saw some smoke floats astern and tried to get to them as

► A welcome sight. A US Navy 'blimp' comes out to take over the anti-submarine task from the Swordfish of 'A' Flight, No. 836 Squadron, as MV *Empire McCabe* approaches New York towards the end of 1944. (Vic Smith)

▼ Swordfish LS218 'D3' of 'D' Flight, No. 836 Squadron, was one of the aircraft damaged during bad weather in the deck park on MV *Empire MacKay* when the ship rolled heavily on 26 December 1943. (Dennis Foley)

I'd heard they were good flotation aids. But as I touched them they kept spinning away. The aiming vanes were off at least two of them but they hadn't detonated.

Then the kite nosed over and went down, I think it took less than a minute. I'd had no sensation of alarm or of the severe cold and wet and fully appreciated that I must get to the dinghy quickly. I'd wasted energy trying to get to the smoke floats and turned towards the dinghy. My Mae West wasn't very buoyant and I must have naturally turned over on to my stomach and tried to breast-stroke towards the dinghy. I saw it was upside down and Nick the AG was there trying to right it. It must have been about 30 yards from me and I was getting nowhere with my breast strokes. Then I got wise and turned over onto my back, making better progress. The cold water was getting me and I felt pretty tried. I rested and promptly went under. That shook me up and I thrashed out and caught hold of the dinghy. Martin was in it with Nick around the other side. By now the water had got Nick and I, and I couldn't move my legs from the hips. My fingers wouldn't grip but they bent and jammed on the beckets and held me. I couldn't raise myself into the dinghy but I could still bellow for a haul and this seemed to give the others the strength to heave me aboard.

There were ice floes around and the water was very cold. We had been told that survival time if wet was a matter of minutes and were relieved to find, although we couldn't feel much, that only a little sea had got inside our Sidcots. The emergency pack had broken away from the dinghy and we could do nothing to repair a small leak which kept bubbling noisily. We huddled together frozen literally stiff and forcing each other to stay awake. The fog stayed with us and fortunately the sea was calm.

After eleven hours, with only seagulls for company, by sheer luck we were eventually picked up by the Canadian frigate HMCS *Montreal*, which nearly overran us, and taken to hospital in St. Johns, Newfoundland. The ordeal by cold water was still not over since in hospital we were laid out naked with electric fans blowing on us over blocks of ice to slow down the thawing process. It was nice when it stopped! The greatest thing was to get back to the *Acavus* before it left Halifax for home. After some days we discharged ourselves and scrounged lifts on a Dakota, and then by train, getting back to 'V' flight just before she sailed.

No. 836 Squadron ceased to exist soon after VE-Day and all her Swordfish were sent to Barton, near Manchester, for breaking up, but No. 860 re-equipped with Barracudas and was transferred to the Dutch Navy. Most of the MAC-ships were in relatively good condition and within a year or two they had been reconverted to merchant vessels, some surviving well into the 1960s under various names.

CHAPTER 20

Back to the Continent

By the spring of 1944 British and American forces had built up sufficiently in the United Kingdom for the long-awaited invasion of Europe to become a reality. The Royal Navy would have a major part to play, especially in the initial landings, and the Fleet Air Arm was to be given several vital tasks.

In preparation, four RAF bases on the south coast were taken over during April and May by General Reconnaissance Wings of Coastal Command, whose units included FAA Avenger and Swordfish squadrons which would be land-based for several months. For operations in the English Channel Nos. 155 and 157 Wings flew respectively from Manston and Hawkinge in Kent. No. 155 was essentially a Beaufighter squadron but also included the Avengers of No. 848 Squadron and the Swordfish of No. 819 Squadron, whilst No. 157 Wing had the Avengers of Nos. 854 and 855 Squadrons, these being later replaced by No. 819 Squadron Swordfish and an RAF Albacore squadron. In the south-west, Harrowbeer and Perranporth were used, the former by the Swordfish of No. 838 Squadron in No. 156 Wing and the latter by the Swordfish of No. 816 Squadron and the Avengers of Nos. 849 and 850 Squadrons.

Operating off the coasts of Belgium, France and Holland, the aircraft executed a considerable number of shipping strikes and attacks on E-boats in addition to carrying out anti-submarine sorties and other varied tasks. At Manston No. 819 Squadron Swordfish had the advantage of new ASV Mk. X radar in radomes under their fuselages, enabling the operators to have a panoramic display of a wide area of coastline and of any ships present. This squadron also had the task of laying a smokescreen over the Allied invasion fleet on D-Day.

For a time several naval fighter squadrons were also involved. At Culmhead in Somerset the 24th Naval Fighter Wing under Lt Cdr N. G. Hallett, RN, which comprised Nos. 887 and 894 Squadrons equipped with Seafire IIIs, spent three weeks during April and May escorting RAF Typhoons on softening-up sweeps over Normandy and Brittany, on occasion operating independently of the RAF aircraft. During the actual invasion the several Seafire and Spitfire-equipped squadrons of the 3rd Naval Fighter Wing were to operate from Lee-on-Solent as an Air Spotting Pool, having earlier undergone special bombardment spotting and tactical reconnaissance training.

►Rocket-equipped Swordfish of No. 816 Squadron, resplendent in invasion stripes, undertook Channel operations around D-Day from their base at Perranporth in Cornwall. (P. Snow)

◄One of a number of black-painted Swordfish which carried out night patrols over the English Channel around D-Day. (Vic Smith)

Together with the Spitfire-equipped Nos. 26 and 63 Squadrons RAF, and VCS-7 of the US Navy, these made up the 34th Tactical Reconnaissance Wing of the 2nd Tactical Air Force.

In an attempt to avoid tragic errors in identification by 'friendly' gunners and air crew, all Allied aircraft operating in the invasion area were painted on the eve of battle with broad black and white bands on the wings and fuselage. The first two spotting Seafires took off from Lee at 0441 on D-Day, 6 June 1944, and by the end of that day the 3rd Wing had carried out 153 sorties out of a total of 435 performed by aircraft operating from that grossly overcrowded station. Inevitably there were losses, one being Sub-Lt (A) H. A. Cogill, RNVR, of No. 808 Squadron, flying Spitfire EN821, whose machine was hit by an enemy aircraft; he failed to escape as it dived into the sea. Another loss was Sub-Lt (A) A. H. Bassett, RNVR, of No. 885 Squadron in Seafire NF533, shot down by enemy flak over France, but more fortunate was Lt (A) W. A. Wallace, RNVR, who was picked up by an American headquarters ship when his Seafire NF537 crash-landed after being hit by light flak. Another survivor was Lt (A) C. L. Metcalf, RNVR, who escaped with only a broken arm when he had to bale out of his Seafire over the Isle of Wight.

Operations continued the next day, with instructions now to avoid attacking defended targets in order to concentrate more economically on the main spotting task. Several more aircraft were lost, including Seafire NF541 of No. 886 Squadron piloted by Lt (A) D. B. Law, RNVR, who had been spotting for a naval vessel before he was hit by flak; he survived the crash-landing and five days later was back in action. Not so lucky was Lee-on-Solent's Commander Flying, Cdr (A) J. M. Keene-Miller, RNVR, flying Seafire NF486 of No. 808 Squadron, who was shot down too far away from the Allied beach-head and was taken prisoner.

Not all the losses were due to enemy action, despite the distinctive black and white stripes. On D-Day plus one Lt Cdr P. E. I. Bailey, RN, the CO of No. 886 Squadron, in Seafire NF534, was hit by fire from Allied ships and forced to bail out. Fortunately he landed on an Allied beach, his only injury being a sprained ankle from a land-mine which he set off. On 10 June Sub-Lt (A) R. G. Kennett, RNVR, of No. 885 Squadron, in Seafire NF542, was attacked by enemy aircraft and lost his life when he crashed in the sea off Deauville.

By the time the 3rd Wing was withdrawn on 15 July it had carried out 1,230 sorties for the loss of only fourteen aircraft, four pilots having been killed, two being missing and one having been taken prisoner. The airfield had an equally impressive record, having handled 2,223 operational sorties between D-Day and the end of June with only one minor landing accident.

One of those involved with No. 808 Squadron was Lt (A) A. W. Bradley, RNZNVR, who carried out a number of flights between D-Day and 13 July, including spotting sorties for naval ship gunnery, resulting on eight occasions in the destruction of the enemy gun positions concerned. On 8 July, when he flew Spitfire EN964 '1H', his log book records 'Anti midget submarine patrol. Scored hits. Kill. By minesweeper.' The submarine had been sighted in the Le Havre estuary and was damaged by fire from his aircraft, being later destroyed by a minesweeper. Of subsequent events, he recalls:

> At the completion of spotter duties, the four naval squadrons which had been involved were either disbanded or re-equipped with newer aircraft. All No. 808's Spitfires had to be returned to RNAS Lee-on-Solent. We took off from RAF Ballyhalbert, Northern Ireland, in

◀ **Lt (A) A. W. Bradley, RNZVR, of No. 808 Squadron, seen here in the cockpit of his Spitfire, attacked and hit a midget submarine in the Le Havre estuary. (A. W. Bradley)**

pairs. However, myself and my wing man were forced to land at RAF Calveley, in Shropshire, due to heavy fog. Next morning we obtained our met report for the rest of our journey and were advised that six-tenths cloud would prevail for a short time, patches of fog up to 5,000 feet for another 50 miles and clear beyond.

So much for met reports! We experienced scattered cloud all right, but they didn't tell us that it would be a solid cloud bank up to 11,000 feet! We hit the cloud bank, me keeping an eye on my wing man (very difficult to see), called him on my R/T – no response. I later found that my radio was not receiving. I pushed on up through the cloud mass, breaking clear at 11,000 feet with a brilliant blue sky and not a cloud to be seen!

OK. I had an idea about where I was, but without confirmation. I checked my petrol gauges and realized that if I didn't get down soon that was it. I decided to do a square search, reducing time on each leg, but found nothing. I extended my last leg time in the same direction, and was being prepared to bale out, as my petrol was getting too low to proceed. All sorts of things were going through my mind – including how to bale out. I knew all along, of course, but when it comes to making up my mind to do it . . .!

Well, my worry was solved shortly afterwards. I saw a hole in the cloud, put my wheels and flaps down and proceeded to keep an opening in sight. My blood pressure was well up by that time, and then it happened – I broke cloud base and in a short distance saw a wind sock! Into fine pitch and across the grass, across wind, and taxied up to the control tower. A squadron leader in dark blue uniform came down to get me in my Spitfire. Alas, I knew the uniform – that of a bloody Aussie! When he saw me with my New Zealand shoulder tabs up, he said 'I know Kiwis can't fly, but this is ridiculous. This is RAF Edgehill, the highest drome in England, and is an RAAF Operational Training Unit, using Wellingtons, and we haven't flown for four days, and you just pop down out of the clouds and make bloody fools of us!'

Well, eventually I carried my procedures out, duly informing Lee-on-Solent of my whereabouts. Apparently my wingman had opted out of the clouds and landed at an American Air Force aerodrome. We eventually checked my radio and repaired it, filled my tanks with petrol and parked my Spit. The Aussies gave me hell that night in the mess. I think I got rather plastered. Morning duly arrived and I said goodbye to my newly acquired Aussie mates then headed for Lee-on-Solent, dodging the barrage balloons as I arrived.

The squadrons attached to Coastal Command continued to operate for a time, but No. 156 Wing disbanded on 8 August, followed on 19 September by No. 155 Wing. No. 157 Wing, however, remained in existence, moving to the Continent to operate its Swordfish from an aerodrome on the Belgian coast until after VE-Day.

▼ **A still shot from the cine film taken by Lt (A) A. W. Bradley, RNZNVR, during an attack in his Seafire on a midget submarine in the Le Havre estuary, 8 July 1944. The submarine was subsequently finished off by a minesweeper (A. W. Bradley)**

CHAPTER 21

Japan Enters the War

A day which will live for ever in the annals of naval history is 7 December 1941, when the Japanese Fleet, in a surprise air raid on America's Hawaiian naval base at Pearl Harbor, wiped out a large proportion of the US Navy before war had been declared. At a stroke, the long-feared threat to British bases in the Far East became a reality and, Singapore being too vulnerable, Colombo, in what was then Ceylon (now Sri Lanka), became the main base for the Eastern Fleet, commanded by Admiral Sir James Somerville. Within four months this fleet could boast ninety carrier-borne aircraft in eight squadrons, aboard the three carriers *Formidable*, *Hermes* and *Indomitable*, with a further three squadrons ashore.

Bill Crozer, then a petty officer, was involved very early with the Japanese, being at that time the pilot of a Walrus (R6587) aboard HMS *Repulse*, with PO Damerell as observer and LA Rose as air gunner:

> The ship sailed at 1730 on 8 December 1941 from Singapore, which had been bombed by the Japanese earlier in the day. She was in company with *Prince of Wales* and several other British and Australian warships. Next day we were given an evening briefing and told to stand by for a catapult launch at first light.
>
> At 0900 on 10 December we were launched to search for possible landings at Kuantan and to carry out an anti-submarine patrol, being instructed to maintain radio silence. We spotted only one merchant ship and saw no sign of any invasion. At about 1115, however, we made a distant sighting of what could have been a number of small ships or barges, so we closed on *Repulse* and from a height of about 1,500 feet requested instructions using an Aldis lamp. An enemy bomber formation then approached at above 10,000 feet and the ship's anti-aircraft guns opened fire. We promptly dived to sea level between the fleet, only to be fired on by one of our own destroyers, so we circled the fleet and then climbed to 1,000 feet.
>
> We saw the first salvo of bombs envelope *Repulse* but she appeared to be all right except for some smoke from the catapult deck. We decided to clear the fleet and make a decision as to whether to stay with it or return to Singapore while we still had sufficient fuel. We then saw the first torpedo attack take place, though at the time we thought it was a low-level bomb attack as drops were being made at about 500 feet and at quite high speed. Two of the Japanese aircraft appeared to have been shot down and we thought *Prince of Wales* might have been hit because of a sudden erratic turn with *Repulse* following.
>
> At about 1300 we decided to head for Singapore but we had stayed on the scene too long and were now short of fuel so we broke W/T silence to send a mayday signal to Singapore with our approximate position. We then force-landed on the sea between the coastline and Pulau Tioman island. After landing safely we decided that the Japanese might possibly have landed and occupied the coastline. We tried to sail away from the shore using a parachute, then attempted to paddle using emergency flares as makeshift paddles, but this was useless so we streamed sea anchors and settled to wait.
>
> Eventually a flying boat from Singapore passed over us, dropping some water cans in a Mae West, to which we then had to swim to recover. After dark the searching destroyer *Stronghold* made contact and we were taken in tow for Singapore. We all stayed in the Walrus but the weather deteriorated and the destroyer had to reduce speed from 8 knots to 4 knots. Her skipper finally decided this was too dangerous, due to the likelihood of Japanese submarines, and would therefore take us on board and abandon our aircraft. However, the Walrus was equipped with what was probably the only ASV radar set in the Far East at that time so on second thoughts it was proposed to leave it on tow to take its chances. The destroyer then increased speed and eventually we arrived off the slipway at Seletar aerodrome, Singapore, after 12 hours in tow. Despite the buffeting it had received, the aircraft was still intact and was taken ashore. We had apparently been reported missing but we were able to join up with the survivors from our ship, which had been sunk, as had *Prince of Wales*.
>
> After servicing at Seletar we were able to air-test our Walrus but then only flew a few local trips due to our short range compared with the RAF Catalinas. The situation in Malaya was deteriorating meanwhile, and it was a great relief when HMS *Exeter* arrived, short of one aircraft and pilot, and I was ordered to join her with my aircraft. The ship was detailed to escort evacuation convoys heading for Java. Owing to W/T silence, and except for patrols, I was employed dropping weighted messages on the decks of convoy leaders giving navigation instructions etc.
>
> During a Japanese air attack off Sumatra, in

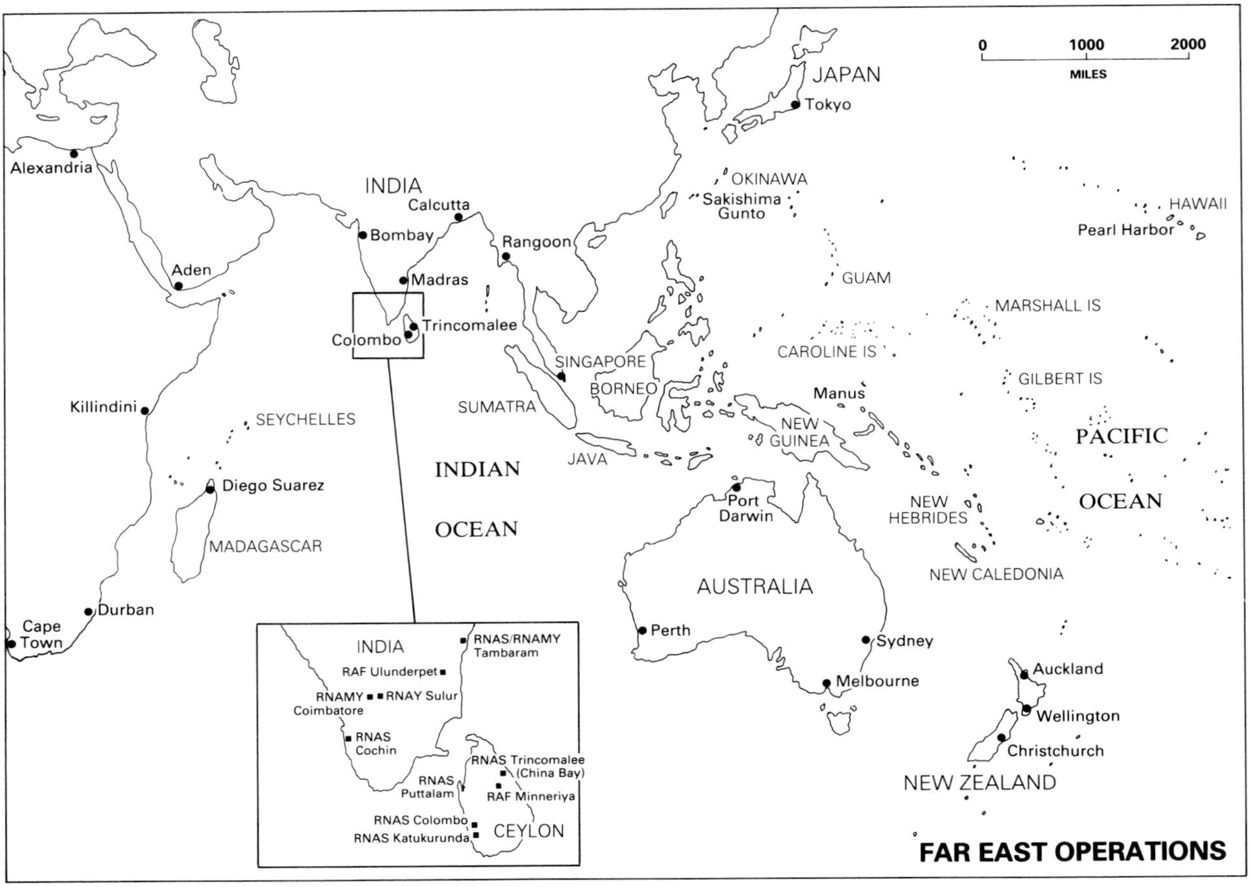

FAR EAST OPERATIONS

the Banka Straits, a near-miss severely damaged one set of mainplanes on my aircraft, which was on the catapult at the time. Arriving in Batavia, orders were given to disembark the damaged aircraft and one crew. As the opinion was that the Japanese would soon occupy Java it seemed likely that the disembarked crew would become, at the very least, prisoners-of-war. The other pilot (a petty officer named Blackwell, now deceased) tossed a coin and I lost. Ironically the *Exeter* was sunk in the Java Battle and Blackwell did four years as POW.

After a short spell in Java we were informed that if we could get the aircraft on board a 100-ton merchant ship called the *Bulan* we might be able to get back to Ceylon. Trouble arose with her Captain, who said the aircraft on deck would attract Japanese air attacks, but after great difficulty taxying with mainplanes on only one side the aircraft was hoisted aboard and covered with a tarpaulin. *Bulan* had a Chinese crew and was infested with large flying cockroaches. The proposed duration of the trip was seven to ten days, during which we were only allowed half a cup of water per day for all purposes, plus a rice ration. We spent most days in the aircraft hull, supplementing the diet with biscuits from the emergency rations, washed down with Drambuie supplied by Royal Marine commandos who were also aboard. We eventually arrived in Ceylon in early March 1942, there joining 'X' Swordfish Squadron, this being later designated No. 788 Squadron. The squadron had twelve Swordfish, of which six were detailed as torpedo-carriers and six as dive-bombers, myself being pilot of one of the latter.

On 5 April 1942 Japanese carriers arrived off Ceylon, making a strike that day on Colombo and later sinking the cruisers *Cornwall* and *Devonshire* in a dive-bombing attack. Following replenishment the Japanese fighters again struck at Ceylon, this time in the early morning of 9 April. However, a patrolling RAF Catalina reported the enemy fleet's apparent intention of attacking Trincomalee, and all shipping, including *Hermes*, was ordered to leave the anchorage. The carrier possessed no fighter aircraft and the Swordfish of No. 814 Squadron were ashore at the time. She was observed at sea by Japanese aircraft and later that day she, two escorting corvettes and two fleet auxiliaries were all sunk. *Hermes* was to be the only Royal Navy carrier sunk in an air attack. No. 814 Squadron remained ashore, available for anti-

► The French sloop *D'Entrecasteaux* after being sunk at Diego Suarez on 5 May 1942 by Swordfish of No. 829 Squadron from *Illustrious* during the invasion of Madagascar. (Reg Torrington via T. W. Boughton)

submarine duties until disbanded at the end of the year.

Bill Crozer says of this period:

> Our six torpedo-planes were shot down in the Easter Day raid on Colombo. Approximately 50 per cent of the air crew were killed and we heard that some of the bodies were recovered and buried by villagers north of Colombo. *Hermes* was sunk and oil tanks destroyed at China Bay. We searched for survivors from *Hermes*. Then *Warspite* arrived short of one aircraft and pilot, and as the only amphibious pilot on the island I went as replacement, later disembarking to the Seychelle Islands to carry out dawn and dusk patrols.

The Japanese carriers now switched their attention to the Pacific but it was feared that they might have set their sights on Madagascar, the large Vichy French island off the coast of East Africa. A Japanese occupation here had to be averted at all costs. The obvious way was to take possession first, and a combined operation was set up, to commence on 5 May 1942. At dawn that day aircraft from *Indomitable* carried out a surprise attack on local airfields, naval fighters preventing defending French fighters from taking off whilst the Albacores of Nos. 827 and 831 Squadrons created havoc on the airfield, setting fire to a hangar.

Spotting duties were carried out by the Walruses from the cruiser *Devonshire*, whilst *Illustrious*, which had sailed to the Indian Ocean from the United Kingdom two months earlier, covered the invasion area, her fighters keeping patrol overhead and her Swordfish attacking selected targets. One group of Swordfish attacked the French sloop *D'Entrecasteaux* and succeeded in blowing up the armed merchant cruiser *Bougainville*, whilst a second group sank the submarine *Bévézières* with depth-charges. A final group dropped leaflets and an ultimatum, then bombed a gun battery and carried out another attack on the now beached *D'Entrecasteaux*. A Swordfish of No. 810 Squadron and Albacore X8950 '5G' of No. 827 Squadron fell victim to defending AA fire but both crews were eventually rescued. Another submarine, *Le Héros*, was sunk by No. 829 Squadron after being caught at sea in the vicinity of the transport convoy.

The battle was not prolonged, the order to cease fire coming through on the afternoon of 7 May. This gave the Allied forces firm control of the whole of the whole northern end of the island since they had achieved their main objective, which was the capture of the large and important harbour at Diego Suarez. It was to be another four months, however, before the remainder of the island was subjugated, following a week of attacks on the southern end of the island in mid-September, the invasion force being covered by *Illustrious*. In the event the Japanese never put in an appearance.

Meanwhile the battered US Navy was heavily occupied in a fierce struggle for the islands in the Pacific, which were much coveted by the Japanese. Little enough could be spared at that stage of the war to help them but it was agreed to send *Victorious* when she emerged from a refit at Norfolk Navy Yard early in February 1943. Whilst there No. 832 Squadron re-equipped with US Navy Grumman TBF-1 Avengers, becoming the first Fleet Air Arm squadron to use this type. The carrier was delayed by damage caused when one of the Avengers crashed on deck after she arrived at Pearl Harbor, but in mid-May she finally arrived in New Caledonia, where she joined USS *Saratoga* at Noumea in Task Force 14.

In June Operation 'Toenail', an invasion of the Japanese-held island of New Georgia, was set in hand. Two carriers were available, and it was decided that all the strike squadrons, including the Avengers of No. 832 Squadron, would operate from *Saratoga*, whilst *Victorious* would take responsibility for the British and American fighter squadrons, all of which were equipped with Wildcats. The task force set sail on 27 June and during the course of the invasion the fighters flew over 600 sorties, the carriers being stationed 250–300 miles from the beaches. Little opposition was met and on 25 July the force was able to return to Noumea, the carriers then regaining their normal aircraft complements.

With the Japanese now on the defensive it was possible to build up British naval strength in Ceylon and southern India. A number of naval air stations were set up for operational training purposes, as were aircraft storage and maintenance units. At sea, trade protection for convoys was provided by CVEs in the area, namely *Battler*, *Atheling*, *Begum*, *Shah* and *Ameer* at various times between October 1943 and the end of 1944. The Swordfish of No. 834 Squadron aboard *Battler* were particularly successful, the German tanker *Brake* being located off Mauritius on 12 March 1944 and then sunk by HMS *Roebuck*; in addition, squadron aircraft sighted two U-boats, one being claimed as probably damaged by rocket projectiles.

Eric Morton was aboard *Battler* at that time:

> In March 1944 the chance for which the ship's company of *Battler* and air crew of No. 834 Squadron had been patiently waiting came at long last. We were the first escort carrier to be operational in the Indian Ocean and Bay of

► Swordfish HS164 '2F' of No. 810 Squadron from HMS *Illustrious* seen during the Madagascar operations. This aircraft was eventually lost when it had to ditch on 18 January 1943. (Cdr R. N. Everett)

▼ Swordfish HS665 of No. 834 Squadron about to take off from the flight deck of HMS *Battler*. (Via E. V. Morton)

Bengal and for months on end we carried out tedious routine A/S patrols from bases at Mombasa, Colombo and later Trincomalee.

No. 834 was a composite squadron of Swordfish and Wildcats (Martlets) and one day in March our patrolling aircraft sighted a ship with two refuelling U-boats alongside. This proved to be the German supply tanker *Brake* but, for some reason that we could never understand, when the sighting was reported, we were forbidden to attack.

Time dulls memory, but there was much anger, disappointment and a total lack of understanding over this lost opportunity. Our aircraft had a good chance of attacking and sinking this fairly easy target of supply ship and U-boats in such a vulnerable state, but no 'strike' could be flown off. There was, I recall, a near-mutiny amongst the incensed air crews, particularly amongst the RNZNVRs, of which there were several in the squadron – splendid chaps they were too.

Why had we not been permitted to do our job and attack, and why was this vital chance missed? Subsequently *Brake* was sunk by the destroyer HMS *Roebuck* but the U-boats had by then disappeared. Inevitably gossip was rife amongst the ship's company and there was much 'tooth sucking'. We blamed Naval Command in Ceylon, squadron blamed the 'fishheads' and so on.

Forty years later a brief article appeared in *Naval Review* by John Winton which may well provide the answer to this mystery. The code name 'Ultra' was given by British Intelligence to the secret decoded signals which resulted from our possession and understanding of the German 'Enigma' machine cypher system, the signals being designated 'Ultra secret'. It is said that, unknown to the Germans, a copy of this highly secret and complex coding machine was brought to England at the beginning of the war by a brave and resourceful Polish patriot. A complete and fully functioning machine was also retrieved from the captured submarine *U-11* (believed by the Germans to have been sunk) and a set of cypher keys were captured from a German trawler/weather ship before she was sunk. Subsequently, thanks also to the expertise of a brilliant team of crypto-analysts from Bletchley Park, it became possible for the Chiefs of Staff and the Prime Minister himself to receive a steady flow of top secret German operational signals. The problem then, of course, was how to put this vital information to good use without letting the German High Command know that we had free access to some of their top secrets.

As John Winton wrote, 'When one player consistently knows which cards his opponent holds, how much and how often dare he go on winning before his opponent suspects and changes the cards – or even the game?' Access therefore to information received through 'Ultra' was very severely restricted, but despite this, a series of events occurred which might well, and indeed should, have made the Germans suspicious.

In 1941 a substantial number of weather ships, supply ships and U-boats were sunk by the Allied Forces because we knew from 'Ultra' signals where they were likely to be at a given time. The Germans, it is now known, did become suspicious but still believed their 'Enigma' coding system to be inviolate. Apparently in 1942 the enemy learned that Montgomery had foreknowledge of Rommel's plans in the desert campaign and even of his illness (obtained via 'Ultra). By 1943 it seemed that 'Ultra' had to be compromised and throughout that year signals derived directly from and quoting verbatim from decoded German messages continued to be sent to ships in the Mediterranean, the North Atlantic and finally the Indian Ocean. Various operational commands and senior officers were guilty of quite reckless indiscretions over this very secret information despite repeated warnings. Happily for the Allies, 'Ultra' in fact remained secure but, as John Winton concludes, this was due to 'luck and the amazing stupidity of German Intelligence as regards the unbreakability of their cypher'.

Here then, at long last, may be the true story

▲ **Swordfish LS274 '1F' of No. 818 Squadron from HMS *Unicorn* flying over Ceylon during early 1944. (Charles N. Bates)**

behind the events which led to so much frustration and mystery over HMS *Battler* and our encounter with the *Brake*. It now transpires, as told by John Winton (*Naval Review*, Vol. 72, p. 121, 1984: 'How the Navy nearly lost Ultra'), that earlier, in February 1944, as a direct result of 'Ultra' information, the German supply tanker *Charlotte Schliemann* was sunk in the Indian Ocean by HMS *Relentless* and shortly afterwards a U-boat was sunk by *Roebuck*. In an attempt by the Allies to avoid German suspicion, each of these incidents was provided with a cover story to avoid compromising 'Ultra' and to explain why on each occasion we had once again managed to be in the right place at the right time. Taken together these successful actions, where three enemy ships had been caught by the Royal Navy and sunk at the very time and place where carefully chosen secret rendezvous had been arranged, must have appeared suspicious to the enemy.

I remember well that after our sighting of the *Brake* much public credit was accorded to our admirable and very competent met officer for the successful location of the tanker in that vast ocean space. It was claimed that, by carefully studying the likely weather and sea conditions over the months, he had predicted the most likely time and locality which would be suitable for a supply ship/U-boat rendezvous. His prediction was said at the time to have led us to the very area where the sighting was actually made.

Was this then the official 'cover story'? All these years later it would be churlish to deny Met his triumph, but maybe it should after all be shared with 'Ultra'. It could, I suppose, have been argued that if our aircraft had attacked and one of the submarines escaped to tell the tale, then 'Ultra' might have been compromised, but one still wonders why, if this suggestion is correct, the same considerations did not apply to *Roebuck*'s subsequent and successful attack. Unfortunately my memory fails to tell me just how long after our sighting and in what location the *Brake* was finally sunk. Certainly both U-boats did escape.

At all events, can there be a better explanation for the undoubted facts that our Swordfish from *Battler*, having at last found the enemy we had been seeking for so long, were at the vital moment refused permission to attack and destroy? Why else were our ship and aircraft withdrawn and a destroyer subsequently sent in to sink the tanker, I wonder? It is certainly intriguing to speculate on this old story and it may well be regarded as a true 'Enigma'!

Around the same time, Telegraphist Ai Gunner George Rock had a spell a Katukurunda, then embarked in *Begum*:

We nineteen FAA personnel travelled to Cape Town by HMS *Falmouth*, a flat-bottomed sloop, arriving before Christmas 1943. In May we embarked on another troopship, the *Nevassa*, bound for Ceylon via Mombasa.

After a two weeks' acclimatization period at HMS *Bherunda* (Colombo Racecourse) we were given a jungle posting, which turned out to be HMS *Ukussa* at Katukurunda in No. 756 Squadron, a crewing-up squadron. Life was interesting, plenty of trips viewed from above and plenty of paddy fields including one at each end of the metal roll-up runway. Italian collaborators were busy improving the areas each side of the runway; they worked like Trojans and appeared to be quite happy. I remember their sergeants were dressed very smartly like brigadiers. On more than one occasion I enjoyed a nice cup of Italian-made coffee when on the way back to our own room (an ex-native hut) after landing.

I was to be crewed up with Peter Getting as pilot and Sammy Manchett as observer. I couldn't have wished for a better pilot or a better observer – I had complete faith in both of them. Sam could always be relied on to get us back to base and later on to our carrier and Peter always gave us a smooth ride and nearly always caught the second arrester wire, which was reassuring as our carrier flight deck was very short.

Whilst at Katukurunda, Peter, Sammy and myself were sent with our plane to China Bay, Trincomalee, for a few weeks to carry out submarine patrols whilst the larger carriers, which had assembled there in mid-1944, left harbour on their way to the Japanese oil refineries.

Finally we were drafted to No. 832 Squadron on the *Begum*, a 'banana boat' classed as an escort carrier or 'baby flat-top'. We were on board then until we got home in February 1945. Our main duties were in the Bay of Bengal on anti-submarine patrols dawn and dusk – a very small squadron of Avengers with four Wildcats.

No. 832 was a happy squadron. We met our fellow air crews (pilots and observers) in the crew room which was a room under the wooden flight deck high above the hangar deck. Of course my fellow TAGs were in the same mess as myself, the PO Mess. We were fortunate to have three-tier bunks hinged to poles and hanging on chains, which could be used to hook up the bunks out of the way when not being used. My fellow TAGs were Alf Snellgrove, Fred Goodman, Fred Shelley, Mark Allen (later killed over Scapa Flow), Joe Hughes, Spike Hughes (both since died), Alwyn Smith and W. Hewitt.

We usually only met our ground crews on the flight deck on take-off or landing. I regret not getting to know them better and when we had more time to mingle on the way home we left them behind in Ceylon where I believe most were destined for Australia.

On our first patrol on leaving the crew room I remember that Sammy Manchett, who had experienced many catapult take-offs from the *Sheffield* in Walruses, said to us new boys to assisted take-off 'Get some cordite up your

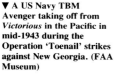

▼ A US Navy TBM Avenger taking off from *Victorious* in the Pacific in mid-1943 during the Operation 'Toenail' strikes against New Georgia. (FAA Museum)

backside'. Perhaps he thought someone was looking a little apprehensive (although in those days I think we just took everything in our stride). The crunch came when we did take off on the booster for the first time. I did everything my experienced colleagues had told me, i.e. Mae West Keypore lining over the gunsight, left arm on top and face on that forearm looking at Commander (Flying) on the bridge, and right hand on the centre lever of the barrel turret side, ready to ditch the side in the unfortunate event of a ducking.

The flag went down, the engine was revving and we were off. It seemed we had gone just a few feet, and I was trying to sit up, having slid down in my safety belt (a single horizontal belt), and ready to push that side off, as I was sure we had only gone a few feet, and ready to go over the front. I got up quickly, looked over the side and saw the *Begum* like a toy boat below – we had travelled a long distance in a short time. Sammy, like the other observers, favoured take-off and landing from the radio section of the Avenger below and behind the turret, and I could see him from the turret as there was a space all round the spring-loaded armour plate which closed up once the TAG was inside.

I looked down at Sammy who had slackened his grip on the handles at the time of take-off and was surrounded by smoke floats. Our airframe fitter made brackets for these as well as flask holders and pencil holders to make sure we were comfortable. We had every faith in him and our even younger engine mechanic from Birmingham known as 'Tiger'. After that, take-offs and landings were part of normal routine.

The ship's company were mostly Merchant Navy personnel in the Navy; I think they were called T124X ratings. They were a happy crowd. Also the PO cooks used to get up before our dawn patrol and make us a nice bowl of tea and fill flasks, all voluntarily.

A typical day for a TAG aboard *Begum* at the time I was aboard was for those on dawn patrol to be called early, bowl of tea, meet crews in ready room, out to aircraft already lined up for the booster, take off at first light about six planes, one in standby on deck. Not sure where we were going, the observer and pilot knew all that, keep a good look-out for that periscope like a feather in the ocean, and then after searching the allocated area others were doing the same in parallel return, hoping the ship was where it should be. There would be wireless silence as we were in the Burma War Zone. I would take off my parachute harness and crawl from the radio compartment up to the second cockpit (originally designed for the observer and I believe used by the US Navy), taking the flask and passing a cup of tea to the pilot as there was just enough space between his head-rest and the canopy to give access.

Apart from the dawn and dusk, patrols were fairly tedious and not very exciting. Occasionally we would get back to where the carrier should be and if very cloudy a square search would be called for, but I never had any fear of not getting down OK. And the weather was so bad that all the other planes returned but we pressed on regardless and returned at the end of our patrol only to find an attendant destroyer sending an Aldis lamp signal – most unusual. It read 'Dr. Livingstone I presume'.

We seemed to be going round in circles in the Bay of Bengal. As TAGs we knew little of the difficulties but have since found out that the pilots and observers were also not much better off; our senior officers were obviously keeping things pretty well tight to their chest. I do remember one day the skipper, 'Jackie' Broome, announcing over the tannoy that he had just sent a message to Admiral Mountbatten at Kandy that we would follow that particular submarine into Rangoon harbour if necessary. Don't know if it was supposed to be a morale booster or just the opposite. We did occasionally find our way into Vizagapatum on the east coast of India for supplies and we quite often refuelled our four attendant vessels at sea. One would wake up one morning when there was no flying and find an escort vessel behind being refuelled.

By April 1944 *Illustrious*, together with a number of escort carriers, was available to the Eastern Fleet and the time had come to give serious thought to a carrier attack on Japanese-held territory. An obvious strategic target was the island of Sumatra, and for this first operation the Fleet had the loan of USS *Saratoga*. Arriving in the target area early on 19 April, *Saratoga* commenced flying off her SBDs at 0515, followed fifteen minutes later by the Barracudas of Nos. 810 and 847 Squadrons aboard *Illustrious* with their respective Hellcat and Corsair escorts. Their target was the harbour of Sabang at the northern end of the island and the SBDs and Barracudas struck within one minute of each other, destroying harbour installations and a radar station as well as aircraft on the airfield in the area and on a neighbouring island. Surprise was achieved and flak was ragged and inaccurate, no losses being sustained in the attack despite two of the Barracudas' having to make a second attack because their bombs failed to release in the first dive. One US Navy Hellcat was lost, the pilot being rescued by a submarine.

On 17 May a similar attack was carried out on the island of Java, the target this time being the oil refinery at Soerabaya, but success was minimal. Further sporadic strikes took place in the ensuing months both by Barracudas and Avengers, a second raid on Sabang being made on 25 July, following which *Illustrious* underwent a two-month refit at Durban and was replaced by *Indomitable*.

The next major attack was again to be Sumatra. *Victorious* had now joined the Fleet

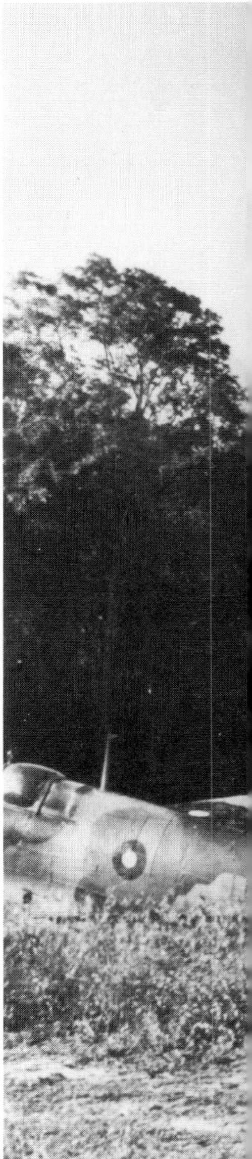

▼ Seafires in reserve storage at Puttalam airstrip in Ceylon about April 1944. (FAA Museum)

and on 24 August the two British carriers sent two waves of Barracudas to inflict heavy damage on a large cement works at Indaroeng as well as the harbour at Emmahaven and various shipping. The squadrons involved were No. 831 from *Victorious* and Nos. 815 and 817 from *Indomitable*, the latter pair comprising the 12th TBR Wing. A further attack on the island by these two carriers on 18 September was much less successful and before the next operation the squadrons were sent ashore for a course of intensive weapons training.

The island of Car Nicobar was to be the next objective and airfields as well as harbour installations and shipping at Nancowry were heavily attacked in two raids on 17 and 19 October under the code-name Operation 'Millet'. The first of these attacks cost the two carriers one Barracuda and two Corsairs to flak and, during a fight with Nakajima Ki-43 'Oscar' fighters on the 19th, two Corsairs and a Hellcat were lost for seven of the Japanese fighters. These proved to be the last operations in this theatre by Barracudas, which were then replaced in both ships by the Avenger.

Following this operation the fleet carriers were transferred to a new British Pacific Fleet and the escort carrier strength in that area became part of a new East Indies Fleet.

CHAPTER 22

The East Indies Fleet

When the East Indies Fleet formed at the beginning of 1945 its air strength was minimal, comprising only the Hellcats of No. 804 Squadron (*Ameer*) and the Avengers of No. 851 Squadron (*Shah*). Its initial task was to support the Fourteenth Army in Burma by attacking Japanese communication lines both at sea and ashore.

The aircraft were soon involved in a major exercise when, on 21 January, the Hellcats were asked to help provide cover for landings by the 26th Indian Infantry Division on Ramree Island off the Burmese coast. In addition to combat air patrols they undertook bombardment-spotting for the covering warships, continuing these tasks for some days and taking in a similar landing by Royal Marines on nearby Cheduba Island on the 26th.

By 3 February *Ameer* was back at Trincomalee with the Fleet and the Hellcats disembarked to China Bay. The next task was to be an urgently needed strategic reconnaissance of various areas where further landings might be possible, extending through Sumatra and Malaya to Singapore. The original intention had been to employ photographic-reconnaissance variants of the Spitfire for this task but instead it was decided to use the PR Hellcats of No. 888 Squadron. These were an adapted version of this aircraft, fitted with specialized photographic equipment. Each machine carried four vertically mounted cameras, comprising two British F52s fitted with 36in lenses, set to overlap by ten per cent and having 500-shot magazines; an American K17 service camera of 9in × 9in format and with a 6in lens; and an American K18 intelligence camera of 9in × 18in format and with a 10in lens. Much of the armour was removed, and guns were not installed except for low-level work, the combined effect of these changes making the aircraft very tail-heavy. To minimize the possibility of detection the Hellcats were given a coating of a special shade of locally concocted blue paint.

Shah, on her way to Durban for a refit, was temporarily absent but her place had been taken by *Empress*. The Fleet left port on 22 February with No. 888 Squadron, the Avengers of No. 845 Squadron and four Hellcats of No. 804 Squadron embarked in *Empress* and the remainder of No. 804 Squadron aboard *Ameer*. The PR Hellcat pilots flew their first sorties four days later, climbing well above 30,000ft in clear conditions and sometimes as high as 42,000ft but dropping down to around 8,000ft if there was cloud cover. In successive trips they covered the Kra Isthmus, Penang, Phuket Island, northern Sumatra and various other areas, with particular emphasis on potential landing beaches. To avoid giving away the location of the Fleet they would fly a dog-leg course in each direction, the first and last 80

◄Hellcat 'K3P' of No. 800 Squadron takes off from HMS *Emperor* about May 1945. (N. S. Painter)

► Seafire III 'D6S' of No. 809 Squadron grabs a few wires while landing aboard HMS *Stalker*. (Via P. H. T. Green)

miles at near sea level, navigating by dead-reckoning with the aid of a knee pad. They were away for up to six hours and in theory could rely on a YG homing beacon to aid their return to the parent ship, which could have sailed a considerable distance in the meantime. In practice, the necessary aerial had a habit of being knocked off the aircraft as they jettisoned their long-range drop tanks so they were allowed to land on any carrier they could find.

The carrier strength of the Fleet was steadily built up and by the time it departed from Trincomalee on a further PR sortie on 8 April it had been augmented by *Emperor* and *Khedive*. This time the Hellcats concentrated on Malaya, sorties being flown over Port Dickson, Kuala Lumpur and the Malacca region to photograph airfields, beaches and ports though the weather was often uncooperative and the time over the target areas was limited by the fact that the Fleet kept well offshore, sometimes as much as 300 miles away. A sad loss was that of an American pilot, Sub-Lt (A) J. W. Thomlinson, RNVR, of No. 888 Squadron, whose aircraft, JX683, suffered an engine failure ten miles west of Port Dickson. He landed safely in the sea and was picked up by a fishing boat, only to be later beheaded by the Japanese after being taken into captivity. On the credit side, the Hellcat fighters of No. 808 Squadron from *Khedive* disposed of three Japanese aircraft which attacked the Fleet, though even this was only achieved at the expense of three of their own aircraft in a landing accident, JV144 bouncing on landing on 10 April and putting paid to JW719 and JV298, the latter unfortunately taking with it the pilot, Lt (A) P. A. Sherry, RNVR, who lost his life.

The carrier strength of the Escort Carrier Squadron (as it was known for a time) continued to increase and towards the end of April it became the 21st Aircraft Carrier Squadron, consisting at that stage of *Emperor*, *Hunter*, *Khedive* and *Stalker*. These were all involved in Operation 'Dracula', an assault on Rangoon. Fighter aircraft flew 110 sorties on 2 May, the day of the invasion, encountering very little opposition whilst they strafed ground objectives and dropped bombs in support of the amphibious landings. Poor weather prevented their participating during the next two days, though in any event the landing parties were meeting considerably less opposition than they had anticipated. When conditions improved, therefore, on the 5th and 6th, the Fleet moved further south so that the aircraft could attack airfields there as well as shipping off the Tenasserim coast.

Although things had gone well there had been a fear that Japanese air units based in the Andaman and Nicobar Islands might fly to resist the invasion. To prevent this eventuality the 3rd Battle Squadron, with *Empress* and *Shah*, had carried out diversionary attacks from 30 April. During eight days of activity rocket and bombing strikes were carried out by Hellcats, Avengers and Seafires on Japanese airfields and on shipping in the area, a total of more than 400 sorties being flown for the loss of only one pilot, Sub-Lt (A) J. A. Scott, RNVR, of No. 804 Squadron in Hellcat JX803 falling to enemy anti-aircraft fire.

After returning to Trincomalee to refuel, the ships sortied to carry out further strikes against the Nicobar Islands, though No. 851 Squadron Avengers aboard *Shah* had to transfer to *Emperor* when the former's catapult went out of action on 11 May. Four days later, while searching for a dinghy containing air crew from an aircraft hit

by enemy flak, a squadron aircraft found the Japanese cruiser *Haguro*. Operating difficulties prevented more than three Avengers (FN939, JZ147 and JZ210) from being launched from *Emperor* but these aircraft mounted a dive-bombing attack although only one near miss was achieved. However, the enemy vessel did not survive for long, falling victim early the next day to torpedoes of the 26th Destroyer Flotilla.

Continuous action then began to take its toll, and by mid-June only *Ameer*, *Khedive* and *Stalker* were available out of the eight escort carriers by then allocated to the East Indies Fleet. Unobtrusive Hellcat PR sorties commenced over southern Malaya and the Penang area on 18 May and then two days later, this task safely completed, the fighters went into action, 29 aircraft from three squadrons carrying out devastating attacks on shipping, airfields and communications in southern Burma and Sumatra. One unfortunate loss was that of the recently appointed commanding officer of No. 808 Squadron, Lt Cdr (A) C. F. Wheatley, RNVR, whose Hellcat, JW868, went down in flames over Medan after being hit by anti-aircraft fire during an attack on airfields.

Between 5 and 11 July Hellcats from *Ameer* and *Emperor* sought out such Japanese aircraft as they could find on Car Nicobar as well as attacking shipping in the area, another squadron losing its commanding officer on the 7th when Lt Cdr (A) R. M. Morris, RNVR, of No. 896 Squadron went into the sea after running into light anti-aircraft fire. From 24 July three days of similar work were undertaken in northern Malaya, cover also being provided for a minesweeping operation off Phuket Island, and this ended the operational activities of the 21st Aircraft Carrier Squadron. Plans for a strike by five carriers on Penang were cancelled and the only other activity of note was after VJ-Day, when five of the ships anchored off Singapore on 10 September during Operation 'Zipper', the re-occupation of Malaya.

By the time of the Japanese surrender the 21st Aircraft Carrier Squadron had thirteen CVEs and during the last six months of the war had been responsible for destroying about a third of all Japanese aircraft in the Burma, Malaya and Sumatra areas. It was, together with the destroyers and submarines of the East Indies Fleet, also responsible for strangling the coastal traffic in the area.

▲ A photograph taken from an Avenger of the first flight of No. 857 Squadron from HMS *Indomitable* during an attack on 29 January 1945 on Songei Gerong oil refinery, Palembang. The refinery is protected by barrage balloons. (Official)

CHAPTER 23

The British Pacific Fleet: The First Phase

The new British Pacific Fleet ended 1944 with a further attack on Sumatran oil fields on 20 December, this time at Pangkalan Brandan under the code-name Operation 'Outflank'. In the event cloud obscured the target and the striking force diverted to an alternative target at Belawan Deli, a port serving Medan, though with poor results.

The first strike having achieved very little, a further attempt was mounted under the code-name Operation 'Lentil' and the Fleet sailed on New Year's Eve with three fleet carriers. *Indefatigable*, *Indomitable* and *Victorious* each carried an Avenger squadron as well as two fighter squadrons, these being equipped respectively with Seafires, Hellcats and Corsairs, in addition to six PR Hellcats of No. 888 Squadron and the twelve new Fireflies of No. 1770 Squadron aboard *Indefatigable* – a total strength of nearly 200 aircraft. The target area was reached on 4 January and this time their luck had improved, the skies being clear.

To prepare the way for the main strike a preliminary offensive sweep, or 'ramrod', was carried out by sixteen of the Corsairs and Hellcats, which took off at 0610 for a surprise attack on inland airfields in which seven out of 25 aircraft were destroyed at Bindjai, Medan, Tandjonpoera and Troemon. At Medan Lt (A) L. D. Durno, RNVR, and Sub-Lt (A) J. H. Richards, RNZNVR, both flying Corsairs of No. 1834 Squadron, shot down a Mitsubishi Ki-46 'Dinah' reconnaissance aircraft which was attempting to land and shortly afterwards the former also shot down a Mitsubishi Ki-21 'Sally' bomber approaching the airfield.

The main striking force, comprising 32 Avengers and Fireflies escorted by 32 Corsairs and Hellcats, left one and a half hours later. The Fireflies went in first, using their rockets to hit electrical and oil installations in the port of Pangkalan Soe Soe before the Avengers released 30 tons of bombs. There was very little flak and five of about a dozen attacking Nakajima 'Oscar' fighters were accounted for by the escort. Losses were correspondingly light. Only one Avenger suffered damage from the fighter attacks and Firefly DT943 flown by No. 1770 Squadron's Commanding Officer, Maj. V. B. G. Cheesman, RM, had to ditch after running out of fuel while in the landing circuit although both crew members were picked up safely by a destroyer.

The Fleet then returned to Trincomalee but on 16 January 1945 it sailed for Australia, where Sydney was to be used as the main base for future operations. The fleet carriers were now grouped as the 1st Aircraft Carrier Squadron, which also included *Illustrious*. They were to be soon in action again, however, as targets in Sumatra were to be attacked en route in an operation code-named 'Meridian'. The first phase, 'Meridian I', suffered from more weather problems but the clouds had cleared sufficiently by the early morning of 24 January for Admiral Vian in his flagship *Indomitable* to give the order to proceed with the planned operation. After forming up, the main force and its escort departed at 0704 and an hour later were at 12,000ft over the mountains. The 'ramrod' Corsairs took off in a second range but their late departure on this occasion gave the enemy time to get some of his fighters off, with consequent losses to both the striking force and their escort. Another hazard was the sudden appearance of a balloon barrage which rose up to 5,000ft as the Avengers dived to attack. Despite this they succeeded in inflicting heavy damage, most of the oil tanks being burnt out and production badly affected for the next three months. Two of the attacking Avengers and five other aircraft were lost but fourteen Japanese aircraft were destroyed.

Lt Cdr (A) D. R. Foster, DSC, RNVR, the Commanding Officer of No. 849 Avenger Squadron from *Victorious*, made this report after the attack:

Operation Meridian (1). Report by Squadron Commander.
0634 Airborne (First T.B.R. from *Victorious*). 0645 *Victorious* group joined up. 0656 Joined Main Strike. 0704 Set Course. 0718 Crossed Coast. 0802 Fireflies join Strike. 0811 Started deployment. 0814 Attacked. 0822 Arrived at R/V. 0826 Strike left R/V. 0916 Crossed Coast. 0928 Strike broke up into carrier groups.

A very successful operation, which should have caused appreciable damage. There were the following faults:

1. I am still not satisfied with some aspects of the strike. The main criticism I have is over the cover afforded Avengers between the target and the Rendezvous. I have raised this before and the only improvement that is evident is that the Fireflies are doing an exceptionally good job, but are not being sufficiently assisted by other fighters. Today a Flight of Hellcats were supposed to be covering our withdrawal. Out of my seven aircraft, three were attacked by Tojos, two being lucky to get back. Not one pilot remembers seeing a Hellcat, although most profess to have seen Fireflies along this route. Avengers will not always be attacked, in this theatre, when in squadron or group formation; they will, however, always be attacked when singly or in pairs. Therefore, one of the most essential places for fighter protection is along that ten miles stretch from target to R/V. At the moment it appears that the signal for bombing is also the signal for some fighter squadrons to go and find a target of their own.
2. The climb was neither one thing nor another. No surprise – no fast climb to 12,000 feet, and then a fast descent.
3. I did not deploy according to plan, coming in from 260° instead of 230°. I also again bombed before the latter half of 857 who have a strange reluctance to get into their dive. The flight who had a Nick formating behind them can consider themselves lucky that for some unknown reason he fired only one short burst. Presumably the Strike Leader went so far North to wait for the destruction of the balloons, I was probably in a better position to see that there were none in a position to comply, and the best policy seemed to be to get in before they were raised higher, and the defence became stiffer.
4. R/T Discipline – due to unserviceability I switched off my V.H.F. early in the flight. From all accounts, I was fortunate.

The lessons were quickly learnt and a number of improvements were incorporated in the plan for 'Meridian II', a similar attack on the oil refinery and installations at Soengei Gerong on 29 January. This time the 'ramrod' Fireflies left earlier, the route from the target area to the subsequent rendezvous area was designed so as to avoid likely flak areas and a greater proportion of the fighter strength remained behind to protect the Fleet. Bad weather prevailed on this occasion but the attackers were eventually airborne by 0640, crossing the coast at 0752 and climbing to 10,000ft. They came under heavy attack from enemy fighters, the Japanese defenders having also learned lessons from the previous attack, and losses were suffered; No. 849 Squadron from *Victorious* was particularly unfortunate in losing its escort before carrying out the attack. The Avengers nevertheless dived through the now inevitable balloon barrage, which accounted for two of their number, a particularly sad loss being that of Lt Cdr W. J. Mainprice, DSC, RN, of No. 854 Squadron, the Wing Leader in JZ112 'Q4A', who had only recently been awarded the DSC for his successful leadership of the squadron in its invaluable work in the English Channel during the Normandy invasion.

Maj. Cheesman has provided this account of these raids:

Towards the end of 1944 the British Pacific Fleet forgathered at Ceylon and we immediately commenced intensive training in operating all these ships and aircraft as one compact unit. This, I might say, is no mean feat in itself since considerable skill is required in manoeuvring four or five carriers, together with their attendant support ships, at 30 knots and having to turn the whole force into the wind every time an aircraft wishes to land.

Apart from this, when flying off so many aircraft from so many ships the sky is very soon full of planes flying in all directions. An extremely high degree of airmanship and squadron drill is required and we had only had a limited time in which to attain the perfection required before we were to make our presence felt on the Japanese.

Within ten days we were ready and the moment I had been so long awaiting had arrived. We were to strike and destroy the Japanese refineries at Pangkalan Brandan and Palembang in the Dutch East Indies island of Sumatra (now Indonesia). These enormous refineries were producing and supplying the Japanese with all their liquid fuel requirements for their armed forces in this theatre. To destroy them would paralyse enemy movements over their entire field of operations, and in particular ground all their aircraft. What a target! And what widespread effects it could have.

And so, one January evening in 1945, our Task Force sailed from Ceylon and finally arrived in the operational area a few days later. All air crews had been preparing in detail for this attack. Our intelligence officers had models and photographs of the whole target area, these having been obtained from the Intelligence Department of the Admiralty for our close scrutiny, and we studied them until we knew every inch by heart. Every pilot of every plane had his allotted target so that the whole refinery could be covered and destroyed.

Zero hour and 'Fly off aircraft'. From all the carriers the heavily laden aircraft streamed off into the murky sky. The form-up, with some 300 planes, was a very tricky business but, thanks to the practices with rigid flying discipline, the whole Air Group was airborne within minutes and on course for the target.

On arrival over the mainland we suddenly emerged into a brilliantly clear sky. This was exactly what we wanted. 'Starboard 30 – target 30 miles – Formation B for Baker – Go', as the squadrons deployed to their attack formations. And there were the barrage balloons all round the target. The best lead in was from the north.

▲ Avenger JZ383 'P1X', of No. 849 Squadron, participating in an attack on oil refineries at Palembang during Operation 'Meridian'. On 5 February 1945 this aircraft was lost when it went over the port side of the ship while landing on. (FAA Museum)

'Bandits left up 10 miles' and our fighters wheeled to attack the Japanese fighters sent up to intercept us. 'Bandits right 90 level closing' – bandits here and bandits there – the battle was on.

We approached the target and in we went.

'Attack–attack–attack'. Now don't rush it – take careful and accurate aim. Remember how those bombs hit *Cornwall* – don't muck it up at the last minute by being over-enthusiastic or you'll miss with your eight HE rockets, I tell myself. Down we go – 300 knots – closing fast – sights on – hold it, hold it, fire! *Phut*, *phut*, *phut*, *phut*, *phut* – I hear my rockets go. Switch to cannon and a burst of cannon shells – all on their way to the target – a tower of machinery known as the 'cracking plant', which should be full of petrol – and by Jove it is! – as an enormous explosion takes place and sheets of flame reached up into the sky.

Watch out – a Jap fighter trying to get on my tail. Avoiding action and trying to get on to his, but he's away now. The whole place is flame and smoke and chaos. With bombs and rockets away there is no point in hanging around here. 'Form up' – and within minutes the course is set for home.

Our fighters overhead drove off pursuing enemy planes as we headed out to sea for our carriers. They were already steaming into wind and ready to receive us. 'Land on' and within minutes the whole striking force had landed, with the fleet turning west into the protection of a dark misty pall.

What incredible luck about the weather. The cloud layer that had threatened our operation in the morning had become our ally by the evening, for only a short time later we heard the enemy air formation searching for us whilst we were safely tucked away under a strata of thick cloud in dense fog.

The next day we repeated the attack on the other refineries at Palembang, and then again on the original target at Pangkalan Brandan – until the whole place was in confirmed ruins and no more aviation fuel flowed for the Japs from these refineries for a long time.

We then sailed for Australia, and from there to the Pacific to join the US Navy for the onslaught on the homeland of Japan itself.

These two raids were probably among the most successful of the Fleet Air Arm's operations in the Second World War and with the earlier 'Lentil' raid accounted for around 140 Japanese aircraft as well as providing a considerable strategic victory with its massive blow to the enemy's oil supplies. After the third attack the Fleet continued on its way to Australia, docking first at Fremantle on 4 February and then sailing for Sydney where it arrived six days later.

The Fleet was then beset by mechanical problems, and an industrial dispute at Sydney docks did little to help, but on 27 February it sailed again, albeit at reduced strength. This time it headed for the Admiralty Islands,

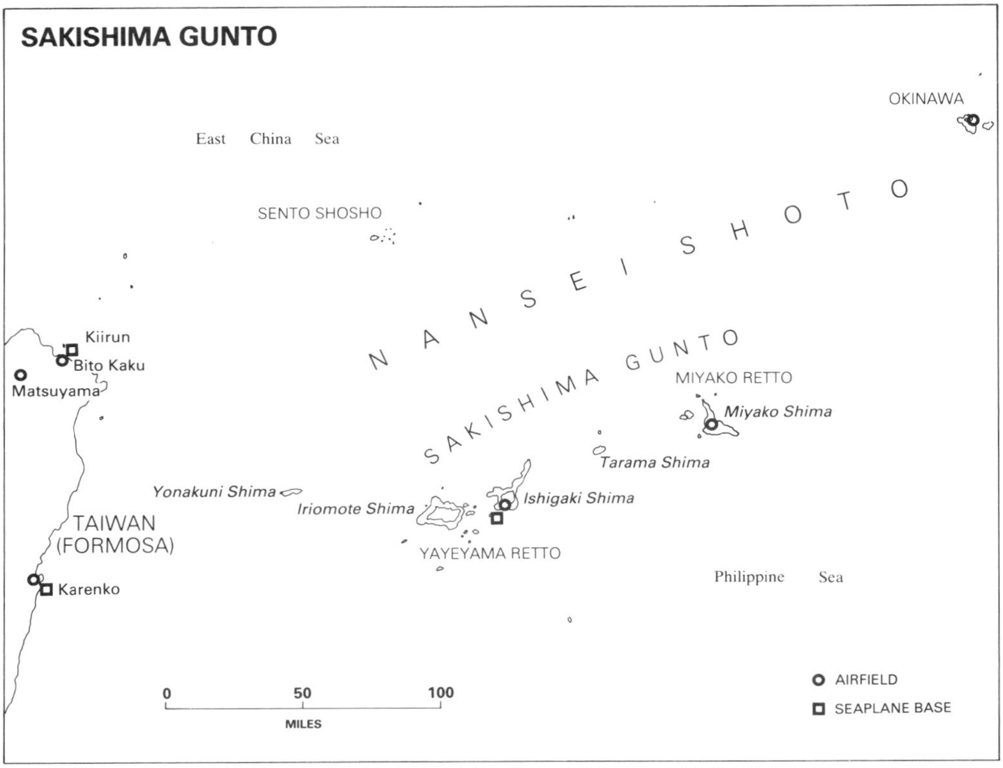

where Manus was to be used by the Fleet as a forward base. The 1st Aircraft Carrier Squadron arrived on 7 March and after replenishment left for Ulithi in the Caroline Islands, where it arrived on the 20th to become Task Force 57 under the operational control of Admiral Spruance's US Fifth Fleet. The objective this time was to be much nearer the Japanese mainland, namely the Sakishima Gunto group of islands situated in the East China Seas between Okinawa and Formosa.

A series of raids was planned as part of the American invasion of Okinawa, which had the somewhat inappropriate code-name Operation 'Iceberg', commencing on 26 March. The targets were six airfields on the main islands of Ishigaki Shima and Mujako Shima and, in all, 548 sorties were flown, 64 tons of bombs dropped and 151 rockets fired. The penalty had been high, however, with a loss during the two days of seventeen aircraft and nine air crew. Moreover, the attackers had inflicted no lasting damage to the runways as the Japanese quickly adapted by filling in the craters overnight. The presence of a night intruder squadron might have prevented this but none was available at this time.

The battle for Okinawa was to be a long and bitter one and the task force was now set to play its role by carrying out a series of similar attacks which would continue for two months. A pattern developed of the Fleet carrying out two days of attacks before withdrawing to refuel and replenish, after which it would return to spend a further two days in the battle area. However, the Japanese were quick to react and on 1 April, the second day of further raids, up to twenty Japanese aircraft attacked the Fleet whilst the 'ramrods' were en route to Ishigaki. Two were shot down but a new tactic made its appearance that day when Sub-Lt (A) R. H. Reynolds, RNVR, of No. 887 Squadron, who had fought a Mitsubishi A6M 'Zeke', saw the doomed aircraft make the first successful kamikaze or suicide attack on the British Pacific Fleet.

Further such attacks were intended but Reynolds stayed aloft long enough to shoot down two other 'Zekes' before descending to make a precarious landing on the somewhat battered flight deck of *Indefatigable*. Such suicide tactics were to be a feature of the enemy's defence against the carriers until the end of the war and were never really overcome, though the British carriers, with their armoured flight decks, fared better than those of their American allies, which were fitted with wooden decks. One major difficulty was that of distinguishing between enemy kamikaze raiders and returning friendly aircraft, and this led to a destroyer or two being stationed at each end of the line, with a Hellcat flying overhead, for identification purposes. Returning pilots were not allowed to land until they had been given clearance by these, a practice soon nicknamed 'de-lousing' by the Americans though officially code-named 'Tomcat'.

Lt Cdr Foster made a much less critical report of this later raid:

Operation 'Iceberg II'. Strike 'Baker', 1st April 1945.
Report of Commanding Officer, No. 849 Squadron – Strike Leader.

1220 Airborne (2nd T.B.R., from *Victorious*); 1227 *Victorious* group formed up; 1239 Strike took departure; 1241 Commenced climb; 1313 Landfall Ishigaki; 1315 Attacked Ishigaki Airfield; 1327 Left R/V for base; 1410 Sighted Fleet.

1. The forming-up was good, although three flights took part instead of only two. There were no incidents on the way to the target. R/T discipline was good, although there was a lot of interference on Button B, which may have been enemy jamming.
2. Landfall was made at the S.E. of Ishigaki, which was moderately clear of cloud. The flights were deployed to starboard, and the attack made from the East, working round to the North. Flak was again light. Fighters were not sent down, as there did not seem to be any serviceable enemy aircraft in the dispersals. The primary target for all three flights was the runway and the taxi tracks leading to it. The bombing was good. Four sticks were definitely seen to burst on the runway, while the control tower was hit by at least one stick. The administration buildings, south of the airfield, were not left undisturbed.
3. The return journey was without incident.

Remarks. The one or two carriers, of which *Victorious* is not one, who flash their identity letters to approaching strikes are a great help; the sooner they flash the more it helps. It gives the Strike Leader a chance to manoeuvre his strike, so that individual flights or squadrons can get to their waiting positions quickly and without confusion. It also lets him know that the strike has been recognised as friendly.

The planned invasion of Okinawa had commenced on 1 April, which made these attacks on the Sakishima airfields even more imperative, to prevent their use for staging aircraft back from other theatres for the defence of that island. After four days' replenishment the Fleet was back in action on 6 April for a further two days of operations, commencing with a dawn sweep by Hellcats over Ishigaki and Miyako followed by an

▼ Fleet carriers conducted a series of raids against Japanese airfields in the Sakishima Gunto during March and April 1945. Here Miyako airfield is being neutralized by Avengers from HMS *Victorious*. (Cdr R. C. Hay)

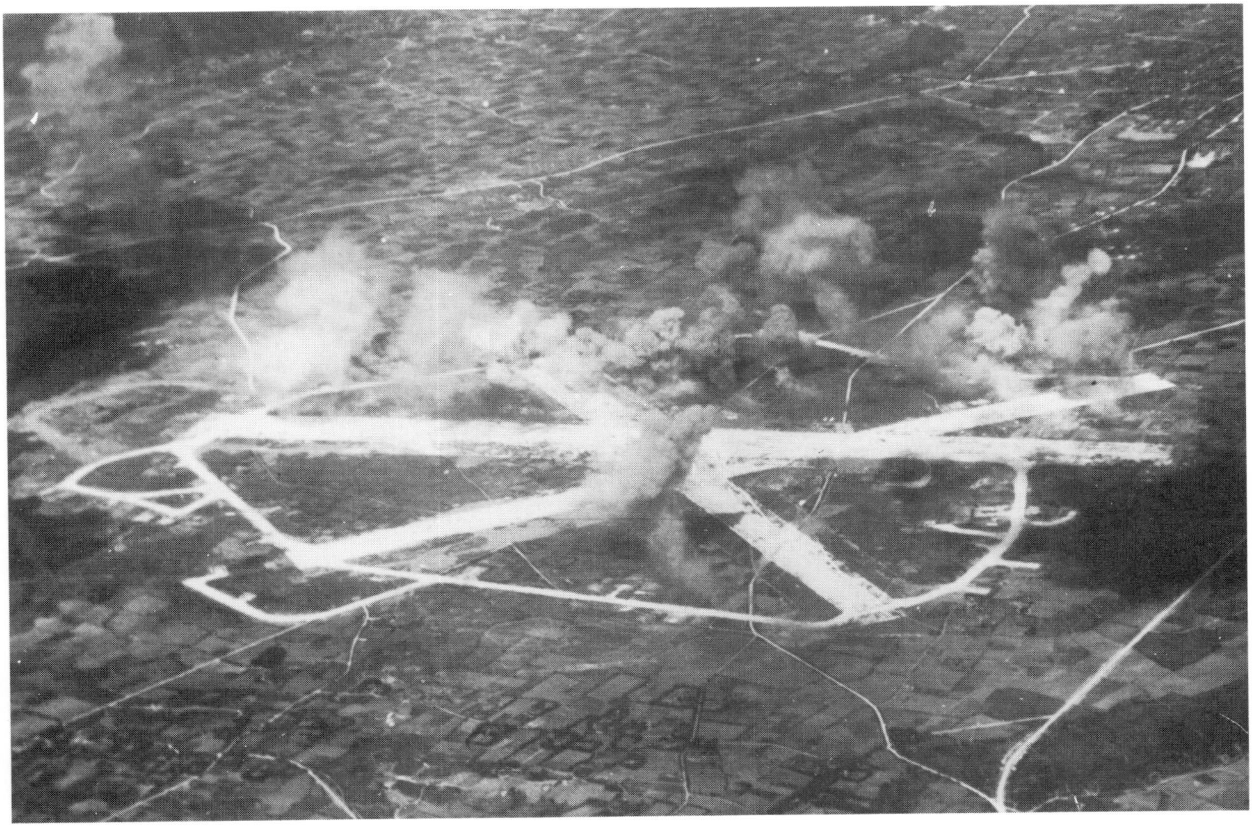

Avenger attack on Hirara town and various airfields and installations. Back at the Fleet, however, further kamikaze attacks had begun, one of three Yokosuka D4Y 'Judy' dive-bombers succeeding in penetrating the AA fire and fighter screen for a near-miss on *Illustrious* which inflicted some damage and caused the loss of two parked Corsairs. Identification was still a problem as a No. 894 Squadron Seafire (NN454) in pursuit was itself shot down in mistake for another suicide attacker, Sub-Lt (A) N. V. Heppenstall, RNVR, losing his life.

The Fleet then withdrew once more, planning to return again on 10 April, but instead they were diverted to attack airfields on Formosa in an attempt to curtail the activities of kamikaze raiders flying from that island to attack the more vulnerable American carriers off Okinawa. Bad weather led to the first such raid being postponed but on 12 April, under the code-name Operation 'Iceberg-Oolong', strikes were mounted against Shinckiku and Matsuyama and the harbour at Kiirun in northern Formosa. Similar attacks were mounted the following day and considerable damage was inflicted. The Fleet came under heavy attack from enemy aircraft, but the combat air patrols succeeded in shooting down a considerable number of these.

Following this the Fleet once more withdrew to replenish, the opportunity being taken for *Formidable* to join, allowing *Illustrious* to return to Sydney and eventually sail back to the United Kingdom for a badly needed refit. Two-day attacks were then resumed on the Sakishima Gunto group, first on 16/17 April and then again on 19/20 April, after which a withdrawal was made to Leyte in the Philippines for a full replenishment, the fleet train ships being by then almost empty of fuel and stores.

Arriving on 23 April after a voyage of 1,000 miles, the Fleet had been continuously at sea for over a month, then a record in British naval history since Nelson's time. The main objective of neutralizing Sakishima airfields during the invasion of Okinawa had been achieved and a total of 2,444 sorties of all kinds had been flown; 412 tons of bombs had been dropped and 325 rockets fired. Losses were, however, heavy, 47 aircraft having failed to

return from operations although many of the crews had been saved by submarines and aircraft of the superb US Navy rescue organization and only 29 men were listed as killed or missing.

There was no time to spare for a proper rest and on 1 May the Fleet was back at sea, heading once more for the Sakishima group. The Japanese were well ready for them this time, having taken full advantage of the respite to do some useful repair work. Attacks recommenced on 4 May and AA fire was as heavy as before, an Avenger of No. 857 Squadron from *Indomitable* soon falling victim. Shortly after 1100 about twenty Japanese aircraft came in to attack the carriers and although eight of these were shot down three succeeded in getting through to score hits. At 1131 a kamikaze 'Zeke' created a two-foot hole in the flight deck of *Formidable*, with considerable other damage and severe casualties, and *Indomitable* also suffered minor damage from two other 'Zekes' shortly afterwards. The armoured decks stood the test well, however, and by 1700 *Formidable* could signal that she was able to land-on aircraft.

▼ Corsairs of Nos. 1834 and 1836 Squadrons lined up for take-off aboard *Victorious*. (Author's collection)

Similar onslaughts continued until 9 May, the last day on which a kamikaze attack was made on the British Pacific Fleet. On this occasion *Formidable* was again the victim and, although eighteen Avengers and Corsairs were wrecked, all fires were extinguished within fifteen minutes and the ship was operating aircraft again. In all, four carriers had been hit in these attacks, two of them twice, but all continued in service. Attacks continued against the Sakishima group in the same pattern until 25 May and then the Fleet sailed for the Admiralty Islands, putting in at Manus on 30 May having successfully completed this phase of the operations.

Maj. Cheesman says of this period:

> As our task force joined the US Fleet at sea the Battle of the Island of Okinawa was in full swing and proving particularly costly to the Americans. The next island on the American invasion list was Formosa and we were ordered to soften up the defences before the landings were to take place. This task we performed day after day, refuelling and receiving our supplies at sea every third day so that full pressure could be maintained without a break. In these attacks we sank ship after ship, until the Japanese found themselves so short of supply ships that they resorted to the use of wooden junks. These we found and sent, with our rockets and cannon shells, to the bottom one after the other. Everything Japanese had to be sunk – and it was.
>
> The Allied forces were getting nearer and nearer to the Japanese homeland – how they wished they had never started this war in the East! – and they were becoming more and more desperate. How could they stop this ceaseless onslaught from the Allied carriers around their home waters?
>
> And so were born the kamikazes – suicide planes, where the pilot volunteered to give his life for his country and his ancestors.
>
> It was not long before we too were to experience these attacks and consequently our squadron spent many hours seeking and shooting these kamikazes out of the sky. Whilst on deck one morning I only just got out of the way of one as he dived into the *Indefatigable*, but fortunately the flight deck of our ships consisted of several inches of armoured steel which meant that the bomb seldom pierced the deck and consequently never reached the hangars full of aircraft below – but they always made a nasty mess of everything they hit on deck. Nevertheless, flying operations were never delayed for more than twenty minutes through any of the hits we received from these fellows and so the principle of the armoured deck was upheld.

These attacks had cost the Royal Navy 41 air crew killed and 44 on board the ships. Some 160 aircraft were written off through enemy action, kamikaze attacks and accidents.

CHAPTER 24

The British Pacific Fleet: The Finale

The Fleet had taken quite a battering and it was necessary for it to stay at Sydney for some weeks while repair work was carried out and stores replenished. Large numbers of new aircraft were by now arriving in Australia and the squadrons took the opportunity to re-equip and work up on their new mounts.

In the meantime *Implacable* had arrived to join the Fleet and on 12 June she left Manus with the escort carrier *Ruler* and an escort of five cruisers for an attack on Truk Atoll in the Caroline Islands as Task Force 111/2, to work up her Air Group prior to joining the Fleet. For Operation 'Inmate', as it was named, 80 aircraft were available, these including Avengers, Fireflies and Seafires. The attacks were carried out on 14/15 June though targets were not as plentiful as anticipated because most had already been wiped out by the Americans in Task Force 58. Nevertheless over 200 sorties were made, including 'ramrods' and strikes against shipping, airfields and installations. Some of the No. 880 Squadron Seafires from *Implacable* flew photographic-reconnaissance sorties and six Avengers dropped flares to carry out a night attack on the second day. A number of Seafires flew CAPs from *Ruler* but that ship's main task was to provide a spare deck for aircraft queuing up to land on *Implacable*, this saving several pilots from a ditching.

The only loss amongst the Seafires was that of Sub-Lt (A) M. H. Payne, RNVR, of No. 801 Squadron in PP975, the last to attack in a strike on the first day, who was shot down by flak. Three Avengers were lost as a result of engine failure, the observer of one of these aircraft Sub-Lt (A) A. S. Moseley, RNVR, of No. 828 Squadron being fortunate to escape when, after struggling out of the aircraft's glass house under water, he found himself close to *Implacable*'s propeller but managed to remain submerged until the ship had passed, although he suffered a collapsed lung as a consequence.

No. 828 Squadron had been plagued by these engine failures and their CO, Lt Cdr (A) F. A. Swanton, RN, and his crew were lucky to survive when their aircraft was cut in two by *Implacable* after ditching on take-off for a raid. It subsequently transpired that the wrong type of spark plug had been fitted to the aircraft but this was not discovered until after thirteen squadron aircraft had been lost in ditchings from this cause.

On 16 July the British Pacific Fleet joined the American Third Fleet, though it was allowed to operate independently because of the considerable experience it had now acquired. The fleet carriers were grouped as the 1st Aircraft Carrier Squadron, as part of Task Force 37, for the culminating phase of the war, which was to be a series of strikes on the Japanese home islands. Accompanying them would be Task Force 112, the fleet train. The CVEs *Arbiter*, *Chaser*, *Ruler*, *Speaker* and *Striker* of the 30th Aircraft Carrier Squadron carried replacement aircraft and also provided defence for the oilers and replenishment ships. The forward British Pacific Fleet base at Manus now boasted an aircraft repair and assembly unit on the airstrip while in the lagoon were anchored the aircraft repair carriers *Unicorn* and *Pioneer* and other ships, providing a complete mobile aircraft, engines and components repair organization.

The air power now available was massive, the American Task Groups having 1,200 aircraft in sixteen carriers. The first American strikes early on 17 July were recalled owing to bad weather, it being by then the height of the typhoon season, but at 0350 the first British machines took off from *Victorious* and *Implacable* when they were 250 miles north-east of Tokyo. Amidst accurate and intense flak they fired rockets, dropped bombs and strafed airfields on the east coast as well as attacking railways and junks. Further attacks were made during the day and, in all, 226 sorties were flown, including CAPs and ASPs. That night the Hellcats of No. 1844 Squadron provided CAP for *King George V* which, with American battleships, shelled industrial targets north of Tokyo. Similar attacks the next day were curtailed by bad weather, and anti-aircraft fire was again intense, but Seafires and Corsairs managed to destroy twelve Japanese aircraft and damage eighteen others on the ground.

After two days of refuelling and replenishment, followed by further bad weather, act-

▶ Corsair KD215 'R6L', piloted by Sub-Lt P. G. Howell of No. 1851 Squadron, after the engine caught fire in a barrier crash aboard *Venerable* on 12 June 1945. (H. A. Smith)

ivities resumed on the 24th, *Indefatigable* having now rejoined the Fleet after having stayed behind at Sydney to deal with mechanical problems. A total of 260 targets were attacked on the first day, in and around Japan; 416 sorties were flown, including ASPs and CAPs, though a Seafire and an Avenger fell to the almost solid hail of flak put up by nearly 200 anti-aircraft guns around the Tokushima airfields. This day was notable in seeing the only attack ever to be made by the Fleet Air Arm on an enemy aircraft carrier, and a successful one at that, as recorded at the time in the diary of No. 849 Squadron, by then commanded by Lt Cdr A. J. Griffith, DSC, RNVR:

> Fleet arrived in the operations area in the early hours of the morning. Ramrods, CAPs were flown off. 'A' Flight were to fly as first Avengers strike of the day, and were ready to take off at 0900, briefed to bomb Okyama airfield. This strike, led by the CO, was ordered, at the last moment, to deal with some tankers just south of original target. Weather conditions were bad involving the combined strike to split up, only five of our aircraft reaching the target area.
>
> En route a Japanese CVE was sighted and duly bombed, scoring two hits out of 16 bombs. The honour went to Sub-Lt Cawood. No flak was encountered until after the attack had been pressed home. All our aircraft landed on safely. Other ramrods and CAPs were flown throughout the day.

The enemy ship was *Kaiyo*, a converted passenger liner, which was left ablaze with her back broken. She was later attacked by American aircraft, beached at nearby Beppu Bay, Kyushu, and subsequently scrapped. That evening No. 1844 Squadron Hellcats from *Formidable* shot down three Aichi B7A 'Grace' torpedo-bombers which they intercepted at 20,000ft heading for the British Task Force. A fourth was damaged and the remainder turned back without making their planned attack.

After replenishment, further operations commenced on 28 July, a dawn attack by twenty Avengers on Harima dockyard being one of several strikes on targets in the Inland Sea, which also included fighter raids on airfields and the naval base at Maizuru, north of Kyoto on Honshu, the main island of Japan. After a spell of bad weather on 29 July

activities resumed the following day despite fog in the Tokyo area, 336 sorties being flown and heavy damage caused to Japanese warships.

When the first atomic bomb was dropped on Japan the Fleet was ordered to stay out of the Hiroshima area, but improved weather conditions enabled strikes to resume on 9 August (the day the second such bomb was dropped on Nagasaki), 267 offensive sorties being flown in addition to 140 CAPs. The Fleet Air Arm gained its second Victoria Cross that day, again posthumously, when Lt (A) R. H. 'Hammy' Gray, RCNVR, of No. 1841 Squadron in Corsair KD658 '115/X' from *Formidable* was shot down while leading an attack on the escort ship *Amakusa* in Onagawa on Honshu island. He had pressed on despite his aircraft being hit and set on fire, crashing near to the escort.

Targets were becoming much harder to find and the next day carrier-borne aircraft roamed at will over Honshu. On the 11th all the carriers except *Indefatigable* left for Sydney for urgent maintenance, to be ready for the coming invasion of the Japanese homeland. Four days later, in the Fleet Air Arm's final fighter combat of the war, eight of a formation of twelve Japanese fighters were shot down by Seafires of the 24th Naval Fighter Wing which were escorting an Avenger strike. A Seafire and an Avenger were lost, the gunner of the latter disposing of another Japanese fighter before ditching. At 0700 that day, 15 August 1945, all further strikes were cancelled, the Japanese having surrendered.

Alan Swanton fought with No. 828 Squadron throughout this period:

After the Barracuda, with which we had previously been equipped, the Grumman Avenger was a great step forward. The Americans had designed their aircraft specifically to operate from aircraft carriers. We British on the other hand, with such a small force to equip, and a budget to match, had to make do with aircraft which had been adapted for use at sea. In fact fighter aircraft aboard HMS *Implacable*, even at that late stage of the war, were Seafires – an adaptation of the Spitfire with folding wings and an arrester hook. It was a splendid little aircraft but, with its narrow undercarriage and very limited endurance, it couldn't compete with the rugged fighter aircraft designed and built in the United States specifically for carrier operations.

At first sight the Avenger TBR (Torpedo-Bomber-Reconnaissance) looked a huge aircraft to me but I very soon learned to appreciate it. No longer those delays on deck after landing while a hookman struggled to disengage the hook from the arrester wire and others manually folded the wings in winds over the deck that almost blew them off their feet.

I got quite a kick out of being able to retract the hook by a flick of a switch and fold the

◀ **Avengers of No. 848 Squadron from *Formidable* on their way to attack a kamikaze airfield. (Official)**

mainplanes while taxying forward into the deck park, knowing that the next aircraft to land on would be relying on me to clear the landing area in the shortest possible time.

When the United States entered the war we learned that the signals employed by their deck landing control officers not only differed from ours in that they were mandatory rather than advisory but, worse still, their signals 'go higher' and 'come lower' had precisely the opposite meaning to those we were using. We literally had to change overnight. I can't help feeling that while they were at it, what a pity they didn't insist that we drove on the right side of the road, instead of allowing us to cling to the left and virtually becoming the odd man out in Europe!

A little over a month after VE-Day we reached our operational area in the Pacific and learned that our first strike was to be against the Japanese-occupied island of Truk. We had heard rumours that the inhabitants of this beleaguered island were so desperately short of food that they had been forced to resort to cannibalism. I'm not quite sure what I had in mind as I strapped on my revolver over my flying suit but presumably I aimed to avoid appearing on some Jap menu if it was humanly possible. In the event it did little to buoy up my spirits.

Came the day and we were briefed for our daylight operation while up on the flight deck our aircraft were being ranged for take-off.

A fleet carrier can accommodate around four squadrons and practically every serviceable aircraft was taking part. Even though they were packed as tightly as possible there wasn't room for those at the head of the range to make a free take-off. It had already been planned that the Seafires and Fireflies would be launched by catapult.

As I climbed into the leading Avenger and strapped myself in I knew by the number of fighters ahead of me that I should have some time to wait before it would be my turn to be flagged off.

On a signal from the bridge we all started engines and while they were warming up we carried out our various cockpit checks and prepared for take-off.

Slowly the carrier altered course into wind and increased speed. I could see Charles Lamb, the flight deck officer, standing near the catapult on the port bow while preparing to flag off the first of the fighters as soon as the ship steadied into wind. No sooner was the first one off than the next was being brought into position for loading on to the catapult. Everything seemed to be going like clockwork as far as I could see and every now and then I glimpsed the green flag being waved aloft as another fighter opened up to full throttle. Then down would come the flag and a split second later the aircraft would hurtle forward and sail into the air.

The whole sensation of being catapulted is quite unlike anything I have ever experienced. From start to finish the launch lasts no more than a second or two and in that

▶ **Lt 'Hammy' Gray, a Canadian serving with No. 1841 Squadron, was posthumously awarded the Victoria Cross for his courageous efforts in leading a Corsair attack on a Japanese escort ship on 9 August 1945. (FAA Museum)**

short time the aircraft is accelerated from a standstill to flying speed. The acceleration is quite smooth but so rapid one feels powerless in the grip of such a giant force. For those few seconds one is scarcely capable of blinking. In fact, during my earliest launches I used to think to myself, 'If this lasts much longer, I can't stand it'. Then suddenly it's over – you're briefly imbued by a feeling of complete euphoria.

Just occasionally something goes very wrong and that is what happened during the launch of our strike on Truk. Charles Lamb was at the point of despatching an aircraft when, for some unaccountable reason, it fell off the catapult cradle. As it hit the deck the wooden propeller shattered and a part of one of the blades hit Charles and almost severed one of his legs. It took a little time to lift the damaged aircraft by crane and clear of the flight deck so that the operation could proceed. The rest of the fighters were catapulted successfully and then it was my turn, as CO of No. 823 Squadron, to carry out the first free take-off.

The Avengers were powered by Pratt and Whitney air-cooled engines and they had all been running for quite some time – not too fast or they would overheat and not too slowly or the plugs might oil up.

I was waved forward to a position on the centre-line of the deck. Being the first meant I should have the shortest run, so I held the aircraft on the brakes while I ran the engine up to full throttle. Even so the engine still seemed a bit sluggish and I noted that the revolutions weren't building up as fast as they should. By

◀HMS *Victorious* is near-missed by a kamikaze. (A. G. Clayton)

the time we were abreast the island I was fairly certain we weren't going to make it with our full bomb load. For the first time in my life I decided to abort a deck take-off. Snapping the throttle shut I braked hard, but an oil or glycol spillage from a previous accident may have left the deck a bit greasy. Instead of coming to a halt somewhere near the bows I found to my dismay that they were getting alarmingly close. Sadly I just couldn't stop in time and the aircraft truckled gently over the bows and dropped into the sea directly ahead of the ship which was cleaving its way through the water at somewhere around thirty knots.

As it hit the sea the aircraft righted itself momentarily and quite automatically I started to carry out the drill we had often practised. Releasing my safety harness I abandoned the cockpit and was groping my way towards the dinghy release panel when the ship's bows sliced through the aircraft like a knife through butter. The next few minutes were a battle for survival but fear didn't seem to enter into it. The water all the way down the ship's side was naturally very turbulent and I swallowed quite a lot of it as a succession of eddies sucked me downwards. At one point as I was on my way down I encountered what I think must have been the port wing of the aircraft going the other way. I made a grab at it and was dragged back up again. Unfortunately, as the broken wing surfaced it straightened out and trapped my fingers. I was very fortunate they weren't severed. As it happened the damage wasn't serious although I carried the scars for years.

Up on the bridge there wasn't much the Captain could do to avoid slicing us up in the ship's propellers. He didn't even know if we had all been swept down the same side. As it happened my senior observer, Lt Nigel Matthews, and Chief Petty Officer Telegraphist/Air Gunner Ward both found themselves in the sea on the starboard side of the ship. We all met up together bobbing around in the wake. Fortunately neither of them were injured and I was grateful for the help they gave me in inflating my life jacket. While doing this they discovered that I was being weighed down by my personal dinghy which was attached to me by a lanyard. They soon had this inflated too and having shoved me into it they hung on to the sides. By then, of course, the worst part of our adventure was over and we didn't have long to wait before the destroyer, HMS *Terpsichore*, which was acting as safety vessel, came alongside and picked us up.

The ship's doctor patched up my damaged fingers for me but for some reason or other the experience seemed to have shaken me up rather more than the other two. When they were transferred back to the carrier I was kept on board till the following day. I certainly felt pretty grim and a bout of seasickness as well didn't improve matters much.

By the time I was transferred to *Implacable* I discovered that Nigel had taken part in a second strike against Truk. It had me wondering what sort of squadron commander I appeared in the eyes of all my young aviators. It was a bad start to our Far Eastern operations and the last thing I wanted was to be thought chicken-hearted or lacking in moral fibre. Nigel on the other hand had shown the right spirit in getting back to his ship and on with the job. If he had any misgivings in his Commanding Officer he certainly never voiced them. He had already come off second best during our earlier operations off Norway and had received a painful wound when we ran into AA fire after successfully torpedoing a fully laden merchant ship.

Truk was just the 'curtain raiser'. Our real hostilities began a few weeks later after a brief spell ashore on the airstrip at Ponam in the Admiralty Islands. By this time the Japs had their backs to the wall and there was a very real threat from kamikaze attacks which had already wrought havoc among some US carriers. Every precaution was taken to keep these suicide attacks at bay. Returning strikes could only approach the Task Force from seaward and even then only after being checked by the fighter defence to make sure that no uninvited guests were tagging along with us.

Strikes continued throughout July against shipping and harbour installations. We also flew inland and attacked airfields and industrial targets. There seemed to be no shortage of aircraft on the ground, and I for one was only too happy that most seemed to remain there. One could only conclude that an acute shortage of fuel or something of that sort kept them grounded. On the other hand there was no shortage of ammunition and the anti-aircraft fire took its toll all too frequently.

During one of our briefings we were warned

on no account to jettison bombs on Hiroshima or Nagasaki. Since none of our targets had been as far south as either of these towns I felt that was hardly likely, though I thought it possible there might be POW camps in that area which we should avoid. However, I didn't have to wait long in order to find out that these two towns had been selected for the most devastating air attacks of all time. The first atomic bomb was dropped on Hiroshima on 6 August and three days later Nagasaki was given the same treatment.

I am not sure that we aboard our carrier had any knowledge of this historic event till some days later. In the meantime we continued on as before. On 9 August we carried out two strikes and were in the air for a total of eight hours. On the following day we made our last attack on the Japanese mainland against an airfield at Koriyama. It seemed particularly tragic that we should have lost an Avenger, two Fireflies and a Corsair on what was, for us, the very last day of World War Two.

The ceasefire came into effect on 15 August and the war was formally ended in a ceremony aboard the US battleship *Missouri* on 2 September 1945.

In the final weeks before VE-Day there had been a steady build-up of British carrier strength in the Far East. It was planned to reorganize the aircraft squadrons and form new ones to build up to a total strength of twenty-two Carrier Air Groups for the intended final onslaught against Japan. The new light fleet carriers *Colossus*, *Glory*, *Venerable* and *Vengeance* had arrived in Australia during July and August, these forming the 11th Aircraft Carrier Squadron under Rear Admiral C. H. J. Harcourt, who flew his flag in HMS *Indomitable*. They were equipped with two squadrons of aircraft, one each of Barracudas and Corsairs, 162 in all, but they arrived too late to see action.

Not every Japanese was inclined to accept the surrender and on 31 August and 1 September aircraft from *Indomitable* and *Venerable* carried out attacks on suicide boats around Hong Kong Island. With this last task accomplished the Fleet Air Arm could at last return to a peacetime existence.

▼ Work begins on clearing up the debris on the flight deck of HMS *Formidable* soon after her first kamikaze attack on 4 May 1945. (FAA Museum)

CHAPTER 25

The Ladies

An invaluable aspect of the activities of the wartime Fleet Air Arm was the increasing role played by women. Numerous members of the Women's Royal Navy Service served on naval air stations, and here are the tales of two of them:

Monica Marriott, then Monica Baxter, writes:

I had joined the Wrens on New Years Day 1942 and was one of the first six cinema operators to be trained at the Gaumont British School for Projectionists, which adjoined what was left of the bombed-out Holborn Empire. I was chosen for this new category not because I was adept at the mysteries of electricity but because I had been educated at a convent, and the powers that be considered that if nuns had taught me needlework I might be trainable to thread a film through a Kalee 8 Projector. I still have my certificate from Gaumont British to prove that their theory was correct!

After a course lasting two weeks, during which we were exempted from the carrot- and potato-bashing at Westfield College with the other new recruits, I was sent down to Parkeston Quay to the destroyer base. Two of the six girls were drafted with me and we worked in an old wooden Customs shed which had been converted to a cinema. There, during the day we showed instructional films to the crews from the ships at the base, to men from the MTBs from across the river at Felixstowe and to various detachments from the other forces in the area. At night we did two 'houses' of entertainment films, with three changes of programme each week, and the place was always full. Here the men from the mine-sweepers and the destroyers and corvettes as well as the base personnel could come and relax for a couple of hours whilst still being on call over the loudspeaker system. The ratings sat on the ground floor and the petty officers and officers were on the balcony, in the middle of which was the 'ops box' made of corrugated iron and like a furnace to work in with two projectors running on carbon arc lamps.

With the photographic memories of youth, we soon knew every word of the aircraft recognition films and *Duties of a Look-out* with the admonition to report 'anything seen, or thought to be seen'. Films such as *The 49th Parallel* were better, but the musicals were the best of all, and we would sing at the top of our voices, thinking that the noise of the machines' running would drown our efforts. On one occasion, when we were showing *100 Men and a Girl*, the base captain knocked on the door of the re-wind room at the end of the show and informed us that he had paid 1s. 9d. to hear Deanna Durbin sing an excerpt from *Traviata* and not our rendering of same!

Two more Wrens were sent to help and we did a lot of work on the Dome Teacher, an igloo-like structure simulating conditions under which anti-aircraft guns were in action. Then, with a hook on my arm and an engagement ring on my finger, I was recommended for a commission and thus made my way to HMS *Condor* at Arbroath.

Again I was one of six Wrens selected for a course in Dead Reckoning Navigation, to be attached, when commissioned, to the Observer Training School to analyse the Navigation Exercises, or 'Navexes' as they were called. At this point I found the Fleet Air Arm very strange after being on a destroyer base for two years, amidst so many friends and doing a familiar job. The course was difficult, or at least I found it so, and I am sure we tried the patience of the chiefs and petty officers who taught us. They were all very experienced observers, mostly from HMS *Glorious*, and obviously they had not trained girls before. Neither had the rather brusque Commander RN who lectured us in the mysteries of meteorology. When told that one of us had a degree in science, he remarked drily that he thought it must be in domestic science! We spent days in the classroom, more of them out on the airfield, compass-swinging in the biting wind that must only blow in that part of Scotland straight from the Arctic. Eventually we were sent up in a Stinson Reliant for our first Navex, and then later in a Swordfish, fixing on Buddon Ness and flying up towards Aberdeen over Glamis Castle.

Then, with successful exams behind us, the six of us went to the Royal Naval College at Greenwich for the Officers' Training Course which lasted for three weeks. During this time I had the joy of being able to meet up with my father on several of his business trips from Nottingham and he would take me out to dinner at the Trocadero.

Being the father of girls rather than boys, the odds at 5–1, I like to think that he was proud of me in my little round hat with the white band round it denoting the fact that I was a cadet officer. Greenwich was fun, and interesting, and we had green vegetables rather than mashed swedes – the staple diet at Arbroath.

Then it was back to Scotland again and the start of our duties in the Observer School, with two of us attached to each course going through. When the charts came in at the end of an exercise one realized how much the young

▲ **WRNS Air Mechanic trainees move a Sea Hurricane in June 1943 at Milmeece, otherwise HMS *Fledgling*, near Stoke-on-Trent. (Via Mollie Brown)**

officers had to learn and how vulnerable they would be when eventually sent to a carrier. Many of them appeared so young even to me, and I at that time was just twenty-two. A lot of them were very air-sick and the charts would come in bearing evidence of this, and of the fact that their compasses had been jabbed into their fingers instead of into the paper. The course was intensive and tough, with the occasional fatal flying accident common to all Fleet Air Arm stations.

Life in the wardroom was never dull, with a cross-section of women from all walks of life and in all circumstances. I think the ones that impressed me most were the widows. They were so earnest and intent and so dedicated. Amongst us there was a Battle of Britain widow, and also the widow of a submariner, and I would look at the sapphire and diamond ring on my finger and wonder if my fiancé would make it. He was on convoy duties to Gibraltar and Malta on either a destroyer or a corvette, and we snatched leaves together whenever we could.

In April 1944 I was appointed to HMS *Nightjar* at Inskip and I can remember how delighted I was to be moving a little nearer home and into an area where I had contacts. This delight continued when I realized what a happy establishment it was, and the memories of the personalities I met there are clearer in my mind than others. The station was divided into two camps, Wharles and Inskip, both being pretty remote except from the airfield, and we cycled miles and miles. On Saturday afternoons, which were normally free, we would speed off into Kirkham, park our bikes for sixpence in the yard attached to a funeral director near the station and catch a train into either Blackpool or Preston.

Inskip was a happy station and reflected the efficiency of its Captain, J. B. Heath. We worked hard, and played hard, and I think that friendships made there have stood the test of time. I remember it being announced from the control tower that the Second Front had been opened in June 1944 with the D-Day landings, and we celebrated VE-Day and VJ-Day whilst I was there. Hopes were rising, and although we knew there was a long way still to go the atmosphere of life was different and we 'forced on' with an extra smile of hope for the future.

At first I was quartered in a Nissen hut cabin together with five other Wren officers, and then as numbers increased a derelict farmhouse was taken over for additional accommodation and I moved in there together with an army of mice who delighted in making their nests in our underclothing drawers. Whilst in the cabin for six, the Director of the WRNS came round and inspected the camp and did the rounds of our quarters. The other five girls had photographs of their beloveds on their various lockers and they ranged from a Commander through various branches and ranks of the combined services down to my ever-loving in the square rig of a leading seaman. Ignoring the shoulder pips and gold braid, Dame Vera swept down into my corner and demanded to know who the 'delightful young man belonged to'. This delightful young man was, I swear, the only naval rating to be allowed to bath in Wren Officers' quarters by courtesy of the officer in charge, a formidable lady from Belfast but with a heart of gold. Accommodation in Wharles village was minimal but I managed to find one cottage where the head of the house was serving a prison sentence, thus freeing a bed for a PG! But no bath. So, when we were all out at our various duties on the airfield, as long as he was in civilian clothes my sailor was spirited in for his ablutions.

We in the women's services were rarely in mortal danger. We suffered much less from the rigours of war than many civilians. We were not destined to perform heroic flights from the decks of aircraft carriers or take part in landings on enemy territory. We were prepared to leave it to the 'stars' of the show to do that. But in every show there is something called a 'supporting cast'. Now, some forty years on, I would like to think that together with many others in the WRNS I played some part, however small, in that role.

Leading Wren Air Radio Mechanic Sheila McCloy, now Mrs Clark, recollects:

I joined the Women's Royal Naval Service on 30 September 1942 at the age of twenty-one. My instructions were to report to Mill Hill, London, for two weeks' probationary course. Recruits were free to change their minds about entering the service during this initial training.

Mill Hill was a huge concrete building, possibly an unfinished hospital. The stairways and floor were of raw cement. Our days were filled with squad drill, lectures on naval life and terminology, very good meals and hours and hours on hands and knees rubbing the floors with cloths wrung out in buckets of cold water. I remember a girl who wore gloves to do this was greatly scorned by her shipmates.

We were keen volunteers – I only met one Wren during my service who had entered as a conscript. Sadly, she was killed in a Barracuda crash.

Cabins and kit, wakey-wakey and pipe down, liberty boats and NAAFI all became familiar. The dormitory cabins with double bunks would have held about fifty girls. Once, after lights out, some were whispering and giggling. It had been a tiring day. Suddenly I bellowed 'Pipe down!' The immediate silence was most gratifying.

From Mill Hill I went to a former theological college in Finchley Road, North London, to do the first three months of training as a radio mechanic. The entry was divided into two watches, each working alternate weeks late into the evening. We were instructed at Chelsea Polytechnic in the fundamentals of wireless and in practical metalwork. So we learnt how to make good soldered joints and to fashion spanners out of metal bars. There was a weekly test and we had a text book to study.

Our first home leave occurred during this time and I went down to my parents in Cornwall. At some stage I must have been in contact with chicken pox. The spots appeared the evening I reported back from leave. Then followed a miserable week of solitary confinement in a small cabin. My only visitor, after a doctor had confirmed chicken pox, was a sullen VAD. She brought meals and emptied my slop pail. Eventually kind-hearted 3rd Officer Pelly lent me her portable radio and this made all the difference to my morale.

The class instructor told my watch that I would probably move down to the next entry. In fact I had been spending many hours swatting the *Fundamentals of Wireless* and the results of the first test on my return to work (I had refused a chance of sick leave) were better than any preceding tests.

By now we all talked in radio jargon and applied the terms indiscriminately. The water jets in the urinal of this normally male college had a 'pulse recurrence frequency'. We coined a mnemonic relating to measurements of voltage, current and capacity: 'Henry's inducements are not far advanced, but his eye (i) lacks potential'.

The next part of the six-month Air Radio Mechanics' Course took place at HMS *Ariel*, Culcheth, in Lancashire. We now lived in a hutted camp on the same terms as the seaman radio mechanics. We were issued with bell-bottomed trousers, navy shirts and a box of tools. We also had heavy navy jerseys and ribbed knee-length woollen knickers.

The entry was split between wireless telegraphy and air–surface vessel radar, which was my line. Each group was told to elect a leader. Pauline Gompers was chosen for the W/Ts and I became spokesman for the ASVs.

Living was pretty basic at HMS *Ariel* and the food was not good. On days off Wrens would hitch lifts on lorries heading for Manchester or Liverpool. The great treat was to have a meal in style at the Liverpool Adelphi or Manchester Midland Hotel and get a glimpse of some gracious living. We wore uniform at all times; No. 1 rig was the navy jacket and skirt with a white shirt and black tie and, of course, sailor hat with the ship's ribbon.

A couple of incidents may be of interest to recall. There was a rumour, started in our case by the instructor PO, that the very high frequency wave length of ASV was dangerous for women and could cause infertility. Pauline Gompers and I agreed that this was a case where we became operational as class leaders. We reported the story to the senior Wren officer, who promptly said 'Rubbish!' Pauline and I accepted that there was no reason to believe the rumour but said we thought some action should be taken. In due course there was an official notice from the First Sea Lord stating that 'In the opinion of the Medical Director General there was absolutely no truth in the allegation that ultra high frequencies were injurious to health'.

The other event took place at divisions one morning. A rating was called out before the whole ship's company. A punishment sentence was read and his badge of rank (Leading Seaman) was ripped from his sleeve. We later learnt that his notes of secret wavelengths, made probably in preparation for an exam, had been picked up in a dance hall in the local town.

We were, of course, given some secret information, and our classroom notes were handed in at the end of daily lectures.

In May 1943 we were posted as newly rated Leading Wren Air Radio Mechanics to various naval air stations. Two of the brightest girls went to Malvern, where research was carried out. One of them, Joy Windsor, reached the rank of 2nd Officer, Air Radio, in due course. I was sent, with Paddy Hurst, to RNAS Evanton near Invergordon, on the shores of the Moray Firth.

This was a small repair and maintenance unit which used the runways of RAF Evanton. Our work involved installing ASV in aircraft. Electricians carried out the wiring and riggers and fitters set the short-wave aerials in position. The Wren radio mechanics, having fitted the transmitter and receiver into their supporting frames, connected the aerial system and soldered the joints. The ASV would then be tried out on the ground.

Following this the Wren mechanic was taken for a flight by Chief Petty Officer Jaggard, the station pilot. Her job was to direct him to 'home in' by means of the ASV.

The receiver would be tuned in flight to pick up a 'blip' from the 'squegger' (a radio beacon set at ground level on the approach to the airfield). This was seen as an intermittent rectangular pulse at right angles and on either side of the vertical central line of the cathode ray tube. The pilot then followed the directions to port or starboard called by the radio mechanic through the 'Gosport tube'. When the 'blip' was correctly aligned and the receiver tuned to 'pin-point' the aircraft would be on course to fly directly over the squegger to the runway and thus show that the ASV was functioning correctly. When in use on operations this apparatus was required to pick up a signal, or blip, reflected by the beam of the ASV transmitter from a vessel on the surface of the sea.

Repairs to ASV involved checking the receiver for a fault by means of an oscilloscope which would show up a break in the circuit. This was corrected by replacing a valve, resistor or capacitor. Transmitters had only two strange valves with metal cooling fins and a deceptively simple circuit consisting mainly of a pair of lecher bars. Repair work was carried out in the mechanics' workshop and it was here that we made the proverbial 'rabbits' during slack times, lampstands, ashtrays, letter openers and so on.

In the course of my time at Evanton I went up in Swordfish, Albacores, Walruses and Barracudas. It is hard to describe the excitement and feeling of privilege to be flying over the glens and mountains of the Eastern Highlands of Scotland as a small part of the Navy at war.

There were about seventy Wrens, in various categories, at Evanton. We were housed about a couple of miles from the base in a hunting lodge called Novar House. It was deep in a beautiful forest that lay beneath the mountain Fyrish. There was a single Wren officer, 1st Officer Buckland, a kindly and capable lady. The food was very good. We slept in cabins with four or six beds. Wood off-cuts could be collected from the forest, which was being felled by a community of Newfoundlanders, and we would make log fires in the bedrooms. This was luxury indeed.

For entertainment there was occasionally a dance in the hall of Novar House, even fancy dress sometimes. There were regular film shows in the great hangar at RAF Evanton. It was very moving when the audience joined in the popular wartime songs relayed on the tannoy before the performance. There was the usual topical variety show with script and songs made up by the local talent.

My time at Evanton came to an end when I was recommended for the Officers' Training Course. In April 1944, at Stoke Poges, the metamorphosis from Leading Wren to 3rd Officer took place, and after that service life became something completely different.

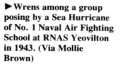

►Wrens among a group posing by a Sea Hurricane of No. 1 Naval Air Fighting School at RNAS Yeovilton in 1943. (Via Mollie Brown)

CHAPTER 26

Medical Aspects

Much has been written about the operational aspects of air warfare from the point of view of the air crews involved but it is interesting to read of the experiences and viewpoints of two members of the medical profession who served aboard wartime carriers.

Surgeon Commander Robinson was aboard HMS *Ark Royal* from May 1940 to November 1941:

> The general health of the ship's company was in my opinion extraordinarily good. The 'Ark' was very steady in rough weather. The number of decks made her a particularly cool ship in the tropics and gave plenty of space to sleep in the open air. The flight deck gave great facilities for exercise of every sort. Deck hockey, gymnastics, PT, fencing and boxing and, above all, walking were possible. When the ship was in harbour inter-part football and hockey were played. On the whole surprisingly little swimming was done by the sailors although the age average was low.
>
> The morale of the ship's company was as good as any Captain would wish. This was due to loyalty to their Captain and the fair name of their ship, and in no small measure to the trust which all hands had for the Flag Officer Commanding Force H, Admiral Sir James Somerville. Of grumbling there was much, but I know that few would have accepted individual relief from the ship.
>
> *Ark Royal*, during the most intensive part of her career, was a very hard-worked ship, and her activities fell into three main periods: October 1939 to March 1940 – South Atlantic; May and June 1940 – Norway campaign; June 1940 to November 1941 – Mediterranean. I joined the ship in June 1940, after the Norwegian campaign had ended. I thus have no personal experience of that period, but my observations are accurate, based as they are on close daily contacts with air crews.
>
> The ship was suddenly recalled from the relative peace of the Mediterranean and plunged straight into intense activity. Due to the long hours of daylight in this latitude, aircraft were being operated for nearly twenty-four hours a day. Swordfish and Skuas made bombing attacks on land objectives, encountering enormous difficulties of terrain,

▼ Swordfish on the flight deck of HMS *Ark Royal* in the South Atlantic during 1940. (Cdr R. N. Everett)

and under constant threat of attack by enemy aircraft or of losing the carrier through fog and bad weather. The Skuas, particularly in their dual role of fighters and bombers, were called upon to endure very prolonged and heavy stress, but they were always considered by pilots to be too slow and of a design which made aerobatics in air combat very unsafe. Yet their crews performed wonders, and it was only in their last operation, against the *Scharnhorst* in Trondheim harbour, that they had serious casualties.

With it all there was little sign of cracking amongst the surviving aircraft crews at the end of the campaign. Two factors I think militated against this. The first was the shortness of this period of action, comparative that is to the final period of the ship's life. The very action itself seemed to carry them along, and worry and fatigue were forgotten. There just wasn't time for them to think of the future. The second factor was the return which the ship made at fairly frequent intervals to a home port, with the opportunity this gave for relaxation. Aircraft personnel and ship's company alike were able to go ashore, play games, visit the local pubs and cinemas in an atmosphere of comparative peace and tranquility.

The ship entered upon the third and final phase of her existence in June 1940. Immediately she had completed her part in the Norway campaign she was despatched direct to Gibraltar. With the exception of a brief fortnight in September 1940 spent in Liverpool, her ship's company saw no other port but Gibraltar for eighteen months. During this eighteen months she was occupied in bombing attacks on Italian ports, convoy work in the Atlantic, interception of raiders, protection of Malta convoys and keeping that island supplied with RAF fighter aircraft. All this time everyone in the ship was subject to the stress of war but the main weight fell on the flying personnel.

There are three main causes of stress among air crew, the first of which is monotony, which I would put as the cause of inefficiency of some airmen. The description of war being periods of intense boredom interspersed with periods of intense action was perfectly exemplified in the 'Ark'. The routine of anti-submarine patrols, fighter training, air-light-torpedo attacks, deck-landing training and reconnaissance was broken at intervals by bombing attacks (invariably done at daybreak) and convoy runs. During the latter the Swordfish crews were grounded and had the experience of feeling what it was like to be the bombed instead of the bomber. On return to port the air crews had little opportunity to release from the monotony because life in Gibraltar was itself intensely monotonous. Thus there were two circles of unvarying routine, one at sea and the other ashore. One got so used to both that the change from ship to shore gave no relief. What was badly needed was not so much a rest as a change of scene. I am convinced that a visit to any other port, even for a day, would have had a most beneficial effect upon everyone's spirits.

The good effect of a rest and a change of environment was strikingly exemplified in the case of some members of one TSR squadron. This squadron had been well over a year in the 'Ark' and were told that they were to be relieved and sent home. The relieving squadron duly arrived, but instead of going home as they expected the squadron relieved were divided into three. One part went home (being routed in a slow convoy and torpedoed on the way), one part was sent to Trinidad, while the third lot were attached to the new squadron as reserve crews. It was little wonder that the effect of this move had bad results. The men left behind had at one stroke lost their squadron, their friends and their chance of a well-earned rest. Surgeon Commander Williams took the step of recommending that these officers should be sent to Tangier for ten days. With the backing of Captain Maund this was arranged. The result was most successful. The party were extremely well cared for by the British residents there and duly returned to the ship quite on the top line and fit for anything.

A second cause of stress is war risk. In a very few cases there was an early deterioration in efficiency due to this factor. These (and there were very few of them) seemed to chuck their hands in almost at the outset of experiencing stress. They presented no problem, for they were invariably sent home as unlikely ever to prove good flyers. The large majority of the FAA improved steadily with action in which they took part, thus becoming increasingly dependable and useful to their squadrons. But in this lay their undoing. Having, so to speak, got their 'First Fifteen' colours they were automatically selected for every ensuing operation. Thus the willing horse was regularly flogged. When they had topped the crest of their efficiency and were beginning to feel the effects of the strain, every subsequent operation served to accelerate the process of deterioration.

A third cause is the type of aircraft. This is rather outside the province of these remarks but nevertheless a contributory factor to the deterioration of efficiency was the obsolete or obsolescent types of aircraft in which they carried out their duties. The Skua was always considered by the fighter pilots to be a slow, unsafe and undergunned machine. The advent of the Fulmar made them much more contented though they still yearned for the fast single-seater such as the Hurricane or the Martlet, and events proved that they were quite right. The Swordfish crews were more satisfied because they knew that they had a reliable machine whose very lack of speed was sometimes an asset. All the FAA, however, felt that they were neglected as a service in respect of the machines they flew.

Detection of deterioration in air crew by an FAA Medical Officer needs a combination of qualities – qualities which I wish I could say I possessed. He must know all the flying personnel, not only by name but sufficiently well to be able to form a good degree of knowledge of their characters, their professional ability, position in their squadrons and something of their jargon and of the stress to which they are subjected. He must be able to detect quickly a change in their outlook or habits and yet must never have the appearance of spying on them. He must stand in the light of a friend to whom they can turn for sympathy and advice. He must be prepared to listen to their grumblings without too obviously siding with or opposing them. He must be able to give friendly warnings without arousing antagonism, and advice without being sententious. Lastly, when it falls to his lot to ground a pilot or observer, or send him home for rehabilitation, he must be something of a diplomat. For he must at one and the same time provide hope for the airman's future and rob his enforced treatment of the imputation of being a failure. In this duty of looking after the flying personnel the MO's difficulties are halved if the Commander (Flying) and the squadron COs are thoughtful and understanding.

There are a number of frequent symptoms to guide him. A recurrent feature which I noticed in a good many reports was dread of flying over the sea, this being often the first symptom elicited on questioning. In the case of pilots, a lack of faith in their observer was sometimes elicited, though this never happened where the crew had been flying together for a long time.

Poor deck-landings, if recurrent in an experienced pilot, were often significant of a nervous deterioration. A 'bottle' from Commander (F) or his squadron CO did not help a pilot much in recovering his efficiency.

Mounting wine bills quite often were a sign of strain. This however was the case more often with the 'tired horse' than the newly joined officer.

Incidentally, it was in our opinion a great pity that the annual medical examinations were dropped. This examination proved a useful opportunity for a general check-up and often the flying people welcomed the official confirmation that they were A1B1.

The commoner symptoms of anxiety state were nearly always present: insomnia, moodiness, irritability, emotionalism and physical signs were all very constant features.

We had a very much smaller percentage of nervous cases from the non-flying personnel. These cases tended to fall into three classes, namely (a) the anxiety states and hysterias, (b) the constitutional inferiors and (c) malingerers. Amongst the commoner symptoms encountered in class (a) were dread of gunfire. Claustrophobia varied with each case. Some had a fear of any enclosed space while others were quite happy in their mess-decks but dreaded going below the waterline. Oddly enough, I do not remember a single case amongst the flying people where this symptom was mentioned.

The constitutional inferiors were all misfits who should not have been taken into the service at all. It was sometimes possible to find them a niche where they could be of some use. Usually, however, they had to be sent home.

I can only remember one case of malingering amongst the patients under my care. In this case, after we had made many endeavours to improved his morale he was surveyed from the station – much too kind a fate for him.

As to treatment, latterly a rest camp was established ashore to which we sent needy cases. A short period of change of routine proved most beneficial in a large percentage. Some who were suffering from having been kept too long at sea were sent home.

All told, the neuro-psychiatric cases in the *Ark Royal* were very few in number. This was, I think, due to the excellent team spirit which pervaded the ship and to the implicit trust we all had in our Captain and Admiral.

On the FAA side I gave regular instruction to the flying personnel of each squadron on the contents and use of the first-aid kit contained in each aircraft. In my lecture I explained the working of the tubonic ampoules of morphia, two of which were in each kit. Some time after this one of the Fulmars on fighter patrol got lost. The crew, after giving their position approximately, had to force-land in the sea. Both the pilot and air-gunner scrambled out, but as occasionally happens, the dinghy failed to emerge, so that they were left supported only by their Mae Wests and a small piece of wood. The water was cold and rough and their prospects were gloomy. After some hours they became so despondent that they decided that it would be better to drown quickly. However, they sighted the first-aid kit, which had floated clear of the sinking plane, and found that the morphia was still dry. They remembered my descriptions of the numbing effect of the drug and decided that it might ease their position a little. Accordingly they injected each other with one-sixth of a grain and awaited results. The pilot, who told the story to me afterwards, said that the first thing they noticed was a decrease in the feeling of chill, then their mood of despondency and resignation changed to marked optimism. They felt so cheerful that they decided to hang on through the night. About an hour later they were sighted and rescued by a Sunderland sent out from Gibraltar for the purpose of looking for them.

Towards the end of the war, Eric Morton was serving in HMS *Pursuer* and had a very different experience:

Our squadron in *Pursuer* was No. 898, equipped with Grumman Hellcat fighters. We were a happy crowd, though in retrospect one regrets the division between Fleet Air Arm and ship's officers, and in particular the T124X agreement officers and ratings who made up most of the engine room and supply staff including the stewards. Technically they were Merchant Navy serving with the RN under the T124X agreement which they had signed, although in fact some of them would never have been accepted by a reputable Merchant skipper.

Our squadron, like many fighter squadrons, had a number of New Zealand pilots, and the salt of the earth they were, all volunteers. Good pilots, friendly, cheerful and great lads for a party. Despite their occasional transgressions everybody liked them, even the more responsible RN executive officers, whose peacetime Dartmouth standards of 'officer-like behaviour' and discipline were occasionally shattered. Typical of the 'Kiwi' pilots was Ken McCrea, Sub-Lieutenant (A) RNZNVR, a tall, rangy, somewhat quieter New Zealander. I learned after he left us and joined a fleet carrier in the Pacific that his aircraft was hit by Japanese anti-aircraft fire over the island of Ishigaki, badly damaged, and Ken's leg was virtually severed by a shell fragment. Nevertheless he managed to maintain control and awareness and find his way back to the carrier. He crash-landed on the flight deck and was lifted out of his cockpit unconscious, but survived following amputation of the leg, and I believe awarded the DSO.

In retrospect there can be little doubt that thousands of British and Allied lives (possibly my own included) were saved by the atomic bombs being dropped on the Japanese mainland on 6 and 9 August, and I for one am grateful for that cataclysmic intervention by the Americans which, following on the decisive Japanese defeat in Burma by the Fourteenth Army, was sufficient to ensure that they sued for peace forthwith and surrendered unconditionally. Consequently the events described below can indeed be described as 'light-hearted'. Happily the much more serious campaign for which we were preparing did not take place.

In the event, news of a likely Jap surrender came through on 11 August and Mountbatten, our 'Supremo', suspended all operations, land, sea and air, on 15 August but subsequently decided to proceed with the invasion as planned. It was considered uncertain as to whether or not the large numbers of Japanese forces widely scattered over a vast area would obey the surrender orders. Probably also the invasion plans were so complex and far reaching that it was easier to allow them to proceed according to schedule than to abort and reorganize a reoccupation. Operation 'Zipper' therefore went ahead largely as planned.

For *Pursuer*, however, things were changed. Our Hellcat squadron disembarked on 18 August and we then became a communications ship for the landings around Port Swettenham.

We embarked a naval landing party, a contingent of Royal Marines and senior Naval, Army and Air Force personnel for the landings, and sailed from Trincomalee on 4 September. Meantime the formal surrender of the Japanese took place in Tokyo Bay on 2 September 1945.

HMS *Pursuer* in company with a large convoy was soon approaching the western coast of Malaya. We were preparing for what we still feared might be an opposed and bloody landing

▼ The escort carrier *Pursuer*, which served mainly in Far Eastern waters. (E. V. Morton)

– at least in some areas. We had learned not to trust the enemy but to respect their fighting qualities and in particular their well-known preference for death rather than defeat or surrender.

In *Pursuer* our own fighting capabilities were reduced drastically as a result of the loss of our principal weapon, the squadron. Our main justification now was the sophisticated communications systems, radio and radar with which we were equipped. We had also hastily prepared our own invasion force from among the ship's company, known colloquially as 'Bromwich's Brigands'. Lt Cdr (A) 'Scruffy' Bromwich, a well known FAA character, was Commander (Flying) in *Pursuer*. He was reputed to have been the first pilot to deck land a Sea Hurricane IB, and pronounced it 'easy'.

To Commander (F), with no flying duties, was assigned, totally in character, the organization of an armed landing party consisting of two jeeps and trailers and a company of sailors armed with rifles and Lanchester sub-machine guns. The jeeps were fitted with temporary Lewis gun mountings and practice drills and manoeuvres were carried out on the flight deck. What were the official terms of reference of this force I never knew, but clearly 'Scruffy' Bromwich was delighted at the prospect of such an independent practical assignment.

We arrived at the entrance to the creek which leads up to Port Swettenham on the night of 8 September and anchored undisturbed while the main convoy remained offshore and prepared for the next day's landings, which were scheduled for the beaches at Port Dickson to the south and Morib to the north at first light. Still uncertain of the Japanese reaction, we, in common with the rest of the convoy, maintained full blackout and remained closed up at action stations.

At about 2100 *Pursuer* received a signal from one of the troopships, SS *Wingsang*, reporting a suspected case of bubonic plague on board and requesting urgent medical assistance. This was a most surprising and unwelcome communication and it appeared that *Wingsang* was anchored about three-quarters of a mile from us in one of the nearby creeks of which there were many in the approaches to the port. She had stores and Indian pioneer corps embarked ready for the next day's landings. My task was to find and board the merchant ship, examine the patient and take what steps I felt were necessary in the light of my findings. This was a great event, and at last I felt that I was involved in the real action and off we went in the motor cutter with armed boat's crew to find *Wingsang*. It was the first and last time that I paid a medical visit carrying an automatic pistol but it certainly gave me some confidence as we set off into what seemed very much 'the unknown' pitch-black tropical creeks, teeming – or so we imagined – with mosquitoes, crocodiles and hostile Japs! Luckily we encountered only the former.

In fact we had some difficulty in finding the blacked-out *Wingsang* in the dark but eventually our hail was appropriately answered and we came alongside. A ladder was thrown down and I climbed up to what seemed a towering height with terrible thoughts of plague in my mind. I was surprised to find that all seemed quiet and peaceful and was welcomed on the boat deck by the first mate, a splendid Norwegian, Chris Petersen, and conducted with due formality to the Captain's cabin. No sign of panic, no worried OC troops, no ship's doctor, no patient. We settled in the Captain's cabin and drinks were served by the steward.

It transpired that the ship's doctor had made this unlikely but potentially disastrous diagnosis of plague in one of the sepoys, but not unreasonably the Captain was suspicious and wished confirmation. In due course the doctor was summoned. He was a sad, grey haired Indian with several day's growth of grey stubble, rather soiled white ducks and an unconvincing manner and I was not surprised at the Captain's lack of confidence. After the normal professional courtesies he took me below.

We traversed several companionways and troop decks, stifling hot and crammed with sleeping Indian soldiers and to my surprise instead of finding our patient isolated in the sick bay, we found him in a corner of one of the troop decks surrounded by his fellow soldiers. He was frightened, febrile and looked ill. The swollen inguinal glands or 'Bubo' were confirmed, but were unilateral – happily for our peace of mind, for the entire invasion force and probably for history. It took only a moment to locate the causative suppurating and dirty lesion on his foot which was clearly responsible for the illness and typical local glandular reaction. I still have to see my first case of bubonic plague!

Having established the diagnosis, advised on treatment and done my best to reassure and preserve the poor Indian's morale, we repaired once again to the Captain's quarters for my report and for more drinks in a much happier mood, with Yellow Jack (quarantine flag) safely stowed away. This time the Captain's steward produced what became an evocative drink, forever associated with memories of *Wingsang* and the plague that wasn't. He appeared with a tray of cocktails containing brandy, crême de cacao and cream served in frosted wine glasses, rims encrusted with sugar and known in the trade I think as an Alexander – all served in the early hours in a far distant Malaysian creek, the night before an uncertain amphibious invasion to repossess an entire peninsula, in the company of an English Merchant captain, his Norwegian first mate and an incompetent, but relieved, unshaven, elderly Indian doctor. To an excited and somewhat immature young surgeon-lieutenant this was 'romance' and not far removed from the worlds of Conrad and Somerset Maugham. It was an experience and a night to remember.

Next morning we proceeded up to Port Swettenham itself while the beach landings went ahead as planned and unopposed. Happily the Japanese observed the surrender

▲ **The Japanese surrender on Kuala Lumpur airfield in September 1945. (E. V. Morton)**

terms punctiliously. Beach-heads were established at Morib and Port Dickson and the plan was for the Army with armoured support to converge on Port Swettenham and Kuala Lumpur, occupying the former, disarming the Japanese garrison before the arrival of *Pursuer* so that all would be ready to receive our headquarters team of VIPs due to go ashore at 0830.

Alas, things did not go according to schedule and our ceremonial landing in the event proved to be almost Gilbertian as viewed by us through our binoculars from the flight deck of the carrier.

The ceremonial landing party set off for the shore as arranged, in the motor cutter, at 0830. There should have been time for the GOC and staff entourage from *Pursuer* to be properly received, as they landed, by the Allied forces. In fact the staff, together with the Royal Marine guard forming the official landing party, presented quite a splendid sight as they left the ship. All officers in their No. 1, clean, neatly starched white, khaki and Air Force blue drill, it was also about the only time that I had seen our Royal Marine contingent in full parade gear.

As the motor cutter with white ensign flying threaded its way through the multitude of sampans, praus, canoes and other small boats that had come out to greet us we scanned the quayside for signs of our victorious and triumphant landing force but only row upon row of Japanese troops lined up in full battle kit on the dockside could we see.

The whole town seemed to have come out to greet us and innumerable sampans and other small craft containing smiling half-naked Malays or equally smiling Chinese including some beautiful and colourfully dressed ladies surrounded the carrier and our motor boat, and there was no doubt about the sincerity and joyful nature of our welcome.

We were anchored some 500 yards from the solidly built quay and we watched anxiously as the motor boat came alongside, half expecting to hear a sudden burst of automatic fire and the ceremony turn in an instant from near-comedy into bloody tragedy and disaster as some wretched 'son of heaven' decided on a last desperate action to save the dishonour of surrender. Happily all that we saw was a number of obsequious Japanese soldiers break ranks, run across the quayside and with much bowing and scraping assist our ceremonial party up from the launch on to the quayside. A

helping hand to the Admiral and Brigadier and reaching down to take the rifles and the machine guns from our gallant Marines while they scrambled ashore. Nothing could have been less tragic or less violent in the way of an invasion and occupation of enemy territory! The formal surrender of several hundred Japanese troops was accepted by our small landing force and all was well. I wondered if our Royal Marines guard had in fact even loaded their rifles for the landing. They certainly had nicely shining and burnished bayonets, and spotless uniforms!

The vanguard of our main landing forces drove down into Port Swettenham an hour or two later to find the surrender complete and all well – a happy contrast to the years of bloodshed and tragedy that had gone before.

The reason for the delayed arrival at Port Swettenham was not entirely unexpected to some. There had always been some debate as to the suitability of the beaches chosen for our main landings, and in fact they did prove to be less suitable than had been hoped because of the presence of soft sand and muddy approaches. As a result the heavy vehicles were considerably delayed on landing and many became bogged down; in fact some were lost and I believe there was a small loss of life. It was fortunate that the landings were unopposed.

A few weeks previous to the invasion I had spent some time at the Royal Marine Commando Camp 39, a few miles from Trincomalee where, incidentally, the hospitality of the Marines and their medical officer my old friend Surgeon-Lieutenant Gerry Little was unequalled.

Among other functions Camp 39 was the base for a special boat section which had been responsible for many landings on the Malayan coast. Marines with their Folboat collapsible canoes were taken by submarine across the Bay of Bengal and had surveyed possible invasion beaches. They told us that they had concluded that the Port Dickson beaches were too soft and the approaches unsuitable for heavy vehicles. However, aerial photographic surveys by the RAF had shown what appeared to be nice firm sandy beaches, and this had finally influenced the planners.

Our indefatigable head brigand, 'Scruffy' Bromwich, appropriated several crates of ex-RAF and other stores during his various forays. I recall crates of aircraft compasses, rifles and other equipment and a complete untouched brand-new Tiger Moth still unassembled in the original crates that had been shipped out from the UK before the Japanese occupation. Most of this was returned ashore at the commander's orders but I suspect some of it remained unobtrusively stored in the hangar deck.

The Tiger Moth certainly remained, and over the next few weeks was carefully and lovingly assembled by a number of our maintenance air engineering staff, including my friend Lieutenant 'Dickie' Guillaume, RNVR, our air engineering officer. The plane had one successful flight before I left the ship, but broke its wooden propeller as a result of a careless flight deck accident while turning the engine. I heard later that when ultimately the ship returned home to the Clyde with our Tiger Moth safely stowed in the hangar a new propeller was fitted and the plane took off with Commander (F) at the controls.

▲ Bromwich's Tiger Moth is assembled on *Pursuer*'s flight deck in Port Swettenham harbour, 1945. (E. V. Morton)

CHAPTER 27

Fleet Air Arm Training

When the Fleet Air Arm took over responsibility for much of its own training in May 1939 it was ill-prepared for the task. In contrast to RAF practice, training units were all given squadron numbers; they were referred to as second-line squadrons, and were numbered in the 700-series. As the war progressed a variety of such units developed and by 1945 several dozen were in operation for a variety of tasks.

While the majority of training units were based in the United Kingdom, quite a number were established overseas, generally near to naval bases. They were to be found in Canada, the United States, the West Indies, East Africa, South Africa, India, Ceylon and Australia. Pilot training, however, was still largely the prerogative of the Royal Air Force, with pupils progressing through Elementary Flying Training Schools and Service Flying Training Schools both at home and in Commonwealth countries under the British Commonwealth Air Training Plan, sometimes referred to as the Empire Air Training Scheme, before progressing to FAA schools to be trained for naval flying. Other aspects of training were also entrusted to the RAF.

Home-based training units tended to be situated in more remote parts of the British Isles so as to be well away from enemy activity and to leave airfields in the east and south-east free for operational use. Thus, after an initial dispersal at the beginning of the war, such units were generally to be found in the West Country, in the north-west of England, in Scotland or in Northern Ireland. The following accounts relate to just a few of the many activities of the Fleet Air Arm schools.

George Rock was one of many hundreds who were accepted for training as a telegraphist air gunner:

I was a 'hostilities only' (HO) sailor – or should it be airman? Having been inspired by the gallant actions of the six Swordfish crews that attacked the *Scharnhorst*, *Gneisenau and Prinz Eugen* during their Channel dash, I decided at 17½ that I wanted to choose which service I went into rather than wait to be called up at 18. I therefore volunteered to be a pilot in the FAA, joining under the Royal Navy Youth Entry scheme. I was accepted as a telegraphist air gunner and told that there would be an opportunity to retrain as a pilot later.

In September 1942, just three weeks after my eighteenth birthday, I joined HMS *Royal Arthur* (Butlin's Holiday Camp at Skegness). Memories are few: plenty of square-bashing and physical training; Lord Haw Haw claiming HMS *Royal Arthur* being sunk; cleaning chalets and inspections. 'How clean was my chalet' was the signature tune of the course.

After six weeks we moved to HMS *St Vincent* at Gosport for more square-bashing, and basic training, Morse code, semaphore and flags

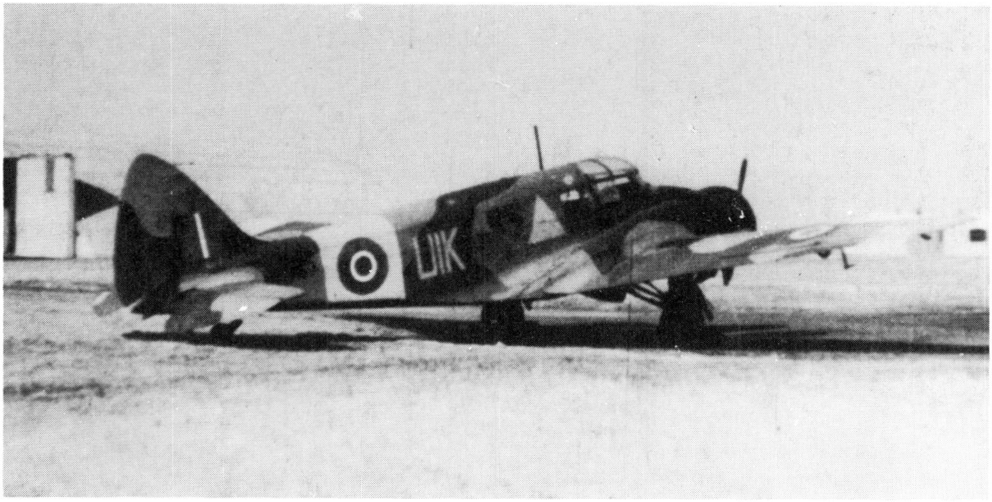

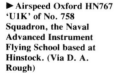

► Airspeed Oxford HN767 'U1K' of No. 758 Squadron, the Naval Advanced Instrument Flying School based at Hinstock. (Via D. A. Rough)

recognition, aircraft recognition, boat drill and swimming. Memories here of the Senior NCO, 'Chiefie' Wilmott, as he was so affectionately called. We were by now a group of young men experiencing great comradeship, moulded in the first instance at Skegness by Leading Seaman Brown and now a well-disciplined, levelled-out group, names I remember besides CPO Wilmott being PO Savings who taught us square-bashing and a PO Labross who taught us Morse code.

After eight weeks, and just one week before Christmas 1942, 35 of us moved to HMS *Kestrel* at Worthy Down, the rest becoming the first TAGS course to be trained in Nova Scotia at No. 2 TAG School. Our disappointment was partly offset when we met up with some of them over a year later in Ceylon and found out that apart from leave before setting out to Nova Scotia they had not had home leave, most of them going the other way round the world and joining South-East Asia Command.

The main part of our course at Worthy Down was spent firstly on the ground learning wireless theory, with daily sessions and daily tests in Morse code. Coded messages included foreign language which we wrote down so fluently if we got the spaces in the right place and yet couldn't understand if we tried to read what we had written. We then graduated to flying, mainly in Proctors, Sharks, Lysanders and the odd Seamew or Kingfisher.

We, the pupils, would turn our transmitter to the frequency given to contact the ground station and would be given a 'TO' (take-off). Our 'drivers' were a very mixed bunch, mainly on rest after operations, some being Air Transport Auxiliary civilians. I can well remember one of the latter not having flown a Shark before, standing with one foot on the wheel saying 'Let's see what plane this is' and then looking at his Pilot's Notes to see the details he needed to fly it!

After getting a 'TO', taking off and retuning the transmitter, which was necessary after reeling out a trailing aerial, one would, when successful in again contacting the ground station, be given a 'GO' go and then proceed on a route which would finish back at Worthy Down. The TAG pupil would send the aircraft

► Swordfish of No. 745 Squadron, part of No. 1 Naval Air Gunners' School at Yarmouth, Nova Scotia, trained telegraphist air gunners for the Fleet Air Arm. (Via C. White)

▼ Blackburn Shark L2359 'F' of No. 775 Squadron, which undertook telegraphist air gunner training at Worthy Down. (Via D. A. Rough)

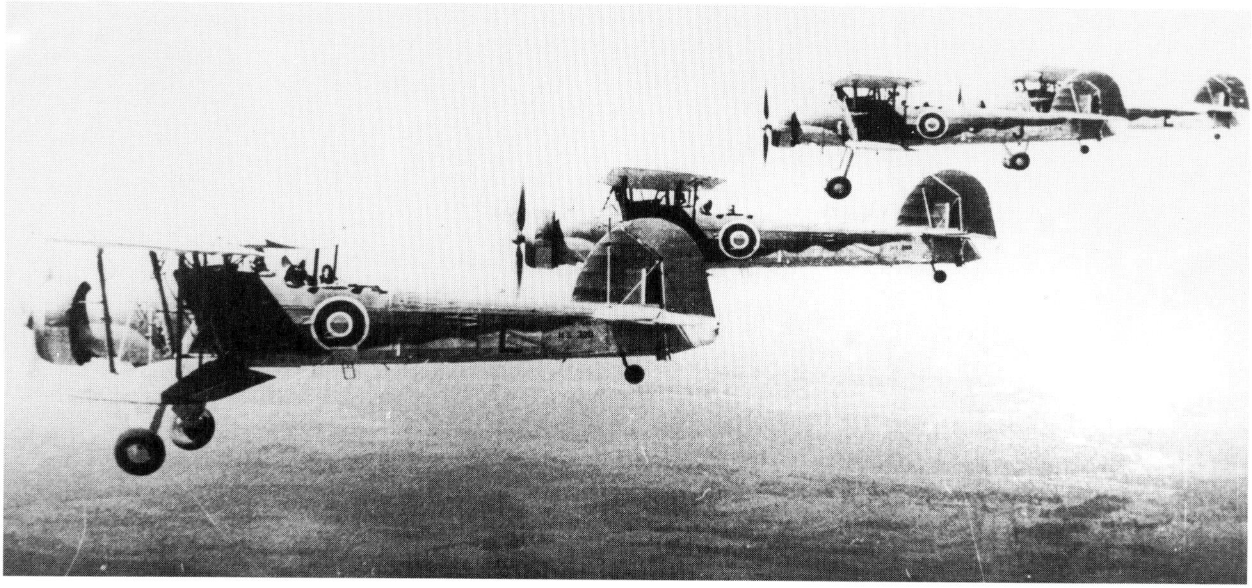

position back to Worthy Down ground station, which would give him a new frequency. This would involve changing some very large coils in the transmitter and re-tuning, contacting the ground station operator on that frequency who would give him another frequency to change to. The whole process would be repeated until we returned to base. Similar frequency change operations had been carried out in huts spread around the perimeter of the airfield with two radio sets and two pupils to each prior to flying training.

We were a happy crowd. Our course instructor was Charles Hewson. Some memories – one pupil from our course was killed on landing in a Proctor. Shortly afterwards Joe Hughes (who was to travel the same ground and squadrons as myself for the rest of the war) failed to return, and we went to bed that night not knowing his fate. Next day we learned that the propeller of the Shark he was flying in came off, Joe heard the engine rev, looked up and saw the prop flying over his head. The pilot, an ATA pilot, put the Shark into a dive and pulled up quite safely in a ploughed field.

We then moved to HMS *Vulture* at St Merryn, in Cornwall, for the whole of August 1943 for air gunnery training. Memories there were firstly being put into the 'Wrennery', the previous course not yet having vacated their hut as they were going on leave before being drafted to various places. I hasten to add that the corridors separating the Wren's huts from ours were bricked up – I wonder why?

Another memory from St Merryn was during our first lecture by 'Tanky' Hearnshaw, being told that when we flew to fire at towed drogues one of us would be in the observer's cockpit and one in the TAG's cockpit. After the latter had fired two pans (400 rounds) of ammunition we would then change cockpits in mid-air. Quite exhilarating to us 18-year-olds, but I shudder to think of it now when you consider the height of the division between cockpits and the small size of each.

One of the pupils would have his bullet tips dipped in paint the night before and in those days the paint was still tacky enough to mark the bullet holes in the drogue. Anyone unfortunate enough to shoot through the drogue towing line would have to fork out 2s. 6d (12½p) to the young Cornish lad that retrieved it and brought it to the camp gate.

Our course was then over and I thought I was lucky to be sent back to Worthy Down with two others as 'tarmac instructors' to help pupils to get their TO, whereas the other course members were drafted to squadrons mainly in Scotland. The truth dawned when, within a month, the three of us were drafted to Cape Town via HMS *Waxwing* in Scotland en route to Gourock where we embarked on an RAF troopship.

▲ Sea Hurricane P2886 'M2H' of No. 768 Squadron from Machrihanish carries out deck-landing training aboard HMS *Argus* in the Firth of Clyde. (Via Capt. H. L. St J. Fancourt)

J. D. Kelsall recalls:

It was Sunday 2 May 1943. At the time I was serving as an instructor with No. 748 Squadron, a Naval Operational Training Unit at St Merryn. In addition I was responsible for supervision of the maintenance of the unit's aircraft, and we had been going through a bad patch with many aircraft unserviceable and continuous hard work by the ground crews, all of which had kept me on the ground when I should have much preferred to be in the air. It was a glorious day, and two of the other instructors were about to leave on an exercise with Whitley bombers from an RAF OTU at a neighbouring airfield.

Escaping briefly from the maintenance worries in the hangar for a quick smoke in the open air, I listened enviously to the sound of Merlin engines as our Hurricanes and Spitfires taxied out for the exercise. I looked up at the blue sky and thought how wonderful it would be to be up there away from all my worries about aircraft serviceability. And suddenly I thought: 'Dammit, why not?'. I shouted for our squadron flight sergeant (though a naval unit, we had a sprinkling of RAF personnel on the ground staff). 'Flight, I'm going up. What can I have to fly?' He shook his head. 'Sorry, sir. What serviceable cabs we've got are on this exercise and there's nothing else you could have.' A thought occurred to me. 'What about the CO's aircraft? He's away on weekend leave and he won't be needing it?' Flight looked worried. 'I don't know that you ought to take that one, sir. You know what the CO thinks of it.' (I did. The aircraft was a brand-new Spitfire which had been received as a replacement for another written off in an accident. The CO had appropriated it as his own and guarded it jealously.) 'Never mind, Flight,' I said. 'The CO will never know I flew it today. I'll take it in five minutes.'

I nipped into my office, pulled on my white flying overalls, collected parachute and helmet and went out to the aircraft. I settled myself in the narrow cockpit, and the rigger, standing on the wing, helped me to get my safety harness on. I closed the small door-flap on the side of the cockpit, looked across to the fitter who was crouched over the starter battery trolley to one side. 'All clear?' I called and he gave me a 'thumbs up' signal. 'Contact!' I called, opened up the throttle a little, switched on and pressed the starter button while operating the primer pump. With a bang and a puff of blue smoke from the exhaust the Merlin fired. I set the throttle to a fast tick-over and checked through the cockpit while the engine warmed up. Finally I ran the engine up to check the magnetos and the operation of the constant-speed Rotol airscrew. All OK. I contacted flying control on the radio for clearance to taxi out and take off, and waved away the chocks under the wheels.

Up the taxi track, on to the airfield perimeter track and round towards the downwind end of the runway in use, which faced into the light north-west breeze. Small white clouds drifted across the blue sky while in the middle distance I could see the blue of the sea. This was going to be fun – I would fly up towards the exercise area and see if I couldn't 'jump' one of the pilots taking part. If I could catch an instructor I could take a beer off him in the wardroom at lunch-time! Arriving at the end of the runway I had a final word with flying control, carried out my pre-take-off checks and turned into wind. I opened up smoothly to take-off power. Check revs and boost – 3000rpm and +12lb of boost, the aircraft accelerating swiftly along the runway. She feels light on the wheels. A quick glance at the airspeed indicator, 100mph, ease back on the control column and she lifts off like a bird.

I was just reaching for the lever to raise the undercarriage when suddenly it happened – the engine cut dead! I was no more than 20 feet off the ground. My immediate reaction was 'It can't be happening to me!' The shattering realization was 'But, by God, it is!' What on earth should I do? Ahead of me lay the short length of runway remaining, followed by grass and the main road past the airfield, with a wall of concertina barbed wire along the top of the bank above the road. Beyond the road was an area of rough ground sloping down to the half-buried protected communications block, a concrete structure. Not a propitious area for a belly landing! And then, in a fraction of a second, there flashed before my eyes a section from the Pilot's Notes for the Spitfire: 'In the event of engine failure during take-off, do not attempt to turn back. Retract the undercarriage, lower the flaps and land straight ahead.' My hand was already on the way towards the undercarriage lever, and I selected 'up', which would at least release the locks and allow the wheels to fold up when the aircraft hit the ground. I selected 'flaps down'; being pneumatically operated they came fully down at once. Then it was back, back, gently on the control column and . . . will she touch within the airfield or will she go over the wire into the road? And, good God, there's a car coming . . . and I'll hit it if she does!

Suddenly the spinning disc of the airscrew in front of me splintered and diminished as it touched the ground. There was a grinding, slithering crunch, a bumpety-bump, and we were down. The nose of the aircraft was sticking through the concertina wire into the road and a grey-faced, goggle-eyed car driver was pulling up just to one side of me, having clearly believed that his last moment had come seconds before.

Everything had happened so quickly that I had had no time to be afraid, but now reaction set in and I found myself trembling violently. The crash tender and ambulance came careering across the grass and pulled up beside me. The young doctor seemed quite put out that I was uninjured. What my Squadron Commander said when he returned from leave that evening is another story. He, too, was quite put out . . .!

Hanging on the wall beside me as I write is the splintered, yellow-painted tip of an airscrew blade and inscribed on it are the words 'Seafire IIC 114, May 2nd 1943 – cut on take-off.' It is a small reminder of a very tense few seconds!

Of a later period in his career, when serving with No. 760 Squadron, J. D. Kelsall relates:

In 1944–45 I was CO of an outfit at RNAS Inskip, in the Fylde of Lancashire, which was equipped with Hurricane IIs. Our job was to train pilots in the techniques of ground attack with 20mm cannon and rockets (then known as RPs) on a range in Morecambe Bay, off Cockerham. At that time these weapons had not reached the stage of technical development which they have today and 'hangfires', when the rocket declined to depart when the firing button was pressed, were not all that uncommon. In consequence there was a safety drill laid down to cope with such situations. One switched off all the relevant circuits, pointed the aircraft out to sea for fifteen minutes and informed Inskip on the radio. If, after fifteen minutes, nothing had happened one again informed Inskip and returned to the airfield, where, presumably, everyone was in a state of twitch just waiting for the accident to happen!

On one occasion I was doing a firing detail myself and had a 'hangfire'. I went through the standard drill and in due course turned and began to head back to the airfield. On that occasion I had a load of rockets fitted with 60lb concrete practice heads. Suddenly, when I was about half a mile off Fleetwood and heading directly for the town, whoooooosh! . . . and away went my 'hangfire'. Panic stations! The thing disappeared, leaving its long trail of smoke, directly for the centre of Fleetwood. I called up Inskip on the radio and told them what had happened, suggesting that they had better contact Fleetwood police and find out how many people I had killed.

I landed in a state of acute concern and went straight to the control tower. 'Tell me the worst,' I said miserably. 'Nothing whatever so far from the police,' I was told. I sat there for an hour, waiting for the bad news – but it never came. Believe it or not, I had parked 60 pounds of concrete somewhere in the middle of Fleetwood at high velocity and there wasn't a squeak from anyone! I'd love to know where it landed!

As the war developed, instrument flying began to play a vital part in training, as related by Philip Moss:

After some six years as a radio officer in the Merchant Navy I joined Jersey Airways Ltd in the mid-thirties, becoming a chief radio officer of the company about the same time that Johnny Pugh joined as one of the pilots.

When the Germans occupied the Channel Islands in June 1940 Jersey Airways Ltd closed down and several air crew members joined the Fleet Air Arm, the majority being posted to No. 782 Squadron at Donibristle. Some weeks later I was asked if I would join No. 782 as a civilian, to fly with them and also advise on Aviation Electronics because, to put it bluntly, in 1940 the Navy did not know a lot about avionics. This I did until I was commissioned as Sub-Lieutenant (A) RNVR, to do Link Trainer instructing until the Air Radio Branch was founded in the spring of 1942, when I then became a founder member of the Branch.

Among those who went to No. 782 was Lieutenant (A) J. B. W. (Johnny) Pugh, RNVR, as he had become. After a while he became worried about the standard of instrument flying of the newly trained pilots who had gained their wings in America or the Caribbean, rarely having seen a cloud during their training. From these conditions they were pitched into North Atlantic and UK weather and numbers of them were lost before they ever saw an enemy aircraft.

Johnny began to bombard the Admiralty with suggestions for improving the level of instrument flying and for a long time this provoked no response. In April 1942, however, he had received permission to form an Instrument Flying Training Flight, and was given three Oxfords and a Tiger Moth and told to form up the flight at Donibristle. He was also given a half ring. He also asked for, and got, four other pilots of his choice, Lieutenants Luxton, Watson, Pridham and MacDonald, Engineer Lieutenant Pleydell-Bouverie, Lieutenant Bill Street (to become Air Traffic Control Officer) and myself as his air radio officer.

He started to train the other pilots in the gentle art of instructing, while Pleydell-Bouverie began to lick his Engineering Department into shape. Bill Street and I were despatched to inspect a grass, ex RAF satellite landing strip in north Shropshire, which was to become our future home, and to make arrangements for the billeting of personnel until such time as we could have appropriate accommodation built. We finally moved down to Hinstock (later HMS *Godwit*), near Market Drayton, in August, the officers flying down in the Oxfords and the Tiger while the ratings and the equipment we had accumulated travelled down by road. We requisitioned a local country house, Hinstock Hall, to become the officer's mess and had the extensive stabling block modified to accommodate the first course of pupils, which was expected in November. Meanwhile accommodation for the ratings and Wrens was also requisitioned and Instructor Training continued.

The first trainees duly arrived and it was agreed that the first two or three courses could be 'milked' of pupils who were considered suitable to become instructors, and so our expansion began. We were given Oxfords and a couple more Tiger Moths and attained squadron status – No. 758.

During 1943 Johnny was given his 'brass hat' and an OBE to go with his AFC in the King's Birthday Honours List. 'Lucky' Luxton, the Chief Flying Instructor, was given his half ring. By now we were expanding rapidly and taking three two-week courses of pilots at a time. In addition we were running several other courses, including one for senior naval officers (Captains and upwards) to enlighten them on the work and running of the Fleet Air Arm. For this particular course the heads of each of the station's departments gave a talk for some ninety minutes on the work of his division, followed by questions from the very senior and often rather elderly 'students'.

By 1944 Johnny Pugh had been promoted to Captain (A), RNVR, as Commanding Officer of the Naval Advanced Instrument Flying School. We had by then acquired two additional grass satellite airfields and taken over the neighbouring RAF Peplow, all of which were equipped with the Standard Beam Approach (SBA) blind-landing system, as was Hinstock. Peplow, compared with Hinstock, was a magnificent airfield, having been laid down as a heavy bomber training station, with three long concrete runways and ample accommodation, workshops and hangars. By then the School had well over 100 aircraft, including Harvards, Ansons (Calibration Flight), Harrows and Wellingtons (Flying Classrooms) on its strength. No. 758 had been divided into several sub-squadrons, some of which were sent, on loan, to other naval air stations, and one was despatched to Ceylon. Meanwhile the School Headquarters Staff had expanded to something over two hundred officers and a correspondingly large number of ratings and Wrens.

No. 739 Squadron, the Blind Approach Development Unit, was attached to us for seven or eight months and No. 702 Squadron joined us for the last few months of the war, as did No. 734 Squadron, the Engine Handling Unit. No. 758 was disbanded in April 1946 and Hinstock was closed down in early 1947, but Peplow continued to function until the end of 1949.

The Naval Advanced Instrument Flying School never shot down any enemy aircraft or sank any enemy ships but I am convinced that it saved the lives of many FAA air crew. During its existence there was only one fatal accident, which is amazing considering the thousands, if not tens of thousands, of take-offs and landings which took place, often in visibility down to a hundred yards. In fact, one day, Johnny made a successful landing in fifty yards' visibility, just to show it could be done.

Of the technical side, Hugh Langrishe writes:

The wartime development of technical training for officers and ratings was done virtually from scratch as none existed under naval control until the Admiralty won back their air arm. Even then, it was still necessary to send large numbers of trainee naval air artificers, air fitters and air mechanics to RAF schools throughout the war – indeed, trainee officers as well. Partly as a result of this, naval type-training was hit or miss and men could be posted to units operating aircraft types they had never seen and had to be trained on the job.

Assistance was given to some squadrons during working-up on new aircraft by parties known as Special Servicing Units. These were self-contained, having their own MT, tools and special equipment. They moved from one air station to another as the working-up programme required, providing technical help and on-the-job training by type-experienced maintenance personnel, under the command of a sub-lieutenant (A) (A/E).

In my own case I did two courses at the RAF School of Aeronautical Engineering at RAF Henlow in 1942 and 1943 as a sub-lieutenant. After completing my training at St Merryn, which was occupied by fighters and second-line squadrons operating obsolescent first-line and training types, I went to Fearn and was put in charge of the Aircraft Repair Section, servicing and repairing nothing but Barracudas. After that I was appointed to take charge of the Servicing Unit specializing in Avengers. Neither I nor my PO technicians had worked on the Avenger before, and hardly any of us had ever seen one! We went to Australia with MONAB 1 [Mobile Naval Air Base No. 1] without any type-training, to provide specialist back-up to operational squadron personnel.

▲ **Seafires IBs of No. 736 Squadron, the School of Air Combat, seen flying over the West Country in the autumn of 1943. (Via Peter Arnold)**

For the best part of four months we did no aircraft engineering at all.

It may not be appreciated how many strains and difficulties were caused in aircraft maintenance by the acquisition of American aircraft. So far as I can recall, even up to 1944 the standard toolbox of FAA ratings only included British Standard spanners, and a very basic range at that. American standards required different spanners, none of which were interchangeable with British tools. It was improbable that British tool manufacturers were producing US-standard spanners at that time. Certainly those we were eventually supplied with for our Avenger Servicing Unit were American-made.

The air stores system used in the FAA was the same as in the RAF, and very good it was. I don't think the US aircraft types were ever fully integrated into our system. The American services used manufacturers' part numbers for type-unique items and a series of Army and Navy numbers for standard parts – in our parlance, 'AGS parts' – but each had its own series. We found by experience that to be sure of obtaining a particular part we had to quote every number we could find: aircraft manufacturer's, sub-contractors and both USAAF and USN numbers.

I recall an early embarrassment when ordering a hydraulic jack for undercarriage operation. The airframe parts list part number was quoted, but the wrong jack arrived. It was only wrong because it originated from a different sub-contractor. We discovered that the Avenger hydraulics were supplied complete by two manufacturers and because of detail differences none of the jacks were interchangeable. I never met such incompatibility on British aircraft.

I am reminded of another instance of this which might seem incredible. After minor tailplane damage to a TBF Avenger, we indented for a replacement against the part number from the appropriate list. What we received did not fit; attachment points were as much as a bolt diameter out. Stores department had supplied the right part made by the wrong manufacturer – General Motors instead of Grumman! I must say that I was never impressed by this particular aspect of American production engineering.

In connection with replacement parts for airframes, I have come across captions on several photographs where the interpreter tries to place some significance to the colour of a wing-tip or tail-unit part, linking it with carrier identification. As I see it there is no secret. British replacement parts came in light green primer, and if there was urgency to get the aircraft into service with a new wing-tip it flew in that paint condition. Likewise, after the US Navy changed to 'midnite' blue, all replacement external airframe parts were supplied in this colour. If fitted to a green/grey camouflage aircraft in the field there was no time to repaint to match.

CHAPTER 28

Postwar Run-down

With victory achieved in both the European and Pacific theatres, the inevitable run-down began. On VJ-Day the Fleet Air Arm had 74 first-line squadrons in service, and 59 assorted aircraft carriers were available for them. Aircraft strength amounted to 3,700 machines and the service boasted more than 72,000 officers and men. The number of shore bases had dramatically increased and there were now 56 naval air stations at home and abroad. The latter included a series of Mobile Naval Air Bases (MONABs) set up in Australia for intended island-hopping as the Pacific War progressed but rendered unnecessary after the dropping of two atomic bombs brought hostilities to a sudden end. Two of the MONABs were, however, subsequently used for a time in Hong Kong and Singapore.

The service was far too large for likely peacetime needs. There was a large aircraft

▼ Firebrands of No. 813 Squadron on the flight deck of HMS *Implacable* in February 1950. (RAF Museum)

carrier construction programme under way, which included four *Ark Royal* Class, ten light fleet carriers (all launched by July 1944), six *Majestic* Class (all launched by September 1945), eight *Hermes* Class (five cancelled in October 1945) and three *Malta* Class. Of these, two of the *Ark Royal* Class would be completed to become HMS *Ark Royal* and HMS *Eagle*, three of the *Hermes* Class were launched postwar and all three of the *Malta* Class (super carriers of 57,000 tons) were cancelled in November 1945, one being scrapped on the slipway.

During the twelve months following VE-Day drastic changes took place. Airfields were closed down or reduced to a 'care and maintenance basis'. Carriers were taken out of service, many for scrapping or, in the case of American-built escort carriers, returned to the USA, where a large number were converted to merchant ships. Wartime types of aircraft went out of service, those of American origin mostly disappearing from the scene. The RNVR was run down and those of its air crew who were retained under a short-service scheme joined the RN (Air) Branch.

Overleaf: Vampire LZ551 'G', piloted by Lt Cdr E. M. 'Winkle' Brown, takes off from the flight deck of HMS *Ocean* in December 1945. (RAF Museum)

By the beginning of 1947 there were only twelve first-line squadrons in existence, mainly grouped in pairs as Carrier Air Groups, and available to them were just six light fleet carriers, all of which commissioned in either 1945 or 1946. Six of the squadrons were based at United Kingdom airfields but two of these would soon sail to the Mediterranean in *Triumph* and two more to the Far East in *Theseus*. Already in the Mediterranean were two squadrons in *Ocean*, and with the British Pacific Fleet were two squadrons each in *Glory* and *Venerable*. None of the escort carriers remained, but the light fleet carrier *Vengeance* would shortly re-enter service and a larger ship would become available the following year when the wartime fleet carrier *Implacable* completed a programme of modernization.

The equipment of these squadrons largely comprised Fireflies and Seafires, the latter being the postwar Mk XV and Mk XVII versions. One exception, however, was the shore-based No. 811 Squadron, which was equipped with Sea Mosquito TR.33 twin-engined torpedo-bombers. On the horizon were the large Blackburn Firebrand torpedo-bomber, the Hawker Sea Fury day fighter and the twin-engined Sea Hornet day and night fighter, all single-seaters. Piston-engined aircraft were to serve with the Fleet Air Arm for some years to come but in the offing were jet aircraft, which would present a quite different challenge.

Carrier trials with jet aircraft had begun in 1945 using a specially modified De Havilland Vampire, Lt Cdr E. M. 'Winkle' Brown becoming the first pilot in the world to land a jet-powered aircraft on the deck of a carrier when he brought LZ551 'G' down safely on the flight deck of HMS *Ocean* on 3 December 1945. There were many misgivings, however, about the possibility of operating jet aircraft routinely from carrier decks and this machine soon afterwards went to Farnborough to begin, with others of its type, a series of trials using rubber decks with which it was proposed to absorb most of the impact of the aircraft. Much time and effort was spent on this concept, which in the end proved unnecessary.

The initial assessment that jet aircraft were likely to be unsuitable for operation from carriers was to prevail for some time in the

Royal Navy and there were numerous difficulties to be overcome before they could be assimilated into carrier service. One major problem was the slow acceleration of a gas turbine engine, which would entail the development of new flying techniques. Approach speeds would be greater, and it would no longer be simply a case of opening up the throttle and going round again; moreover, the carriers then in service would be too small for jet aircraft operations and large new carriers would be required. On the other hand there would be no torque from a propeller, and cockpits could be placed much further forward, resulting in greatly improved visibility. This was all in the future, though, and in the meantime piston engines prevailed.

By 1947 it had become apparent that the spread of world communism presented a major challenge to freedom which had to be met. A fresh arms build-up was becoming necessary and as part of this both the Royal Air Force and Fleet Air Arm needed some form of readily available back-up in case fresh hostilities should break out. Both services were therefore permitted to set up a series of reserve squadrons and consequently a number of RNVR squadrons were formed around the country. At first equipped, like their first-line counterparts, with Seafires and Fireflies, the units were manned by volunteers drawn from former wartime air crew and ground personnel, who responded with enthusiasm, giving up their weekends for training as well as attending the annual fortnight-long training camps, often overseas.

In April 1949 No. 702 Squadron re-formed at Culdrose as the Naval Jet Evaluation and Training Unit, equipped with De Havilland Sea Vampire F.20s and Gloster Meteor T.7s. This unit spearheaded the introduction of jet aircraft into naval service, but piston-engined aircraft were destined to be used throughout the Royal Navy's first postwar use of its aircraft in anger.

▼ Sea Hornet VZ708 '456/C' of No. 801 Squadron from *Implacable* flying over the Rock of Gibraltar in March 1950. (RAF Museum)

CHAPTER 29

Fleet Air Arm Operations in Korea

At 0400 on 25 June 1950 the 38th Parallel, which had been established as a demarcation line, was crossed in a large-scale attack by North Korean Communists. The United Nations voted to come to the aid of South Korea and in the ensuing conflict the Fleet Air Arm played a small but invaluable role.

Many British warships were in Japanese waters that summer, and they were immediately placed at the disposal of Vice-Admiral C. T. Joy, USN (COMNAVFE). Among them was HMS *Triumph*, which had embarked the 13th Carrier Air Group comprising twelve Seafire F.47s of No. 800 Squadron and twelve Firefly 1s of No. 827 Squadron. Plans were laid for a combined British and American force to move into the Yellow Sea for strikes against targets in North Korea by aircraft from USS *Valley Forge* and *Triumph*. For this purpose Rear Admiral Hoskins, USN, commanding the US 3rd Carrier Division, would be in tactical command, flying his flag in *Valley Forge*. It soon became obvious that US forces had difficulty distinguishing between a Seafire F.47 and Yak-9, and all FAA aircraft were later painted with black and white stripes.

On 2 July the two ships rendezvoused and sailed north at about 22kt and the first strikes were flown off the following morning. Twelve Fireflies and nine Seafires from *Triumph* attacked Haeju airfield and carried out rocket attacks on hangars and buildings, no aircraft being sighted and only slight damage suffered from small-arms fire. Further strikes were made the next day on targets of opportunity, including a railway bridge and a column of troops, and one aircraft was damaged by flak.

The choice of targets for British aircraft was severely limited by the Firefly's strike radius of 120 to 130 nautical miles. The American aircraft were proving much more versatile, both the Skyraider and Corsair being capable of carrying mixed loads of bombs and rockets and drop tanks, and they could be catapulted with any of them.

The replacement and upkeep of aircraft was likely to be a problem and rather than employ a shore-base in the forward area it was decided to use HMS *Simbang*, the FAA shore-base at Sembawang, Singapore. The Air Repair Department of the supply carrier *Unicorn* was disembarked, together with workshop equipment and stores, *Unicorn* then becoming a replenishment ship only. For storage and major work a repair and maintenance base was set up at Iwakuni in Japan.

Triumph provided combat air patrols (CAP) and anti-submarine patrols (ASP) during strikes by *Valley Forge* two weeks later but had to return to Sasebo on 22 July for repairs. Then at midnight on 24/25 July she sailed as part of Task Force 77, to head for the area north of Quelpart Island. *Valley Forge* made numerous attacks on the west coast during the next few days though was handicapped by air-to-ground communication difficulties. *Triumph*, however, was again restricted to the CAP and ASP roles, averaging 42 sorties (84 flying hours) on each of the four days that strikes were carried out. Unfortunately a USAF B-29 shot down a No. 800 Squadron Seafire (VP473) on the 28th, possibly mistaking it for a Yak-9, but Commissioned Pilot White was picked up by a US destroyer.

On 30 July *Triumph* left the US Seventh Fleet and sailed for Kure for further attention to a troublesome stern gland, after which the ship launched a series of air searches and strikes on military targets in the west-coast port areas, there being no worthwhile shipping targets. A tragic accident occurred on 29 August when a Firefly missed the wires on landing and its propeller broke on the barrier. Half a blade, with the root, went through the scuttle of the operations room, killing Lt Cdr I. M. MacLachlen, RN, the CO of No. 800 Squadron.

Operating from about 60 miles east of Wonsan, the aircraft attacked various road and rail targets during 8 and 9 September, despite bad weather. Around this time several Seafires became unserviceable through a wrinkling of the skin – an old Second World War complaint. Returning to Sasebo on 10 September, the ship sailed again two days later to provide air cover for landings around the south-west corner of Korea. Aircraft took off before dawn on the 15th, six Fireflies being fitted with two 45-gallon overload tanks which gave them two hours over the target. Having helped to ensure the success of the Inchon invasion, *Triumph* returned to Sasebo, its air group now reduced to eight Fireflies and three Seafires, all obsolescent and at the end of their operational life. Four days later the ship departed for the United Kingdom.

On 5 October *Theseus* arrived as a replacement, carrying the 17th Carrier Air Group with more modern equipment comprising the 21 Sea Fury FB.11s of No. 807 Squadron and the twelve Firefly AS.5s of No. 810 Squadron. On 9 October the Fleet Aviation Officer (Cdr E. S. Carver) visited the local Tactical Air Control Centre at Kimpo to make sure the personnel there knew the general plan and the types of aircraft operating, only to find that the US Fifth Air Force had not informed them of any British carrier operations in the area. On 10 October Fireflies destroyed the two centre spans of a railway bridge near Changyan but subsequent attacks on road bridges were not so successful. Sea Furies attacking a stores depot encountered considerable light AA fire; Lt S. Leonard was shot down but rescued five miles from the target by a USAF helicopter in the face of opposition.

By 13 October it was clear that the enemy had largely evacuated the Haeju-Ongjin area and the attack was switched to the port of Chinnampo, where on the 13th and 14th three strikes with bombs and rockets caused much destruction to dockside stores and buildings. The Fireflies' dive-bombing was highly accurate, and the Sea Furies attacked two mine-laying junks at Ho-do, blowing the stern off one and riddling the other. Similar attacks were carried out on Mongumpo, Sariwon and Chinnampo on the 16th and 17th. Air operations were then suspended briefly to clarify the position ashore, where UN troops were advancing rapidly, and bad weather intervened on the 19th. During the next two days *Theseus* was able to operate her aircraft over the Sinanju-Chougju area, the only unrestricted region on the west coast. She then returned to Sasebo. The increased radius of the new Sea Furies and Firefly AS.5s was proving a most welcome advantage, as was the ability to launch Fireflies with bombs regardless of natural wind. The Sea Furies demonstrated their accuracy with rockets but in the later stages tier stowage had to be abandoned owing to damage to rocket posts and mainplanes on firing.

▲ **Chinnampo under attack from Fireflies of 810 Squadron from HMS *Theseus*. (Via F. C. Lynn)**

◀ **A Sikorsky S.51 planeguard helicopter of the US Navy coming in to land aboard HMAS *Sydney*. (Author's collection)**

By early December the situation in Korea had deteriorated, thanks to the arrival of Chinese forces, and the British and Commonwealth sea forces had to be redeployed to give close support to the Eighth Army and 1st US Marine Division in their desperate retreat to the sea and subsequent evacuation by sea on the 6th. Following the evacuation, *Theseus* provided air cover over the task group and armed reconnaissance north of the bomb line. As all the American carriers were fully employed on the east coast only *Theseus* was available for all flying duties on the west coast. Winter had by now set in and conditions at sea were appalling, with frequent gales, intense cold and low visibility, but despite this 332 sorties were flown between 7 and 15 December without accident or damage. For its activities during 1950 the 17th CAG was later awarded the annual Boyd Trophy for the finest feat by the Fleet Air Arm during the year.

The year closed with the continuation of the Chinese offensive. *Theseus* had retired to Kure but by 7 January 1941 she was off the west coast of Korea and carried the duties of the Air Support Element for the next ten days, working in close support of the US 25th Division on the left flank of the line southward from Osan. This was the first time such support had been provided by the FAA and control was mainly by airborne controllers in USAF Harvards. It worked well despite some congestion on the radio frequency in use.

USS *Bataan* arrived on the west coast during January, enabling the two ships to operate alternately on an eighteen-day cycle. *Theseus* relieved her on the 25th, meeting improved weather conditions, and in the ensuing eight days of operations flew 408 sorties, providing close support for the US 1st Corps and the usual reconnaissance of coasts, airstrips and roads. Casualties were not infrequent but there were several instances of ditched pilots being rescued by Canadian and American ships.

By early April it was apparent that Communist preparations for another major offensive were almost complete, with an estimated 70 divisions south of the Yalu. Indications that China might be contemplating an assault on Formosa caused the US Seventh Fleet to keep most of its heavy carriers in that region. Both *Bataan* and *Theseus* were therefore operating in the Sea of Japan, the first time since *Triumph* left eight months earlier that a British carrier had worked with another deck. Friendly rivalry was to produce a general speeding-up of flying operations. *Theseus* with one catapult was usually able to launch more quickly than *Bataan* with two, and the catapulting intervals for Sea Furies dropped to 40-42 seconds.

Flying operations were carried out from 9 to 15 April and these included a daily reconnaissance across Korea of the Choppeki area. On the east coast, strikes were carried out on road and rail bridges, rolling stock, marshalling yards, supply dumps and warehouses at various places, bombardment spotting took place in the Wonsan and Songjin areas and armed reconnaissance flights were made as required. Battle casualties were the highest experienced, five Sea Furies and one Firefly being lost or badly damaged, and on the 10th two Sea Furies were attacked in error by US Marine Corsairs, one being severely damaged.

Theseus sailed for home on 25 April, having achieved 3,446 operational sorties in 86 operational flying days in seven months. In her place arrived *Glory*, carrying the 14th Carrier Air Group consisting of the 21 Sea Fury FB.11s of No. 804 Squadron and twelve Firefly 5s of No. 812 Squadron, plus a Dragonfly rescue helicopter, this being the first operational use of the helicopter by the Fleet Air Arm. Her arrival coincided with the start of the anticipated Chinese spring offensive. Concentrating on air support to the army, it was thought that there would be massive air opposition, but in the event there was only an attack on 22 April by four Yaks on two Corsairs from *Bataan*; three of the enemy aircraft were shot down and the fourth heavily damaged.

Glory was relieved by *Bataan* on 19 May but she was back in the operational area by 3 June, only to have to return to harbour eight days later because of heavily contaminated aviation fuel. The press printed rumours of sabotage but in fact the culprit was the supply ship RFA *Wave Premier*, whose supply pipe from her tanks to the forward position had not been used for several years and had consequently become contaminated. During this period further losses were incurred. On the next patrol, four Sea Furies, though plainly marked, were attacked on 25 June by four American F-80s but fortunately escaped without damage after taking evasive action.

Having completed 2,892 sorties, *Glory* now gave way to HMAS *Sydney*, whose air group comprised Nos. 805 and 808 Sea Fury Squadrons and No. 817 Firefly Squadron, a US Navy helicopter being also loaned to the ship. On 11 October the Australian ship equalled *Glory*'s record of 89 sorties, finishing up with an attack by sixteen Sea Furies on at least 2,000 enemy troops caught digging in on the

▼ Sea Fury FB.11 VX730 '109/K' of No. 805 Squadron, Royal Australian Navy, aboard HMAS *Sydney* during the Korean War. This particular machine survived to become an exhibit at the Museum of Applied Arts and Science in New South Wales. (Via S. Brett)

hills covering the beaches; over 200 were killed and an ammunition dump was seen to blow up as the ships withdrew.

Returning to the fray on 18 October, the Fireflies attacked railway bridges and tunnels with considerable success whilst the Sea Furies struck at coastal shipping and troop concentrations. The most popular task, however, was close support for the Commonwealth Division and particularly, of course, the Australian Regiment, though it was on this duty that the heaviest flak was encountered. That afternoon five Fireflies ran into intense flak while attacking tunnels south of Sariwon and one aircraft crash-landed near the target. The downed crew were some distance from the ship, and nightfall was near, but *Sydney*'s helicopter was despatched, with support from Sea Furies and also Meteors of No. 77 Squadron RAAF. As it landed, Aviation Mechanician's Mate C. G. Goulding, USN, jumped out and shot two of the enemy who had crept to within fifteen yards. An hour later the helicopter landed safely at last light at Kimpo airfield with the crew of the Firefly aboard.

Winter then set in but on 20 and 21 November the ship took part in Operation 'Athenaeum', an attack on targets in the Hungman area during which 113 sorties were flown. During a clear spell early in December support was laid on for anti-invasion operations in the Choda-Sok area, including constant combat air patrol (TARCAP) over the target. Many of the ship's company had never seen snow in any quantity and as they left the battle area on 7 January they made good use of it in a traditional snow fight. Since her arrival on the station HMAS *Sydney* had spent a total of 64 days in the operational area, during which 2,366 sorties were flown, and she was now replaced by *Glory*.

The ship relieved the US escort carrier *Bairoko* on 24 February, and despite the intense cold the weather was good for flying except for a few periods when snowstorms lessened the visibility. For some time past it had been found that the 60lb rockets carried by the Sea Furies lacked sufficient explosive power for many of the available targets and during the patrol in April they were fitted to carry two 500lb bombs instead. The Sea Fury proved to be an accurate dive-bomber, particularly against well dug-in gun positions. The bombs were fused for a 30-second delay, which enabled the pilot to deliver his attack from a lower altitude with a corresponding increase in accuracy.

In May *Ocean* took over. Aboard her was the 17th CAG comprising No. 802 Sea Fury

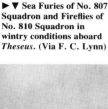

►▼ Sea Furies of No. 807 Squadron and Fireflies of No. 810 Squadron in wintry conditions aboard *Theseus*. (Via F. C. Lynn)

Squadron and No. 825 Firefly Squadron, which soon began to suffer casualties, several aircraft being lost on the first patrol. The ship's second patrol started on 29 May and the weather was generally favourable. The supply of bombs and rockets was limited, however, so sorties were restricted to 68 a day, any shortfall due to bad weather being made up the following day. A total of 544 sorties were flown in the eight days of the patrol but engine reliability proved a problem, No. 825 Squadron suffering three connecting-rod failures in their Griffon engines.

June saw a change of policy regarding aircraft targets in North Korea, and on 18 June previous restrictions on attacks on electrical power installations were lifted. Five days later successful coordinated attacks were carried out by the US Fifth Air Force and Task Force 77 on the main complexes of Chosin, Fusen, Kyosen and Suiho. Fog then hampered operations but on 9 July positions were attacked in the Taedong estuary, each strike being preceded by flak suppression and bombardment.

In late July poor weather prevailed in the normal operating area but 70 miles north entirely suitable conditions were encountered, with the northern part of North Korea clear. This well illustrated the inherent advantage of a carrier over an airfield as an operating base. For the first time, however, probably encouraged by the knowledge that the US Fifth Air Force was grounded, enemy MiG-15s attempted to interfere with *Ocean*'s aircraft and a Firefly was lost on the 26th.

The next patrol started on 8 August, and MiG-15s were encountered, operating mainly over the Hanchon–Chinnampo–Pyongyang triangle – strategically the most important area for the enemy in the whole of western Korea. On 9 August Lt P. Carmichael, RN, in WJ232 '114/O' was leading four Sea Furies when they were attacked by eight MiGs north of Chinnampo. No Sea Fury was damaged, but one MiG was shot down, exploding on hitting the ground. This was the only enemy aircraft shot down by the Fleet Air Arm throughout the Korean campaign and the only example of a jet aircraft being shot down by a piston-engined fighter. The next day Lt Carmichael's flight was attacked again by eight MiGs, two of which were hit before they withdrew, one on fire; no damage was sustained by the Sea Furies.

On 16 September it was reported that all rail bridges on the main line between Pyongyang and Chinnampo had been destroyed. The following day Sea Furies dropped 500lb and 1,000lb bombs on sluice gates in three positions at the mouths of rivers, during a period of spring tides. All the gates were breached and a number of delayed-action bombs were dropped to discourage attempts to repair them at the next low water.

Indications that the enemy might be using road transport at night led to night reconnaissance. A number of lorries with burning headlights were detected and immobilized and first light revealed numerous laden oxcarts on the road. Further attention was paid to this traffic on subsequent patrols.

Glory then returned for her third Korean tour, carrying No. 801 Sea Fury Squadron and No. 821 Firefly Squadron. During her first two patrols bad weather was encountered and a sudden drop in the temperature during December had a marked effect on serviceability, especially that of the Fireflies. On 15 December the ship's Dragonfly

►*Sydney* battles through stormy conditions off Korea. (Author's collection)

helicopter was caught in a cross-wind on the flight deck and, despite an attempt at a snatch take-off, it toppled into the sea with the loss of both crew members.

Improved weather then allowed more information from photographic interpretation; this was invaluable in selecting rocket targets for the Fireflies, the main effort of the Sea Fury attacks being directed at bridges. Poor weather again reduced activities in the New Year of 1953. The enemy took advantage of the frozen ground and rivers to drive easily round any damage so the attacks were concentrated on railway lines in inaccessible parts of the routes, 33 rail cuts of this nature being effected.

In February special attention was paid to villages south-south-west of Chinnampo, said to be housing about 1,400 troops, and to the Ongjin peninsular, where troops were reported to be massing with rubber boats for attacks on friendly islands. Pre-dawn strikes on 8 and 14 February caught a large number of lorries with their lights on and did considerable damage.

By this stage good liaison was being achieved with the partisans. On 2 March an attack at short notice by two Sea Furies on CAP in bad weather achieved such success, in support of partisans who were being attacked on an island north of Sunwi-do, that the planned follow-up strike proved unnecessary. Later that month the spring thaw was exploited as much as possible and attacks on road and rail targets were carried out. On 23 April four Sea Furies were attacked by four unidentified aircraft with swept-back wings, one Royal Navy aircraft suffering superficial damage.

On 17 May *Ocean* arrived at Sasebo to take over, carrying No. 807 Sea Fury Squadron and No. 810 Firefly Squadron. Poor visibility hampered operations on the carrier's first patrol but despite this 560 sorties were flown against enemy communications, stores, troops, guns and buildings. Close air support was provided on demand for the Commonwealth Division and partisans, as was bombardment spotting for USS *New Jersey* and HMS *Newcastle*.

Ocean carried out her last patrol of the war between 15 and 23 July. Once again the weather was unfavourable and only 434 sorties were flown, but during the patrol the one-thousandth accident-free landing was made and by the end of it 1,197 had been achieved. A small unit consisting of three Fireflies fitted with APX-6 (IFF Mk 10) was disembarked on 17 July to K6 airfield forty miles south of Seoul. These aircraft undertook 26 operational hours as night fighters against low-flying enemy aircraft but achieved no kills.

On 27 July 1953, three years and thirty-three days after the outbreak of hostilities, an armistice was signed at Panmunjom, and this is still in force. During the conflict many lessons were learnt and much experience gained. In particular, the helicopter came into its own as a short-range rescue aircraft over both land and sea. As a planeguard it was unrivalled for efficiency and economy.

The five British carriers involved had between them steamed 279,000 miles during the conflict. Their ten squadrons had flown nearly 23,000 operational sorties, during which 22 air crew had lost their lives in attacks on troop concentrations and other targets and another 13 had been killed in accidents.

CHAPTER 30

The Old Order Changeth

The Korean War over, the way was now clear for a complete reorganization of both the equipment and working methods of the Fleet Air Arm. With the advent of jet aircraft the days of the existing types of carrier were numbered, though it was to be some time before the last of the light fleet carriers departed from the scene. The first jets to be flown by the Fleet Air Arm were adaptations of RAF aircraft but in August 1951 No. 800 Squadron recommissioned under Lt Cdr G. C. Baldwin, DSC, RN, with Supermarine Attackers. This new jet fighter was specifically designed for carrier operations, though even it was based on a design originally intended for possible RAF use.

At around the same time the wartime carrier *Indomitable* came back into service after an extensive refit, though she was never to carry jet aircraft. The privilege of being the first to do this fell to *Eagle*, a brand new carrier which commissioned at the beginning of March 1952 and very soon embarked the 13th Carrier Air Group, then comprising the Attackers of No. 800 Squadron and the Firebrands of No. 827 Squadron. This CAG later included No. 803 Attacker squadron and also No. 849A Flight equipped with Douglas Skyraider AEW.1 airborne early warning aircraft supplied from US Navy reserves under the Mutual Defence Assistance Program. An adaptation of the Douglas AD-4W, the Skyraider was a defensive aircraft equipped with special radar under the fuselage capable of detecting enemy sea and air forces at a considerable distance from the fleet and also able to direct counter-attacks. The massive bulge under the fuselage was quickly likened to that on a pregnant female guppy fish and led to these aircraft being given this nickname.

Eagle was one of two fleet carriers laid down during the war but not completed until several years later, the other being *Ark Royal*; both of these ships resurrected the names of carriers sunk during the Second World War. They were fitted out to a completely new standard, including, for example, a cafeteria for junior ratings in place of the time-honoured system whereby sailors slept and ate on their own mess-decks.

From very early after the Second World War until the present day it has been regular practice for the Fleet Air Arm to participate each winter in NATO exercises in northern Norway. One such was Exercise 'Polar Mist' during the early part of the winter of 1954 in which the Sea Furies of No. 801 Squadron were involved. The aircraft left Ford on 20 September, refuelling at Valkenburg and Stavanger/Sola before arriving at Trondheim/Vaernes for an overnight stay. The next morning they flew up the coast to their destination at Bardufoss, where the former wartime Luftwaffe aerodrome had been recently enlarged for use as a NATO base and some work was still in progress. The neighbouring terrain was somewhat hazardous, the airfield being surrounded by 3,000ft-high mountains, but open fjords allowed two routes in from the sea which could be safely followed even if the mountains were covered in cloud.

The weather remained clear throughout the exercise, which was rather fortunate especially as the nearby mountains largely negated the direction-finding equipment. The living quarters were centrally heated wooden huts but the British airmen were not too happy with the Norwegian rations which largely consisted of tinned herrings and sardines. The only hot meal of the day was also usually fish so the squadron were pleased when their own cook, who had travelled with the other ground crews and the stores in one of two Transport Command Hastings, managed to draw extra supplies of food and provide a hot meal more to their taste.

The exercise started at 0001 on 26 September, Norwegian F-84s of No. 337 Squadron acting as the 'enemy'. Mock strikes were carried out throughout the day against such targets as ferries, jetties, radio stations and radar stations and the 'enemy' Army headquarters at Harstad. Six aircraft made a strike on the opposing airfield at Bodø, resulting in a dogfight with the F-84s, of which two were claimed as 'shot down' without loss to themselves. During a mock naval engagement the next day, in which an 'enemy' raider force attempted to break through into

▶An Attacker comes in to land aboard *Eagle*, June 1952. (RAF Museum)

Vaags Fjord, the Sea Furies were bounced from above by four F-84s, whose pilots claimed several of the Sea Furies as 'shot down'. Despite bad weather having set in by then, the aircraft set off home on 30 September, again staying overnight at Vaernes before reaching Ford at 1715 the next day.

On 15 June 1953 the Fleet Air Arm had an opportunity to show its strength when it participated in the Coronation Review of the Fleet at Spithead before Her Majesty Queen Elizabeth II. A total of nine carriers were assembled for the occasion. Headed by *Eagle*, they comprised the wartime fleet carriers *Illustrious*, *Implacable*, *Indefatigable* and *Indomitable* as well as the light fleet carriers *Perseus*, *Theseus*, *Magnificent* and *Sydney*, the two last belonging respectively to the Royal Canadian Navy and the Royal Australian Navy.

A fly-past of three hundred naval aircraft was led by a Sea Vampire piloted by Rear-Admiral W. T. Couchman, DSO, OBE, the Flag Officer Flying Training, and the 37 squadrons taking part included those of the RNVR. Many of the participating pilots had fought in the Korean War and the aircraft included Fireflies, Sea Furies, Seafires, Attackers, Vampires, Skyraiders, Sea Hornets, Meteors, Avengers, Gannets, Wyverns, Sea Venoms, Sea Hawks and Dragonflies.

Here at last were signs of re-equipment. The Avengers were refurbished and modernized US Navy aircraft, supplied under the Mutual Defence Assistance Program and eventually equipping a number of regular and RNVR squadrons in the anti-submarine role as a stop-gap measure while the new Fairey Gannet was being developed. The Westland Wyvern, which was never a great success, was to replace the Firebrand as a torpedo fighter, perpetuating the concept of a single-seat aircraft in this role. Both the Gannet and the Wyvern were powered by turboprop engines. To fulfil the pure jet fighter task, the single-seat Hawker Sea Hawk would shortly

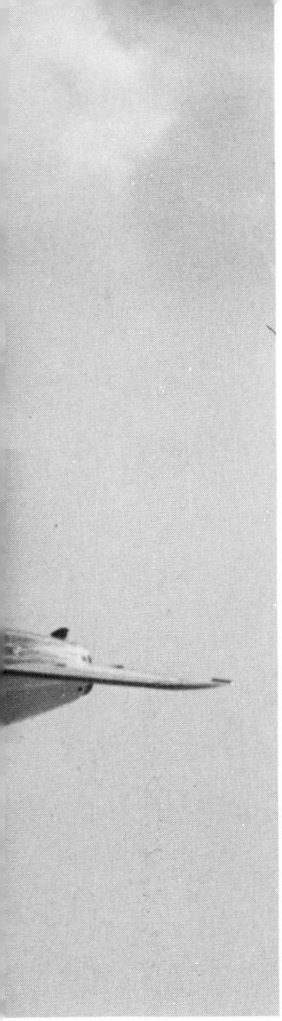

▲ A flight of No. 800 Squadron Attackers flying from Ford in 1951, during work-up prior to joining HMS *Eagle*. (RAF Museum)

Overleaf: HMS *Ark Royal* at sea in October 1955. On the flight deck are the Sea Hawks of No. 898 Squadron as well as a Skyraider, a Gannet and a Whirlwind. (RAF Museum)

supersede the Attacker, while the twin-boomed De Havilland Sea Venom was to enter service as a two-seat radar-equipped all-weather fighter.

The first production Gannet had flown only six days before the fly-past and this type was destined to remain in service for a quarter of a century, its primary role originally being to search for and help keep track of the several hundred submarines which the Russians had by then built. Later the AEW.3 variant was developed, to replace the Skyraider, and this proved to be the longest-lived version.

Lt Cdr N. C. Manley-Cooper, RN, was in command of one of the Avenger squadrons, No. 824:

> In the summer of 1953 the Fleet Air Arm had two Avenger squadrons, Nos. 824 and 826, both based at Lee-on-Solent. As there were no carriers available we carried out exercises all around the UK until 19 May 1954 when we all went on spring leave. Whilst on leave I received a phone call from the Admiralty asking how many tons of stores and spares the squadron would need if we were to go to Gibraltar for three months. I said I had no idea but was told that this was urgent as it had Churchill's priority. I went back to Lee and got hold of the Air Engineer Officer and asked his opinion. I think he said something like 30 tons. The squadron was recalled from leave and we soon found ourselves flying out to Marieux in southern France on the first leg of our journey. From there we hopped to Algeria, then to Oran and from there to Gibraltar, where we arrived in time for Exercise 'Switchback II'. As I recall, this was something to do with pinpointing all merchant ships entering the Straits of Gibraltar within a certain radius. I believe it was in connection with a new asdic then being sorted out, all highly top secret.
>
> Whilst we were at Gibraltar we were the only representatives of the FAA, there being still no carriers available. We were entertained in turn by the Army, the Navy and the RAF and the problem was how to return their hospitality with our own limited resources. A young sub-lieutenant, Vic Sirret (later to become an Admiral), had found that one could bring sherry across the border from Spain. I asked him how much it would cost, and he said it would work out at only 4d. a glass. So I said 'Right, let's give a sherry party'.
>
> On the appointed day we lined up our Avengers at North Front aerodrome to form three sides of a square, leaving them fuelled, as it would have been more dangerous to defuel them. On the fourth side of the square we arranged for the band of the Duke of Wellington's Regiment to be lined up. We had invited the top brass from the other services, including the Air Officer Commanding and the Admiral Commanding, and the whole thing went with a swing. It was well run, though I say it myself.
>
> The exercise ended on 15 June and we then left for home. We again stopped at Marieux to refuel, remaining there overnight. The ratings were billeted in the best hotel whilst the officers were put up in the local brothel – which I hasten to add was cleared out of its usual inhabitants!

New carriers were also coming into commission at this time. The wartime ships were either scrapped or sold, with the exception of *Victorious* which was undergoing extensive modernization. In their place came the new *Centaur* Class of light fleet carriers, *Albion*, *Bulwark* and *Centaur* all being completed in 1953 and 1954. They were in fact somewhat larger than the wartime light fleet carriers, having an overall length of 737ft compared with 695ft for the *Colossus* Class which preceded them. Bunks replaced the time-honoured hammocks and, like *Eagle*, they had a cafeteria system, equipped with refrigeration capable of storing four months' supply of food. There was a 200-seat cinema, a fully equipped laundry and a sick bay which was virtually a small hospital with four wards and an operating theatre.

The new *Ark Royal* finally commissioned in February 1955, nearly twelve years after being first laid down, her first commander being Capt. D. R. F. Cambell, DSC, RN. She was of a vastly different configuration from that originally envisaged, however. Her 803ft flight deck incorporated such new ideas as a pair of steam catapults, a partially angled deck, a port-side deck lift and a mirror landing device. The ship had another technological innovation in that it incorporated its own television network, via which live shows could be transmitted throughout the ship. The Captain and officers could speak to the ship's company, for instance, to brief them on forthcoming exercises, and when in range of shore transmitters the network could provide current BBC and ITV programmes or their counterparts elsewhere.

Credit for the angled deck, now universally accepted among the world's carriers, must go to Captain Cambell, who was formerly Deputy Chief Naval Representative at the Ministry of Supply and who, three years prior to this, had developed the concept in conjunction with Lewis Boddington of the Royal Aircraft Establishment at Farnborough. Since 1939 it had been the practice for the forward end of the flight deck to be reserved for catapult take-offs, the remaining two-thirds being available for landing-on. As aircraft came in they were placed in a forward deck park before being struck down on the forward lift. To protect landed aircraft from any following machine which failed to pick up any of the series of the

XE374

athwartships arrester wires a safety barrier was raised during landing operations. This was a cumbersome arrangement and aircraft in trouble had been known to go into the deck park despite the barrier. The angled deck was a basically simple idea which would revolutionize carrier deck operations. By offsetting the line for take-off and landing a few degrees from the centreline (5½° in the case of *Ark Royal*), barriers could be dispensed with because there was now sufficient space for the pilot to increase engine power and go round again if the wire was missed. In its crudest form, it was only necessary to obliterate the original deck markings and apply new ones with white paint, this method being used for the early trials in *Triumph* in 1952. More sophisticated applications later saw additional areas built on to the port side of the flight deck of some carriers.

In practical terms the angled deck gave the landing aircraft a free unobstructed 'runway' for almost the full length of the flight deck, at an angle to the centre-line. The pilot made his approach at a high angle of attack with power on, maintaining this attitude until he caught a wire, then closed his throttle and stopped by using his brakes and the arrester wire. Should he overshoot the wires his speed could be increased by pushing forward on the stick, thereby reducing drag, and he could fly off without recourse to the throttle, thus overcoming the problem of slow engine acceleration. The traditional barrier need now only be rigged in an emergency, such as critical fuel shortage or damage to the arrester gear of either the aircraft or the ship. At a stroke the deck park was safe from overshoots, and it would be possible to taxi into it more quickly (thus making room for following aircraft) and it could also be increased in size.

To assist heavily loaded aircraft to take off from carrier decks, reliance had until now been placed on an accelerator, or 'booster', which used a combination of compressed air and hydraulics. This equipment, however, while perfectly adequate for prewar and wartime aircraft, lacked sufficient power to cope with the much heavier machines now coming into service. The new short-stroke steam catapults, developed by C. C. Mitchell of MacTaggart, Scott & Co. Ltd (the main suppliers of catapults to the Royal Navy) and tested in *Perseus* in 1951, launched aircraft using steam drawn mainly from the ship's boilers and was capable of boosting off even the largest aircraft; moreover failures, or 'cold shots', became much less frequent.

Yet another British invention, also to be quickly adopted by other nations, was the

► A Sea Hawk of No. 806 Squadron, arrester hook down, comes in to land aboard *Eagle* during the 1954 spring cruise. Astern is the fast minelayer *Apollo*, and the carrier's planeguard Dragonfly is in attendance in case of mishap. (RAF Museum)

◄ Gannet AS.1s of No. 820 Squadron aboard HMS *Bulwark*. (RAF Museum)

mirror landing aid, which was to replace the Deck Landing Control Officer whose vital and sometimes dangerous task was becoming increasingly difficult as landing speeds became progressively higher. These speeds had crept up from the 50kt of the Flycatcher, for instance, to nearly double that in its piston-engined successors. In place of the prewar method of a fairly steep approach at just above the stall, followed by a flare-out and engine cut, a faster and more level approach had become the norm. The advent of the new jets meant that approach speeds were once again raised, nearly trebling those of the 1920s to a round 140–150kts.

The new landing aid was the brainchild of Lt Cdr H. C. N. Goodhart, RN, and was tried out on board *Illustrious* in 1952 when 48 successful Vampire landings were completed. The pilot was no longer dependent on the traditional 'batsman', with the ever-present possibility of a dangerous situation developing during the time-lag between a signal being given and the pilot responding. Through his reflection in the gyro-stabilized mirror and the attitude of the indicating lights he became the master of his own destiny and could react instantly. The mirror was stabilized so as to produce a visual glide path which would allow the pilot to fly straight on to the deck without the need for a flare-out or a reduction in engine power before the arrester wire was engaged, thus allowing him to go round again if necessary.

Albion had mirrors fitted in 1954 for a spell in the Mediterranean, one being on the port side just beneath flight-deck level and the other on the starboard side just abaft the island. Both were gyro-stabilized in pitch but not in roll, and could be stabilized by hand in the event of a gyro failure. On each side of the mirror were seven green lights to provide a datum line, and each mirror could be raised or lowered to allow for the pilot's being seated at varying heights in different types of aircraft. The port mirror was normally used; the starboard mirror was generally reserved for practice though it could be brought into operation if, for example, the use of the port mirror led to sun-dazzle problems. A correct approach would result in No. 3 wire being picked up, but a pitching deck could present difficulties, as could a tendency to flare out as the wires were entered or to disregard the mirror as soon as the round-down was passed.

The air crew were themselves better protected, too. New headgear in the shape of Cromwell helmets, nicknamed 'bone-domes', made them less vulnerable in the event of an accident, and the adoption of an audio airspeed indicator combined with a head-up display on the windscreen allowed the pilot to maintain sight of the mirror throughout the landing period. Rubberized fabric immersion suits gave protection in the event of a ditching, particularly where sea temperatures were low. Should it become necessary to bale out, Martin-Baker ejection seats provided an additional measure of safety, these being first fitted as standard equipment in the later production batches of Sea Venoms.

ROYAL NAVY
111
WM969
107
WM920
104
103

CHAPTER 31

The Helicopter Era Dawns

◄ **Sea Hawks of No. 898 Squadron bank over *Albion* in September 1954. (RAF Museum)**

The helicopter role in the Fleet Air Arm grew from very small beginnings and at that time it could not have been foreseen how predominant this class of aircraft would eventually become. The Royal Navy pioneered the use of military helicopters, becoming the first service in the world to order them for operational use when a contract was placed in 1943 for 45 American-built Sikorsky VS-316s, these having the US designation R-4 and the British name Hoverfly I. Training was carried out initially in America during 1944 with a view to using the helicopters from ships of the Royal Navy against U-boats. Only one practical trial was carried out, two aircraft being carried aboard the British merchantman *Daghestan* on a special platform for an eastbound Atlantic convoy early in 1944. Heavy seas permitted only one take-off and landing during the crossing and the aircraft was deemed unsuitable in the anti-submarine role at that stage of development. The R-4s were shipped to the United Kingdom, and an order was placed for 150 of an improved version, the R-6, although this was subsequently cut back to 31; these, in the main, went into service with the RAF as the Hoverfly II, only three seeing service with the Fleet Air Arm. The Admiralty had in fact placed a wartime order for no fewer than 250 Sikorsky R-5s for anti-submarine convoy protection but the design (later known as the Sikorsky S-51) was not ready before the approach of the war's end and the order was therefore cancelled. The Navy preferred to wait for the more advanced machines being developed by Sikorsky.

The handful of naval 'choppers', as the breed became universally known, provided the nucleus of the Fleet Air Arm's later vast experience in this form of flying. They were very much in the development stage during 1945 and as such were entrusted to an assortment of independent flights to be assessed for a variety of tasks which included hydrographic survey, torpedo-dropping and gunnery spotting. By 1946, however, the aircraft had largely been centralized in No. 771 Squadron, a Fleet Requirements Unit based at Gosport.

It was now becoming obvious to both the Royal Navy and the RAF that helicopters were here to stay, but the problem was one of supply. Ideally a British manufacturer would have provided a suitable machine, and the Royal Aircraft Establishment at Farnborough had in fact provided some support for the development of rotary-wing aircraft as far

► **One of the Fleet Air Arm's small number of Sikorsky Hoverflies seen at RNAS Bramcote during a Navy Day display. (Author's collection)**

back as the First World War. Trials had been carried out intermittently with a series of helicopters and autogyros produced by such designers as Brennan, Isacco, Cierva, Hafner and Kay but none had proved an outstanding success.

Despite Britain's pioneering role in this field, America was by now well in the lead with helicopter development and in 1947 Westland Aircraft decided to import six Sikorsky S.51s for development work. Although larger and more powerful than the Hoverfly, the S.51 still did not have the performance for anti-submarine work, but it was fully capable of undertaking air-sea rescue work and it was also suitable for some types of civil operation. Westland took out a licence for its production at Yeovil and thus made the first step towards becoming exclusively a manufacturer of helicopters.

With the prospect of helicopters becoming a permanent feature of naval aviation the helicopter element of No. 771 Squadron broke away in May 1947 to become a new No. 705 Squadron, or Helicopter Fleet Requirements Unit, at Gosport. This was to be the sole operating authority for all naval helicopter flying, carrying out such varied tasks as training pilots, crewmen and maintenance personnel, evaluating helicopter equipment, developing techniques, carrying out special trials and undertaking communications work.

Progress with 'anglicizing' the S.51 was slow, a shortage of dollars being partly to blame, and it was not until October 1948 that Westland was able to fly a British-assembled machine. Fourteen months later the first of these aircraft, now known as the Dragonfly, arrived at No. 705 Squadron. This first version was designated the HR.1, and by the end of 1950 the last of the Hoverflies had been withdrawn.

The training task of the squadron was then widened to include that of providing experienced crews to man small helicopter flights, both for planeguard duties on aircraft carriers and for search and rescue at shore bases. The first such carrier-borne unit embarked in *Indomitable* early in 1951 and only three months later another in *Glory* was on its way to participate in the Korean War, where four pilots were to be rescued from the sea and another four from behind enemy lines.

► Dragonfly HR.3 VX600 '531' from No. 705 Squadron, the Fleet Requirements Unit at Lee-on-Solent, flying over *Ark Royal*, about 1957. (RAF Museum)

ROYAL NAVY
531
R06

The knowledge that such help was readily available did much to maintain morale in the carrier squadrons.

The Dragonfly served in some numbers with both the Fleet Air Arm and the RAF, early variants being powered by a British-built 540hp Alvis Leonides engine. The design was progressively improved and the fabric-covered rotor blades of the HR.1 were replaced in the HR.3 by all-metal ones with hydraulic servo controls. This all-naval version entered service in 1952 and a few machines were later brought up to HR.5 standard, with increased engine power and improved instrumentation.

The Fleet Air Arm's first major use of helicopters in the search and rescue task occurred in January 1952 when the freighter *Flying Enterprise* broke down and went adrift in the Western Approaches. Flying in what until then had been thought to be impossible conditions, a Dragonfly refuelled at RNAS Culdrose to make a valiant but unsuccessful attempt to rescue the master, Captain Carlsen, and his mate. This episode was eclipsed a year later when, in February 1953, No. 705 Squadron performed an invaluable service following the flooding of much of the east coast of England and large areas of Holland. During two weeks of rescue work around six hundred Dutch people were rescued by Dragonflies of the FAA and other services with the loss of only one squadron machine. While operating near Gilze Rijen, Lt R. R. Crayton, RN, in WG748 made a landing with reduced revolutions on a narrow road on top of a dyke but the aircraft skidded and toppled on to its side into 12ft of sea water. The crew, fortunately, were saved. In June 1953 twelve Dragonflies were in the vanguard of the Coronation Review of the Fleet at Spithead. The type continued to give sterling service until 1965, having paved the way for the more advanced machines of the future.

The Dragonfly had stood both the RAF and the Fleet Air Arm in good stead, but a larger machine was now needed. There were still no suitable British helicopters available, and therefore American Sikorsky machines again filled the gap. Westland Aircraft took out a licence for the production of the S.55, which would be known as the Whirlwind in British service. It would take some time, however, to anglicize the design and get production under way, and in the meantime 25 S.55 variants were provided under the Mutual Defence Assistance Program. Ten of these were US

► Men of No. 42 Royal Marine Commando rapidly de-plane at Worthy Down from a Whirlwind HAS.7 of No. 848 Squadron in a snowstorm, early 1960. The men are about to embark in HMS *Bulwark*. (RAF Museum)

◀ **A Whirlwind at dispersal on the edge of the jungle. (Author's collection)**

Marine HRS-2s, designated Whirlwind HAR.21 in British parlance, and intended for search and rescue work. The remaining fifteen were US Navy HO4S-3s, designated Whirlwind HAS.22 for anti-submarine duties.

The HAR.21s arrived in November 1952, and all ten were allocated to the newly re-formed No. 848 Squadron at Gosport. The HAS.22s did not arrive until the following September and were used by a number of units, notably No. 706 Anti-Submarine Helicopter Squadron, also at Gosport. Trials were carried out with sonar equipment at both Portland and Belfast. No. 848 Squadron was immediately tasked with providing helicopter support in Malaya, where since 1948 Communist guerilla troops and terrorists had been attempting to take over the country. On 10 December 1952 the Whirlwinds were embarked in the ferry carrier *Perseus* and on 8 January 1953 they were disembarked to RNAS Sembawang on Singapore island for an intended 3½-week work-up period. Even this short period had to be truncated, however, when the RAF Dragonfly unit was beset by mechanical problems, and on 24 January No. 848 Squadron became operational. Six of the aircraft were placed on immediate alert, three at Sembawang and three at Kuala Lumpur, the remaining four being retained in reserve at Sembawang along with most of the maintenance personnel. Both operational detachments were soon at work, three wounded soldiers being lifted the very next day by the Kuala Lumpur detachment from a jungle clearing to the British Military Hospital at Kiurara. This first casualty evacuation (casevac) sortie was soon emulated by the Sembawang detachment, which on 27 January winched a Gurkha casualty to the similar hospital at Singapore.

During that first year the small number of naval Whirlwinds undertook a variety of tasks in support of the ground forces in addition to its casevac activities. For the first time soldiers could be transported to and from dense jungle to a precise map reference within a matter of minutes instead of having to hack their way through for several days or even weeks. Up to ten soldiers, though usually fewer in practice, could be carried in each aircraft and a shuttle service could either drop them in or recover them from a jungle clearing which was often barely large enough to clear the rotors. If necessary the troops and their supplies could be winched down from just above the tree-tops. Tracker dogs could be lowered to help round up bandits, supplies and personnel dropped by parachute, leaflets dropped, prisoners taken back to base and a myriad

▲ ***Bulwark* soon after her recommissioning early in 1960 as a commando carrier. (RAF Museum)**

other tasks performed which had never before been possible.

Another pioneering task with long-term effects was that of undertaking Commando operations. In Operation 'Bahadur' four Whirlwinds each made four sorties to drop 75 Gurkhas into a landing zone, and having demonstrated the practicability of this new method a much larger action was mounted at brigade level. Operation 'Cato' was a response to an intelligence report of a meeting of Communist delegates in the Benta area in Western Pahang. No. 848 Squadron was to carry out 183 sorties in all, during which it flew in 650 soldiers as well as 4,000lb of equipment and supplies. This first large-scale operation amply demonstrated the ability of the Whirlwinds to deploy large numbers of troops and their trappings at short notice, though on this occasion their efforts were rewarded by only a small number of terrorists being killed or captured.

For its efforts during 1953 the squadron was later awarded the annual Boyd Trophy. By the end of the following year it had logged up 6,000 hours of operational flying during which it had transported 18,000 men as well as 363,000lb of stores and ammunition. The squadron was eventually disbanded towards the end of 1956, having made a significant contribution to a successful campaign. Its key role in the defeat of the terrorists was recognised by the Malayan Government, which awarded the squadron a suitably inscribed silver kris, this curved dagger being the country's national symbol.

No. 706 Squadron, meanwhile, had become No. 845 Squadron at Lee-on-Solent on 14 November 1955. In addition to the American Whirlwind HAS.22s it also had Westland-built Whirlwind HAR.3s and later HAS.7s, taking part in night hovering and sonar dunking trials aboard *Bulwark* during the autumn of 1957. Both of these later Whirlwind variants were also used for planeguard duties aboard carriers, replacing the earlier Dragonflies.

CHAPTER 32

The Suez Affair

The ending of the Malayan Emergency in 1956 came shortly after the Fleet Air Arm's involvement in another Eastern conflict. For some years relations with Egypt had become progressively more difficult and matters came to a head in July 1956 when President Nasser nationalized the Suez Canal. Both British and French interests were at stake, and a joint operation was planned to attack the Canal Zone of Egypt with the intention of securing the waterway, which provided the only economical means of obtaining vital commodities – particularly oil – from the Persian Gulf and Far East. 'Supertankers' did not exist at that time; indeed, these monsters were only conceived as a means of circumventing the need for the Canal.

The attack, which led to much subsequent controversy and bitterness, also involved the Israelis and was mounted under the code-name Operation 'Musketeer'. The main action would of necessity be carried out by ground forces but air support on a large scale was essential. However, the nearest land bases available to the RAF for their bomber and fighter attacks were in Malta and Cyprus and the provision of close support could therefore only be by carrier-borne aircraft. Fortunately a number of carriers were still in service and as the Fleet Air Arm was in the throes of a re-equipment programme these could be equipped with the most modern fixed-wing naval aircraft and helicopters. All participating British and French aircraft carried black and yellow identification stripes around the rear fuselage and outer wing sections, similar in style to the black and white invasion stripes used during the Normandy invasion and later the Korean War.

The plan was to carry out the attack in stages, all involving the FAA. The first objective was to destroy the Egyptian Air Force on the ground before it could intervene. On 1 November aircraft took off from the carriers *Albion*, *Eagle* and *Bulwark* to make a surprise attack on Egyptian airfields. Typical was an early morning raid by twelve Sea Hawks from *Bulwark* on Cairo West airfield in which Egyptian Air Force Lancasters and Russian-built 'Beagle' bombers were subjected to a devastating attack. Other airfields to be attacked included the former RN airfield at Dekheila, near Alexandria, as well as Abu Sueir, Fayid, Kabrit and Kasfareet. Aircraft would climb to 20,000ft, fly over the sea towards their target, then descend to rain bombs, gun fire and rockets in profusion on aircraft, hangars and control towers, after which they sped back just above the ground until reaching the coast, at which point they would climb up to 5,000ft before making a more leisurely return to the ship.

By the second day photographic reconnaissance showed that for all practical purposes the defending air force no longer existed and the FAA squadrons were free to turn their attention to other targets. Numerous attacks were carried out on military installations of various kinds as well as bridges, roads and railways, and by 5 November the Egyptians had lost not only their air defence but also much of their ground equipment as well as the communications infrastructure. Nearly 1,300 sorties had been undertaken by fixed-wing aircraft from the three carriers involved, many of the pilots having made four individual sorties in a single day. *Bulwark*'s aircraft alone claimed to have disposed of over 100 Egyptian aircraft, destroyed or badly

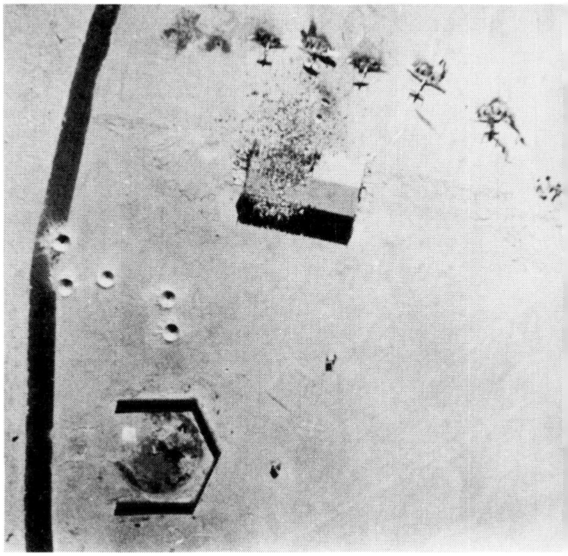

▶ An aerial view of blitzed hangars and burnt-out Lancaster bombers of the Egyptian Air Force after a strafing and bombing attack on Cairo West airfield by Sea Hawks of No. 810 Squadron from HMS *Bulwark*.

damaged, as well as two E-boats, eighteen tanks and assorted guns and transport.

The way was now clear for the British and French ground forces to be landed, and on that same day parachute troops were dropped, the carriers sailing close in to provide continuous air support. By nightfall the outskirts of Port Fuad and Port Said had been occupied, helicopters from *Ocean* and *Theseus* carrying ashore food and ammunition in a continuous shuttle service. At first light the next day, 6 November, beach defences were attacked and Commandos put ashore, after which the two helicopter carriers sent off the machines of No. 845 Squadron and the Joint (Experimental) Helicopter Unit, which transported ashore the five hundred men of No. 45 Marine Commando together with their equipment and ammunition.

This was the first time helicopters had been used in such a role and it turned out to be no easy task. The Marines were looking forward to getting ashore without wetting their feet but as their helicopters sped towards the intended landing zone it was seen to be veiled in smoke. The pilots veered westward to seek out a clear area and a successful landing was made in the Egyptian Stadium by the machine carrying the reconnaissance party, the pilot, Lt Cdr R. R. Crayton, RN, apparently oblivious to assorted bangs and thumps that could be heard around as he approached (it subsequently transpired that he had not heard them through his 'bone-dome'!). A sudden appearance by the Egyptian Army over the walls surrounding the stadium led to a rapid take-off but a hasty return was made to rescue the reconnaissance party which did its best to create a record for the two-hundred-yards sprint. A safer landing point was found west of De Lesseps' statue, the first wave landing at 0615, and by 0738 a total of 415 men and 23 tons of stores had been landed, though not without losses. The reconnaissance machine was riddled with bullet holes and had to be grounded because of a leak from the petrol tank and two other machines were damaged.

Having completed their Commando task the Whirlwinds were now free to be used in the casevac role, standing patrols by the fixed-wing aircraft providing cover. Things went well everywhere and by nightfall on the 6th the Anglo-French troops had captured Port Said and were well on the way to taking the Suez Canal. This was not to be, however, as the international political battle had already been virtually lost, and at midnight that night a ceasefire came into effect, all the British and French forces eventually having to withdraw. Nevertheless the Fleet Air Arm had taken full advantage of the first real opportunity to show its paces in a large-scale operation since the end of the Second World War and it had done so with enthusiasm, carrying out all its allotted tasks with precision and competence. This was to prove the last major operation by a large British carrier force.

▼ Wyvern S.4s of No. 830 Squadron, fresh from participating in the Suez attacks, lined up on the flight deck of HMS *Eagle*. (Via B. J. Lowe)

CHAPTER 33

Change and Minor Wars

After the Suez ceasefire the Royal Navy carriers remained in the Mediterranean area for a time but by March 1957 they were all back home. This, however, was a sad month for the Fleet Air Arm as it saw the disbandment of all the RNVR squadrons as part of a programme of cuts in defence spending. During their decade of existence these units had grown in number from four to eleven and their equipment had progressed from Seafires, Fireflies and, later, Sea Furies to Sea Hawks, Attackers, Avengers and Gannets.

Typical of the minor flare-ups in which the Royal Navy was likely to be called upon to play a part was an episode in 1958. On 1 February that year Egypt, Sudan and Syria joined together as the United Arab Republic under President Nasser of Egypt, and thirteen days later Iraq and Jordan were united to form the Arab Federation. On 14 July, however, news came through of a military coup in Iraq in which King Feisal II and his young son were murdered. King Hussein of Jordan was declared head of state but two weeks later he dissolved the short-lived Federation and appealed for help from Britain under a defence treaty.

Eagle was in the Mediterranean at the time and two days later she arrived at Cyprus from Malta to help provide support for King Hussein. The ship was given the task of taking over protection of part of the route of an air lift from Cyprus to Amman. Two days later the Sea Hawks of No. 802 Squadron arrived from the United Kingdom, having left Ford the previous day and refuelled on the way at Dijon, Practica de Mare, Hal Far and El Adem before arriving at Akrotiri. The Sea Hawks, and the Sea Venoms of No. 894 Squadron which were already aboard, then operated around the clock, Skyraiders of No. 849A Flight maintaining airborne early warning patrols against possible attacks by low-flying aircraft or motor torpedo boats. The Gannets of No. 814 Squadron were also available and these undertook protective anti-submarine patrols over an area of some 40 square miles around the carrier and its escorts. By the time the airlift ended on 23 July around 500 sorties had been flown, a number of United Arab Republic aircraft having been intercepted and escorted until they were clear of the force. The pilot of one Il-14 on its way to Damascus airport thought he was under attack, as did one from Syria, and each promptly turned back until reassured as to the intentions of the Sea Hawks flying alongside each of them. *Bulwark* also participated towards the end of the operation, having been recalled to Aden from a South African cruise, and *Albion* played a role as a troop transport.

At about the same time FAA helicopters were brought in to help against terrorist activities in Cyprus. The four Whirlwinds of No. 728C Flight had been sent to Nicosia in mid-June 1958 from their base in Malta, embarking with No. 45 Royal Marine Commando as deck cargo in the cruiser HMS *Bermuda*, and a month later they found themselves in action. At 0330 on 11 July the aircraft descended in line astern to a field north of the village of Lefkoniko and set down the Marines. The passage over the Kyrenia Mountains had been somewhat bumpy and the landing was rather tricky due to a 40kt wind coming over a steep wooded ridge behind the village. Operation 'Springtime', as it was termed, was intended to contain and then round up seven terrorists believed to be hiding near the small village of Akanthou in northern Cyprus, and also participating in the attack would be RAF Sycamores of No. 284 Squadron and soldiers from the Royal West Kents. The attack took place on 13 July and the aircraft flew across mountainous country to the area where the terrorists were believed to have their hide. One of the Whirlwinds deposited its Marines only 50yd from the hide, landing beneath a 200ft rock face on a small ridged area with a slope of 1:4. The hide was empty, however, and despite a search lasting several days, covering the ground inch by inch and laying trip flares, no trace was found, but the helicopters were useful in dropping food and water to the troops. On 26 July the Flight was shipped back to Malta in HMS *Reggio* (formerly *LST 5311*), having gained invaluable experience but without any real success for its mission.

The following year *Victorious* came back

into commission after an eight-year refit. Completely transformed, she now boasted a fully angled deck, two steam catapults, mirror sights and the most advanced operations room of any of the world's carriers. The latter was linked to a large Type 984 radar above the island which provided detailed information on any aircraft in the vicinity. Towards the end of 1959 the new carrier *Hermes* came into commission, also fitted with a fully angled deck and Type 984 radar, whilst *Bulwark* was withdrawn for conversion to a commando carrier, to be equipped only with helicopters.

New fixed-wing aircraft were also in the offing, the Supermarine Scimitar being issued in June 1958 to No. 803 Squadron for service aboard *Victorious*. Replacing the Sea Hawk, this powerful new fighter was fitted with two Rolls-Royce Avon engines and had four 30mm Aden guns in addition to a provision for underwing bombs or rockets. In 1959 came a replacement for the ageing Sea Venoms in the all-weather role in the shape of the twin-boomed De Havilland Sea Vixen, equipped with Firestreak guided missiles, a Ferranti pilot attack sight and a GEC radar system which was locked on to the ship's Type 984 radar. The Sea Vixen's capacity to defend the fleet was increased by the introduction of specialized air-direction frigates fitted with improved radar surveillance equipment. At about this time a new version of the Gannet also came into service, the AEW.3 being fitted, like the Skyraider which it replaced in No. 849 Squadron, with an underbelly 'guppy' type radome.

On the lighter side, the Royal Navy entered two teams for the Blériot Air Race from the Arc de Triomphe to Marble Arch in July 1959. One included a Scimitar piloted by Cdr I. H. F.

◀ **Sea Venom FAW.22s of No. 894 Squadron from *Albion* display their 'shark's teeth' markings at Yeovilton in 1960. (B. J. Lowe)**

▼ **Scimitar F.1 XD236 '150/V', of No. 803 Squadron, after entering the barrier aboard *Victorious* on 20 March 1959. Fortunately the asbestos-suit-clad emergency fire party were not needed on this occasion. (Admiralty)**

Martin, RN, as competitor, and the other a Sea Vixen with the observer, Lt W. J. Carter, RN, as competitor. The attempt by the Scimitar took place on 15 July and involved Martin being taken by a French motorcyclist from the starting point to Issy, from where he was whisked by Whirlwind to Villacoublay, quickly cleared Customs then flew to Wisley in 20 minutes, once more clearing Customs. From there he had another Whirlwind ride to land on a lighter off Cadogan Pier, then a journey by launch and finally a five-minute ride on the pillion of a Royal Marines' motor-cycle to end up with an overall time of 47 minutes, achieving sixth position in the race and being the fastest single-seat competitor.

The helicopter element of the Fleet Air Arm was the next to be used operationally, however. In 1961 Iraq threatened to annex the independent Sheikhdom of Kuwait, a country vital to Britain's oil supplies and with which there was a defence agreement. Within twenty-four hours of a call for help the newly converted *Bulwark* had arrived from Karachi with No. 42 Royal Marine Commando and No. 848 Squadron, the latter now re-equipped with Whirlwind HAS.7s. In adverse weather, and in temperatures up to 120°F, 600 Marines were quickly put ashore by the squadron Whirlwinds together with all their supporting equipment, providing ample proof of the value of such a force. *Bulwark* was soon joined by *Victorious*, which was recalled from passage to Hong Kong, and the RAF also played a significant role. These measures were sufficient and in the event no shots were fired.

By now *Albion* had also been converted to a commando carrier, and the Whirlwind was being replaced by the larger Westland Wessex HAS.1. The latter was yet another 'anglicization' of a Sikorsky design, this time the S.58. The helicopters were soon to be in action, as towards the end of 1962 the Sultan of Brunei in North Borneo asked for help against guerrilla attacks from Indonesian territory, both across the border with Sarawak and by sea. As it happened, *Albion* was carrying No. 40 Royal Marine Commando from Mombasa to Singapore and she was immediately re-routed to Kuching, where the troops were put ashore.

The so-called 'confrontation' was to last 3½ years and the Wessexes and Whirlwinds of Nos. 845 and 846 Squadrons were to play a vital role. Conditions were very similar to those experienced a decade earlier in Malaya but this time there were two commando carriers available to act in turn as a floating base; in addition a forward base was set up at Nanga Gaat, near the Indonesian border, where the Fleet Air Arm became a part of the local community, learning the language and sometimes wearing the local dress. The helicopters performed a similar task to that in the Malayan episode, flying many thousands of sorties to transport troops into dense jungle, paddy fields and mangrove swamps, handicapped by unreliable maps, a lack of proper weather forecasting and relatively primitive radar equipment. As in Malaya, troops and stores were landed in small jungle clearings, or winched down from above the trees if none was available, often in torrential rain. When the squadrons finally left in October 1966 there were several days of local festivities. For their achievements No. 846 Squadron received the annual Boyd Trophy award in 1963 and the following year it went to No. 845 Squadron.

The helicopter was able to demonstrate one of its happier roles late in 1961 when No. 825 Squadron, by then equipped with Whirlwind HAS.7s, was called upon to provide flood relief in East Africa. On 22 November its aircraft were put ashore in Kenya from *Victorious*, which happened to be in the vicinity, and the ship then continued on its way to the Mediterranean. A headquarters was set up at the former wartime FAA base at Port Reitz, near Mombasa, and two detachments of two aircraft each operated from Malindi airstrip and Lamu sea wall, respectively 80 and 160 miles north of Mombasa. During the next few weeks the helicopters undertook reconnaissance flights, dropped food and evacuated casualties. On 30 November and the following day 140 cattle were lifted across the swollen Subaki river which had temporarily changed its course, to augment dwindling meat supplies in Mombasa, further such air lifts then becoming unnecessary when the water returned to its normal course. The Lamu detachment had a particularly difficult task as

► De Havilland Sea Vixen FAW.2 XN706 '135/E', of No. 899 Squadron (*Eagle*), comes in to land during 1970. (MAP)

▼ Blackburn Buccaneer S.2 XV867 '611/LM', of No. 803 Squadron from Lossiemouth, and equipped to carry Martel air-to-surface missiles, undertakes a low flypast during 1969. (Via B. J. Lowe)

maps of the area were inaccurate. The terrain was a mixture of open forest, semi-tropical forest and dry open bush and there were very few roads or tracks. The main objectives were to help prevent the spread of disease and to stockpile food, the helicopters usually operating at their near-maximum all-up weight for the latter task. Landing in such conditions near isolated villages with little real idea of wind direction could be risky and on three occasions night landings had to be made on return to Lamu with the aid of improvised goose-neck flares and a Very pistol. By the time No. 824 Squadron from *Centaur* took over the task on 9 December, 343 hours' flying had been put in during sixteen days of intensive activity.

▼ Gannet AEW.3 '072/E' of No. 849 Squadron's 'D' Flight banks towards *Eagle*. (Via B. J. Lowe)

Meanwhile further fixed-wing re-equipment arrived in mid-1962 in the shape of the new Blackburn Buccaneer, a powerful, purpose-built, low-level, high-speed strike aircraft. Much technological development had been incorporated in its design. The fuselage had an area-rule configuration to reduce drag while boundary layer control was provided in the wings, resulting in a doubling of lift and a consequent reduction in approach speeds. The Buccaneer was designed for extended operations at high speeds near sea and ground level, beneath enemy radar coverage, where air turbulence was likely to be encountered, and therefore steel components were used extensively, many being machined from solid metal to counteract fatigue. Its electronics and weapons system allowed the accurate delivery of either conventional or nuclear weapons, both by normal methods and by newly developed 'toss bombing' techniques whereby the aircraft could turn well away from the impact area while the bombs continued on a ballistic trajectory.

Fleet Air Arm helicopters were involved again when trouble flared up once more in the Gulf States during May 1964. British forces were due to be withdrawn from Aden but fighting had broken out between the South Arabian Federation and the Yemen. No. 45 Royal Marine Commando was put ashore by the Wessex helicopters of No. 815 Squadron to operate from the difficult Radfan area. Conditions were often appalling, with turbulence among the mountains, dust storms and heavy rains, but nevertheless four Wessexes succeeded in transporting 550 men and all their equipment into the battle zone in one day. Three weeks later, on the successful completion of the operation, the force withdrew and *Centaur* sailed back to Singapore.

Two years later came the Rhodesian crisis and the need to set up a blockade to prevent oil tankers sailing to the port of Beira. The Beira Patrol came into being with first *Eagle* and later *Ark Royal* taking up station in the Mozambique Channel. While the crisis lasted Gannets, Scimitars and Sea Vixens helped to maintain a constant vigil. Towards the end of her turn of duty one of *Ark Royal*'s Sea Vixens, XJ520 '014/R' of No. 890 Squadron, was lost in unfortunate circumstances. On 10 May 1966 the aircraft had completed a normal oil-tanker patrol and was returning to the ship when the port engine flamed out and there was a rapid loss of fuel. The pilot, Lt Alan Tarver, radioed the ship, which immediately sent up Lt Robin Munro-Davies in a Scimitar tanker. He met the stricken aircraft at 15,000ft some forty miles from the ship but Tarver was unable to manoeuvre the Sea Vixen's refuelling probe into the Scimitar's hose.

The second engine ran out of fuel when they were in sight of the ship but there was little hope of the Sea Vixen gliding the few remaining miles. Tarver ordered his observer. Lt John Stutchbury, to eject when down to 6,000ft but the ejection mechanism failed to operate. Shouting to tell him to bale out, manually, the pilot saw Stutchbury, a large man, become stuck in the narrow hatchway.

▲Blackburn Buccaneer S.2 XT279 '322', of No. 809 Squadron, flying above the clouds near Lossiemouth around 1969. (Official)

▼De Havilland Sea Vixen FAW.2 XP918 '122/E', of No. 899 Squadron, comes in to land aboard HMS *Eagle* during 1971; a Wessex planeguard is in attendance. (C.F. Motley)

▼► Sea Vixen FAW.1 XJ583 (No. 892 Squadron) on fire aboard *Victorious*, 8 February 1961. The flames were extinguished, but not before the aircraft had been seriously damaged by both fire and salt water. It was shipped back to the United Kingdom aboard *Hermes* to end its days as a ground instructional airframe at Arbroath. (Author's collection)

Now down to 3,000ft and only travelling at 200kt, he inverted the aircraft in the hope that gravity would do the trick but to no avail; a second roll was equally ineffective. Lowering the flaps and reducing the speed to 130kt, almost at the stall, reduced the slipstream and gave Stutchbury a chance to manoeuvre himself out along the top of the fuselage, but something still held him in and despite Tarver's frantic last-minute efforts to reach across and free him the two men were both on board when the aircraft finally flicked over into the sea.

Munro-Davies, who had been watching all this helplessly from overhead, radioed back that Tarver could not possibly have survived as he was unable to leave the Sea Vixen until the last second. He was wrong, though, as the pilot's parachute had partially deployed on entering the sea and he was able to get free despite being stunned. Twenty minutes later he was returned to the carrier's deck by courtesy of a planeguard Wessex, and he was subsequently awarded the George Medal for his valiant attempts to save his colleague's life.

CHAPTER 34

The Helicopter Begins to Take Over

The mid-1960s saw two significant developments in the increasing helicopter element of the Fleet Air Arm. One was the introduction into service of the Wessex HU.5, a twin-engined derivative of this type designed specifically for troop carrying and capable of transporting up to sixteen fully armed Marines from a carrier deck to a beachhead or forward area. It also had sufficient power to be able to lift, slung beneath it, such heavy loads as Land Rover vehicles, artillery, fuel and ammunition and deposit them where needed. A hundred were built, and they were eventually to equip four FAA Commando squadrons, Nos. 845, 846, 847 and 848, the first of these having detached flights operating from both Radfan and Borneo by May 1965. The planeguard and shore-based SAR flights also re-equipped. Earlier marks of Whirlwind were replaced in some instances by HAR.9s, these being conversions of HAS.7s fitted with more powerful Bristol Siddeley (later Rolls-Royce) Gnome engines in place of the Alvis Leonides Major. These in turn gave way first to the Wessex HAS.1 and then to the Wessex HU.5.

Of equal importance was the introduction of the Westland Wasp. The company had at last produced a successful all-British helicopter, albeit essentially one it had inherited from the Saro company via Faireys. Nearly 100 were eventually built for the Royal Navy and for the first time since the demise of the catapult seaplane it became a practical proposition to operate an aircraft from a warship other than a carrier. In March 1964 No. 829 Squadron formed at Culdrose as the parent unit for what was to become a host of seaborne Wasp flights, moving its headquarters eight months later to Portland which, a quarter of a century later, is still the home for all such units. The Wasp was a lightweight machine with an anti-submarine capability, able to operate from a deck platform. It could remain on patrol for up to an hour and was able to drop homing torpedoes or depth charges. Four years after its introduction it was also equipped to carry French-built Nord air-to-surface guided missiles for defence against fast patrol boats. The aircraft was mainly used in 'Tribal', *Leander* and *Rothesay* Class frigates, the first Wasp Flight being formed aboard HMS *Leander* in November 1963.

Other new helicopter-carrying ships were coming into commission at that time. These included two assault ships, *Fearless* and *Intrepid*, specially designed for use in amphibious warfare and with a dock aft for housing landing craft above which was a large helicopter deck. The two ships were each fully equipped to act as Naval Assault Group Brigade Headquarters.

A major blow fell in 1966 when the Government of the day decided to place an overall limit of £200 million on the Defence Budget. This brought the immediate cancellation of the new strike carrier CVA-01, which was to have been a large new replacement for the wartime class of carrier still in service, and effectively killed off the long-terms prospects of the fleet carrier in the Royal Navy. CVA-01 would have had a wide deck with a three-lane arrangement making the fully angled deck unnecessary but in order to accommodate the fast and heavy aircraft by then in service with the Fleet Air Arm its size, and therefore cost, had become prohibitive within the newly imposed limits on Defence spending.

Fixed-wing flying was nevertheless to be a feature of British naval aviation for some years to come. *Victorious* was paid off in 1967 for a refit, though an accidental fire led to her being eventually broken up. However, *Eagle* came back into service in 1967, allowing *Ark Royal* in turn to be withdrawn for a refit. Many improvements were needed, including the modernization of engines, boilers, air conditioning and machinery, as well as a complete renewal of 1,200 miles of the electrical cabling. The angle of the landing deck was increased to 8½°, entailing the removal and repositioning of the starboard catapult which was then increased in length to 199ft. Both it and the existing 154ft port catapult were fitted with jet blast deflectors, the surrounding deck areas being given water cooling, and both were fitted with Van Zelm arresting gear which could retrieve the costly catapult bridles for further use. With all these alterations, the FAA was ready to go

▼ Whirlwind HAR.9s of the Search and Rescue Flight at Culdrose carried out many rescues around the Cornish coast before being withdrawn in 1975. (RNAS Culdrose)

supersonic in the shape of the McDonnell Douglas Phantom, destined only to serve in *Ark Royal*. This ubiquitous all-weather strike fighter was much modified for Royal Navy service, power for the 'anglicized' version being provided by two Rolls-Royce Spey turbojets fitted with re-heat. In the meantime further developments in the helicopter field had seen the Royal Fleet Auxiliary *Engadine* come into service during 1967 as a helicopter support ship while in 1969 HMS *Blake*, a *Tiger* Class cruiser, recommissioned as a helicopter cruiser able to accommodate four anti-submarine or assault helicopters; she was followed later by HMS *Tiger* herself.

The Fleet Air Arm had a moment of glory

▲ **Wasp HAS.1 XS564 '466/AT' from No. 829 Squadron's flight aboard the *Leander* Class frigate *Argonaut*, 1973. (MAP)**

when, in March 1967, the large tanker *Torrey Canyon* foundered off the Scillies. There were fears for the pollution hazards her cargo might create and the Fleet Air Arm was heavily involved in the consequent activities. Wessex HU.5s of No. 848 Squadron based at Culdrose flew oil reconnaissance and casualty evacuation. They transferred men and equipment to the stricken ship and flew detergent and special clearance teams to the beaches in addition to helping the media give adequate coverage. Buccaneers of Nos. 800 and 736 Squadrons carried out an unsuccessful attempt to combat the pollution by setting fire to the oil on board the ship in a bombing attack and the task was completed by napalm bombs from RAF Hunters.

No. 848 Squadron, now flying Wessex helicopters, was involved later that year in the British military withdrawal from Aden. During October and November, based in *Albion*, they carried around 11,000 passengers and almost 2½ tons of stores and on 29 November, the day Aden gained her independence and ceased to be a protectorate, 500 Marines of No. 42 Royal Marine Commando were lifted from defence positions around the RAF airfield at Khormaksar in an operation covered by *Eagle*.

By the late 1960s the annual NATO winter exercises in Norway had become the prerogative of the helicopter squadrons. In February 1969, for example, No. 848 Squadron embarked four of its Wessex HU.5s in RFA *Engadine*, flying off to Bardufoss on 14 February after a five-day voyage into the Arctic Circle to participate in the annual Exercise 'Clockwork'. It was bitterly cold when the ship sailed into Sorreis Fjord and she was soon covered in ice and salt spray frozen on to the foredeck. A cautious start was made on testing the flying conditions. Landing soon proved to be hazardous because the relatively mild winter (by Norwegian standards) had left the snow quite soft, with the result that a descending machine was likely to create its own local snowstorm. Fresh snow fell a few days later and it then became possible to try out a new design of helicopter ski which had been brought along for trials. During the second week operations began in conjunction with No. 45 Royal Marine Commando, based 20 miles to the east at Skjold. After evolving drills to cope with the bulky equipment carried by the troops and to prevent the men getting frostbite due to the bitterly cold downwash from the rotor blades, they were airlifted up into the surrounding mountains where they carried out training in warfare in winter conditions. The period concluded with a large-scale joint exercise involving the Norwegian Army and Air Force as well as the RAF. On 16 March, after five weeks ashore, the squadron rejoined *Engadine* and sailed home.

► **Wessex HU.5 XT456 'VA' of No. 846 Squadron demonstrates its military load-carrying ability aboard *Bulwark* circa 1978. (HMS *Heron*)**

VA
NO PUSH
ROYAL NAVY
21 FM 25
23 FM 90

CHAPTER 35

The Seventies

The 1970s were destined to be the final decade in which the Fleet Air Arm would have an operational fixed-wing carrier force. *Ark Royal* emerged from her refit in early 1970 and among her complement were the Phantoms of No. 892 Squadron, the only first-line unit to receive the type. The previous May three squadron aircraft had taken part in the *Daily Mail* Transatlantic Air Race and one of these distinguished itself by setting up a new west–east record of 4hr 46min 57sec, the aircraft concerned being piloted by Lt B. Davies, RN, with Lt Cdr P. M. Goddard, RN, as observer. This record, which represented a true air speed of 1,100mph, was achieved with the help of RAF Victor tanker aircraft from No. 55 Squadron and was to stand for five years. The Phantoms had also flown from the US carrier *Saratoga* later that year whilst in the Mediterranean. During 1974 they were modified by having fin-top housings fitted, for passive electronic countermeasures.

Ark Royal became the centre of an international incident on 9 November 1970 while participating in Exercise 'Lime Jug' in the Mediterranean. Russian naval ships loaded with assorted electronic gear had for some years shadowed and monitored such exercises, the shadower on this occasion being the 'Kotlin' Class guided missile destroyer *365*, sailing on a parallel course. Night flying was planned and the first Phantom took off quite normally at twilight when the ships were about 110 miles west of Crete. Just as the second machine was about to depart, however, the Russian ship suddenly changed course to port, across the bows of the carrier, quite contrary to international regulations which provided that all other ships must keep clear of a carrier when she is operating aircraft. Fortunately the aircraft had not been released and Captain Raymond Lygo promptly cancelled the launch and ordered full astern; but there was insufficient time to avoid a collision. Had he not reacted so quickly the destroyer would almost certainly have been cut in two, but in the event she was badly scraped and damage was caused to her superstructure. *Ark Royal* got away with some minor damage above the waterline and the first Phantom was ordered to land ashore. There were no casualties aboard the British vessel but seven Russian seamen

◀ Phantom XT862 '722' from No. 700P Intensive Flying Unit during landings and take-offs aboard *Hermes* in 1968. (Via B. J. Lowe)

▲ Sea King XV703 '050/R' of No. 824 Squadron, *Ark Royal*, airlifting Wasp HAS.1 XS542 of No. 829 Squadron's *Falmouth* Flight around 1976. (RNAS Culdrose)

were either flung overboard on impact or jumped into the sea, only five of these being recovered in the subsequent search. The Soviet Government afterwards made a formal protest but refused to give any indication as to why their ship was sailing dangerously close to the British carrier. Lygo was rightly absolved from any blame and subsequently gained promotion to Admiral before retiring, later becoming Chief Executive of British Aerospace.

On a more mundane but nevertheless vital level, Whirlwind HAR.9s of SAR flights were by now operating from naval air stations around the coast. In February 1973, for example, the Lee-on-Solent SAR Flight took over from the RAF the responsibility for an area extending approximately from Beachy Head to Lyme Bay. This extremely busy strip of coast included both Southampton and Portsmouth, with daily activity by everything from ocean liners, 'supertankers' and large naval vessels down to yachts and smaller craft. Three aircraft were operated, one being in immediate reserve, with four crews and maintainers working shifts around the clock. One crew, comprising a pilot, an aircrewman and a diver, had to be on standby from dawn until dusk, the whole year round. From the start, rescues of all kinds were required with great frequency, particularly during the summer 'silly season', many victims requiring medical attention. During the first year well over 100 incidents occurred, the peak month being August when 38 missions were flown.

The year 1970 saw the introduction of an even larger Westland helicopter. Like its predecessors the Sea King HAS.1 was yet another 'anglicization' of a Sikorsky design, in this case the S.61B. With a range of 690 miles it could search an area four times that of the Wessex and remain aloft for up to four hours. Powered by two Rolls-Royce Gnome engines driving a five-bladed rotor, it had a comprehensive range of equipment which included an integrated radar and sonar tactical display, a fully automatic flight-control system and wide range of weapons which could include four homing torpedoes or the same number of depth charges. Both *Ark Royal* and *Eagle* had squadrons of Sea Kings aboard and *Blake* and *Tiger* were each capable of taking four of these aircraft.

The new helicopter was quickly in active service, Sea Kings of No. 814 Anti-Submarine Squadron operating from *Hermes* (now a commando carrier) being involved in the rescue of around 1,500 civilians from a beach near Kyrenia during the Turkish invasion of Cyprus in July 1974. The Sea Kings are still in use, having been progressively updated, and are likely to continue in service well into the 1990s. Like the Wessexes before them, they have regularly participated in NATO exercises, including those in the Arctic region of northern Norway.

The fixed-wing capability of the Fleet Air Arm was meanwhile in decline. After 20 years' service *Eagle* was decommissioned at Devonport on 26 January 1972 and on 4 December 1978 *Ark Royal* returned to Plymouth for the last time, thus ending six decades of fixed-wing carrier flying by the Royal Navy. With her demise there was no longer any need for the Fleet Air Arm to retain its Phantoms, Buccaneers and Gannets and these were all phased out. The first two types were transferred to the RAF and have continued to give good service for many years. The Gannets, however, were scapped (a decision which was later to have tragic and unforeseen consequences), their radar being passed to the RAF for the Shackleton AEW.2 programme. With this reduced need, Brawdy and Lossiemouth were both transferred to the RAF, and only Culdrose, Lee-on-Solent, Prestwick and Yeovilton were left as naval shore bases, all still in use at the present time.

▼ Sea King HC.4 ZA295 'VM/B' of No. 846 Squadron from *Bulwark* about to lift a field gun at Yeovilton. (HMS *Heron*)

CHAPTER 36

Tragedy and Triumph

The commando carriers *Bulwark* and *Hermes* remained in service for helicopter operations but the Royal Navy had no fixed-wing carrier capacity. In prospect, however, was the new *Invincible* Class light aircraft carrier, the first ship of which was to commission in July 1980. The primary task of the *Invincible* Class was to be air-sea warfare, with a secondary assault role, though it was originally conceived as a 'through-deck' cruiser escort for the CVA-01 Class carrier to replace *Tiger* and *Blake*. The new carriers were allocated to Atlantic Ocean work for NATO and equipped with vertical take-off Sea Harriers for the defence of ships and convoys when they were outside the range of land-based fighters; they would afford protection against Russian long-range reconnaissance and anti-submarine aircraft, particularly those equipped with stand-off missiles.

The Sea Harrier, which was developed from the RAF's Harrier, was well suited to shipborne operations. Unlike previous fixed-wing carrier aircraft it required no catapult or arrester wires, nor was it necessary for the parent ship to head into wind during aircraft movements and so leave herself vulnerable to enemy submarines. It could be used to reconnoitre a wide area around a fleet or convoy, looking for hostile fighters or bombers, and it was equally useful in attacks against enemy ships or submarines. If necessary, it could easily be flown ashore for beach-head operations. All of these characteristics would soon be put to the test.

After a period of intensive flying trials, two Sea Harrier squadrons formed at Yeovilton on 31 March 1980, No. 800 being allocated for service in *Invincible* whilst No. 899 Squadron acted as the headquarters unit. A year later *Bulwark* was paid off, leaving the Royal Navy with just two carriers. However, at about this time tests were being carried out at the Royal Aircraft Establishment at Farnborough with a so-called 'ski jump', an upswept deck platform which would enable Sea Harriers to undertake a fairly normal take off and thus carry a greater load of fuel and armament than if they were taking off vertically. The system was the brainchild of Lt Cdr D. R. Taylor, who had developed the theoretical concept during a year's sabbatical at Southampton University. The tests proved successful and large ramps were soon added to the forward decks of both *Hermes* and *Invincible*. The changes were made not a moment too soon, for in 1982 Britain became involved in another war – one that was to have a significant effect on both the morale and standing of the Fleet Air Arm and was to prove how vital a service it still was.

On 2 April 1982 Argentine forces invaded the Falkland Islands which, they declared, would henceforth be Argentine territory and known as the Malvinas. This move appeared to have caught the British Government of the day by surprise, though all the signs were there: in fact they had probably themselves triggered off the chain of events that led to the invasion when they had announced that the Arctic Survey ship *Endurance* was to be withdrawn from the area and not replaced.

For many years Argentina had been making threatening noises against the islands, having never recognized British sovereignty of the Falklands or South Georgia. Britain's presence in the islands was fairly minimal, consisting, apart from a traditional small Marine detachment and occasional visits by RN ships, of the visits during the Arctic summers of a survey ship, originally *Protector* and later *Endurance*. These vessels were jointly manned by civilians and the Royal Navy and equipped with two Fleet Air Arm helicopters. But the Argentine threats had not been taken very seriously and so even the survey ship was about to be withdrawn. This optimistic viewpoint turned out to be misplaced. The Argentinians interpreted the withdrawal as a lack of interest in the islands and on 2 April they launched an invasion against the lightly defended Falklands and also South Georgia, very quickly occupying them.

The islands were 8,000 miles from Britain, a distance which would present considerable difficulties in re-taking them. Nevertheless a task force was hastily set up, and the Royal Navy would of necessity have the major role to play. The RAF was very limited in its ability to assist because of the distances involved, and direct air support could therefore only be

▲ **Sea Harrier FRS.1 ZA191 '18' of No. 800 Squadron lashed down on *Hermes'* heaving deck during the Falklands War; a replenishment ship is just visible in the background. (Ministry of Defence)**

provided by the Fleet Air Arm, which now had only two small carriers left in service plus the assault ships *Fearless* and *Intrepid*.

Within four hours of news arriving that Argentine troops had occupied Port Stanley, the Falklands capital, No. 800 Squadron had re-embarked in *Hermes* at Portsmouth with eight Sea Harriers, including three hastily transferred from No. 899 Squadron at Yeovilton, the strength being brought up to twelve aircraft by the time of the ship's departure. No. 801 Squadron was similarly reinforced by machines from No. 899 to an increased strength of eight Sea Harriers for passage in *Invincible* and on 5 April the two carriers sailed together with supporting ships. The combined air strength aboard the various ships added up to a total of twenty Sea Harriers and 45 assorted helicopters – and Operation 'Corporate' was under way.

Ascension Island, which lies just over halfway between Britain and the Falklands, was to be used as a staging post, having both a large airfield and a good anchorage. Already heading there were eight destroyers and frigates involved in Exercise 'Spring Train', which had been abruptly terminated for the real thing. Wideawake airfield soon began to be the focal point for massive air activity in the South Atlantic. A Naval Air Support Unit was set up and a number of helicopters were to be flown there in both RAF and chartered transport aircraft, the first naval machines to arrive being two Wessex HU.5s brought in by chartered Belfast from Yeovilton.

At home the newly re-formed No. 809 Squadron started working up with further Sea Harriers, two new Wessex squadrons were formed (Nos. 847 and 848) and also a Sea King squadron (No. 825), these all forming from

▲ **A Sea King airlifts stores at the stern of HMS *Hermes* whilst Sea Harriers and Harriers stand ready for take off in the South Atlantic. (Ministry of Defence)**

second-line training squadrons. The container vessels *Atlantic Causeway* and *Atlantic Conveyer* were meanwhile requisitioned and hastily converted to aircraft transports. The machines carried were to include the Harriers of No. 1 Squadron RAF and the Chinook twin-rotor helicopters of No. 18 Squadron, RAF.

The task force's long voyage to the South Atlantic afforded an opportunity to undertake exercises, so that it would arrive as an integrated fighting unit. This was particularly useful for the Sea Harrier pilots, a number of whom had come straight from conversion to VTOL aircraft. On 12 April the British Government announced an exclusion zone of 200 miles around the Falklands against Argentine ships and aircraft. The fleet arrived at Ascension on 16 April and within 24 hours the helicopters had flown more than 300 sorties, helping to get men and equipment in the correct ships for the coming counter-attack.

The two carriers and their escorts sailed again on 18 April, following an advance group of ships which was already heading for the Falklands. Except during particularly bad weather, ASW Sea Kings of the two squadrons involved would fly a continuous screen around the carrier battle group until the campaign ended four months later. On 21 April the Sea Harriers made their first contact, a Boeing 707 of the Argentine Air Force, which they escorted from the area. This surveillance continued, and on 24 April the Argentine Government was given formal warning that such aircraft were at risk, after which they only appeared when weather prohibited flying by the Sea Harriers.

Ascension was too far from the Falklands to be a convenient base and therefore, as a first

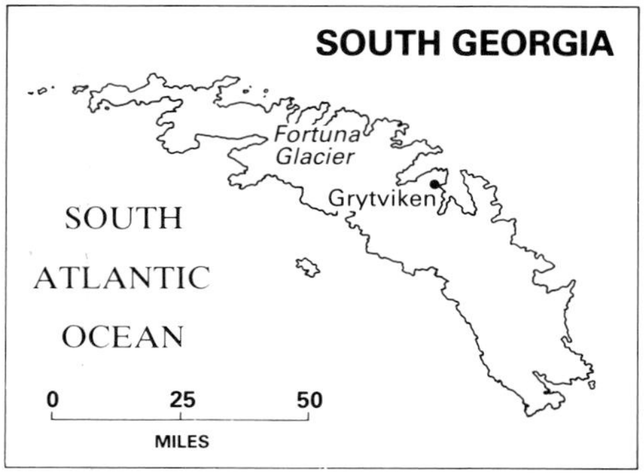

step, British forces set out to re-occupy South Georgia. On 21 April, in poor weather, Wessexes from the guided missile destroyer *Antrim* and RFA *Tidespring* helped put ashore an advance detachment of troops on Fortuna Glacier; however, the weather deteriorated dramatically and in the subsequent evacuation the following day two machines crashed, fortunately without serious injury to crews or passengers. The main attack was scheduled to take place on 25 April but an intelligence report that morning of an Argentine submarine in the area resulted in a search by ships and helicopters of the Task Group. *Antrim*'s Wessex 3 was successful in sighting the 'Guppy' Class submarine *Santa Fe* on the surface, five miles off South Georgia, for which it was making. The helicopter promptly dropped depth charges, resulting in a stream of oil and smoke as the enemy vessel then tried to head for the comparative safety of the main settlement of Grytviken. Before it could get there a Wasp of *Endurance* Flight carried out a further attack with AS.12 missiles and it ended up beached alongside a pier at Grytviken. The way was now clear for the ships to sail in, and helicopters then proceeded to carry out numerous support tasks, including bombardment spotting, searching out Argentine troop positions and airlifting British troops ashore. By the end of the day the island was again in British hands, providing a safe base for the forthcoming activities some 800 miles from the Falklands.

▼ *Hermes* in the South Atlantic during the Falklands War, with Harriers, Sea Harriers and a Lynx on deck. A replenishment ship, probably RFA *Fort Austin*, is visible in the background. (Ministry of Defence)

The first attack on the main island came at dawn on 1 May. Following an attack by a single Vulcan on the runway at Port Stanley, nine Sea Harriers of No. 800 Squadron from *Hermes* raided the airfield, three others attacking the airstrip at Goose Green. The CAP Sea Harriers of No. 801 Squadron succeeded in shooting down two Argentine Mirage fighters, a Canberra and a Dagger bomber, and a Pucará close-support aircraft was destroyed on the ground at Goose Green. In the afternoon three warships bombarded Port Stanley airfield to give the impression that an amphibious attack was imminent.

The following day the Argentine cruiser *General Belgrano* was sunk by a British submarine as she neared the exclusion zone, after which enemy surface ships ceased to participate in the war though Argentine submarines continued to be a threat. In the evening of 2 May a Sea King of No. 826 Squadron homed the Lynxes from *Coventry* and *Glasgow* on to an Argentine patrol boat. In the first use of Sea Skua missiles the two aircraft attacked and badly damaged the *Alferez Sobral*, though at the time they thought they had attacked two separate patrol boats and damaged one of them.

The first major British loss came on 4 May when the guided missile destroyer *Sheffield* sank after being hit by an Exocet missile from a Super Étendard aircraft of the Argentine Navy, twenty of her crew members being killed. This served to highlight the folly of abolishing the Royal Navy's airborne early warning capability only a short time before. Combat air patrols by the Sea Harriers were unable to provide adequate protection against such low-level approaches by Argentine aircraft and this problem remained throughout the campaign. The FAA suffered its first Sea Harrier loss on 4 May when Lt Nick Taylor of No. 800 Squadron in XZ450 was killed during a bombing attack on Goose Green airstrip in East Falkland. Two more were lost on 6 May, probably in a collision during bad weather, when Lt. Cdr J. E. Eyton-Jones in XZ452 and Lt W. A. Curtis in XZ452, both of No. 801 Squadron, failed to return from a CAP.

Meanwhile between 30 April and 5 May eight Sea Harriers of No. 809 Squadron had flown non-stop from Yeovilton to Ascension, refuelled en route by Handley Page Victor tankers – the longest flight made by this type of aircraft. Nine Harrier GR.3s of No. 1 Squadron RAF made a similar flight. On 6 May all the No. 809 Squadron aircraft and six from No. 1 Squadron landed on the container ship *Atlantic Conveyor* for ferrying to the Task Force off the Falklands. En route one No. 809 aircraft was held at readiness on board for defence purposes – in Second World War MAC-ship fashion! On meeting the Task Force, No. 809 gave up four aircraft each to Nos. 800 and 801 Squadrons whilst the RAF Harriers joined *Hermes*; in addition RFA *Fort*

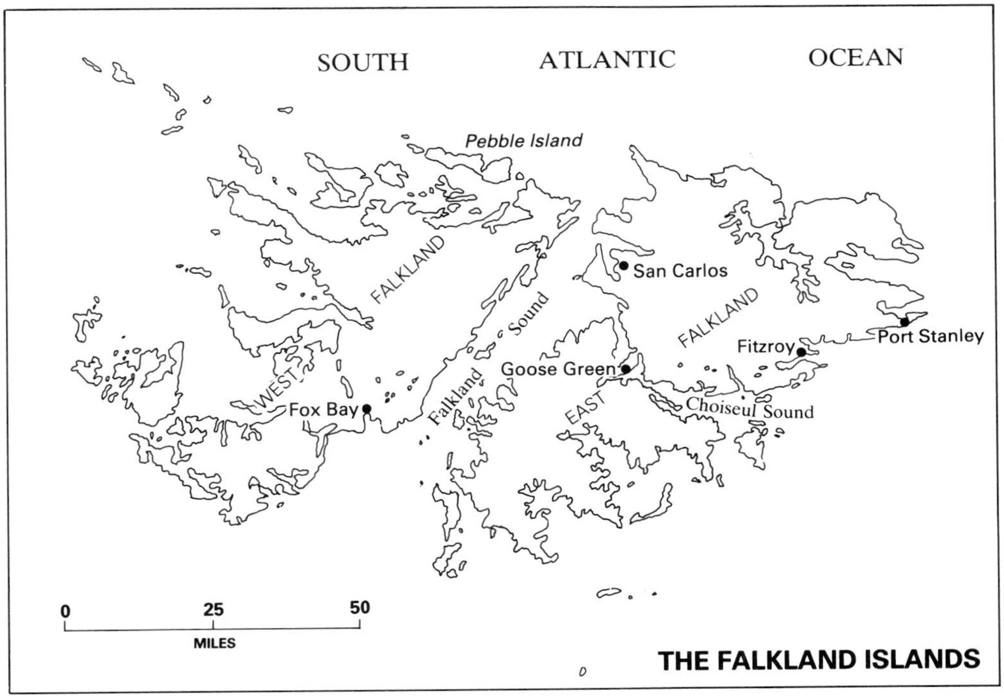

Austin brought four Lynxes equipped with electronic equipment to serve as Exocet decoys, two each for *Hermes* and *Invincible*.

Bad weather intervened for a few days but on 12 May it had improved sufficiently for the Sea Harriers to commence both high-level and low-level bombing over Port Stanley airfield. That same day, however, Argentine A-4 Skyhawks carried out an attack in two waves of four on *Brilliant* and *Glasgow*, the latter being sufficiently damaged to be withdrawn from the operational area. Nevertheless by mid-May the task force had achieved its initial objective of transporting all the necessary troops to the South Atlantic; moreover, despite occasional harassment from the Argentinians it had succeeded in gaining control of the seas in the immediate area.

The way was now clear for a start to be made on recapturing the islands, the main initial objective being East Falkland, and this could only be achieved by ground forces. The area around the capital at Port Stanley was heavily defended, however, and it was consequently decided to mount an amphibious attack via the more lightly defended San Carlos Water anchorage on the opposite side of the island. There was a possible danger from Pucará strike aircraft on nearby Pebble Island, but the SAS, transported there by Sea Kings of No. 846 Squadron, destroyed eleven of the aircraft in a daring night raid on 14/15 May. On 16 May two pairs of aircraft from No. 800 Squadron attacked the supply ships *Bahía Buen Suceso* at Fox Bay and *Rio Carcarana* in Falkland Sound, both being damaged and abandoned.

On 19 May came the amphibious assault on San Carlos under cover of fire from British warships. British helicopters were extremely active throughout, Wessexes and Sea Kings of Nos. 845, 846 and 848 Squadrons being employed ferrying ashore large quantities of stores, weapons and ammunition whilst No. 826 Sea Kings from RFA *Fort Austin* undertook ASW and anti-surface vessel patrols and frigate-based Wasps and Lynxes kept watch on the numerous nearby coves and inlets. The Argentinians carried out a substantial number of fierce air attacks on the landing area on 21, 23 and 24 May but lost 23 of their aircraft and were unable to prevent the beach-head being established. The two carriers were too vulnerable to come in close to assist but their Sea Harriers flew numerous patrols over the battle area, preventing the Argentinians from mounting a counterattack.

Other warships had of necessity to approach the landings, leading to the loss of the frigates *Ardent* and *Antelope* on 21 and 24 May respectively and of the container ship *Atlantic Conveyor* and the cruiser *Coventry* on 25 May. The loss of the container ship, which succumbed to Exocet missiles fired by one of two Super Étendard aircraft, was a particular blow as a Lynx, three Chinooks and the six Wessexes of No. 848 'D' Flight went down with her, nineteen men being lost. Other British aircraft losses in this period were not of the same order as the enemy's, amounting only to one Sea Harrier, one RAF Harrier, *Ardent*'s Lynx and two Royal Marine Gazelles.

From that point the pattern was one of relentless advance by the military, with the Fleet Air Arm playing a major supporting role. On 28 May troops of the 2nd Battalion The Parachute Regiment carried out a successful assault on Darwin and Goose Green in the narrow central region of East Falkland, with Harrier support. During the course of the next few days further advances were made in a pincer movement towards Stanley, full use being made of helicopters.

◀ **Sea King HAS.2A XV700 '264' of No. 825 Squadron, piloted by Lt Cdr Hugh Clark, the unit's CO, amid blinding smoke during the rescue operation from RFA *Sir Galahad* at Port Pleasant, East Falkland, 8 June 1962. (Ministry of Defence)**

◀ **Wessex HU.5 XS512 'WT' of No. 848 Squadron's 'D' Flight and five others of its type could not be retrieved after an Exocet missile had struck *Atlantic Conveyor* on 25 May 1982. (Ministry of Defence)**

The loss of the RAF Chinooks aboard *Atlantic Conveyor* had added to the difficulties and as a consequence a sea passage became necessary for the attack on Fitzroy, tragically resulting in the loss on 8 June of the RFAs *Sir Tristram* and *Sir Galahad* during an Argentine air strike by A-4B Skyhawks. Naval helicopters were to hand, and time after time they went close to the smoke and flames pouring from the latter ship, which was carrying the 1st Battalion Welsh Guards, and it was largely thanks to their efforts that only 50 men lost their lives in the stricken ship. Sea Harriers were meanwhile continuing their patrols and later that day destroyed four Argentine Mirages above Choiseul Sound. *Sir Tristram*, which had been abandoned, was later retrieved and repaired but the remains of *Sir Galahad* were afterwards taken out to sea and sunk as a war grave.

Three days later the final stage of the operation began, with ground forces closing in on Port Stanley again supported from the air. The guided missile destroyer *Glamorgan* was hit by shore-mounted Exocets while withdrawing after bombarding shore positions during the night of 11/12 June but she was able to continue operations after extinguishing a number of fires, although her Wessex helicopter was lost. This was the last occasion during the campaign that a British vessel was attacked. By 14 June British troops were on the outskirts of Port Stanley and shortly afterwards white flags appeared. General Menendez then offered the surrender of the Argentine troops.

In all during the campaign the Fleet Air Arm lost 23 aircraft, amounting to six Sea Harriers, five Sea Kings, nine Wessexes and three Lynxes, including those lost aboard ships which had been attacked. In addition the RAF lost four Harriers and three Chinooks and the Royal Marines one Scout and three Gazelles, making a total British loss of 34 machines. There were far outweighed by the Argentine losses, which amounted to exactly 100 aircraft, including those destroyed on the ground and captured. Numerous awards were made in due course to members of the Fleet Air Arm for their gallantry during the campaign.

One of the biggest difficulties facing the task force had been the lack of airborne early warning radar since the demise of the AEW Gannet. As a temporary measure two Sea Kings (XV650 and XV704) were fitted by Westland within eight and half weeks with modified Searchwater equipment and assigned to a newly-formed 'D' Flight of No. 824 Squadron aboard *Illustrious*, the second of the new carriers which had only commissioned on 18 June. She sailed to the Falklands to relieve *Invincible* on guard duty until Port Stanley airfield had been repaired and the defence of the island assumed by the RAF. The AEW deficiency was one of many lessons which had to be learned the hard way, and the Fleet Air Arm would take good care that it was never again without this capacity.

▶ **A reconnaissance patrol returning to Port San Carlos settlement in Wessex HU.5 XT450 'V' of 'C' Flight, No. 845 Squadron, shortly before the Argentine surrender. (Ministry of Defence)**

CHAPTER 37

The Fleet Air Arm Today

With the ending of the Falklands conflict the run-down of naval aviation was resumed. No. 809 Squadron was disbanded on 17 December 1982 after the return from the South Atlantic of *Illustrious* (or 'Lust' as she is affectionately nicknamed), its aircraft being dispersed among the other three Sea Harrier squadrons. No. 899 Squadron returned to its role of headquarters unit but the other two units rotated between the new carriers, this class being completed on 1 November 1985 with the commissioning of the new *Ark Royal*. The air group for each of these small carriers initially comprised sixteen aircraft, made up of five Sea Harriers, eight ASW Sea Kings and three AEW Sea Kings, but this has recently been increased to eight Sea Harriers and twelve Sea Kings. During exercises, where it has been possible to spare two carriers, one usually takes the responsibility for air cover whilst the other operates as a commando carrier in support of landings.

The carriers have to be ready to deal with any emergency, and to this end Disaster Relief Training (DISTEX) is undertaken. If so required, casualties can be evacuated and essential services such as medical facilities and supplies, electrical power and fresh water can

▲ Sea Harrier FRS.1 ZX493 '001/N' from Yeovilton displays the fin code of HMS *Invincible*. (No. 801 Squadron/Nigel B. Thomas)

be provided. Another task is search and rescue, as instanced in May 1985 when *Illustrious*'s helicopters plucked five survivors from MV *Thalathia* in the English Channel. In another incident in September 1988 involving the same carrier, which at the time was returning from Exercise 'Teamwork 88', 49 survivors from the burning oil platform *Ocean Odyssey* were airlifted after the rig had caught fire as a result of a massive gas explosion.

The Sea Harrier FRS.1 is due for uprating to the FRS.2 version, which had its maiden flight at Dunsfold in September 1988. Featuring Ferranti Blue Vixen multi-mode fire-control radar and other advanced modifications, it is to enter service in the early 1990s. With regard to helicopters, the Wessex has now been withdrawn and the workhorse of the modern Fleet Air Arm is therefore the Westland Sea King in its many variants. Following the Falklands War, Westland took on the task of installing more permanent Searchwater radar in the Sea King and the result was the AEW.2 variant, several aircraft being modified to this standard. Once these became available it was possible to form two further AEW flights within the newly recommissioned No. 849 Squadron, thus reviving the number of the original AEW squadron.

The basic role of the Sea King, though, is that of anti-submarine work, and most machines have been gradually modernized through several stages, the HAS.5 variant being the most prolific at present. Fourteen of these are allocated to No. 706 Squadron at Culdrose, to provide trainee pilots with their first experience of this large aircraft after being trained on smaller machines. The next phase of training involves a spell of learning how to land on a ship under the auspices of No. 810 Squadron; RFA *Engadine* is generally used for this task but is due to be replaced by the new aviation training ship RFA *Argus*, a converted roll-on/roll-off container vessel. As they progress, the pupils move on to ASW training and after they have mastered all aspects of a Sea King's work they are posted to one of the first-line squadrons allocated to various ships, where they could find themselves undertaking one of a variety of tasks such as commando support or anti-submarine warfare; alternatively they might find themselves posted to No. 819 Squadron at Prestwick where they are likely to spend much of their flying time over the Irish Sea, exercising with submarines under training, interspersed with occasional rescue missions in the area. In 1989 the squadron commenced trials at Prestwick with the new Sea King HAR.6.

Support for the Royal Marines is provided by the Yeovilton-based Nos. 845 and 846 Tactical Assault Squadrons, which are equipped with the Sea King HC.4 variant as is the second-line No. 707 Squadron which provides helicopter advanced flying training at Yeovilton. These Sea Kings can carry eighteen fully equipped troops or a small vehicle or other underslung stores. They have, however, had a number of spells afloat, generally in RFAs (though they can operate from carriers

◀ Gazelle HT.2s of No. 705 Squadron, the Basic Helicopter Training Unit, lined up at Culdrose. (RNAS Culdrose)

or various other suitable naval vessels), and have seen much active service, including a period with the peacekeeping force in Lebanon, another troubled area. No. 845 Squadron is primarily a support unit for No. 3 Commando Brigade Royal Marines, conducting regular training exercises within the Arctic Circle, whilst No. 846 Squadron operates similarly with No. 45 Royal Marine Commando. A Sea King replacement is now under development by Westland and its partner Augusta of Italy in the shape of the EH.101, now named Merlin by the Royal Navy.

Smaller helicopters in use by the present-day Fleet Air Arm are the Westland/Aérospatiale Gazelle and Lynx, both the product of an Anglo-French collaborative agreement signed in February 1967. Since 1974 the Gazelle has been the mainstay of No. 705 Squadron, the Basic Helicopter Training Unit at Culdrose. For display purposes the instructors of this unit operate a team known as the 'Sharks'.

Commencing in 1976 the Lynx gradually took over from the Wasp on small ships' flights, operating mainly from various classes of destroyer and frigate, around 50 of which are so equipped. Training is undertaken by No. 702 Squadron at Portland, after which pilots move to a ship's flight, coming under the auspices of either No. 815 or No. 829 Squadron. The current version is the Lynx HAS.3, many earlier machines having also been brought up to this standard, but the helicopter is being progressively modernized and a future development will be the Mk. 8 with improved weaponry and radar.

Naval pilots start their flying careers on the forty-year-old De Havilland Chipmunk T.10, of which around a dozen are still maintained in service with the Flying Grading Flight at Roborough, near Plymouth. Here they are assessed for flying training suitability and once accepted they then move on to the Royal Naval Elementary Flying Training School (within the RAF's No. 1 Flying Training School at Linton-on-Ouse) for a 60-hour *ab initio* training course on RAF Bulldog aircraft. From here they split away to train for their intended roles. Those destined for Sea Harriers remain at Linton-on-Ouse for basic flying training on Jet Provosts. They then go to No. 4 Flying Training School at RAF Valley to

▶ The latest carrier to bear the name HMS *Ark Royal* seen after commissioning, with one of the surviving Swordfish displayed on deck. (HMS *Ark Royal*)

▲ **Lynx HAS.2 XZ235 '403' of No. 815 Squadron's *Battleaxe* Flight, nicknamed 'Asterix' after the French cartoon character. (No. 815 Squadron, via Lt L. W. Halliday)**

convert to high-speed jets in the shape of British Aerospace Hawks. Next they move to No. 2 Tactical Weapons Unit at RAF Chivenor, again training on Hawks but this time to fit them for flying in an operational environment. Having completed this stage they are now ready for the real thing and, after a brief introduction to helicopters (in this case Gazelles), they would previously have returned north, to No. 233 Operational Conversion Unit at RAF Wittering for conversion to Harriers. By then, having amassed about 400 hours' flying time, they would be ready for No. 899 Squadron at Yeovilton, where they would undertake advanced training on the Sea Harrier, learning to use it as an operational machine. From the beginning of 1989, however, this Wittering phase was cut out of the programme and instead trainees now go straight to No. 899 Squadron, which provides similar tuition using Sea Harrier T.4s. Finally they become fully operational, progressing to either No. 800 or No. 801 Squadron for service aboard carriers.

Future helicopter pilots move to Culdrose for basic training on Gazelles with No. 705 Squadron, and after obtaining their wings they are streamed to anti-submarine warfare with Nos. 810, 814, 815, 820, 824 or 829 Squadrons, commando flying with Nos. 845 or 846 Squadrons, search and rescue with No. 819 Squadron or airborne early warning with No. 849 Squadron. Observer pupils undertake basic training at Culdrose, coming either direct from Dartmouth or from fleet service. A preliminary course is undertaken in aviation medicine and survival, then after arrival for the Basic Observer Course at Culdrose they receive instruction in airmanship, navigation, radar and communications, the course including 100 hours of airborne training on the sixteen British Aerospace Jetstream T.2 'flying classrooms' of No. 750 Squadron. After completing the seven-month-long course they move on to advanced and operational flying training squadrons.

Aircrewmen ratings also undertake basic training at Culdrose. The Aircrewman School employs the Sea Kings of No. 706 Squadron for a thirteen-week course, then pupils go to Portland for flying training with No. 772 Squadron, returning to Culdrose for sonar-operating training before being posted to first-line squadrons. Those going to commando squadrons are, in addition to their aircrewman duties, trained to fly their aircraft in the event of an emergency and also to navigate.

The Fleet Air Arm of today thus comprises a well-trained force of twenty-one first and second-line squadrons. Though a comparatively small service by historical standards, it has proved itself well capable in battle in recent times and remains efficient and ready for whatever the future may bring.

Appendices

APPENDIX I: BRITISH NAVAL AVIATION 'FIRSTS'

The Fleet Air Arm, and its predecessor the Royal Naval Air Service, has many pioneering achievements to its credit. Among them are the following:

2.5.12 First recorded flight from a moving ship (HMS *Hibernia* steaming at 10½kt): Lt C. R. Samson, in a Short S.38 biplane.

28.7.14 First successful torpedo drop: Sqn Cdr A. M. Longmore, in a Short Type 81 carrying a 14in torpedo.

22.9.14 First British air raid on Germany (on the Düsseldorf airship sheds): aircraft of No. 3 Squadron, RNAS, based at Antwerp.

8.10.14 First destruction of a Zeppelin by an aircraft (the newly delivered *Z9* in the Düsseldorf airship sheds): Flt Lt R. L. G.Marix of No. 3 Squadron, RNAS.

21.11.14 First long-range strategic bombing raid (on the Friedrichshafen airship sheds on the shores of Lake Constance): three Avro 504s based in eastern France at Belfort near the German-Swiss border.

21.12.14 First night bombing raid (on Ostend): Wg Cdr C. R. Samson in a Maurice Farman biplane.

25.12.14 First attempt to exert sea power upon land by means of the air (an attack on Cuxhaven on the north German coast): Short seaplanes from the seaplane carriers *Empress*, *Engadine* and *Riviera*.

7.6.15 First victory over a Zeppelin in the air (*LZ37*, shot down near Bruges): Morane Saulnier monoplane flown by Flt Sub-Lt R. Warneford who was subsequently awarded the Victoria Cross.

12.8.15 First occasion a ship had been torpedoed from the air (a 5,000-ton Turkish supply vessel): a Short 184 piloted by Commander C. H. K. Edmonds during the Dardanelles campaign.

6.6.17 First landplane torpedo-carrier completed: the Sopwith Cuckoo.

28.6.17 First successful flight from a turret platform: Flt Cdr F. J. Rutland in a Sopwith Pup from HMS *Yarmouth*.

2.8.17 First carrier deck landing: Sqn Cdr E. H. Dunning on HMS *Furious*.

15.3.18 First carrier with aircraft lifts re-enters service: HMS *Furious*.

14.9.18 First flush deck aircraft carrier enters service: HMS *Argus*.

6.1.21 First carrier fitted with palisades re-enters service: HMS *Argus*.

1.5.23 First ship to be designed from the waterline upwards as a carrier, and first carrier with an island superstructure, enters service: HMS *Hermes*.

1.9.25 First ship fitted with round-down re-enters service: HMS *Furious*.

6.5.26 First night deck landing: Flt Lt Gerald Boyce in a Blackburn Dart on HMS *Furious* off the South Coast.

1.3.28 First carrier to be fitted with transverse arrester gear enters service: HMS *Courageous*.

2.1.33 First carrier to be fitted with hydraulically controlled arrester gear re-enters service: HMS *Courageous*.

16.11.38 First carrier with deck armour enters service: HMS *Ark Royal*.

26.9.39 First German aircraft to be shot down by any of the British services in World War II: a Dornier Do 18 by Lt B. S. McEwen of No. 803 Squadron flying a Blackburn Skua from HMS *Ark Royal*.

25.5.40 First fully armoured carrier enters service: HMS *Illustrious*.

11.11.40 First carrier-based torpedo-bomber attack (on the Italian Fleet in harbour at Taranto).

1943 First service order placed for helicopters for operational use (45 American-built Sikorsky VS-316 Hoverfly Is).

25.3.44 First deck-landing of a twin-engined aircraft: Lt Cdr E. M. Brown, flying a navalized Mosquito on to the deck of HMS *Indefatigable*.

3.12.45	First landing by a jet-powered aircraft on an aircraft carrier: Lt Cdr E. M. Brown flying a modified De Havilland Vampire on to the deck of HMS *Ocean*.
7.51	First trials of steam catapult (in HMS *Perseus*, and developed by C. C. Mitchell of MacTaggart, Scott & Co. Ltd).
1952	First trials of an angled deck (on HMS *Triumph*, and developed by Capt. D. R. F. Cambell in conjunction with Lewis Boddington).
1952	First trials of a mirror landing sight (on HMS *Illustrious*, and invented by Lt Cdr H. C. N. Goodhart).
6.11.56	First ship-based helicopter assault: Suez.
8.2.63	First experimental carrier/VTOL trials (a Hawker P.1127 prototype on HMS *Ark Royal*).
9.8.67.	First radar-fitted anti-submarine helicopter enters service (Wessex HAS.3 with No. 814 Squadron).
9.5.81	First carrier fitted with ski jump re-enters service (HMS *Hermes*, and developed by Lt Cdr D. R. Taylor).

APPENDIX II: FIRST-LINE STRENGTH OF THE FLEET AIR ARM AT THE OUTBREAK OF WORLD WAR II

Ship	**Squadrons**
Home Fleet	
Ark Royal	800 (3 Roc, 9 Skua)
	803 (9 Skua)
	810 (12 Swordfish)
	818 (9 Swordfish)
	820 (12 Swordfish)
	821 (9 Swordfish)
Rodney	702 (1 Swordfish)
Repulse	705 (2 Swordfish)
Newcastle	712 (2 Walrus)
Sheffield	712 (2 Walrus)
Edinburgh	712 (2 Walrus)
Belfast	712 (2 Walrus)
Glasgow	712 (2 Walrus)
Suffolk	712 (2 Walrus)
Channel Force	
Courageous	811 (12 Swordfish)
	822 (12 Swordfish)
Hermes	814 (9 Swordfish)
America and West Indies	
York	718 (1 Walrus)
Berwick	718 (2 Walrus)
Orion	718 (2 Seafox)
Mediterranean Fleet	
Glorious	802 (12 Sea Gladiator)
	812 (12 Swordfish)
	823 (12 Swordfish)
	825 (12 Swordfish)
Malaya	701 (2 Swordfish)
Warspite	701 (2 Swordfish)
Barham	701 (1 Swordfish)
Devonshire	711 (Walrus)
Sussex	711 (1 Walrus)
Shropshire	711 (1 Walrus)
Arethusa	713 (1 Walrus)
Penelope	713 (1 Walrus)
Galatea	713 (1 Walrus)
East Indies	
Manchester	714 (2 Walrus)
Liverpool	714 (2 Walrus)
Gloucester	714 (2 Walrus)
New Zealand	
Achilles	720 (1 Walrus)
Leander	720 (1 Walrus)
South Atlantic	
Neptune	716 (2 Seafox)
Cumberland	712 (2 Walrus)
Ajax	718 (2 Seafox)
Exeter	718 (2 Walrus)
Albatross	710 (6 Walrus)
China	
Eagle	813 (9 Swordfish)
	824 (9 Swordfish)
Cornwall	715 (2 Walrus)
Birmingham	715 (2 Walrus)
Dorsetshire	715 (1 Walrus)
Kent	715 (1 Walrus)
Terror	715 (1 Walrus)
At notice to embark	
Resolution	For 702 (1 Swordfish)
Suffolk	For 712 (1 Walrus)
Emerald	For 702 (1 Seafox)
Enterprise	For 702 (1 Seafox)
Effingham	No sqn (1 Walrus)
Renown	For 705 (2 Swordfish)
Valiant	No sqn (2 Swordfish)

APPENDIX III: FIRST-LINE STRENGTH OF THE FLEET AIR ARM ON VJ-DAY

Home Station		
802	*Queen*	12 Seafire XV
803	Arbroath	12 Seafire L.III
805	Machrihanish	25 Seafire L.III
806	Machrihanish	25 Seafire L.III
810	*Queen*	12 Barracuda III
816	Inskip	12 Firefly I
817	Fearn	12 Barracuda II (ASH)
818	Fearn	12 Barracuda II (disbanding)

822	Belfast	12 Barracuda II (ASH) (for *Campania*)
825	Rattray	12 Barracuda II (ASH)
826	East Haven	12 Barracuda II (ASH)
846	Crail	8 Avenger II
860	Maydown	12 Barracuda III (for Royal Netherlands Navy)
889	Belfast	6 Hellcat II (PR)
891	Nutts Corner	16 Hellcat II (NF)
892	Drem	16 Hellcat II (NF)
1702	Lee-on-Solent	6 Sea Otter I
1703	Lee-on-Solent	6 Sea Otter I
1791	Drem	16 Firefly I (NF)
1792	Inskip	16 Firefly I (NF)
1835	Belfast	21 Corsair IV
1837	Nutts Corner	21 Corsair III
1852	Belfast	21 Corsair IV
1853	Machrihanish	18 Corsair IV (disbanding)

East Indies

800	Trincomalee	6 Hellcat II (PR) (for *Emperor*)
804	*Ameer*	24 Hellcat II
807	*Hunter*	24 Seafire L.III
808	*Khedive*	24 Hellcat IIRP
809	*Stalker*	24 Seafire L.III
815	*Smiter*	12 Barracuda III
821	Katukurunda	12 Barracuda III (for *Trumpeter*)
824	Katukurunda	12 Barracuda II
845	*Shah*	8 Avenger I
851	*Shah*	8 Avenger I
879	*Attacker*	24 Seafire L.IIC/L.III
882	Cochin	24 Wildcat VI (for *Searcher*)
888	Colombo Racecourse	6 Hellcat II (PR)
896	Trincomalee	24 Hellcat IIFB (for *Empress*)
898	*Pursuer*	24 Hellcat II
1700	Trincomalee	6 Walrus

British Pacific Fleet

801	*Implacable*	24 Seafire L.III
812	*Vengeance*	12 Barracuda II
814	*Venerable*	12 Barracuda II
820	*Indefatigable*	16 Avenger II
827	*Colossus*	12 Barracuda II
828	*Implacable*	16 Avenger I/II
837	*Glory*	12 Barracuda II
848	*Formidable*	16 Avenger I/II
849	*Victorious*	16 Avenger I/II
854	Nowra	16 Avenger I/III
857	*Indomitable*	16 Avenger I/II
880	*Implacable*	24 Seafire L.III
885	*Ruler*	24 Hellcat IIRP
887	*Indefatigable*	24 Seafire F.III/L.III
894	*Indefatigable*	16 Seafire L.III
899	Schofields	24 Seafire L.III
1701A	Maryborough	3 Sea Otter I
1701B	Ponam	3 Sea Otter I
1770	Schofields	12 Firefly I
1771	*Implacable*	12 Firefly I
1772	*Indefatigable*	12 Firefly I
1790	Schofields	12 Firefly I (NF)
1831	*Glory*	21 Corsair IV
1834	*Victorious*	18 Corsair II/IV
1836	*Victorious*	18 Corsair II/IV
1839	*Indomitable*	18 Hellcat I/II
1841	*Formidable*	18 Corsair IV
1842	*Formidable*	18 Corsair IV
1843	Nowra	18 Corsair IV
1844	Nowra	18 Hellcat I (for *Indomitable*)
1845	Nowra	18 Corsair IV
1846	*Colossus*	21 Corsair IV
1850	*Vengeance*	21 Corsair IV
1851	*Venerable*	21 Corsair IV

South Africa

881	Wingfield	24 Hellcat II

APPENDIX IV: FLEET AIR ARM CARRIERS AND SQUADRONS IN THE KOREAN WAR

Carrier	Period	Air Group	Sqn	Commanding Officer	Aircraft
Triumph	7.50–9.50	13th CAG	800	Lt Cdr I. M. MacLachlen, RN Lt Cdr T. D. Handley, RN*	12 Seafire F.47
			827	Lt Cdr B. C. Lyons, RN	12 Firefly FR.1
Theseus	10.50–4.51	17th CAG	807	Lt Cdr M. P. G. Smith, DSC, RN	21 Sea Fury FB.11
			810	Lt Cdr K. S. Pattison, DSC, RN	12 Firefly 5
Glory	4.51–9.51	14th CAG	804	Lt Cdr J. S. Bailey, OBE, RN	21 Sea Fury FB.11
			812	Lt Cdr F. A. Swanton, DSC, RN	12 Firefly 5
Sydney	9.51–1.52	20th CAG	805	Lt Cdr J. R. N. Salthouse, RAN	21 Sea Fury FB.11 (805 and 808)
			808	Lt Cdr J. L. Appleby, RAN	
			817	Lt Cdr R. B. Lunberg, RN	12 Firefly 5
Glory	1.52–5.52	14th CAG	804	Lt Cdr J. S. Bailey, OBE, RN	21 Sea Fury FB.11
			812	Lt Cdr J. M. Culbertson, RN	12 Firefly 5
Ocean	5.52–10.52	17th CAG	802	Lt Cdr S. F. F. Shotton, DSC, RN Lt Cdr P. H. London, DSC, RN†	21 Sea Fury FB.11
			825	Lt Cdr C. K. Roberts, DSO, RN	12 Firefly 5
Glory	11.52–5.53	–	801	Lt Cdr J. B. Stuart, RN	21 Sea Fury FB.11
			821	Lt Cdr J. R. N. Gardner, RN	12 Firefly FR.5
Ocean	5.53–7.53	–	807	Lt Cdr T. L. M. Brander, RN	21 Sea Fury FB.11
			810	Lt Cdr A. W. Bloomer, RN	12 Firefly FR.5

* From August 1950. † From August 1952.

APPENDIX V: FLEET AIR ARM SQUADRONS IN THE SUEZ CAMPAIGN

Squadron	Aircraft	Ship
800	Sea Hawk FGA.6	*Albion*
802	Sea Hawk FB.3	*Albion*
804	Sea Hawk FGA.6	*Bulwark*
809	Sea Venom FAW.21	*Albion*
810	Sea Hawk FGA.4/6	*Bulwark*
830	Wyvern S.4	*Eagle*
845	Whirlwind HAS.22, HAR.3	*Theseus*
849A Flt	Skyraider AEW.1	*Eagle*
849C Flt	Skyraider AEW.1	*Albion*
892	Sea Venom FAW.21	*Eagle*
893	Sea Venom FAW.21	*Eagle*
895	Sea Hawk FB.5	*Bulwark*
897	Sea Hawk FGA.6	*Eagle*
899	Sea Hawk FGA.6	*Eagle*

APPENDIX VI: FLEET AIR ARM SQUADRONS IN THE FALKLANDS WAR

Squadron	Aircraft	Ships
737	Wessex HAS.3	*Antrim* (100 Flt), *Glamorgan* (103 Flt)
800	Sea Harrier FRS.1	*Hermes*
801	Sea Harrier FRS.1	*Invincible*
809	Sea Harrier FRS.1	*Atlantic Conveyor*, *Hermes*, *Invincible*
815	Lynx HAS.2	*Alacrity* (206 Flt), *Ambuscade* (219 Flt), *Andromeda* (222 Flt), *Antelope* (216 Flt), *Ardent* (207 Flt), *Argonaut* (211 Flt), *Arrow* (204 Flt), *Avenger* (205 and 240 Flt), *Brilliant* (220 Flt), *Broadsword* (221 Flt), *Cardiff* (214 Flt), *Coventry* (212 Flt), *Exeter* (239 Flt), *Glasgow* (215 Flt), *Minerva* (210 Flt), *Newcastle* (203 Flt), *Penelope* (209 Flt), *Sheffield* (213 Flt)
820	Sea King HAS.5	*Invincible*
824	Sea King HAS.2A	*Olmeda* ('A' Flt), *Fort Grange* ('B' Flt)
825	Sea King HAS.2/2A	*Atlantic Causeway*, *Canberra*, *Queen Elizabeth II*
826	Sea King HAS.5	*Hermes*, *Fort Austin*
829	Wasp HAS.1	*Active* (027 Flt), *Contender Bezant* (029 and 031 Flts), *Endurance* (001 Flt), *Hecla* (012 Flt), *Herald* (010 Flt), *Hydra* (011 Flt), *Plymouth* (027 Flt), *St. Helena* (033 Flt), *Yarmouth* (032 Flt)
845	Wessex HU.5	*Resource* ('A' Flt), *Fort Austin* ('B' Flt), *Tidespring* ('C' Flt), Wideawake ('D' Flt), *Intrepid* ('E' Flt), *Invincible*
846	Sea King HC.4	*Hermes*, *Fearless*, *Intrepid*, *Canberra*, *Elk*, *Norland*
847	Wessex HU.5	*Engadine*, *Atlantic Causeway*
848	Wessex HU.5	*Regent* ('A' Flt), *Olna* ('B' Flt), *Olwen* ('C' Flt), *Atlantic Conveyor* ('D' Flt)
899	Sea Harrier FRS.1	*Hermes*, *Invincible*

Glossary

AA	Anti-aircraft
AEO	Air Engineer Officer
AEW	Airborne Early Warning
AFC	Air Force Cross
AG	Air Gunner
AI	Air Interception (airborne radar)
AMC	Armed Merchant Cruiser
AOC	Air Officer Commanding
Asdic	Anti-submarine underwater detection device (sonar)
ASH	Air-to-surface vessel radar installed in aircraft (American type)
ASP	Anti-submarine patrol
ASV	Air-to-surface vessel radar installed in aircraft (British type)
ASW	Anti-submarine warfare
ATA	Air Transport Auxiliary
BABS	Blind Approach Beam System
CAG	Carrier Air Group
CAM-ship	Catapult-armed merchant ship
CAP	Combat air patrol
Capt.	Captain
Casevac	Casualty evacuation
Cdr	Commander
CGM	Conspicious Gallantry Medal
CO	Commanding Officer
Cobra	Search around convoy at specified distance
COMNAVFE	Flag-Officer Commanding, Far East (US)
CPO	Chief Petty Officer
CVE	Escort carrier (Carrier/Heavier than Air/Escort)
D/F	Direction-finding equipment
DFC	Distinguished Flying Cross
DISTEX	Disaster Relief Training Exercise
DLCO	Deck Landing Control Officer (batsman)
DSC	Distinguished Service Cross

DSO	Distinguished Service Order
E-boat	Small offensive German motor torpedo boat
ETA	Estimated time of arrival
FAA	Fleet Air Arm
FB	Fighter-Bomber
Flak	Enemy anti-aircraft fire
Flt Cdr	Flight Commander
Flt Lt	Flight Lieutenant
FR	Fighter-Reconnaissance
FRS	Fighter-Reconnaissance-Strike
GEC	General Electric Company
GOC	General Officer Commanding
Gosport tube	Aircraft oral intercommunications device
GP	General-purpose (bomb)
Gp Capt.	Group Captain
HA	High-angle (anti-aircraft gun or director)
HAR	Helicopter Air Rescue
HAS	Helicopter Anti-Submarine
HE	High explosive
H/F	High-frequency
HMAS	Her/His Majesty's Australian Ship
HMCS	Her/His Majesty's Canadian Ship
HO	Hostilities Only
HU	Helicopter Utility
IFF	Identification friend of foe (transmitter)
Jaunty	Master-at-Arms (Chief of Ship's Police) (slang)
Kamikaze	'Divine Wind' (Japanese suicide aircraft)
Killick	Leading rating (slang)
LG	Landing ground
Lt	Lieutenant
Lt Cdr	Lieutenant-Commander
MAC-ship	Merchant Aircraft Carrier
Mae West	Life jacket (slang)
M/F	Medium frequency
MONAB	Mobile Naval Air Base
MSFU	Merchant Ship Fighter Unit
MT	Motor transport
MTB	Motor torpedo boat
MV	Motor vessel
NA	Naval Airman
NAAFI	Navy, Army and Air Force Institutes
NATO	North Atlantic Treaty Organization
NCO	Non-commissioned officer
NF	Night-Fighter
OBE	Officer of (the Order of) the British Empire
OC	Officer Commanding
OTU	Operational Training Unit
PMO	Principal Medical Officer
PO	Petty Officer
POW	Prisoner-of-war
PR	Photographic Reconnaissance
RAF	Royal Air Force
RAAF	Royal Australian Air Force
'Ramrod'	Attack on target by bombers or fighter-bombers escorted by fighters
RANR	Royal Australian Naval Reserve
Ret.	Retired
RCNVR	Royal Canadian Navy Volunteer Reserve
RFA	Royal Fleet Auxiliary
RM	Royal Marines
RN	Royal Navy
RNAS	Royal Naval Air Service; Royal Naval Air Station
RNR	Royal Naval Reserve
RNVR	Royal Naval Volunteer Reserve
RNZNVR	Royal New Zealand Navy Volunteer Reserve
RP	Rocket projectile
R/T	Radio telephone
RV	Rendezvous
SAAF	South African Air Force
SAP	Semi-armour piercing
SAR	Search and Rescue
SAS	Special Air Service
SBA	Standard Beam Approach
SBD	Douglas Dauntless aircraft (US Navy)
Sg. Lt	Surgeon-Lieutenant
Sgt	Sergeant
Sommerfeld track	Portable perforated steel runway
Sonar	Anti-submarine detection equipment
Sqn Cdr	Squadron Commander
SS	Steamship
Sub-Lt	Sub-Lieutenant
TAF	Tactical Air Force (as in 2nd TAF)
TAG	Telegraphist Air Gunner
TARCAP	Target CAP
TBF	Grumman Avenger aircraft (US Navy and FAA)
TBR	Torpedo-Bomber-Reconnaissance
TO	Take-off
Tiffy	Artificer (slang)
Tomcat	Visual identification of friendly aircraft by standing patrol over fleet
TSR	Torpedo-Spotter-Reconnaissance
T124X	Articles signed by ex-Merchant Navy men serving with RNR rank in HM ships
UK	United Kingdom
US	United States
u/s	Unserviceable
USAAF	United States Army Air Force
USAF	United States Air Force
USN	United States Navy
USS	United States Ship
VAD	Voluntary Aid Detachment
VC	Victoria Cross
VE-Day	Victory in Europe Day (8 March 1945)
Very light	Pyrotechnic cartridge recognition light fired from a wide-mouthed pistol
VHF	Very high frequency
Viper	Patrol around convoy at visibility distance
VJ-Day	Victory against Japan Day (15 August 1945)
VTOL	Vertical take-off and landing
Wg Cdr	Wing Commander
WRNS	Women's Royal Naval Service
W/T	Wireless telegraphy (signalling in Morse code)
YG beacon	Homing beacon

Bibliography

Admiralty, The. *Ark Royal – The Admiralty Account of Her Achievement*. HM Stationery Office (London, 1942).
Admiralty, The. *Fleet Air Arm – The Admiralty Account of Naval Operations*. HM Stationery Office. (London, 1943).
Admiralty, The. *East of Malta, West of Suez – The Admiralty Account of the Naval Air War in the Eastern Mediterranean, September 1939 to March 1941*. HM Stationery Office (London, 1943).
Beaver, Paul. *Encyclopaedia of the Fleet Air Arm since 1945*. Patrick Stephens (Wellingborough, 1987).
Beaver, Paul. *The British Aircraft Carrier*. 2nd Edn. Patrick Stephens (Wellingborough, 1984).
Bowyer, Chaz. *Eugene Esmonde, VC, DSO*. William Kimber (London, 1983).
Brown, David. *Carrier Operations in World War II*. 2nd Edn. Ian Allan (Shepperton, 1974).
Brown, Capt. Eric. *Wings on my Sleeve*. Airlife (Shrewsbury, 1978).
Burden, Rodney; Draper, Michael I.; Rough, Douglas A.; Smith, Colin R.; and Wilton, David L. *Falklands: The Air War*. British Aviation Research Group; Arms & Armour Press (London, 1986 and 1987).
Chesneau, Roger. *Aircraft Carriers of the World*. Arms & Armour Press (London, 1984).
Flight Deck: Journal of Naval Aviation (Various issues). Ministry of Defence.
Francillon, Rene J. *Japanese Aircraft of the Pacific War*. 2nd Edn. Putnam & Co. (London, 1979).
Friedman, Norman. *British Carrier Aviation*. Conway Maritime Press (London, 1988).
Harrison, W. *Swordfish at War*. Ian Allan (Shepperton, 1987).
Jabberwock (Various issues). The Society of Friends of the Fleet Air Arm Museum.
Jameson, William. *Ark Royal 1939–1941*. Rupert Hart-Davies (London, 1957).
Kemp, Lt Cdr P. K. *Fleet Air Arm*. Herbert Jenkins (London, 1954).
Middlebrook, Martin. *The Fight for the 'Malvinas'*. Viking (London, 1989).
Milne, Lt Cdr J. M. *Flashing Blades over the Sea: The Development and History of Helicopters in the Royal Navy*. Maritime Books (Liskeard)
Poolman, Kenneth. *Night Strike from Malta*. Jane's Publishing Co. (London, 1980).
Poolman, Kenneth. *Escort Carrier*. Secker & Warburg (London, 1983).
Public Records Office. Various documents in the ADM series.
Secretary of State for Defence, The. *The Falklands Campaign – The Lessons*. HM Stationery Office (1982).
Sturtivant, Ray. *The Squadrons of the Fleet Air Arm*. Air-Britain (Historians) (Tonbridge, 1984).
Sturtivant, Ray. *Fleet Air Arm at War*. Ian Allan (Shepperton, 1982).
Thetford, Owen. *British Naval Aircraft since 1912*. 4th Edn. Putnam & Co. (London, 1978).
Till, Geoffrey. *Air Power and the Royal Navy*. Jane's Publishing Co. (London, 1979).
Woods, Gerard A. *Wings at Sea: A Fleet Air Arm Observer's War 1940–45*. Conway Maritime Press (London, 1985).
Waterman, Lt Cdr J. *The Fleet Air Arm History*. Old Bond Street Publishing Co. (London, 1974).
Winton, John. 'How the Navy very nearly lost Ultra'. *Naval Review*, Vol. 72 p. 121 (1984).